THE PRINCIPLES OF ECONOMICS,
WITH APPLICATIONS
TO
PRACTICAL PROBLEMS

First published 1904
This edition published by Lector House in 2025

ISBN: 978-93-6138-790-6
Edition copyright © 2025 by Lector House LLP
All rights reserved under the International Copyright Conventions.

Every possible effort has been made to ensure that the information contained in this book is accurate at the time of going to press and the publisher cannot accept responsibility for any errors or omissions, however caused, in this unabridged, slightly corrected republication of the text of the first edition. No responsibility for loss or damage occasioned to any person, acting or refraining from action, as a result of the material in this publication can be accepted by the publisher. The publisher is not associated with any product or vendor mentioned in the book. The contents of this work are intended to further general scientific research, understanding and discussion, only. Readers should consult with a specialist, where appropriate.

No part of this publication may be reproduced, stored in a retrieval system, or transmitted, in any form, or by any means, electronic, mechanical, photocopying or otherwise, without the prior permission of the publisher.

Lector House LLP
Registered Office: H. No. 96, Block C, Tomar Colony,
Burari, Delhi – 110084, India
info@lectorhouse.com
www.lectorhouse.com

THE PRINCIPLES OF ECONOMICS, WITH APPLICATIONS TO PRACTICAL PROBLEMS

FRANK ALBERT FETTER

2025

LECTOR HOUSE LLP

THE PRINCIPLES OF ECONOMICS, WITH APPLICATIONS TO PRACTICAL PROBLEMS

BY

FRANK A. FETTER, PH.D.

PROFESSOR OF POLITICAL ECONOMY AND FINANCE,
CORNELL UNIVERSITY

TO THE STUDENTS
OF THREE UNIVERSITIES
—INDIANA, STANFORD, AND CORNELL—
FOR WHOM, WITH WHOM, AND BY WHOSE AID
THIS BOOK CAME TO BE WRITTEN

Preface

This book had its beginning ten years ago in a series of brief discussions supplementing a text used in the class-room. Their purpose was to amend certain theoretical views even then generally questioned by economists, and to present most recent opinions on some other questions. These critical comments evolved into a course of lectures following an original outline, and were at length reduced to manuscript in the form of a stenographic report made from day to day in the class-room. The propositions printed in italics were dictated to the class, to give the key-note to the main divisions of the argument. Repeated revisions have shortened the text, cut out many digressions and illustrations, and remedied many of the faults both of thought and of expression; but no effort has been made to conceal or alter the original and essential character of the simple, informal, class-room talks by teacher to student. To this origin are traceable many conversational phrases and local illustrations, and the occasional use of the personal form of address.

The lectures, at the outset, sought to give merely a summary of widely accepted economic theory, not to offer any contribution to the subject. While they were in progress, however, special studies in the evolution of the economic concepts were pursued, and the manuscript of a book on that more special subject was carried well toward completion. That work, which it is hoped some time to complete, was, for several reasons, put aside while the present text was preparing for publication. The economic theories of the present transition period show many discordant elements, yet the author felt that his attempt to unify the statement of principles, in an elementary text explaining modern problems, and consistent in its various parts, helped to reveal to him both difficulties and possible solutions in the more special theoretical field. The unforeseen outcome of these varied studies is an elementary text embodying a new conception of the theory of distribution, an outline of which will be found in Chapter Forty-three. It is, in brief, a consistently subjective analysis of the relations of goods to wants, in place of the admixture of objective and subjective distinctions found in the traditional conceptions of rent, interest, and price.

The beginning of the systematic study of economics, like the first steps in a language, is difficult because of the entire strangeness of the thought, and it is not to be hoped that any pedagogic device can do away with the need of strenuous thinking by the student. The aim, however, in the development of this theory of distribution, has been to proceed by gradual steps, as in a series of geometrical propositions, from the simple and familiar acts and experiences of the individual's every-day life, through the more complex relations, to the most complex, practical, economic problems of the day. The hope has long been entertained by economists that a conception of the whole problem of value would be attained that would coördinate and unify the various "laws," — those of rent, wages, interest, etc. This solution has here been sought by a development of recent theories, the unit of the complex problem of value being the simplest, immediate, temporary gratification.

Possibly some teachers will observe and regret the almost entire absence of critical discussions of controverted points in theory, which make up so large a part of some of the older texts. The more positive manner of presentation has been purposely adopted, and only such reference is made to conflicting views as is needed to guard the student against misunderstanding in his further reading. The author would not have it thought that he doubts the disciplinary value of economic theory or its scientific worth for more advanced students, for, on the contrary, he believes in it, perhaps to an extreme degree; but, for his own part, he has become convinced of the unwisdom of carrying on these subtle controversies in classes of beginners. The inherent difficulties of the subject are great enough, without the creation of new ones.

The fifty-seven chapters represent the work of the typical college course in elementary economics, allowing two chapters a week, and a third meeting weekly for review and for the discussion of questions, exercises, and reports. The subject is so large that the text is, in many places, hardly more than a suggestive outline. In class-room work it should be supplemented by other sources of information, such as personal observation by the students (many of the questions following the text serving to stimulate the attention); visits to local industries; interchange of opinions; examples given by the teacher; study and discussion, in the light of the principles stated in the text, of some such problems as are suggested in the appended list of questions; collateral reading; the preparation of exercises and the use of statistical material from the census, labor reports, etc.; history and description of industries; history of the growth of economic ideas. Suggestions, from teachers, of changes that will make the text more useful in their classes, will be thankfully received by the author.

Lack of space makes it impossible to mention by name the many sources to which the writer is indebted. Special acknowledgment, however, is gratefully made to C. H. Hull, of Cornell University; to E. W. Kemmerer, now of the Philippine Treasury Department, and to U. G. Weatherly, of Indiana University, who have read large portions of the manuscript, and have made many valuable suggestions; to W. M. Daniels, of Princeton University, who has read every page of the copy, and to whom are due the greatest obligations for his numerous and able criticisms both of the argument and of the expression; to R. C. Brooks, now of Swarthmore College, for a number of the questions in the appended list, and for helpful comments given while the course was developing; and to R. F. Hoxie and to A. C. Muhse, whose thoughtful reading of the proof has eliminated many errors. For the defects remaining, not these friendly critics, but the author alone, should be held accountable.

No book on economics can to-day satisfy everybody—"Or even anybody," adds a friend. But with this book may go the hope that what has been written with love of truth and of democracy may serve, in its small way, both to further sound economic reasoning and to extend among American citizens a better understanding of the economic problems set for this generation to solve.

FRANK A. FETTER.

Ithaca, N. Y., August, 1904.

Contents

Chapter   Page

Preface vii

PART I

DIVISION A—WANTS AND PRESENT GOODS

I. The Nature and Purpose of Political Economy 1
- § I. Name and Definition .1
- § II. Place of Economics among the Social Sciences 2
- § III. The Relation of Economics to Practical Affairs 3

II. Economic Motives 6
- § I. Material Wants, the Primary Economic Motives 6
- § II. Desires for Non-material Ends, as Secondary Economic Motives 8

III. Wealth and Welfare. 10
- § I. The Relation of Men and Material Things to Economic Welfare 10
- § II. Some Important Economic Concepts Connected with Wealth and Welfare 13

IV. The Nature of Demand. 15
- § I. The Comparison of Goods in Man's Thought 15
- § II. Demand for Goods Grows Out of Subjective Comparisons 19

V.	Exchange in a Market.	22
	• § I. Exchange of Goods Resulting from Demand	22
	• § II. Barter under Simple Conditions	23
	• § III. Price in a Market	26
VI.	Psychic Income	29
	• § I. Income as a Flow of Goods	29
	• § II. Income as a Series of Gratifications	32

DIVISION B—WEALTH AND RENT

VII.	Wealth and its Indirect Uses	35
	• § I. The Grades of Relation of Indirect Goods to Gratification	35
	• § II. Conditions of Economic Wealth	37
VIII.	The Renting Contract	40
	• § I. Nature and Definition of Rent	40
	• § II. The History of Contract Rent and Changes in It	42
IX.	The Law of Diminishing Returns	46
	• § I. Definition of the Concept of (Economic) Diminishing Returns	46
	• § II. Other Meanings of the Phrase "Diminishing Returns"	50
	• § III. Development of the Concept of Diminishing Returns	52
X.	The Theory of Rent: The Market Value of the Usufruct.	55
	• § I. Differential Advantages in Consumption Goods	55
	• § II. Differential Advantages in Indirect Goods	57
XI.	Repair, Depreciation, and Destruction of Wealth: Relation to its Sale and Rent.	61
	• § I. Repair of Rent-Bearing Agents	61
	• § II. Depreciation in Rent-earning Power of Agents Kept in Repair.	63
	• § III. Destruction of Natural Stores of Materials	65
XII.	Increase of Rent-bearers and of Rents	68
	• § I. Efforts of Men to Increase Products and Rent-bearers	68
	• § II. Effects of Social Changes in Raising the Rents of

Indirect Agents 71

DIVISION C—CAPITALIZATION AND TIME-VALUE

XIII. Money as a Tool in Exchange 75
- § I. Origin of the Use of Money 75
- § II. Nature of the Use of Money 78
- § III. The Value of Typical Money 80

XIV. The Money Economy and the Concept of Capital 82
- § I. The Barter Economy and its Decline 82
- § II. The Concept of Capital in Modern Business 86

XV. The Capitalization of All Forms of Rent 89
- § I. The Purchase of Rent-charges as an Example of Capitalization 89
- § II. Capitalization Involved in the Evaluating of Indirect Agents 92
- § III. The Increasing Role of Capitalization in Modern Industry 95

XVI. Interest on Money Loans 98
- § I. Various Forms of Contract Interest 98
- § II. The Motive for Paying Interest 101

XVII. The Theory of Time-value 105
- § I. Definition and Scope of Time-value 105
- § II. The Adjustment of the Rate of Time-discount 107

XVIII. Relatively Fixed and Relatively Increasable Forms of Capital . . . 113
- § I. How Various Forms of Capital May Be Increased 113
- § II. Social Significance of These Differences 115

XIX. Saving and Production as Affected by the Rate of Interest 118
- § I. Saving as Affected by the Interest Rate 118
- § II. Conditions Favorable to Saving 122
- § III. Influence of the Interest Rate on Methods of Production 123

PART II
THE VALUE OF HUMAN SERVICES
DIVISION A—LABOR AND WAGES

XX. Labor and Classes of Laborers. 128
- § I. Relation of Labor to Wealth. 128
- § II. Varieties of Talents and of Abilities in Men 131

XXI. The Supply of Labor 136
- § I. What is a Doctrine of Population? 136
- § II. Population in Human Society 138
- § III. Current Aspect of the Population Problem 141

XXII. Conditions for Efficient Labor. 144
- § I. Objective Physical Conditions 144
- § II. Social Conditions Favoring Efficiency 146
- § III. Division of Labor. 148

XXIII. The Law of Wages 151
- § I. Nature of Wages and the Wages Problem. 151
- § II. The Different Modes of Earning Wages 153
- § III. Wages as Exemplifying the General Law of Value 155

XXIV. The Relation of Labor to Value 158
- § I. Relation of Rent to Wages. 158
- § II. Relation of Time-value to Wages. 160
- § III. The Relation of Labor to Value 163

XXV. The Wage System and its Results. 166
- § I. Systems of Labor. 166
- § II. The Wage System as it Is 168
- § III. Progress of the Masses under the Wage System 170

XXVI. Machinery and Labor. 173
- § I. Extent of the Use of Machinery. 173
- § II. Effect of Machinery on the Welfare and Wages of the Masses. 175

XXVII. Trade-unions 180
- § I. The Objects of Trade-unions 180
- § II. The Methods of Trade-unions 182
- § III. Combination and Wages 185

DIVISION B—ENTERPRISE AND PROFITS

XXVIII. Production and the Combination of the Factors. 189
- § I. The Nature of Production. 189
- § II. Combination of the Factors 191

XXIX. Business Organization and the Enterpriser's Function 195
- § I. The Direction of Industry 195
- § II. Qualities of a Business Organizer 197
- § III. The Selection of Ability 199

XXX. Cost of Production 201
- § I. Cost of Production from the Enterpriser's Point of View 201
- § II. Cost of Production from the Economist's Standpoint . . 203

XXXI. The Law of Profits 208
- § I. Meaning of Terms 208
- § II. The Typical Enterpriser's Services Reviewed 210
- § III. Statement of the Law of Profits 212

XXXII. Profit-sharing, Producers' and Consumers' Coöperation 215
- § I. Profit-sharing 215
- § II. Producers' Coöperation 217
- § III. Consumers' Coöperation 219

XXXIII. Monopoly Profits 222
- § I. Nature of Monopoly 222
- § II. Kinds of Monopoly 224
- § III. The Fixing of a Monopoly Price 226

XXXIV. Growth of Trusts and Combinations in the United States 229
- § I. Growth of Large Industry in the United States 229
- § II. Advantages of Large Production 233

	• § III. Causes of Industrial Combinations	235
XXXV.	Effect of Trusts on Prices	238
	• § I. How Trusts Might Affect Prices	238
	• § II. How Trusts Have Affected Prices	241
XXXVI.	Gambling, Speculation, and Promoters' Profits	245
	• § I. Gambling vs. Insurance	245
	• § II. The Speculator as a Risk-taker	249
	• § III. Promoter's and Trustee's Profits	251
XXXVII.	Crises and Industrial Depressions	253
	• § I. Definition and Description of Crises	253
	• § II. Crises in the Nineteenth Century	255
	• § III. Various Explanations of Crises	257

PART III

THE SOCIAL ASPECTS OF VALUE

DIVISION A—RELATION OF PRIVATE INCOME TO SOCIAL WELFARE

XXXVIII.	Private Property and Inheritance	263
	• § I. Impersonal and Personal Shares of Income	263
	• § II. The Origin of Private Property	265
	• § III. Limitations of the Right of Private Property	268
XXXIX.	Income and Social Service	271
	• § I. Income from Property	271
	• § II. Income from Personal Services	275
XL.	Waste and Luxury	279
	• § I. Waste of Wealth	279
	• § II. Luxury	282
XLI.	Reaction of Consumption on Production	286
	• § I. Reaction upon Material Productive Agents	286
	• § II. Reaction upon the Efficiency of the Workers	288

- § III. Effects on the Abiding Welfare of the Consumer 290

XLII. Distribution of the Social Income 293
- § I. The Nature of Personal Distribution 293
- § II. Methods of Personal Distribution 294

XLIII. Survey of the Theory of Value 300
- § I. Review of the Plan Followed 300
- § II. Relation of Value Theories to Social Reforms 302
- § III. Interrelation of Economic Agents 304

DIVISION B—RELATION OF THE STATE TO INDUSTRY

XLIV. Free Competition and State Action 308
- § I. Competition and Custom 308
- § II. Economic Harmony through Competition 310
- § III. Social Limiting of Competition 312

XLV. Use, Coinage, and Value of Money 314
- § I. The Precious Metals as Money 314
- § II. The Quantity Theory of Money 318

XLVI. Token Coinage and Government Paper Money 323
- § I. Light-weight Coins 323
- § II. Paper Money Experiments 326
- § III. Theories of Political Money 328

XLVII. The Standard of Deferred Payments 330
- § I. Function of the Standard 330
- § II. International Bimetallism 332
- § III. The Free-silver Movement in America 334

XLVIII. Banking and Credit 337
- § I. Functions of a Bank 337
- § II. Typical Bank Money 339
- § III. Banks of the United States To-day 341

XLIX. Taxation in its Relation to Value 343
- § I. Purposes of Taxation 343

CONTENTS

- § II. Forms of Taxation 345
- § III. Principles and Practice 347

L. The General Theory of International Trade 350
- § I. International Trade as a Case of Exchange 350
- § II. Theory of Foreign Exchanges of Money 353
- § III. Real Benefits of Foreign Trade 356

LI. The Protective Tariff 358
- § I. The Nature and Claims of Protection 358
- § II. The Reasonable Measure of Justification of Protection . 362
- § III. Values as Affected by Protection 365

LII. Other Protective Social and Labor Legislation. 367
- § I. Social Legislation. 367
- § II. Labor Legislation. 370

LIII. Public Ownership of Industry. 374
- § I. Examples of Public Ownership. 374
- § II. Economic Aspects of Public Ownership. 376

LIV. Railroads and Industry. 382
- § I. Transportation as a Form of Production. 382
- § II. The Railroad as a Carrier 383
- § III. Discrimination in Rates on Railroads 385

LV. The Public Nature of Railroads 388
- § I. Public Privileges of Railroad Corporations 388
- § II. Political and Economic Power of Railroad Managers . . 391
- § III. Commissions to Control Railroads. 393

LVI. Public Policy as to Control of Industry. 396
- § I. State Regulation of Corporate Industry 396
- § II. Difficulties of Public Control of Industry 398
- § III. Trend of Policy as to Public Industrial Activity. 401

LVII. Future Trend of Values. 404
- § I. Past and Present of Economic Society 404

- § II. The Economic Future of Society 406

QUESTIONS AND CRITICAL NOTES

Questions and Critical Notes 411

Index 442

PART I

DIVISION A—WANTS AND PRESENT GOODS

Chapter I
The Nature and Purpose of Political Economy

§ I.   Name and Definition

Verbal definition of economics

1. *Economics, or political economy, may be defined, briefly, as the study of men earning a living; or, more fully, as the study of the material world and of the activities and mutual relations of men, so far as all these are the objective conditions to gratifying desires.* To define, means to mark off the limits of a subject, to tell what questions are or are not included within it. The ideas of most persons on this subject are vague, yet it would be very desirable if the student could approach this study with an exact understanding of the nature of the questions with which it deals. Until a subject has been studied, however, a definition in mere words cannot greatly aid in marking it off clearly in our thought. The essential thing for the student is to see clearly the central purpose of the study, not to decide at once all of the puzzling cases.

Natural sciences deal with material things

2. *A definition that suggests clear and familiar thoughts to the student seems at first much more difficult to get in any social science than in the natural sciences.* These deal with concrete, material things which we are accustomed to see, handle, and measure. If a mere child is told that botany is a study in which he may learn about flowers, trees, and plants, the answer is fairly satisfying, for he at once thinks of many things of that kind. When, in like manner zoölogy is defined as the study of animals, or geology as the study of rocks and the earth, the words call up memories of many familiar objects. Even so difficult and foreign-looking a word as ichthyology seems to be made clear by the statement that it is the name of the study in which one learns about fish. It is true that there may be some misunderstanding as to the way in which these subjects are studied, for botany is not in the main to teach how to cultivate plants in the garden, nor ichthyology how to catch fish or to propagate them in a pond. But the main purpose of these studies is clear at the outset from these simple definitions. Indeed, as the study is pursued, and knowledge widens

to take in the manifold and various forms of life, the boundaries of the special sciences become not more but less sharp and definite.

Economics studies some social acts and relations

Political economy, on the other hand, as one of the social sciences, which deal with men and their relations in society, seems to be a very much more complex thought to get hold of. We are tempted to say that it deals with less familiar things; but the truth may be, as a thoughtful friend suggests, that the simple social acts and relations are more familiar to our thought than are lions, palm-trees, or even horses. Every hour in the streets or stores, one may witness thousands of acts, such as bargains, labor, payments, that are the subject-matter of economic science. Their very familiarity may cause men to overlook their deeper meaning.

Many other definitions have been given of political economy. It has been called the science of wealth, or the science of exchanges. Evidently there are various ways in which wealth may be considered or exchanges made. The particular aspects that are dealt with in political economy will be made clear by considering two other questions, the place of economics among the social sciences and the relation of economics to practical affairs.

§ II. Place of Economics among the Social Sciences

Economics contrasted with the natural sciences

1. *Political economy, as one of the social sciences, may be contrasted with the natural sciences, which deal with material things and their mutual relations, while it deals with one aspect of men's life in society, namely, the earning of a living, or the use of wealth.* It is true that political economy also has to do with plants and animals and the earth—in fact, with all of those things which are the subject-matter of the natural sciences; but it has to do with them only in so far as they are related to man's welfare and affect his estimate of the value of things; only in so far as they are related to the one central subject of economic interest, the earning of a living.

Character of the social sciences

2. *The social sciences deal with men and their relations with each other.* The word "social" comes from the Latin socius, meaning a fellow, comrade, companion, associate. As men living together have to do with each other in a great many different ways, and enter into a great many different relations, there arise a great many different social problems. Each of the social sciences attempts to study man in some one important aspect—that is, to view these relations from some one standpoint.

Man's acts, his life, and his motives are so complex that it is not surprising that there has been less definiteness in the thought of the social sciences, and that they have advanced less rapidly toward exactness in their conclusions, than have the natural sciences. This complexity also explains the discouragement of the beginner in the early lessons in this subject. Usually the greatest difficulties appear in the first few weeks of its study. The thought is more abstract than in natural science; it requires a different, I will not say higher, kind of ability than does mathematics. But little by little the strangeness of the language and ideas disappears; the bare definitions become clothed with the facts of observation and recalled experiences; and soon the "economic" acts and relations of men in society come to be as real and as interesting to the student as are the materials in the natural world about him—often, indeed, more interesting.

Economics, politics, law, and ethics

3. *Political economy is related to all the other social sciences, it being the study of certain of men's relations, while politics, law, and ethics have to do with other relations or with relations under a different aspect.* Politics treats of the form and working of government and is mainly concerned with the question of power or control of the individual's actions and liberty. Law treats of the precepts and regulations in accordance with which the actions of men are limited by the state, and the contracts into which they have seen fit to enter are interpreted. Ethics treats the question of right or wrong, studies the moral aspects of men's acts and relations. The attempt just made to distinguish between the fields occupied by the various social sciences betrays at once the fundamental unity existing among them. The acts of men are closely related in their lives, but they may be looked at from different sides. The central thought in economics is the business relation, the relation of men in exchanging their services or material wealth. In pursuing economic inquiries we come into contact with political, legal, and ethical considerations, all of which must be recognized before a final practical answer can be given to any question. Nevertheless the province of economics is limited. It is because of the feebleness of our mental power that we divide and subdivide these complex questions and try to answer certain parts before we seek to answer the whole. When we attempt this final and more difficult task, we should rise to the standpoint of the social philosopher.

§ III. The Relation of Economics to Practical Affairs

Economics is first a science

1. *The ideal of political economy here set forth is that it should be a science, a search for truth, a systematized body of knowledge, arriving at a statement of the laws to which economic actions conform.* It is not the advocacy of any particular policy or idea, but if it arrives at any conclusions, any truths, these cannot fail to affect the practical action of men.

But it touches many practical interests

Political economy, because defined as the science of wealth, has been described by some as a gospel of Mammon. It is hardly necessary to refute such a misconception. Political economy is not the science of wealth-getting for the individual. Its study is not primarily for the selfish ends and interest of the individual. Certainly some of its lessons may be of practical value to men in active business, for many economic "principles" are but the general statement of those ideas that have been approved by the experience of business men, of statesmen, and of the masses of men. Some of its lessons must have educational value in practical business, for political economy is not dreamed out by the closet philosopher, but more and more it is the attempt to describe the interests and the action of the practical world in which men must live. Many men are working together to develop its study—those who collect statistics and facts bearing on all kinds of practical affairs, and those who search through the records of the past for illustrations of experiments and experiences that may help us in our life to-day.

Economic study needed in a democracy

2. *But, in the main, the study of political economy is a social study for social ends and not a selfish study for individual advantage.* The name political economy was first suggested in France when the government was monarchical and despotic in the extreme. As domestic economy indicates a set of rules or principles to guide wisely the action of the housekeeper or the owner of an estate, so political economy was first thought of as a set of rules or principles to guide the king and his counselors in the control of the state. The term has continued to bear something of that suggestion in it, though of late the term "economics," as being broader and less likely to be confused with politics, has very generally come into use. But in the degree in which unlimited monarchy has given way to the rule of the people, the conception of political economy has been modified. In a democracy there is need for a general diffusion of knowledge. The power now rests not with the king and a few counselors, but in the last resort with the people, and therefore the people must be acquainted with the experience of the past, must have all possible systematic knowledge to enlighten public policy and to guide legislation.

Is of growing interest and influence

Moreover, with the growth of the modern state, with the increasing importance of business, and of industrial and commercial interests, as compared with changes of dynasty or the personal rivalries of rulers, economic questions have grown in relative importance. In our own country, particularly since the subjects of slavery and of States' rights ceased to absorb the attention of our people, economic questions have pushed rapidly into the foreground. Indeed, it has of late been more clearly seen that many of the older political questions, such as the American Revolution and slavery, formerly discussed almost entirely in their political and constitutional aspects, were at bottom questions of economic rivalry and of economic welfare. The remarkable increase in the attention given to this study in colleges and universities in the last twenty years is but the index of the greatly

THE NATURE AND PURPOSE OF POLITICAL ECONOMY 5

increased interest and attention felt in it by citizens generally.

To sum up, it may be said that in the study of political economy we are seeking the reason, connection, and relations in the great multitude of acts arising out of the dependence of desires on the world of things and men.

Chapter II
Economic Motives

§ I. Material Wants, the Primary Economic Motives

Feeling urges to economic actions

1. *A logical explanation of industry must begin with a discussion of the nature of wants, for the purpose of industry is to gratify wants.* An economic want may be defined as a feeling of incompleteness, because of the lack of a part of the outer world or of some change in it. Often the question asked when one first sees a moving trolley car or automobile or bicycle is: What makes it go? The first question to ask in the part of the study of economic society here undertaken is: What is its motive force? Without an answer to that question one cannot hope to understand the ceaseless and varied activities of men occupied in the making of a living. The question merits long and careful study, but the general answer is so simple that it seems almost self-evident: The motive force in economics is found in the feelings of men. It is men's desire to make use of men and things about them which calls forth all the manifold phenomena studied in economics.

Animal species shaped by their environment

2. *Wants among animals depend on the environment;* that is to say, the utmost that creatures of a lower order than man can do is to take things as they find them. The imagination and intelligence of animals are not developed enough to lead them to desire much beyond that which is ordinarily to be obtained. And so the environment shapes and affects the animal. The fish is fitted to live in the water and thrives there, and we must believe, enjoys living there. The horse and the cow like best the food of the fields, and so each species of animal, in order to survive in the severe struggle for existence, has been forced to fit itself to the conditions in which it lives. After the animal has been thus fitted, its desire is for those things normally to be found in its surroundings. So different animals desire or want different things, but always it is the environment that determines the want, and not the want that determines the environment.

ECONOMIC MOTIVES

Simple wants of primitive men

3. *In simpler human societies, wants are mostly confined to physical necessities; that is, in the earlier stages of society, man's wants are very much like those of the animals.* Man bends his energies to securing the things necessary to survival. He feels the pangs of hunger and he strives to secure food. He feels the need of companionship, for it is only through association and mutual help that men, so weak as compared with many kinds of animals, are able to resist the enemies which beset them. He needs clothing to protect him against the harsher climates of the lands to which he moves. For the same purpose, to protect himself against the cold and rain, he needs a shelter, a cave, a wigwam, or a hut; for a house is but a larger dress.

Manifold wants in civilized society

4. *In human society, wants develop and transform the world.* In the rudest societies of which there is any record, savages are found with wants developed in a great number of directions beyond the wants of any animals. Man is not a passive victim of circumstances; his wants are not determined solely by his environment; his desires soar beyond the things about him. As men become more the masters of circumstances, their desires anticipate mere physical wants; they seek a more varied food of finer flavor and more delicately prepared. Dress is not limited by physical comfort, for one of the earliest of the esthetic wants to develop is the love of personal ornament. The rude hut or communal lodge to protect against rain and cold becomes a home. Out of the earlier rude companionship develop the noblest sentiments of friendship and family life. Seeking to gratify the senses and the love of action, men develop esthetic tastes, the love of the beautiful in sound, in form, in taste, in color, in motion. And finally, as the imagination and intellect develop, there grow up the various forms of intellectual pleasures—the love of reading, of study, of travel, and of thought.

The various wants of man are sometimes classified as necessities, comforts, and luxuries, but all economists take care to emphasize that these terms have only relative meanings which, in the rapidly changing conditions of modern life, are changing constantly. The comforts of one generation, or of one country, become the necessities in another; and luxuries becoming comforts, are looked upon finally as necessities. And as the desires grow, they more and more alter the world. Man has changed the face of the earth; he has affected its climate, its fertility, its beauty, because, either for better or for worse, his desires have impressed themselves upon the world about him.

Wants must precede wealth

5. *In human society the growth of wants is necessary to progress.* From the earliest times teachers of morals have argued for simplicity of life and against the development of refinements. We do not now raise the moral question, but there is no doubt that the economic effect of developing wants is in the main to impel to greater effort. They are the mainspring of economic progress. In recent discussion of the control of the tropics, the too great contentedness of tropical

peoples has been brought out prominently. Some one has said that if a colony of New England school-teachers and Presbyterian deacons should settle in the tropics, their descendants would, in a single generation, be wearing breech-clouts and going to cock-fights on Sunday. Certain it is that the energy and ambition of the temperate zone are hard to maintain in warmer lands. The negro's content with hard conditions, so often counted as a virtue, is one of the difficulties in the way of solving the race problem in our South to-day. Booker T. Washington, and others who are laboring for the elevation of the American negroes, would try first to make them discontented with the one-room cabins, in which hundreds of thousands of families live. If only the desire for a two- or three-room cabin can be aroused, experience shows that family life and industrial qualities may be improved in many other ways.

But impossible hopes lessen gratifications

Not only in America, but in most civilized lands to-day, is seen a rapid growth of wants in the working-classes. The incomes and the standard of living have become increasing, but not so fast as have the desires of the working-classes. Regret has been expressed by some that the workers of Europe are becoming "declassed." Increasing wages, it is said, bring not welfare, but unhappiness, to the complaining masses. If discontent with one's lot goes beyond a moderate degree, if it is more than the desire to better one's lot by personal efforts, if it becomes an unhappy longing for the impossible, then indeed it may be a misfortune. But a moderate ambition to better one's condition is the "divine discontent" absolutely indispensable if energy and enterprise are to be called into being.

Wants grow refined as wealth advances

It is a suggestive fact that civilized man, equipped with all of the inventions and the advantages of science, spends more hours of effort in gaining a livelihood than does the savage with his almost unaided hands. Activity is dependent not on bare physical necessity, but on developed wants—in the economic sense of the term. Such social institutions as property and inheritance owe their origin and their justification to their average effect on the motives to activity. If society is to develop, if progress is to continue, human wants—not of the grosser sort, but ever more refined—must continue to emerge and urge men to action.

§ II. Desires for Non-material Ends, as Secondary Economic Motives

The real man in economics

1. *The spiritual nature of man must not be ignored in economic reasoning.* There has been much and just criticism of the earlier writers and of their conclusions because so little account was taken by them of any but the motive of self-interest in economic

affairs. Generally it was assumed that men knew their own interest, and sought in a very unsympathetic way those things which would gratify their material wants. Thus man in economic reasoning was made an abstraction, differing from real men in his lack of manifold spiritual and social elements.

Desires for the non-material may become economic motives

2. *The main classes of non-material wants that are secondarily economic are fear of temporal punishment; sentiments of moral and religious duty; pride, honor, and fear of disgrace; and pleasure in work for itself, for social approval, or for a social result.* The first is best illustrated by slavery, where the slave is not impelled to seek wealth for his own welfare, but is driven by punishment to perform the task. The object is to create within the mind of the slave a motive that will take the place of the ordinary economic motive. The feeling of religious or moral duty leads men to act often in direct opposition to the usual economic motive. The taboo is faithfully observed by the members of a savage tribe who suffer as a result the severest hardships. A religious injunction prevents the use of food that would save from starvation. Pride, either of family or of calling; the soldier's honor leading him to sacrifice not only his future but his life; the love of social approval, holding men to the most disagreeable tasks—these illustrate how strongly social sentiments oppose the narrower motive of immediate self-interest as generally thought of. Pleasure in work for work's sake, and pride in the result, may act as motives quite as strong in some cases as desire for the product that can be used. And even where this does not change the kind of work done, it comes in to influence the interest and earnestness with which the work is performed.

Economists must overlook no influence on value

3. *Whatever motive in man's complex nature makes him desire things more or less, becomes for the time, and in so far, an economic motive.* These various social and spiritual motives sometimes work positively, in the direction of magnifying man's desire for things; sometimes negatively, to diminish it. If we are to understand economic action, we must take men as they are. A religious motive that leads men to refrain from the eating of meat or to eat fish in preference on certain days, is a fact which the economist has but to accept, for it is sure to affect the value of meat and fish at that place and time. Moral convictions, whatever be their origin, whether due to the teaching of parents, to unconscious influences, or to native temperament, may be quite as effective as the pangs of hunger in determining what men desire. Therefore, while these various motives are primarily social or moral or religious, they may be said to be secondarily economic motives, and they may become in certain cases the most important influences of which the economist must take account.

Chapter III
Wealth and Welfare

§ I. The Relation of Men and Material Things to Economic Welfare

Man is the center of economic reasoning

1. *The gratifying of economic wants depends on things outside of the man who feels the wants.* Man is to himself the center of the world. He groups things and estimates things with reference to their bearing on his desires, be these what are called selfish or unselfish. If we were discussing the economics of an inferior species of animals, things would be grouped in a very different way. But economics being the study of man's welfare, everything must be judged from his standpoint, and things are or are not of economic importance according as they have relation to his wants and satisfactions. Things needful for any of the lower animals are spoken of as "ministering to welfare" in the economic sense only in case these animals are useful to men. Examples are the mulberry-tree on which the silkworm feeds, the flower visited by the honey-bee. In the same view some men are seen to minister to the welfare of other men and therefore bear the same relation for the moment to the welfare of the others as do material things. In any case we study man's welfare as affected by the world which surrounds him.

Physical nature is an unchangeable fact

2. *Material things and natural forces differ in kind and nature.* This is an axiom which we must take as a basis for reasoning in economics. Things have certain physical qualities quite apart from any action or influence of man. They are operated on by mechanical laws; the force of gravitation causes them to fall at a certain rate under given conditions. They differ in specific gravity, reflect the rays of light, absorb or transmit heat. All these things are for man ultimate physical facts, but unless he knows these facts he cannot take full advantage of the favorable qualities of things or weigh properly their importance to his welfare. Things differ in a multitude of ways in their chemical qualities. Niter, charcoal, and saltpeter, combined in certain proportions, give certain reactions; different combinations give various results.

Solids combine to form gases, and liquids unite to form solids, and these qualities and reactions of material things are for man ultimate truths of chemistry. Likewise many things have certain physiological effects. Sunshine acts on living bodies, whether plant, animal, or man, in certain ways. Some plants are nourishing to man, others are poisonous. If man were not on the earth, things would have the same physical and chemical qualities, mechanical laws would be the same as at present so far as we can conclude. Man cannot change the nature of things; but he can acquaint himself with that nature and then put the things into the relations where a given result will follow.

But economics has to do with psychological effects

3. *As a result of these differences, things have different relations to wants.* These various qualities, physical, chemical, physiological, are important in an economic sense only as they produce psychological effects, that is, as they affect the feelings and judgments of men. We come to some general thoughts which it will be well to define.

Some definitions

Gratification is the feeling that results when a want has been met. Feelings are hard to define in words; the best definition is found in the experience of each individual. We can only say, therefore, that gratification is the attainment of desire, the fulfilment of wants. The word that has usually been employed in this sense in economic discussion is "satisfaction"; but by its derivation and general usage satisfaction means "the complete or full gratification" of a desire, and this meaning is quite inconsistent with the thought in many connections in which the word is used. We shall therefore prefer here the word gratification, and its corresponding verb, gratify.

Wealth is the collective term for those things which are felt to be related to the gratification of wants. The word is applied in economic discussion to any part of those things, no matter how small. We shall have occasion later to define and discuss this term more fully.

Welfare, in an immediate or narrow sense, is the same as gratification of the moment; in a broader sense, it means the abiding condition of well-being. We have here a distinction very much like that often made between pleasure and happiness. If we think of only the present moment, welfare is the absence of pain, and the presence of the pleasureable feeling; but if we consider a longer period in a man's life or his entire lifetime, it is seen that many things that afford a momentary gratification do not minister to his ultimate, or abiding, welfare. Moralists and philosophers often have dwelt on this contrast. The difference is illustrated by the thoughtlessness and impulsiveness of a child or savage as contrasted with the more rational life of those with foresight and patience.

Economics first studies wealth

Wealth, in the general economic sense, is judged with reference to gratification rather than with reference to abiding welfare. It is the first duty of the economist not to preach what should be, but to understand things as they are. He must, in studying the problem of value, recognize any motive that leads men to attach importance to acts and things. He will therefore take account of abiding welfare and of immediate gratification to exactly the degree that men in general do, and the sad fact is that the present impulse rules a large part of the acts of men. Whether tobacco or alcohol or morphine minister to the abiding happiness of those who use them does not alter the immediate fact that here and now they are sought and an importance is attached to them because of their power to gratify an immediate desire.

Then wealth and welfare

5. *In studying the question of social prosperity, however, we must rise to the standpoint of the social philosopher and consider the more abiding effects of wealth.* Wants may be developed and made rational, and the permanent prosperity of a community depends upon this result. Any species of animal that continued regularly to enjoy that which weakens the health and strength would become extinct. Any society or individual that continues to derive gratification, to seek its pleasure, in ways that do not, on the average, minister to permanent welfare, sinks in the struggle of life and gives way to those men or nations that have a sounder and healthier adjustment of wants and welfare. We touch here, therefore, on the edge of the great problems of morals, and while we must recognize the contrast that often exists in the life of any particular man between his "pleasures" and his health and happiness, we see that there is a reason why, on the whole, and in the long run, these two cannot remain far apart. The old proverbs, "Be virtuous and you will be happy," "Honesty is the best policy," and "Virtue is its own reward," have a sound basis in the age-long experience of the world. Cynics or jesters may easily disprove these truths in a multitude of particular cases.

Free men are not economic wealth

6. *Wealth does not include such personal qualities as honesty, integrity, good health.* Some economists speak of these as "internal goods," but it is far better not to speak of free men or of their qualities as wealth. Many difficulties arise from such a use of the term in practical discussion. One of the most important of all distinctions to maintain in economics is that between material things and men. Only in the case of human slavery may persons be counted as economic wealth. It is a different thing, however, to consider human services as wealth of an ephemeral kind at the moment they are rendered. We are, thus merely recognizing that men may bear at the given moment the same relation to our wants as do material things.

§ II. Some Important Economic Concepts Connected with Wealth and Welfare

Popular meaning of useful

1. *Utility, in its broadest usage, is the general capability that things have of ministering to human well being.* The term is evidently one without any scientific precision. It expresses only a general or average impression that we have in reference to the relation of a class of goods to human wants. Every one would agree to the statement that "water is useful," thinking of the fact that it is indispensable to life and that it ministers to life in a multitude of ways. But what of water in one's cellar, water soaking one's clothes on a cold day, water breaking through the walls of a mountain reservoir and carrying death and destruction in its path? The poison that is doing what we at the moment desire, we call useful; that doing what we would prevent, we call harmful. Noxious weeds become "useful" by the discovery of some new process by which they can be worked into other forms, though they may still continue to be noxious in many a farmer's fields. The utility of anything, therefore, is seen to be of a relative and limited nature. The term "utility" in popular speech is very inexact. It can be employed in economic discussion only when carefully modified and defined.

Kinds of goods

2. *Goods consist of all those things objective to the user which have a beneficial relation to human wants.* They fall into several classes. We may first distinguish between free and economic goods. Free goods are things that exist in superfluity, that is, in quantities sufficient not only to gratify, but to satisfy all the wants that may depend on them. Economic goods are things so limited in quantity that all of the wants to which they could minister are not satisfied. The whole thought of economy begins with scarcity; indeed, even the conception of free goods is hardly possible until some limitation of wants is experienced. Practical economics is the study of the best way to employ things to secure the highest amount of gratification. The problem itself arises out of the fact that many things are used up before all wants dependent on them are completely satisfied.

A distinction is often made between consumption and production goods, or it may be better to say immediate and intermediate goods. Consumption goods are those things which are immediately at the point of gratifying man's desires. Production goods are those things which are not yet ready to gratify desires; some of them, being merely means of securing consumption goods, never will themselves immediately gratify desire.

Value is utility given precision

3. *Value, in the narrow personal sense, may be defined as the importance attributed to a good by a man.* The vagueness and inexactness of the word "utility," or the word "good," disappears when we reach the word "value." It is not a usual relation or a vague degree of benefit sometimes present and sometimes absent, but it refers

to a particular thing, person, time, and condition. Value is in the closest relation with wants, and in this narrow sense depends on the individual's estimate. From the meeting and comparison of the estimates of individuals, arise market values or prices, which are the central object of study in economics.

Chapter IV
The Nature of Demand

§ I. The Comparison of Goods in Man's Thought

Wants and goods must be constantly adjusted

1. *As wants differ in kind and degree, so goods differ in their power to gratify wants.* This general and simple statement unites the leading thoughts of the two chapters preceding. Confirmation of its truth may be found in observation and experience. The purpose of this chapter is to show how, starting from the general nature of wants and the nature of goods, we can arrive at an explanation of the exchange of goods. Recognizing the simple but fundamental fact stated at the opening of this paragraph, an exchange may be seen to be a rational and a logical result when men are living together in society.

Ripe and unripe goods

2. *Immediately enjoyable goods are the first objective things whose value is to be explained.* Goods come into relation with wants in a multitude of ways. Some things will not gratify a want until after the lapse of a long time, as ice cut in December and stored for summer use. Other things will never themselves directly gratify a want, but will be of help in getting things that do; such are the young fruit trees planted in the orchard, and the hammer that will be used to drive nails in a house that will shelter men. Still other things are gratifying wants at this moment, or are ready for use and will be used up in a very short time; examples of such are the food on the table and in the pantry, and the cigar in the pocket. All these things are called goods, because of their beneficial relation to man's desires, but the relation is very immediate in some cases, very remote in others. The value of all goods is to be explained, but the explanation will be more or less complex according to the directness or indirectness of their relation with wants. As it is the power of goods to gratify wants that alone causes value to be attributed to them, those goods which are ripest, which are ready to gratify wants, are nearest to the source of an explanation. The value of unripe enjoyments must be traced to some expected gratification as its cause or basis. In order to attack the difficulties one

by one we will, therefore, in the following discussion, deal first with this class of ripe, consumable goods, as food, personal services, enjoyments of any sort that are immediately available. The explanation of these cases of value must precede that of cases in which the relation to wants is less obvious and direct.

The law of diminishing utility

3. *As the amount of any good increases, after a certain point the gratification that the added portions afford decreases.* This is called the law of the diminishing utility of goods or of the decreasing gratification afforded by goods. The reason for the truth of this proposition is found in the very nature of man and his nervous organization. Any stimulus to the nerves, however pleasant at first, becomes painful when long continued or increased unduly. The trumpet too distant at first for the ear to distinguish its notes, may swell to pleasing tones as it approaches, until at length its volume and its din may become absolutely painful. If we were to express the degree of gratification by a curve, we should see the curve rising gradually to a maximum, and then falling somewhat suddenly and becoming a negative quantity, when pain, not pleasure, resulted. The same change could be illustrated by any sensation or by any of men's activities.

The proposition must be understood as applying to the gratification resulting from each added portion of the sensation. There is a maximum point in the gratification afforded by any nerve-stimulus. A man coming in from the winter's storm and holding out his hands before the fire, feels an intense pleasure in the grateful warmth; a few moments later, the same heat becomes unpleasant. In winter we wish for a moderation of the temperature; on the sultry days of summer, we think of a cool breeze as the most to be desired of all things. Whether the temperature rises or falls, there is a point beyond which the change is no longer an addition to, but a subtraction from, pleasure. A man, however hungry at first, may be made miserable if forced to eat beyond his capacity. Each added portion of the good consumed contributes to the gratification up to a certain point. The sum of these pleasurable sensations may be called the total gratification, which finally reaches satisfaction or fullness. Then begins what may be called in algebraic phrase a "negative gratification" which, if it becomes large enough, will make the total gratification a negative quantity. Each added portion, dose or increment beyond a certain point reduces thus the welfare of the user. One may have too much of a good thing.

The marginal utility

4. *Marginal utility is the gratification afforded by the added portion of the good.* The marginal dose, increment, or portion is that which may be logically considered as coming last in the case of any good or group of goods divisible into small parts. In considering the strict theory of the case, in order to get at the principle involved, the doses may be spoken of as infinitesimally small. The marginal utility expresses the importance that men attach to one unit of this kind of goods under the particular circumstances at the moment existing, and not under certain conceivable conditions which do not in fact exist or need to be taken into account

THE NATURE OF DEMAND

by the persons affected. The marginal unit of a homogeneous supply cannot be considered to have a greater utility than any other unit at the moment, and therefore the product of the marginal utility by the number of units, gives the total measure of importance of the supply then and there, and this is the value.

The value of goods, as has been indicated, is the measure of the dependence felt by men on a portion of the outer world, as the condition of gratifying their wants. From the very nature of wants, which reside in feelings, a dependence that is not felt, a relation between things and gratification that is not recognized, can have no influence on value. Now, it is at this margin of supply that dependence is felt. Men do not concern themselves about that which they have in superfluity — unless, indeed, the excess causes them some discomfort. It is well that they do not, for a wise direction of effort can only take place when men think mainly of their need of things that they want, and want most, and direct their efforts toward securing them.

From marginal utility to value

The diminishing utility of successive portions (doses or increments, as they are called) may be represented by a curve of utility.

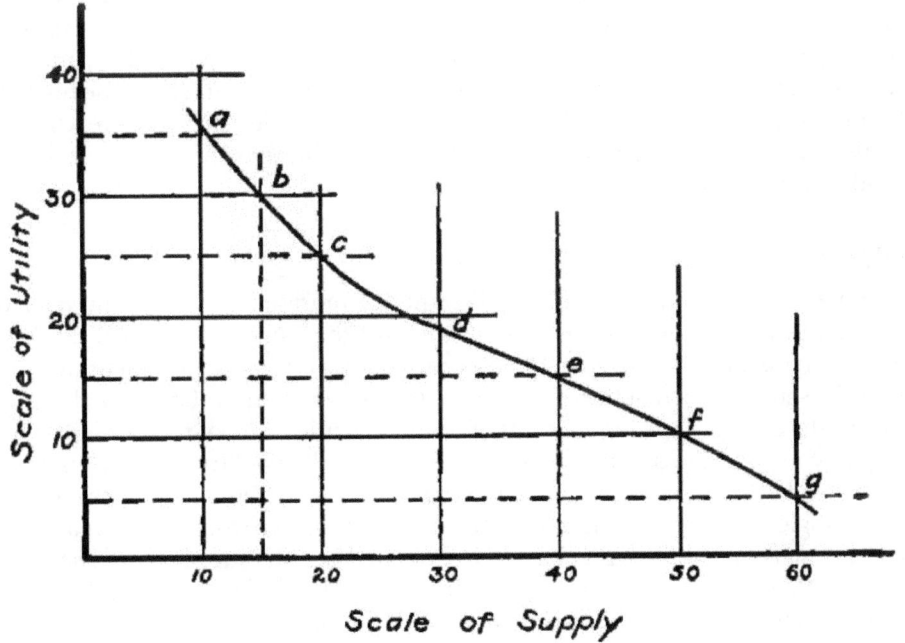

Scale of Supply

The diagram is constructed on the hypothesis that a tenth unit of a certain good would have a utility expressed as 36; a fifteenth unit of 30, etc., and that the value of the whole supply is estimated according to these marginal units. Of course if the conditions were that "all or none" was to be taken, the result would be different.

Unit of Supply	Marginal Utility	Value of Whole Supply
10	36	360
15	30	450
20	25	500
30	19	570
40	15	600
50	10	500
60	5	300

This diagram is frequently used, and it is important to guard against some misunderstandings. The marginal unit of any given supply—for example, ten units—is not any particular unit, it is any one of the ten units. In the presence of nine units of the good the person or persons find all the various wants that are dependent on that good gratified to such a degree that the tenth unit has an importance expressed by 36. But as this last or marginal unit of supply may be used for any of the purposes, the importance of each and every unit likewise will be expressed by 36. Any one of the units, when once present is, in a logical sense, a marginal unit. When, however, it is a question of increasing the supply, some one unit may properly be looked upon as marginal. The dependence felt by men on the whole group is the product of the units by the marginal utility. As the number of units increases, the marginal utility decreases, until at length it may reach zero, and the total value would be nothing. A point of maximum value evidently will be found somewhere between the two extremes.

Only one marginal utility at one moment

Note carefully that on the one diagram are represented a large number of marginal utilities which never exist at one and the same moment. At any one moment there is a given number of units and there is but one marginal utility, and this is the same for each of the units. It is quite erroneous to say that when there are 30 units the utility of the tenth unit is 36; of the twentieth, 25; of the thirtieth, 19. It is equally incorrect to say that when there are 60 units the "total utility" is equal to the area between the right angle and the curve a-g, while the value is equal to the rectangle below and to the left of the point g. The curve from a-g but marks the height of marginal utilities that have no existence when the supply is 30. The "total utility," often spoken of in this connection, if it has any existence certainly cannot be calculated. The diagram must be understood as representing indicatively at any given moment but one marginal utility, the same for every unit of like goods. The other perpendicular lines are expressed in the conditional mood; they are what the marginal utility would be were the numbers of units different.

Changing feelings changes utility

5. *Since goods possess utility only as they gratify wants, it follows that if wants*

change, the utility changes. Utility does not rest unchanging in the goods as something "intrinsic," but it depends on the relation of goods to men. This truth, unrecognized for many centuries, is now seen to be fundamental to the whole problem of value. The portions of a good added later do not appeal to the same man as the earlier portions. The man has been changed by what he has enjoyed. In changing his feelings, goods have also changed his wants. Hence, the added portions of the good are changed in respect to their utility or power to gratify a man's wants. Though physically and chemically, *i.e.*, in every material way, they are exactly like the earlier portions, they cannot have the same want-gratifying power until he again changes, for they are not in the presence of the same feelings.

Wants are constantly shifting; different kinds of goods are compared in man's thought and arranged on a scale at every moment according to their felt utility. An increase in the amount of a good will drop the marginal utility of the added portions down the scale of usefulness for the next moment. When we rise in the morning, we want our breakfast; the breakfast eaten, another breakfast does not appeal to us. Our tasks done, we take a boat-ride or go golfing; then, appetite returning, we are tempted to our dinner. And thus from hour to hour wants are gratified, are altered and are shifted, until, wearied with the day's labor and pastimes, we go to rest. In a well-ordered life, in an advanced economic society, the means for gratifying our wants as they arise are provided in advance. The changing series of desires is met by a changing series of goods. Life has been defined as a constant adjustment of inner relations to outer conditions. Economic life is therefore like physical life, a constant adjustment; and this adjustment of goods but reflects the shifting and adjustment of feelings.

Choice is constantly shifting

6. *The substitution of goods in men's thought is the shifting of the choice from a good that does not give the highest gratification economically possible at the time, to another good that does.* The shifting that takes place on the scale of gratification makes it necessary for man to shift constantly his choice of goods. This again is the problem of "economy." Waste results when goods continue to be used to secure a lower degree of gratification, if they might be used to secure a higher. The change of choice may be because of a change in the man, or because of a change in the quality or the quantity of the goods; or because of a change in the ratio at which the goods can be secured.

§ II. Demand for Goods Grows Out of Subjective Comparisons

Desire may become demand

1. *Demand is desire for goods united with the power to give something in exchange.* An example frequently given to show the difference between desire and demand

is the hungry boy looking longingly at the sweetmeats in the confectioner's window. He represents desire, but not until the kind-hearted gentleman gives him a nickel does he represent effective demand. Desire, therefore, must be united with power to give something in exchange before it can be called demand. It must be for something that is attainable; yearning for something beyond reach, sighing for the moon, is desire that never can become effective demand.

Demand the social expression of shifting choice

2. *Demand is the social aspect of the individual man's comparison of utilities.* It is the expression of the man's wish to substitute some of his goods for some one else's goods in order to get a higher satisfaction. This comparison is often made between two goods owned in different quantities. When men are constantly comparing things in their own possession, it is a short step to compare their goods with their neighbor's.

Demand for consumption goods is thus the manifestation of the man's desire to redistribute his enjoyments. In demand for goods men virtually say: "Part of what I have I am ready to give for part of what you have." The strength of their desire is expressed by the amount of their offer. When he makes this comparison and this offer, man enters into a social, economic relation with his fellows.

The limit of the exchanger's demand

3. *The law of individual demand is: The trader will reduce his stock of a particular good to the point where its marginal utility equals that of the alternative goods.* The greater the divergence in his estimates of the marginal utilities of two goods, the more ready is he to trade the lower utility for the higher one. Exchange is but the effort to adjust goods to wants in the best way. The less useful (marginally viewed) is traded for the more useful. The greater the difference, in the one trader's judgment, between the marginal utilities of the two goods, the greater is the maladjustment, and the greater, therefore, is the motive to seek readjustment by means of exchange. As the quantity of the good parted with declines, its marginal utility increases; and as more of the other good is acquired, its marginal utility declines. The marginal utility of the two exchangeable units must come to equilibrium in the individual's judgment. At this point demand ceases, not because an additional unit of the one good could afford no gratification, but because it would afford less gratification than the other good in which demand must be expressed to be effectual.

The Demand curve

4. *Demand thus varies at different ratios of exchange between goods, and may be expressed graphically by a demand curve.* This would show for any one man the decline of the marginal utility of each added portion of a good, and these individual demand curves may be united into a demand curve for a group of men. The demand curve expresses graphically what a man would be willing to pay at each particular stage in the increase of goods. We have here come to the very threshold of the subject of markets and exchange.

THE NATURE OF DEMAND

Elasticity of demand

5. *Elasticity of demand, in the case of any good, expresses the degree in which a change in its ratio to other goods will increase the demand.* Elasticity varies for different classes of men according to their wealth and to the cost of the goods. If strawberries are a dollar a box in the city market, a slight fall in the price, say to seventy-five cents, will increase the demand but slightly. But if the price is fifteen cents and falls to ten, the increase in the demand will be marked, for the number of consumers to whom a difference of five cents is important is then very great. The demand for the staples is comparatively inelastic. A certain amount of simple food is necessary to support life; an increase in its price will not quickly check the demand. On the other hand, if the price of staple foods falls, no very great increase will take place in the demand.

Chapter V
Exchange in a Market

§ I. Exchange of Goods Resulting from Demand

Reciprocal demand becomes exchange

1. *Exchange in the usual economic sense is the transfer of two goods by two owners, each of whom deems the good taken more than a value-equivalent for the one given.* The comparison of goods that has been discussed above is a kind of exchange. When a person chooses one thing rather than another, one form of gratification may be said to be mentally exchanged for another. This is exchange in that person's mind, or subjective exchange. But the word "exchange" as usually employed means an exchange of goods between persons. It is objective exchange, and when the word is used without modification, it is to be understood in the objective sense. In the last chapter were analyzed the motives of the individual man. Robinson Crusoe on his desert island would in very many ways be acted upon by the same motives in reference to economic goods that men are in society. Yet, it is exchange in society and the complicated problems arising from this transfer of goods from person to person that constitute nearly the whole of the subject-matter of political economy.

Exchange is seen to arise out of the differences in the situations of men with reference to goods. The different subjective valuations give rise to demand, and demand leads to exchange. In early societies differences in natural products were the most usual causes of exchange. Salt, though so essential to life, is found in few places. The metals early became indispensable for weapons of defense or for the chase, and were sought far and wide. Rare shells, feathers, jewels, and the precious metals appealed in early times to a universal desire for ornament. Products like these are the objects of a rude sort of exchange in the first simple efforts made to adjust possessions to wants. Within the tribe, differences in the skill and ability of men to produce arrow heads or weapons or ornaments, bring about the exchange of goods.

Mutual advantage in exchange

2. *The advantage of exchange consists in the raising of the want-gratifying power*

of goods to both parties. It generally was assumed by medieval thinkers that if one party to an exchange gained, the other must lose. The mistaken idea prevailed that value is something fixed in the good, and unchangeable. Where the exchange is voluntary (and only that kind is here being considered), it is mutual advantages which make the exchange rational. Many false conclusions on practical questions still result from a failure to grasp this simple truth. It follows from this that the act of exchange is itself useful, for goods having a small importance to men are given a higher importance by being brought into better relations with wants. Merchants, peddlers, traders, and common carriers of all sorts, therefore, are adding to the utility of goods. This idea has been only slowly apprehended, but is now one of the least disputed propositions in economics.

Demand is supply in another aspect

3. *Barter is the exchange of goods without the use of money.* Either one of the goods traded in cases of barter may be considered as sold, and either one as bought, according as the matter is looked at from the standpoint of the one or the other party to the exchange. Demand, therefore, is supply, and supply is demand when the point of view is shifted from one party to another. The fisherman's demand for venison is expressed in terms of fish; the hunter's demand for fish is expressed in terms of venison. But to the fisherman the venison is the supply offered to him. The term "marginal utility" of a good, therefore, does not refer merely to the demand of the consumer; for it expresses by a single phrase the idea both of demand and of supply. The utility of the goods composing the supply is expressed in terms of the goods that represent demand and vice versa. The only way in which man can give definite, concrete, numerical expression to his desire for goods is to state it in terms of other goods. In expressing numerically, in terms of other objects, an estimate of the utility of an apple, a horse or a house, one inevitably gives expression to a ratio of exchange; demand for one good is the offer of another good.

§ II. Barter under Simple Conditions

In isolated exchange the price is not economically fixed

1. *In isolated exchange, where only two traders engage in barter, their estimates give respectively the upper and the lower figures of the ratio at which the trade can take place.* Let us recall the fact that a difference in the *relative* estimates that men place on goods is the first essential of exchange. Those estimates may be expressed in a ratio; we may say that A will give four apples for one orange, would be glad to give fewer, but will not give more; while B will give one orange for three apples, would be glad to get more apples, but will not take fewer. The outside limits of the ratio at which the exchange must take place will, therefore, be one orange for three or four apples.

A, seller of apples, offers 4 (or fewer) apples for 1 orange.

B, buyer of apples, demands 3 (or more) apples for 1 orange.

There is, in entirely isolated exchange, therefore, a lack of definiteness in the price, much depending on what Adam Smith called the "higgling of the market." In the old-time American horse trade much depended on "bluff"; in such cases it was as important to be able to judge character as to judge horses. A thorough analysis of the trade, however, would probably show that the bargain is concluded at a point which exactly balances the hopes of gain and fears of loss of one of the parties.

Competitive bidding narrows the limits of price

2. *Where one-sided competition exists, the ratio of the exchange will be somewhere between the estimates of the two buyers most eager for the last portion offered.* By competition is here meant the independent seeking of the same thing at one time by two or more persons. Where there is one market price paid by a number of buyers, it may be that no two of the subjective estimates are alike; the exchange value may differ from all of their estimates, and yet must correspond closely to two. Auction sales well illustrate the principle. If there is one ax to be sold and ten possible buyers for an ax, and there is no combination among them, the bidding will go on until the estimate of the buyer next to the most eager, has been reached. The most eager buyer can then secure the ax by bidding just a little above his next competitor. But if there are ten axes and ten buyers who know that there will be ten axes offered, the more eager buyers will refuse to bid much above the less eager ones. A shrewd auctioneer, therefore, often conceals the fact that there is more than one of an article, and having sold it off, brings out a second or a third one of the same kind, thus keeping the buyers in ignorance of the supply and getting somewhere near the estimate of the most eager buyer in each case. Advertisements of "a limited supply," "the last chance," "positively the last appearance," are meant to stimulate the demand of the patrons, and to lead them to buy at once. In general, therefore, where competition exists on one side, price is fixed with greater definiteness than in isolated exchange. Not so much depends on shrewd bargaining, on bluff, or on the stubbornness of an individual. Far more depends on forces outside the control of any one man. The bidders are impelled by self-interest to outbid their competitors, and thus the limits within which the market price must fall are narrowly fixed.

Buyers fix price of perishable goods

If things already brought to market must be sold at any price that can be secured, the buyers may be said to fix the price. This does not mean that they can buy it for any sum that they wish, but it means that when each one is trying to get it as cheap as possible, their bids finally determine how much it will sell for. In such cases, therefore, the competition is for the moment one-sided.

If a part of the supply can be withdrawn and kept without great loss, this will be done if the price is low. Strawberries, fish, and meat may be sold Saturday night at any price that will secure purchasers, but every thing that can be kept with little or no depreciation will be withheld from sale for a time. It may even be of advantage to the seller to destroy a part of the supply, when the increased price of the smaller amount will give a larger total.

The margin of advantage and the marginal pair

3. *Where two-sided competition exists, the bidding goes on until a price is reached where the least eager seller and the least eager buyer have the narrowest possible motive to exchange.* As the market ratio varies from those in the minds of the individuals when they come to the market, there is left a considerable margin to some and a very small one to others. This difference between the market value and the ratio of exchange at which any given individual would continue to exchange for the good may be called the *margin of advantage*. Moreover, the buyers will have a margin and the sellers a margin, and as that margin narrows there is less and less motive to continue the exchange until, finally, the margin disappearing, the buyer or seller, withdrawing from the market, ceases to be an exchanger, at least for that particular part of the goods.

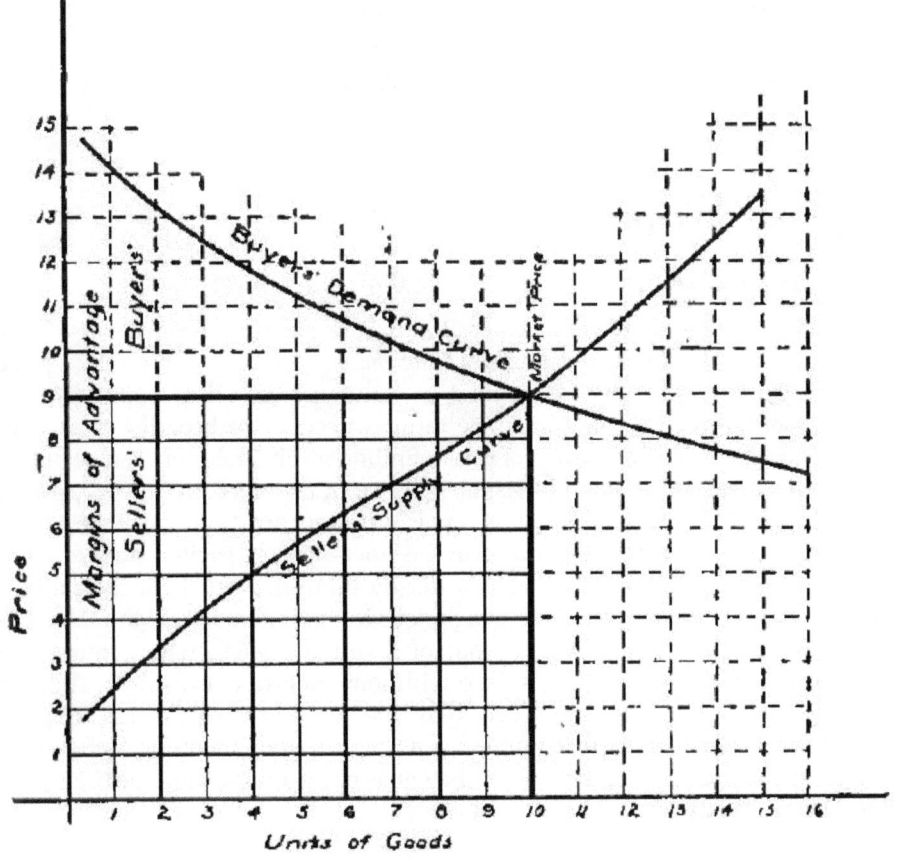

Units of Goods

The least eager buyer and the least eager seller may be called the *marginal pair*. They are the buyer and the seller respectively having the narrowest margin of advantage. Their outside estimates are nearest to the market ratio. If the market ratio shifts slightly in either direction, one of them will drop out of the exchange. It is evident that a buyer who is taking ten units may be on the margin with reference to the tenth unit, and yet may continue to be one of the most eager buyers to secure one unit. Thus, the marginal buyer is to be thought of as that person who, logically considered, is the least eager, or on the margin, with reference to a particular unit of supply, however eager he may be with reference to any other unit of supply. It would be well to recall here the discussion of the nature of wants and the variation in the intensity of demand.

Market values built on individual estimates

4. *Market values are built up on subjective valuations.* The idea of market values, therefore, is that of the want-gratifying power of goods as expressed in terms of other goods, where there are various buyers and sellers. They are not an average of the subjective valuations, nor are they made up of the extremes. They correspond closely with the subjective estimates of two of the exchangers. The other parties to the exchange are willing to accept the market ratio, for it offers them more inducements than it does to either one of the marginal pair.

§ III. Price in a Market

One price in a market

1. *A market is a body of buyers and sellers in such close business relations that the actual price conforms closely to the valuation of the marginal pair.* The word "price" which we have used, may be defined as value expressed in terms of some commonly exchanged commodity. The term is used more broadly of anything given in exchange. The very terms of this definition imply that there can be but one price in a market. This is a somewhat abstract but a useful economic proposition. Very often within sound of each other's voices traders are paying different prices for a good. On the occasion of a break in the stock-market, excited traders within ten feet of each other make bids that differ by thousands of dollars. Retail and wholesale merchants may be purchasing goods in the same room at the same time at very different prices. But within a group of buyers and sellers where competition is approximately complete, price is fixed with some degree of exactness. The more nearly the actual conditions approach to the ideal of a market, the less are prices fixed by higgling, and the more impersonal they become, the buyers and sellers being compelled to adjust their bids to the needs of the market, and not being able to vary them greatly one way or the other.

EXCHANGE IN A MARKET

The earlier markets

2. *Markets are steadily widening through the improvement of means of communication and transportation.* The earliest markets were established on the borders between tribes, villages or nations as a common ground where strangers met to trade. At such markets were brought together from sparsely settled districts a comparatively large number of merchants and customers. Buyers had the opportunity of wide selection both in kind and quality, and the sellers found a large body of customers gathered at one point. Throughout the Middle Ages purchases were made by the more prosperous husbandmen in great quantities once a year at the fairs or markets. As both the buyers and sellers came from widely separated places, there was, in most respects, no combination, and the conditions of a competitive market were present.

The growth of markets

The number of buyers and sellers that can constitute a single market is limited both directly and indirectly by the means of transportation. A dense population cannot usually be maintained without easy means of transportation to bring in a large supply of food, and to carry back manufactured goods great distances. The remarkable growth in the means of commerce since the application of steam to water traffic, and the invention of the railroad, have made it possible for goods to be gathered from most distant points. A market implies a common understanding among traders. Modern means of communication such as newspapers, post-offices, telegraph and cable, trade bulletins, commercial travelers, the consular service, and many forms of special agencies, are diffusing information widely. As a result of these changes, there has been a widening of the village-market to the markets of the province, of the nation, and finally of the world. While a part of every one's purchases continues to be made in the neighborhood, a greater and greater portion of the total business is done by traders who are widely separated and who are indeed members of the world market. Various articles produced in the same locality may seek different markets. The market for wheat may be in Liverpool, while that for fruit and eggs is in the village near the farm-house. If a given product of any community is sold in different markets, the net prices secured must be very nearly equal.

The conceptions normal and market price

3. *Normal price is spoken of in contrast to market price when the actual market price results from exceptional circumstances and probably will not be maintained.* The term "normal price," much used in economic discussion, is the price which, apart from exceptional conditions, is expected to prevail, and to which actual prices seem constantly striving to adjust themselves. As actual prices are nearly always either more or less than so-called normal price, and only momentarily ever correspond with it, the term "normal" would appear to be something of a misnomer. Moreover, as the circumstances of production change, this normal price itself is altered so that what is normal one day may be quite abnormal the next. The thought of "normal price" is an abstract one, but despite the inaptness of the word it is not without

some practical validity. In determining whether he shall continue to produce certain goods, the business man is practically guided by his view of normal price. An example of departure from normal price as above defined, is found in the price of food when an expected ship has failed to arrive at a port with its cargo of grain. A scarcity amounting almost to famine might thus exist in a seaboard city, and the market price would rise; but as this would be due to an accident and would afford a larger gain than usual to those who happened to have a supply of grain, men would say that the market price was above the normal price. The arrival of the expected ship would cause the market price to return to the normal.

Review of the argument

In review, we see that the market value of goods grows out of the different personal estimates made by men. Market value itself being a complex and difficult problem, it can be mastered only by dividing it. First, therefore, must be studied the more general and obvious motives of men, the nature of wants and their effects on man's subjective estimates. The same simple motives that influence the subjective valuations made by individual men, may be traced to the conditions of the complicated market. It is their workings that are seen in the obscurest problems of market price.

Chapter VI
Psychic Income

§ I. Income as a Flow of Goods

The recurrence of wants

1. *Satisfaction and gratification being only temporary conditions, economic wants appear in more or less regularly recurring series.* Impressions are short lived, sensations are temporary, wants that have been satisfied recur. Wants recur for the same reason that they first arose. No impression on the nerves or on the senses is lasting. Man's senses were developed for the purpose of bringing him into relation with the outer world, of enabling him to survive in his struggle with the forces of nature. So, when a good has been enjoyed, the utility to that person of that thing or service for that particular moment, falls, it may be even to zero. To keep wants satisfied is impossible; we cannot do next year's reading or next week's eating now; we cannot live the life of to-morrow. The best results in reading or eating come from taking the right amount day by day. But it is a need in the life of men that wants should recur after a time, otherwise there would be no motive for action.

Series of wants and series of goods

2. *The economic ideal is that this series of recurring wants should be met by a corresponding series of goods.* It is evident that if a series or succession of goods varies, at different times, moments, and conditions, in its power to gratify wants, the closer the correspondence between the two series, that of wants and that of goods, the greater will be the total of gratification. We may liken man's life to a journey in which the supplies of food are gotten at the stations. If any one of these supplies fails, the traveler suffers the pangs of hunger, and if two or three supplies are at one point, they do not serve the needs of man so well as if distributed along the way. This constant inflow of goods is one of the fundamental needs of life. The savage dimly understands this need. Even the birds and the beasts adjust their lives to it either by travel or by toil. The spring and autumn migrations to new feeding grounds are the attempts of the bird to gratify this series of wants as they arise. The ant, the bee, and the squirrel anticipate, and work to fill their

storehouses against the days of need.

Social and private incomes

3. *Objective income consists of the additional sums of goods acquired by individuals or by society during the income period.* The term national or social income may be contrasted with individual or private income in the objective sense. The nature of the acquisition of objective incomes may, in some cases, be different if viewed from the social and individual standpoints. Society, as a whole, may be said to acquire income only when goods are produced; individuals may acquire income by gift, bequest, theft, or other modes of transfer from other individuals. In many cases the two kinds of income, however, agree, the objective income of society being the algebraic sum of the goods acquired or parted with by all the individuals.

We should not understand that either social or private objective incomes include only material goods, for many utilities and labor services that never take on a material or money expression are included in either case. Indeed, we are close here to the conception of psychic income which is to be developed more fully.

Money income

Income of money is not often the same as income of things. Usually many of these subtler utilities are overlooked and omitted from the recognized money income. In this day the use of money is so common that we are sometimes led to ignore the value of things to which the money expression is not given. The money income is merely the money expression of the value of currently acquired goods, and it is the only medium through which such varied sources of gratification can be compared.

Gross and net income

4. *Income in the logical sense must be a net addition, but the term gross income is not without popular and practical meaning.* Gross income is sometimes spoken of in the sense of total receipts, as the total of goods secured; net income is the remainder after deducting expenditures and after replacing the goods employed to secure the income. In order to produce some goods technically, men make use of other goods. While they are storing up a supply of wood or coal it may be looked upon as the income, but they may burn it to help grow hothouse plants. While they gather flowers with one hand, they destroy fuel with the other. Only the net increase in value can be accounted income in the second period. The goods that come into a man's possession in any period are of many sorts: to get some he has destroyed many previously existing goods; while to get others he has not needed to use up the accumulations of the past or to mortgage the future. The one kind is gross, the other net income.

Wealth and income

5. *An income of consumption goods is a part of wealth, but not the whole of it.* The

consumption goods, the "present goods" at the moment available, are the essential part of wealth for the moment's enjoyment. The only essential and immediate conditions of a series of gratifications is a regular series of consumption goods. But many things existing which could be used to secure a gratification are not in fact treated as consumption goods. A crop of corn is not all income. In a time of famine it could be used, but seed-corn was saved from last year, and some must be kept for next year. This is a part of wealth, but not of "present goods" as we understand the term.

Some goods never can become enjoyable goods

Further, in the economic world there is much wealth that never can gratify any want directly; many forms of wealth never can be consumption goods. It is true that everything called wealth is expected to contribute sooner or later in some way to the sum of gratifications. It is for that reason it is called wealth. It is, however, a mere figure of speech to say indirect want-gratifiers become want-gratifying goods. For example, the engine transporting a load of coal is indirectly gratifying wants; if it is transporting a train-load of passengers, the gratification is direct. A machine making cloth for next year is gratifying wants only in a metaphorical sense. A field used to produce food is not a direct want-gratifier until it is transformed into a residence site, a playground, or a tennis-court.

It is necessary therefore to recognize the distinction between present and future incomes. The value of the mass of wealth in possession and yielding income, rests in large part upon its power of contributing to income in some future period. Thus, any durable good may be looked upon as embodying a series of incomes ranging from present to future in varying degrees. This will be fully considered under the subject of capital.

Income from wealth and from labor

6. *Incomes are called funded or unfunded according to the sources from which they are derived.* Funded income arises from the possession of wealth or of claims on wealth, such as lands, railroad stocks, government bonds, etc. The income is "funded" because it corresponds to an abiding fund of wealth. The income arising from current labor is unfunded, because there is no permanent fund of accumulated wealth corresponding to it.

The idea of regularity connected with funded income is not essential to the idea of income in general, *i.e.*, we cannot refuse to call a thing income because it occurs only this year. If it is part of the sum of goods that flows in, that is newly available for the man's use, it is income. But funded income is the more abiding, for income from wages stops when the man dies or fails to perform his work, while the income from wealth continues after he ceases to be active. Thus, families with equal incomes may differ greatly in wealth, the one depending entirely on salaries, the other on rents.

§ II. Income as a Series of Gratifications

Gratification the test of psychic income

All sources of income are productive

1. *The value of consumption goods is derived from the pleasurable psychic impressions which they aid to produce, and these psychic effects constitute the psychic income.* The objective income is sometimes called the "real" income, but certainly it is not income in the most essential sense. Things outside of men cannot be feelings, they can only call out or occasion feeling, and it is the attainment of pleasurable conditions in mind or soul that is the aim of all economic activity. Material income and immaterial income are both related to and reducible to psychic income. Some portions at least of the objective incomes of goods are continually by use becoming subjective incomes of enjoyment. Men talk of material income as consisting of bushels of wheat, head of cattle, etc., and of immaterial income as the uses that durable goods yield directly or that men perform for each other, *e.g.*, those of the singer, physician, teacher, judge—all services that do not take on material form. There was a long-standing dispute in economic literature regarding the difference between productive and unproductive labor. Productive labor was said to be that which embodied itself in abiding material form. The distinction led to some peculiar puzzles and paradoxes. The bartender mixing drinks, adds to the value of those ingredients; in a minute that value is dissipated. According to the distinction in question, he is a productive laborer because his services are embodied in material form, whereas the lecturer is regarded as an unproductive laborer because the results of his labor are not embodied in material form. But whether or not the service has for a moment embodied itself in material form is of no essential economic import. The presence of the waiter is as essential to the well-served dinner as are the polished silver and china, or as the well-cooked food. The distinction in question is not now made by economists, all labor that contributes to value being regarded as productive. But a similar distinction is inconsistently preserved by many writers in the case of material things. A building used as a factory is called productive, but used by the owner as a dwelling it is called unproductive because the service it renders does not appear in material form. But the use of the house, or that of land for a school ground or campus, secures a certain gratification, an immaterial good. Consistency requires that the services of men and the use of material things be judged by their psychic results, the question whether the service takes on a material or an immaterial form being disregarded.

All wealth is logically related to psychic income

2. *Only those things and actions that are in some causal relation to gratifications can have value to man.* This proposition of theory is demonstrated every hour in practical life. The business man always is trying to trace a causal relation between things that do not and cannot themselves directly satisfy wants, and things that do. The vineyard has no value to Tantalus, unable to reach its fruit. A captive, chained to a rock, attaches value only to the things within his reach. Men living in savagery and ignorance starve amid the possibilities of plenty. Chained by their

ignorance and improvidence to a little spot of earth, they do not see clearly, either in time or space, the economic relations about them.

Values of things distant in time

3. *Man's foresight and knowledge enable him to think of many periods at once, and thus his felt dependence on goods extends over a series of future productive agents.* In order to simplify the problem, we have spoken of the economic man as living only in and for the moment. If he had no more knowledge, memory, or imagination than is necessary to compare goods here, only present goods could have value to him. Even the higher animals, and much more the savages, rise above that level of improvidence. With increased intelligence the economic life of man expands, and he attaches importance to things which at the present moment have not, and cannot have, the slightest influence on his immediate gratification. The extension of man's view works a momentous change in his economic estimates. Of the thousands of forms of matter in the world, only a comparatively few ever will make an immediate gratifying impression on man's senses. But many of them are so connected in his thought by chains of association with pleasures or uses, that almost instinctively and most intensely he attaches an importance to them. In most cases it would require close thought to see that the service attributed directly to them was but a reflection of that performed by some other good. Thus, more and more, the estimates placed by men on goods come to depend on knowledge and foresight, and not on immediate impressions and feelings.

Goods related in varying degrees to psychic income

4. *Things are causally related in varying degrees to the psychic income, and have value only as their relation is known and felt.* The explanation of value is not complete till value has been traced back to its source in gratification. Often the complex nature of the problem is ignored. If one discusses the trading of a bushel of grain, to be used by a hungry man for food, for a sheep to be kept for breeding, or for wool to be made into cloth next year, he may overlook the difference in the grade of wants compared. In this case, a gratification of the present moment is compared with a gratification of a very different kind at a future time. The problem involved is complex because of differences in time, in place, and in the nature of the want-gratifiers. The student should endeavor to reduce the problem of value to its simplest form by considering first the exchange, at the present moment, of immediately enjoyable goods. The logical starting-point in the theory of value is in those goods that are in closest touch with feeling, and on this basis may be built up an explanation of values in which reason and forethought have a greater part. Starting from the proposition that psychic income is the foundation of all values, we shall go on, however, to trace causes that give value to all the physical agents, and to the most indirect of want-gratifiers.

DIVISION B—WEALTH AND RENT

Chapter VII
Wealth and its Indirect Uses

§ I. The Grades of Relation of Indirect Goods to Gratification

Technical rank of agents

1. *Goods may be ranked according to their technical relation to wants.* The technical rank of goods (sometimes spoken of as the degree of roundaboutness of the process) signifies the number of steps or processes that intervene between the agent used and the desired form. If one wishing the hickory-nut hanging above his head must first pick up a stick to throw at it, the nut is removed one step from desire. But even among savages the processes are much more complicated. The Indian with a crude knife fashions his bow and arrow, fastens the flint and cord which represent still other processes of industry, and shoots the bird which satisfies his hunger. In modern conditions the relations are vastly more complicated; only at the end of a long series do men arrive at the thing which gratifies their wants.

Time relations of goods to wants

2. *Goods may be ranked by their relation to wants in time.* The relation in respect to time is measured by the period that must elapse before the utility of an agent results in, is converted into, gratification. No agent or influence intervening, a thing may yet be removed a long way from gratification. A tree may not be fitted to bear fruit for ten years to come. Meantime, there are many other possible uses for the tree: it may be used for fuel, or to make a canoe with which to catch fish, or to follow some other indirect method of production. Evidently the technical and time relations of goods are very different. The number of steps has no necessary relation to the time. A number of technical steps may be taken in half an hour, or a process of a single technical step may last a year. In the mechanic arts the technical relations are of primary significance, but in economics the time relations are mainly to be considered.

3. *Economic goods may be classified as immediately enjoyable goods and durable*

agents. Enjoyable goods are goods in a final form, producing gratification or just ready to give gratification the next moment, as the cool draft of air made by a fan on a hot day, the cup of coffee steaming on the table.

Enjoyable goods and durable agents

Many goods of just the same form as the foregoing may not be affording current gratification (except that afforded by thrift and forethought), but are kept because later they will gratify a more intense want or gratify a want better. Apples and potatoes are kept in a cellar so that their use is distributed throughout the winter; cider and wine are kept till they get a quality that appeals more to the palate. Coal, wood, and stocks of goods, are thus kept in the form of enjoyable goods, destined to be physically destroyed when at length they yield a gratification. Evidently they must be storing up meantime a certain additional utility, for otherwise there would be no reason why they should be kept for the future. Such goods as these are sometimes called unripened consumption goods, but until ripened they bear in part the character of durable agents.

Abiding sources of economic enjoyments are called durable agents. The inhabited house is a source of continued gratification in each moment's shelter it affords; but, further, it is the durable source of a series of future uses, as yet unripened. The hammer, the hoe, the tree, the field may all be considered as agents to secure consumption goods. Some of these are but one step removed from direct gratification, as the hoe helping the gardener to get food for his own use. Other agents are bound by many technical links to the ultimate gratification.

Degrees of durableness

4. *This classification of goods is abstract, in that it is a classification, not of concrete goods, but of qualities shared in some degree by nearly all goods.* Most goods unite in some degree both characters, but in varying measure. This is, therefore, a continuity classification, the varying classes of goods grading from those whose durableness is zero (just at the moment of consumption) to those most durable, which yield an endless series of uses or products. Yet the classification is practical, corresponding as it does with thoughts which men have in the use of goods. By repairs and other methods goods become, and are looked upon as, durable sources of a series of uses.

It is to be noted further that the enjoyable goods pass over into psychic income, that is, they are the stream of objective utilities that is each moment detaching itself as income from the great mass of wealth. The durable goods are those utilities which for the time remain, not yet ripened or ready to be converted into psychic income.

§ II. Conditions of Economic Wealth

Income as affected by climatic conditions

1. *The bounty and variety of the natural supply of indirect goods in the material world are the prime conditions of a bountiful income to society.* The effect of climate on the supply of goods available for man is complex. Climate is itself a direct source of gratification. As temperature must be adjusted to man's need, climate satisfies wants directly. Health, energy, the beauty of noonday woods and of sunlit clouds are conditioned on the favor of nature. Climate affects, further, the supply of material economic goods. All the earlier civilizations arose in warmer countries. But, after man had gained a certain mastery over the obstacles of nature, he was able to soften the harsher features of climate, and with better shelter and clothing, with better stocks of winter food and fuel, the more favorable features of the temperate zone could be utilized. So civilization moved northward from Egypt and India to Greece and Rome, to northern Europe and America.

By natural resources

Soil conditions for vegetable life determine first the amount and kind of animal life. Animal life from one point of view is a parasite, living on the vegetable; it is only the vegetable that has power to assimilate most inorganic compounds. Water being a need of plant life, the amount of rainfall is one of the most important conditions of industry. Man, therefore, depends on the resources of the soil directly or indirectly; a fertile soil furnishes him either directly a supply of vegetable food, or indirectly a supply of animal food.

Natural supplies of metals, of coal, and of timber are important consumption goods, but they are also indirectly the condition for a vast variety of other goods. The industry that could exist without iron, copper, and coal would be of a very low grade.

By flora and fauna

The variety of flora and fauna, and their fitness for man's needs, largely condition the possible production. If, in the course of evolution, it had chanced that wheat and corn, the horse and the cow, had been crowded out in the struggle for existence, we should have had a very different civilization. The possibilities of civilization in Peru, and those of all the Indians on the American continent, were limited for lack of domestic animals. Animals that are fit for domestication are a necessary intermediate agent by aid of which man can appropriate and turn to his use the fertile qualities of the soil.

Not content with the material world about him, even when it is at its best, man alters it in many ways. He enriches the soil, improves the varieties of animals, he even in some slight degree affects the climate, and by the use of a multitude of artificial bits of matter called tools, works profound changes in the world in which he lives.

By motion and energy

2. *A large part of the utility of goods is conditioned on motion and energy.* It has been said that man's power in production is limited to moving things. The outer world is to man the sole source of motive forces. He can bring things together and they produce the result. Further, it may be said that nearly every kind of utility is conditioned on motion. It is man's aim to secure a constant inflow of goods. To secure this either he must move to get the goods, or he must cause goods to move toward him.

The law of "conservation of energy" helps to explain economic action; the supply of energy in the universe cannot be increased or diminished, but may take on new forms. So a limited supply in man's control may take on various forms and so have different effects on gratifications. One and the same source of energy may be converted into the different forms of heat, light, motion, electricity, etc. But there must be some source. Man's desire is directed to getting force at the right place and in the right degree. If light or heat is too intense, it causes pain; the glare of the sun blinds instead of giving keener vision. A moderate force applied to any of the senses gives the maximum clearness or pleasure. Man is constantly endeavoring to secure forces from the outer world and to adjust motion so that it will directly or indirectly best serve his purposes.

By food, animals, and fuel

3. *Among the main sources of power used by men are food, domestic animals, and fuel.* In eating food man stores up force in his own body. When he draws the bow he puts force into it to lie latent until liberated at the right moment. There must be a source of energy likewise that mental action may go on, and the power of sunbeams, stored for a time in food, is liberated in the processes of thought.

This first natural mode of liberating energy within their own bodies does not satisfy the growing needs and aims of men. Such a mode is "labor," which becomes at times painful and distasteful. In the earliest societies known, some sorts of domestic animals are found supplementing man's efforts and acting upon the material world to alter it for man. The dog joining in the chase guards his master's safety, and helps to bear his burdens. The draft-beast in the field turns the heavy soil, and aids in the final harvest. The trained elephant does the work of twenty men piling logs, loading ships, or carrying burdens.

Man further increases his control over the material world by making other men do his bidding. Domestic slavery, where wife or child serves the father of the family, or chattel slavery, where the vanquished toils for the victor, are all but universal in early communities. Such a method of increasing one's control over the forces of the world requires only superior strength, no special intelligence in mechanics, and is thus one of the first crude devices in a primitive civilization.

Fuel has been, up to the present time, perhaps the most important source of energy. Fire in the hands of savage man gave him dominion over the forests and over the metals. In this age of steam the liberation of the energy of the sun, stored up in coal in ages past, is still the indispensable condition of our developed industry.

By the energy in wind and flowing water

4. *The greatest and most exhaustless reservoirs of power for man's use are in wind and water.* While the supply of fuel is being used at a progressive rate and will soon approach exhaustion, there are elsewhere exhaustless stores of energy awaiting man's command. To make use of the wind for sailing a boat, only the simplest arrangements are needed; a windmill fixed at one place requires more ingenuity and machinery. The energy of the wind is derived from the sun and will last until the sun loses its heat. If some means can be found for equalizing the flow and for storing the power of the wind, it may yet become a great agency of industry. The force of falling water, long used in a petty way by the old water-mills, is just beginning to be employed on a large scale at such points as Niagara. Where fuel is high, as on the Pacific coast, wave motors have been successfully used in a small way, but wave motion is too irregular to serve well the needs for power. But the constant motion of the tides offers, at some favored points, a source of power that will remain as long as the earth revolves upon its axis.

By the intelligent utilization of all these agencies

5. *Man studies and compares the durable goods that give him command over enjoyable goods, and attaches value to them.* Thus energy is found dissipating itself throughout the world in ways useless to man, and in places where it cannot serve his purposes. As man grows in power of control over nature, he seeks to apply these forces in forms and at places he has selected. If he can arm himself with the energies of mine and torrent, he can react with giant strength on the material world. He ceases to accept passively its conditions, and to live on its grudging gifts; he becomes its fashioner, in a sense its creator. His intelligence and his wants are most important factors determining what the form of the physical world about him shall be.

But all the efforts of men in the most developed economy cannot make to disappear the differences in the quality of goods and agents. Desirable goods to consume are limited in quantity, and they vary in quality; hence they have value and some higher than others. Likewise, durable material agents and sources of power are limited in number and vary in convenience of location and efficiency. As men seek to gratify their desires, they attach importance to these agents of power. Each is valued for its service or its series of services. When anything is seen to contain a series of uses, it becomes a rent-bearer, and the economic problem of rent arises, one step more complex than the problem of valuing simple consumption goods.

Chapter VIII
The Renting Contract

§ I. Nature and Definition of Rent

Temporary use and permanent possession of agents

1. *The temporary use of materials and power and their sources is necessary to bring most enjoyable goods into being.* Indirect goods have value solely because they help to get direct goods. The apple-tree is valued because it bears fruit, and the orchard because the trees give promise of yielding a succession of crops for years to come. There are thus two problems of value in connection with durable goods: that of the value of a temporary use for a brief period, as for a year; and that of the value of a thing itself, the use-bearer, for a long series of years or in perpetuity. To explain what fixes the value of the temporary use is the problem of rent; to explain what determines the value of long-continued use or of permanent control and ownership of a use-bearer is the problem of capitalization.

Origin of the term rent

2. *The term rent is used in a number of senses, which must be carefully distinguished.* The original meaning of rent was any regular income or revenue arising from wealth. The word comes from the low Latin *renta* from *renda*, in turn from *redditus*, that which is given, yielded or given back, or *rendita*, that which is given or returned. The French *rendre* (English render), to give or return that which belongs to one, is used very early. Chaucer used "rente" as an income. "Cattle had he enough and rente," cattle probably meaning property (chattels), and rente income. Rental is a collective term for a number of rents. The total yield of an estate was called its rental or rent-roll, and a list of the various sources of income, including all payments from tenants in money, produce or services, constituted its rental.

Popular and special meaning of rent

3. *The popular meaning of rent is the amount paid for the use of material things which must be returned to the owners after the time of use agreed upon.* We speak of the rent of a

house, boat, etc., using the word as a synonym for hire. In the European languages the word is used more frequently in that sense. In the French *la rente* means the income from any kind of property; but corporate securities and national bonds came particularly to be called *les rentes*, because they are a form of investment yielding a permanent income. The one who has a perpetual income from bonds or rents is called a *rentier*. In German the term *Rente* is used more broadly than in English, as an income of any sort, *Grundrente* meaning the rent of land, and *Capitalrente* the income usually in England called interest.

A restricted meaning has long been applied by economists to the word: the income yielded by lands, etc. This was put in contrast with interest for money and capital, and with wages of labor. This meaning is now being abandoned by economic students.

A wider meaning recently given to the word by many economists turns on the supposed relation of some portions of price to cost of production. Thus, frequent use is made of the expressions: consumer's rent, producer's rent, buyer's rent, seller's rent, etc. In the well-founded opinion of some recent critics this usage rests on a mistaken reasoning. However, in the midst of this wide variety of usage the student must be forewarned and alert. Doubtless agreement will at length be arrived at. Meantime, no economist can dictate what meaning is to be attached to the term, but one may suggest the definition that seems to him most expedient. Throughout this work we shall endeavor to use the term rent uniformly and consistently as it is now to be defined.

The essence of rent

4. *The essential thought in rent, as we shall use it, is that it is the value of the usufruct as distinguished from the value of the use-bearer or thing itself.* The meaning of usufruct is the use of the fruits, or in legal phrase: "the right of using and enjoying the income of an estate or other thing belonging to another, without impairing the substance." The obvious fact is that fruits can be eaten without destroying the tree, the harvest gathered without destroying the field. By a metaphor the word in legal discussion is applied to the use of any product, and we shall employ it, as in common speech, in reference to one's own goods as well as to the goods of another.

Rented agents are looked upon as durable

The qualities whose use gives value are not usually indestructible, but they are treated as undestroyed. There is a famous phrase used by Ricardo, "rent is paid for the original and indestructible qualities of the soil." He said "indestructible," but the word is not apt. There are many qualities in the fertile field that *must* be destroyed when it is used. Every economist since Ricardo's time has recognized this, and many excuses for the inaccuracy have been given. After every harvest, the field is less serviceable than before, and if it is to be of the same grade of efficiency, the fertile elements must be restored. We cannot assert that Ricardo meant *undestroyed*, for he was not quite clear on the question. But it is evident that one can count as true income only that part of the value of product that remains after full repairs have been made. It is only by a fiction that most indirect agents can be regarded as indestructible. Things yielding rent are not indestructible, but generally they are preserved undestroyed.

True rent a net income

5. *A distinction must be made between gross and net, or true and false rent.* Before the usufruct is estimated, allowance must be made for repairs, depreciation, and for various expenses which absorb a good portion of the gross product. When this allowance has been made, the income may be considered as a net sum not due to the sale, or to the using up of any part of the thing rented. This is the essential thought in typical rent—that it is the value of the surplus, or net product, of an economic agent leaving the agent itself unimpaired in efficiency. The total product is sometimes called the "gross rent," but economic rent is "net rent." This thought is made clearer by the following discussion.

§ II. The History of Contract Rent and Changes in It

Economic and contract rent distinguished

1. *Economic rent (likewise called natural, competitive, and sometimes rack rent) is to be distinguished from contract rent.* Economic rent is the market value of the usufruct, and contract rent is the amount a man pays for the use of wealth by virtue of an existing agreement. The one is impersonal or economic; the other is personal or legal, being fixed by agreements between persons. The rents usually spoken of are contract rents.

The two diverge more or less. If the contract has been lately made the two will be nearly the same. Contracts of long standing often bind the tenant or borrower to pay either more or less than the present competitive price. If, after a time, the value of the use is greater than the contract rent, the tenant is fortunate in having his lease. But he is the loser if he is bound by lease or agreement to pay rent in a locality where land has become less valuable.

Economic and contract rent usually diverge also because of the agreement that the owner, or lender, keep up the repairs and pay the taxes. Here it is simply the difference between gross and net rent.

Custom may prevent the owner from charging all the usufruct of the agent is worth. If the contract rent is less than the economic rent, evidently the borrower enjoys a part of the usufruct, without charge, and to that degree is in the position of an owner. The usufruct in this case is divided between the two parties. Such instances were numerous in the Middle Ages in the renting of land, and still are found in many countries.

Contract rent is based on economic rent and tends to conform to it whenever

THE RENTING CONTRACT

there is competition. The existence of economic rent is the basis of the agreement to pay contract rent. Prospective hirers of agents forecast what the use will be worth to them and make their bids accordingly.

The renting contract for the use of wealth

2. *The renting contract is the agreement of a borrower to pay for the use of a thing and, at the end of the time, to restore it in good condition or pay for its complete repair.* In practical business it is necessary to have definite agreements to prevent disputes. Some provide that one party, some that the other party, shall keep up repairs. The form of the renting contract is observed by men in estimating the uses of their own wealth where no contract exists. If they count the gross product of an agent as rent, it is bad bookkeeping. In many cases it is necessary, therefore, to follow the form of the renting contract in order to determine the net yield of indirect goods.

The renting contract in the Middle Ages

3. *In early stages of industry the use of nearly all wealth is estimated under the renting contract.* In the lower stages of culture, in hunting, fishing, or nomadic pastoral tribes, land is not recognized as wealth to be exchanged or owned. But at a later stage, as in the Middle Ages in Europe, land and the things pertaining to it, as ditches, houses, mills, cattle, stock, and the few simple implements, constituted the larger portion of the wealth. Land was granted to the tenant or serf in return for services. The contract was pretty strictly drawn and all items were specified. It was not hard to hold the tenant to his contract to keep the land in about the same condition. There was a certain rotation of crops; the tenant was obliged to keep his stock up to standard; and, moreover, he had a certain interest in the land because his contract rent (as explained above) was less than the economic rent. The landlord, therefore, could count pretty surely on the undiminished power of his land and stock from one year to another.

At that time, truck and barter were the common modes of exchange, and rents were paid in products and services, not in money. The fruits of the soil were consumed on the spot instead of being sold as now. Land was rarely, if ever, sold outright, so that there was no occasion to estimate its total selling value. It was thought of as a place on which to live and as a source of livelihood. Its yearly use was all that was subject to contract, sale, and exchange. Not the land itself but a *rent charge* on the land was sold, the term rent charge meaning an annual sum payable out of the yield of an estate. Many medieval estates were so tied up by legal conditions that they could not be sold outright; all that the owner could do was to sell or mortgage the annual rental. Thus, in the Middle Ages, it was all but universal to look upon most indirect agents as exchangeable only under the renting contract, as subject to renting but not to complete transfer and sale.

The renting contract not convenient in commerce

4. *As industry developed, the renting contract remained almost wholly confined to cases of renting lands and houses.* The materials and appliances needed for

manufacture and commerce are so manifold and varying in quality that the rent-form of contract is very cumbersome and difficult for exchangers to enforce. If a merchant about to embark on a trading journey wished to rent a ship and a stock of goods, the renting contract became most difficult to interpret. He must agree to repay the loan in goods of the same kind and quality as those received, a contract most difficult to execute, and giving occasion to costly tests and countless disagreements. It was much easier for the merchant to get his loan under the interest contract, *i.e.*, a money loan, with which to buy the goods. With the growth of industry and commerce, wealth increased in towns, taking many forms, as those of ships, wagons, tools, and stocks of goods, that could not conveniently be rented.

The thought of it remains associated with a rural economy

In England, the country which developed its industrial system earliest, the idea of rent, therefore, gradually became disassociated almost entirely from the use or hire of any wealth but land and real property. Because in the Middle Ages rent was associated almost entirely with natural resources, they being the only important forms of wealth which men rented from others, there was fostered the idea that the essential mark of rent is the connection with natural resources. It is a simple example of the association of ideas. In the transfer or loan of movable goods, the rent contract was quite overshadowed by the other form of contract, that of a money loan. According to this explanation the essential and primary difference between renting wealth and borrowing money at interest is not in the kind of wealth whose use is thus temporarily transferred, but in the nature of the contract. But as forms of wealth differ in their fitness for transfer under the two forms of contract, there goes on a competition between them, as a result of which each becomes associated with certain groups of goods. In the Middle Ages the renting contract was the dominant form, but it has been progressively displaced by loans in the money form, and its importance is still declining.

Renting contracts most used with land

5. *The main forms of wealth whose usufruct is still sold under long renting contracts are land and its more durable improvements.* In England farms are let under long leases, a very common form being the thirty-year lease. Under the old, almost fixed, conditions in agriculture such a lease was equitable, but when prices are rapidly changing and when new methods are being introduced, it gives rise to great hardships. About twenty-five years ago, the great fall in the price of agricultural products brought ruin to many of the tenant farmers. The land troubles in Ireland have been largely about tenants' improvements. When the lease expired, the landlord could appropriate all the improvements that the tenant had made. In America farms are let usually on shares, and from year to year, but the plan of a money rent is increasingly followed. The difficulty of getting an equitable arrangement between landlord and tenant is recognized by all. The landlord must make the proper repairs or see that they are made; he must specify in the contract whether the products can be taken away or are to be fed on the place so that the soil may not be impoverished, and he must provide for the purchase of

other fertilizers. On the other hand, the tenant under the renting contract has little motive for improvement, and many occasions for discontent. So in America, far more than in the older countries, land changes hands by sale, the purchaser going into debt for it, giving his note and paying interest on the loan rather than rent for the farm.

But many other goods are rented

Many less durable goods are rented for brief periods. Carriages are rented for the day, bicycles by the week or month. Sewing-machines, boats, guns, tents, and even diamond engagement rings, yield their joys under the renting contract. People frequently hesitate between the renting and the purchase of a piano, and in some cases renting is the more convenient and desirable way of securing its use. The purchase of a dress-coat or of a masquerade-suit to be worn but once, involves for some an excessive and needless sacrifice. For a moderate sum its temporary use may be had, and it is then returned, little the worse for wear, to the accommodating clothier.

Economic rent much wider than the renting contract

A final word of caution may be given. Economic rent is not confined to the cases of contract rent. It exists in every case where a more or less durable agent yields a use that is scarce and desirable. The owner who uses a thing himself gets the advantage in the product as clearly as if he collected rent from a borrower. Houses lived in by the owners, house furnishings, clothing, books, all scarce and durable agents, are yielding rents in this logical sense. To the economist, therefore, the problem of economic rent, as one of the grand divisions of the problem of value, remains of undiminished importance, for in these unceasing streams of uses emanating from our environment, is found the basis for the value of all durable wealth.

Chapter IX
The Law of Diminishing Returns

§ I. Definition of the Concept of (Economic) Diminishing Returns

Economic agents contain uses to be obtained only with progressive difficulty

1. The phrase "diminishing returns of industrial agents" is the expression of the fact that there is an elastic limit to the utility any indirect good can afford within a given time. Successive attempts to get additional services from a thing are usually in part successful, but each additional service is gained with more difficulty, or a smaller added service is gained for an equal expenditure of materials or effort. A book stands many hours untouched on the shelves of the library; but if, as often happens, two or more persons wish to use it at the same hour, time and energy are wasted. The book has a potential use during the twenty-four hours, but all this can be secured only at the cost of the greatest inconvenience. The greatest net uses, therefore, are seen to be to the first user and in the first hour, for these uses cost the least time and trouble. If the members of a family will take turns, one chair will serve for all of them; but if all are to be able to sit down together, a chair must be provided for each. Often it will happen that only one chair is in use, the other nine chairs being valued only for their potential uses. I knew two young men who owned a dress-coat in partnership, and as they had different evenings free from business all went well until both were invited to a reception which both were very eager to attend.

This is true of all classes of agents

Illustrations of this principle may be drawn from every class of durable goods. The example generally given is that of a field used for agriculture. It was long ago seen that a larger crop could usually be obtained on the same area, only with greater effort or expenditure; but this fact has been thought to be peculiar to the use of land. The examples given above have been purposely chosen from very different fields, to show that the truth is a general one: a good that affords a given service can be made to increase that service, ordinarily, only on condition that men

THE LAW OF DIMINISHING RETURNS 47

put forth greater effort, or sacrifice more goods.

The decreased utility is most clearly seen in the diminished effect which other agents produce when used in connection with the thing. When several are trying to use the same book, and are wasting time trying to get it, we often say their study hours are less fruitful because of the poor library facilities. Again, we speak either of the diminished returns of the field, or of the labor applied to the field. Either the particular thing is said to show diminished returns or the other coöperating agents are said to show them.

Decreasing technical effectiveness of material things

2. *As the agents used in connection with a fixed amount of any other agent (for mechanical, chemical, physiological, psychological, and other purposes) increase, their objective effectiveness after a given point decreases.* Objective or technical effectiveness means effectiveness independent of the thought or estimate of men. It is not the effectiveness to produce a feeling in men, but to produce results on the material world. In a mechanism, if one part is increased without increasing the other parts, a point is reached where it does not add to the result. If in the building of a bridge the weight of the floor is increased beyond a certain point, the rest of the bridge being left unchanged, the bridge is weakened instead of strengthened. If the weight of the iron in the framework is increased beyond a certain point without strengthening the piers, the structure is weakened. If the pier is greatly enlarged, the bridge may not be weakened, but there is an utter waste of material and effort, and perhaps the main purpose of the bridge is defeated by the damming up of the stream. A bicycle frame, like a chain, is no stronger than its weakest part. If the strength of all parts of the wheel and frame is in equal proportion to the strain they must bear, added weight to any single part weakens the whole machine. The development of the modern type of bicycle, by many experiments, is a good example of the adjustment of materials according to the principle of technical efficiency.

A variation of the same principle is seen in chemical combinations. Exact proportions of materials must be used to get a certain result. Increase of one ingredient will not increase the desired product. Either the added part is rejected, does not enter at all into the compound, or it unites to form another and different product.

That the same principle holds good of the psychological effects of things, we have already fully recognized in discussing wants and marginal utility. A given amount of a good will affect the senses in a pleasurable way, but an increase in the amount will not cause a proportional addition to pleasure of sight, sound, or smell. On the contrary, such an increase may defeat the object entirely. Here we are at the threshold of the economic problem, for we have touched on "feeling."

Economic diminishing returns relate to value

3. *The idea of economic diminishing returns arises when man recognizes these technical facts and their relation to gratification, in his use of a limited supply of indirect agents.* All

economy begins with scarcity. The varying effects produced by different agents therefore require to be studied or the sum or direct goods of enjoyment will not be as great as is possible. Waste will take place. A bridge will have its maximum use with a minimum outlay when the parts are in a certain proportion. Beyond that point, the increase of any part may add something to the usefulness of the bridge, but the agents must be taken from some other and greater use.

The thought of economic diminishing returns always has reference to value. If a particular kind and amount of a certain material is used in varying combinations with other agents, the value of the added product will not always be in the same proportion to the value of the added agent. The bridge-builder must consider not only what the added material will add to strength, but what it will cost, and whether the result will justify this expense. So the economic problem of diminishing returns is more complicated than the mechanical one, for it contains not only the technical but other factors.

The marginal utility in goods

If the value of the product increases less rapidly than the cost of the agents successively added to secure it, a point must at length be reached where the value of the added agents and of the additional product just balance; this is called the point of marginal utility.

If a certain value in labor, fertilizer, or material, be applied to an acre of land, it may be more than recovered in the value of the product. Further applications give a product increased not in equal proportion to the former yield, and so on till the value of the last-added agent just balances that of the added product. This is the best adjustment possible, and beyond this point there will be a deficit in value. Just where the equilibrium is found at any time is the margin of cultivation.

The term "cultivation" is taken from agriculture but must be understood in the broader sense of utilization, as the principle is not confined to the case of land or agriculture, but applies as well to the use of furniture, books, clothing, horses, or any other indirect agents.

Meaning of intensive margin of utilization

The extensive margin of utilization

4. *There are two margins, the intensive and the extensive.* The margin of utilization in the case of a single piece of wealth is called the intensive margin. Any form of indirect wealth, anything kept to use, may be considered as containing a series of uses. Using one thing more and more while uniting other things with it, is using it more intensively.

Getting more use out of the book by effort, out of the farm by applying more fertilizer, out of the house by putting more people into it, is intensive utilization. The earlier uses come easily, naturally; the later ones are gotten with increasing difficulty.

When a number of agents are of different qualities, the point between the

THE LAW OF DIMINISHING RETURNS

one last used and the next unused is the extensive margin of utilization. The best agents that are available are naturally used first, but as they are more intensively used there is increasing inconvenience. Then recourse must be made to the inferior agents, whose first uses, however, are greater than the later, intensive uses, of the better grades. When the step is made to the use of agents that were before unused because inferior, it is extending the margin of utilization. The intensive margin of use is in the particular thing; the extensive margin of use lies outside of this.

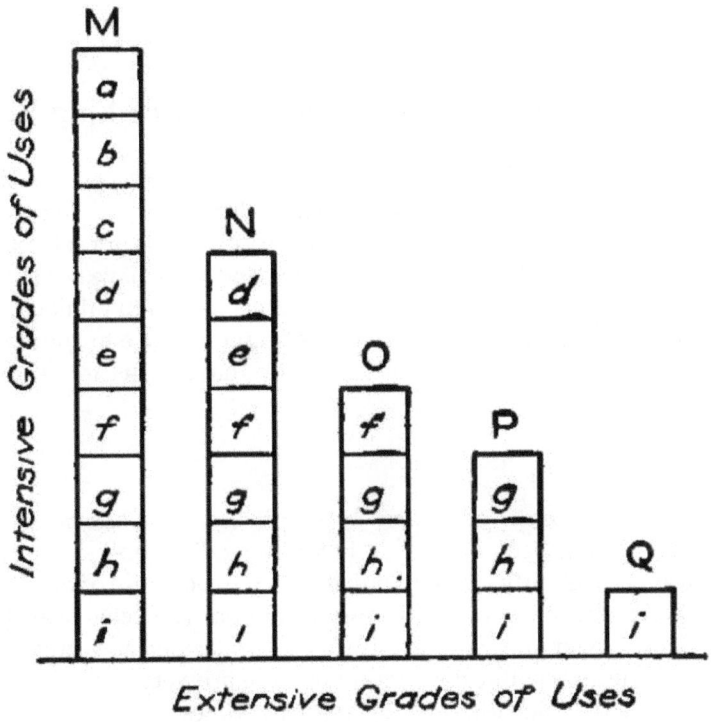

Extensive Grades of Uses

The relation of the two margins may be shown in a simple diagram. Let the better grades of indirect agents be represented by longer rectangles, the upper parts of which represent the more accessible, more easily secured utilities. Each agent consists of many strata of uses. The best uses are grades a, b, and c, in M; but after M has been utilized intensively down to d, N will begin to be utilized at its highest point. When utilization goes down to f, O comes into use, and so on. Therefore it will be seen that until the intensive margin takes in d, M is on the extreme margin of utilization, and N is just outside it; when the intensive margin falls to g and h, P is inside the extensive margin, and Q is just outside.

Equilibrium of the two margins

The marginal utility or effectiveness of added agents tends to be equal on the intensive and the extensive margins. This is simply a case of the substitution of goods in the use of indirect agents. If the value of the added product in the use of a particular good decreases, a point finally is reached where it is better to transfer the outlay to another agent, to change from intensive to extensive utilization, to go over to the use of another field or of another machine not so good. The effectiveness of the labor or capital that men have to apply is being compared constantly in the two cases, and to the extent that this comparison is perfect the effectiveness of the agents tends to be equal on the margin in the two applications.

§ II. Other Meanings of the Phrase "Diminishing Returns"

Does not mean declining prosperity

1. *The phrase diminishing returns is sometimes taken as meaning merely a decrease in prosperity.* Many ideas are connected with this phrase. It is not self-explanatory. It suggests various thoughts according to context and these have not failed to give rise to different uses. The student must be cautious if he is to think clearly about it. If population declines, or industry changes from one place to another, or from one kind of goods to another, it is sometimes said that returns are diminishing in the deserted district.

Nor exhaustion of the soil

2. *A more common misuse of the term is to apply it to the exhaustion of the soil.* If the soil of a district has been robbed of its fertile qualities and smaller crops are raised than was the case fifty years before, it is said to be a case of of the increased difficulty in the extraction of natural stores in mining. The veins near the surface being mined first, later the galleries must be cut deeper and greater expense incurred to get the stores. But the conditions here are very different from those we have considered under diminishing returns. Mines are used not under the renting contract, but under the royalty contract, which permits and contemplates a progressive using up of the limited stores of natural resources.

Fallacious contract between manufacture and agriculture

All industries if limited as to one factor, as area, show diminishing returns

3. *Manufactures are often said to show increasing returns in contrast with agriculture as an industry of decreasing returns.* There is here an inconsistent shifting of thought. Agriculture is thought of as limited to a certain area of ground, whereon evidently diminishing returns will take place. But the fixed limit of ground-space is not thought of in connection with manufactures. Taking the same view of manufactures, commerce, education, etc., that is, assuming each industry to be confined to limited area of ground, each is seen to be subject to diminishing returns. Some ground-space is one of the essentials to carry on any business. If the attempt is made to accumulate a large library in one small room, a point is reached where much energy is wasted in trying to find the books. In a university

THE LAW OF DIMINISHING RETURNS   51

the psychical product, education, may be limited by the need of space. The schoolroom, laboratory, or college class-room could be used at midnight, it is true, but not conveniently; and as students increase, buildings must be added. The same is true of any industry. We cannot conveniently increase the business of a lumber-yard without a larger yard-space, or of a factory without a larger floor-space. But the added space may be gotten by spreading horizontally or piling up perpendicularly. A ten-story building on an acre lot represents ten acres of floor-space. Putting up higher buildings is an expansion in area by the more intensive utilization of the land. Devices like elevators, and more compact appliances, make possible an increasing business in manufacture, trade, or commerce upon the same area of land. All industries, if looked at consistently from this standpoint, are subject to the same condition, though it is true this will make itself felt in varying degrees in different lines of industry. In agriculture some similar devices are possible by the use of greenhouses, but it is true that in it, on account of the need of sun, light, and air, the limits of space are more quickly felt, and are less elastic than in most other industries. The difference, however, is one of degree, and not of kind. Higher factories, larger stores, enable manufacturers to adapt themselves to the law as applied to the surface of land, but not to escape its operations. Neither the law of gravitation nor the law of diminishing returns is violated or broken when materials are lifted to build the upper stories. Both "laws" are at work, even when the building is rising from the ground. Men are merely adapting their conduct to the conditions imposed by gravitation and diminishing returns.

Confused with the question of large production

Manufactures usually are thought of as enlarging by increase of the amount of capital employed, without limitation as to the area covered. But even here a limit is reached in the amount of capital that can be employed at any one location because of the difficulty of widening the market. The question, however, is one of the advantages of large production with large capital, not of the increasing use of a limited area of land. If manufactures and agriculture are to be compared with reference to their economic nature, it is essential to clear thinking that both be looked at with reference to the same conditions, and from the same point of view.

Technical confused with historical diminishing returns

4. *Technical diminishing returns are often confused with historical diminishing returns.* The principle of technical diminishing returns is that at any given moment the uses obtainable from any indirect agent cannot be indefinitely increased without increasing difficulty. Historical diminishing returns occur when, in fact, human effort is less bountifully rewarded in a later period than in an earlier one. If to-day a day's labor in agriculture produced less than fifty years ago, historical diminishing returns would have occurred. In fact, labor is more bountifully rewarded in agriculture than fifty years ago, yet it is true to-day that there are few fields or appliances which, if used more intensively with the prevailing prices of labor and material, would not show a diminishing return to the additional capital applied. Therefore, in the historical sense, increasing returns have prevailed, yet at

every moment it has been necessary to apply resources under the guidance of the principle of diminishing returns.

§ III. Development of the Concept of Diminishing Returns

Recognition of diminishing returns to land

1. *The law of "diminishing returns" was first recognized and expressed with reference to the use of land in agriculture.* There are several evident reasons why this occurred. It is obvious to every farmer and gardener that he cannot indefinitely increase his crop, that two men cannot always produce twice as much as one man, and that in general the product does not always vary in proportion to the labor and materials applied. Moreover, the food supply is a fundamental factor in industry and in the welfare of states. The limit to the supply of food on a given area, cultivated by a given method, early appeared and became a serious practical problem.

The circumstances in Europe in the eighteenth century drew attention to the subject. Population was increasing, and the pressure for food was strong. While all the forms of industry most common in cities were increasing, and the wealth of the cities was growing, poverty was increasing among the peasantry. Especially was this true in England during the Napoleonic wars, 1793-1815, owing to exceptional conditions. The food-supply from abroad was cut off, and when the English farmers, tempted by the high prices, took poorer land into cultivation, and sought to get larger crops from their older fields, a great object-lesson was presented on the principle of diminishing returns in agriculture.

This confused with historical diminishing returns

2. *This truth of diminishing returns in agriculture was confused with the thought of historical diminishing returns.* Circumstances of the time led to the belief that because of lack of food misery must continue among the masses of men. It was thought inevitable that the population would continue to increase and food become more scarce. The idea of diminishing returns became thus a prophecy of what would happen, a social philosophy, that affected the thought of men on every practical social question.

The principle applies to land in all of its uses

3. *The application of the principle of diminishing returns was soon broadened to include land in other than agricultural uses.* This was a natural and inevitable extension of the thought. It was evident that an unlimited use could not be made of a limited area of land, in any industry whatever. There is no explanation of rent of business sites, residences, lots, wharves, waterfalls, etc., unless account is taken of diminishing returns. If it were possible to do an unlimited amount of business upon a limited area of land, it would never get more scarce and could never rise in value. The idea of diminishing returns came properly, therefore, to be applied to land in all

THE LAW OF DIMINISHING RETURNS 53

its uses. It is true, however, that the relatively large areas needed in agriculture make the phenomenon of diminishing returns much more striking in it than in most other industries.

And to all indirect agents

4. "Diminishing returns" should be broadly applied to all wealth having indirect uses. The argument for this view may take both a negative and a positive form. Why should we say that the principle applies to land and not to cases of other industrial agents? Why in the case of a waterfall and not in the case of the water-wheel? Why in the case of the field and not in the case of the trees in the field? Are they not all scarce and desirable goods yielding a limited supply of uses?

Positively it can be argued that the concept of diminishing returns is indispensable to a reasonable explanation of the value of any indirect agents. Anything that could afford an infinite series of uses at once would be an infinite supply. If an infinite number of uses could be gotten out of one hammer in all places at once, it would pound all the nails in the world. One wagon, one acre of land, one ax, one book of each kind, would serve for all men, and duplicates would be valueless. But in the case of every material thing there is a limit of convenient and economic use.

Diminishing returns related to diminishing gratification

5. *Diminishing returns of indirect agents is a special case of the universal law of the diminishing utility of goods.* Diminishing returns have to do with indirect goods, while diminishing gratification has to do with direct or consumption goods. They are two species or aspects of the same general principle. If the supply of certain indirect agents is increased, thereby increasing consumption goods, the utility of the indirect agents per unit diminishes. In such a case a diminishing return is the reflection, back to the indirect good, of the diminishing utility of the direct goods it helps to secure. Any indirect agent, added to a fixed amount of other agents with which it is technically used, is credited with a diminished utility, just as an additional supply of enjoyable goods, coming to meet a fixed demand, falls in value.

The concept of technical diminishing returns has reference to a limited period of time. Though a definite agent may have bound up in it a long series of uses, these cannot be secured at the moment. If a rent-bearer, such as a fruit-tree, were permanent, and men could wait through eternity for its yield, they would get an infinite yield of fruit. But in any finite period, there can be only a limited yield.

The basal law of economics

The concept of diminishing returns is one aspect of the great economic law of proportionality, that is, it is one expression of the fundamental, axiomatic truth, that there is a best or proper adjustment of means and ends. It is, therefore, the central and essential thought in political economy. On it depend all important conclusions with reference to the value of indirect goods. Out of it grow the important economic theories of rent and capitalization.

Chapter X
The Theory of Rent: The Market Value of the Usufruct

§ I. Differential Advantages in Consumption Goods

Connection between gratification, rents, and value of wealth

1. *Both rent and the value of durable wealth are based on the value of the fruits or products yielded by the wealth.* Gratification, afforded directly or indirectly, is the basis of all values. The relation of most kinds of wealth to wants is indirect; but gratification thus afforded indirectly is none the less the basis on which the usufruct of wealth is estimated. Men find the logical or causal connection between direct goods, or final product, and indirect goods, or agents.

To explain the value of the durable wealth, or rent-bearer, a still farther step in thought must be taken. The value of the rent-bearer is based on the series of rents which it affords. To explain how these rents are added to give the value of the indirect agents is the task of a theory of capitalization. This being the relation, a change in the value of the product changes the rent, and this in turn changes the value of the rent-bearer. The theory of rent, therefore, has to begin with a review of the valuation of enjoyable goods.

Effect of scarcity on utility of uniform goods

2. *In a group of consumption goods, all of the same quality, the marginal utility declines as the quantity increases.* If the quantity of an article capable of ministering to man's wants is very limited, its value is high. If the supply of something of uniform quality, for which there is no substitute, is scanty, the value is estimated without reference to any other grade. If a fishing tribe caught very few fish, but these were all equally good, and if no other food were to be had, fish would have a high ratio of exchange with every other kind of goods.

If the quantity increases, the value of each unit of the whole supply falls, as the importance attributed to its parts declines. If an Indian hunting-party met with unusual success, the value of buffalo meat declined. If there is a remarkable potato crop, potatoes fall in value.

Relation of different grades of consumption goods

3. *In a series of consumption goods of different qualities, the lower grades acquire value only as scarcity increases in the higher grades.* If difference in quality between two grades of apples is marked and there is a superabundant supply of the best grade, no importance is attached to the poorer. But if the better grade becomes scarce, the appetite for the poorer grade increases, and finally it, too, will be consumed. In some years the small, knotty apples are allowed to rot on the ground; in other years they are gathered and are sold at good prices. But if there is an abrupt difference in quality, and hence in the marginal utility of the two grades, the value of the better goods may rise considerably before there is any recourse to the poorer. If the differences in quality are very slight, the presence of the lower grades has the effect of limiting the increase of value of the higher grades. Practically in almost all kinds of goods there are gradations in quality. Complete uniformity is of the rarest occurrence. When did one ever see a basket of peaches that were all of the same size, ripeness, color, flavor, and perfection? If the step from the higher to the lower grade is very slight, resort is immediately made to the next lower grade, some of which is substituted for the higher.

There is an independent reason for the value of each grade of goods; each grade would have value if there were none of the other, but they mutually affect each other's value when they exist, side by side, in the same market. The marginal utility of each is lessened by the presence of the other. And thus, two or ten grades constitute for many purposes a single supply as they shade into each other or are merged by substitution.

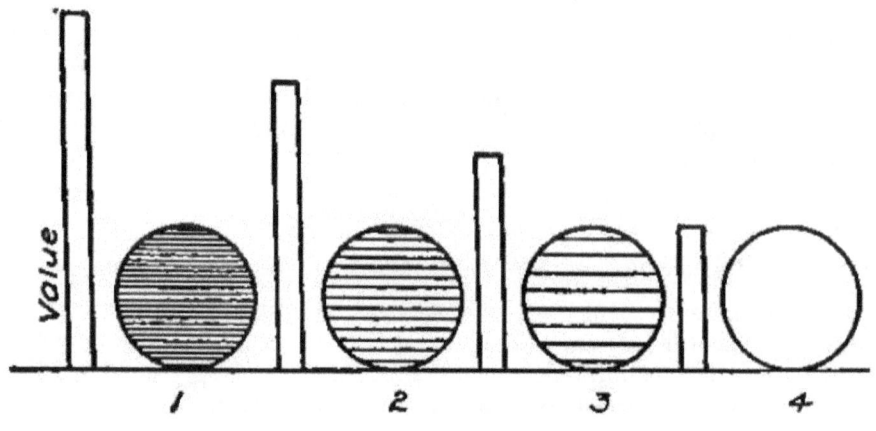

Grades of Consumption Goods by Quality

Free goods are on the margin of utilization

4. *Goods of the lowest grades, having no marginal utility, are free goods.* This is a

simple truth, but it has important bearings. There may be said to be an "extensive margin of utilization" of many consumption goods. The poorer grades of apples, rotting on the ground, the multitudes of waste things not valued, are on the margin of utilization. When a lower grade is used, the margin is extended. The value of goods is measured upward from the margin of utilization, but this is simply to say that their value is measured from zero upward.

Likewise, there is an intensive marginal utility in consumption goods. As the better grade of apples becomes more scarce, they will be used more sparingly and kept to satisfy only the intenser wants. The superiority of some consumption goods, either in quantity or quality, often is exactly analogous to the "differential advantage" spoken of by economists in the case of productive agents. The differential advantage of the highest grade over the grade of free goods, whose value is zero, evidently is the whole value of the highest grade.

§ II. Differential Advantages in Indirect Goods

Differential advantage of agents in the quality of their products

1. *Rent varies with the quality of the products yielded by agents, other things being equal.* Let us take first a simple case where the agent is the sole condition of the product. If there is but one tree bearing a certain luscious fruit, or but one spring yielding a mineral water, the rent of the tree or spring being equal to the value of the products must vary as the quality of the products varies. If two or more trees are standing side by side, they will be compared with regard to the difference in the quality of their fruits. If two fields differ in quality, greater importance will be attached to the field capable of producing the better grade or variety of fruit or product. A peculiar mineral quality in the soil may impart to wine a choice flavor that can at once be recognized by experts; while other fields, distant but a few rods, cannot by any effort be made to produce wine of the same rare quality. There is said to be a marked difference in the success of vineyards lying only a short distance apart on the shores of the larger lakes of New York. Nearness to the water moderates the temperature, often prevents frosts, and hence insures the ripening and quality of the fruit. In the Santa Clara valley, as in other parts of California, there is a frostless belt, sharply marked off from the lands where it is unsafe to attempt to cultivate the delicate orange-tree and other semi-tropical plants. In manifold ways differences in geological formation affect the use of land and the success of many industries. On one side of a little creek is limestone land, on the other shale, the limestone producing a crop larger and of better quality. When the peculiar nature of the one field is found to be the cause of the exceptional quality of its fruits, the difference in value is attributed to it.

The lower grade limits the value of the higher grade

If there is but one grade of agent, it is, of course, valued without reference to any lower grade. The effect of the presence of lower grades of agents is to lower the value of the higher, inasmuch as the lower grades are substituted for the higher. There may be at first enough of the higher grade of agents to produce all the fruit wanted of the better quality. If, then, there is an increasing demand, and the additional yield can be secured only with greater effort, the value of the product will rise. The presence of poorer grades, however, checks that rise, because use can be shifted to them. The value of grade one is not high because grades two, three, and four, which are worse than it, are available, but because they are not of better quality than they are. Poor as they are, their presence reduces somewhat the intensity of demand for the best grade. Indirect agents, therefore, are seen to be subject to just the same comparisons, substitutions, and estimates, when their value is considered, as are direct consumption goods.

Differential advantage of agents in the amount of their products

2. *The rents of two agents differ as do the quantities of goods yielded by them, other things being equal.* In the case just considered, the quantity remained the same while the quality differed; now is to be considered the case where the quantity differs while the quality remains the same. It is possible that one grade of agents is "poorer" because it produces less fruit, not fruit of poorer quality. Consider first the static problem. If both agents yield fruits exactly alike, the value of equal units at the same place and time must be equal, and the usufructs would vary in just proportion with the quantity of product. Now consider the dynamic problem. If the desire for that fruit increases, rent would grow as scarcity became more felt. The agents yielding, under the prevailing conditions, the largest product, would first be used; later, the poorer agents. The possibility of resorting to the poorer agents would keep the better from rising so high.

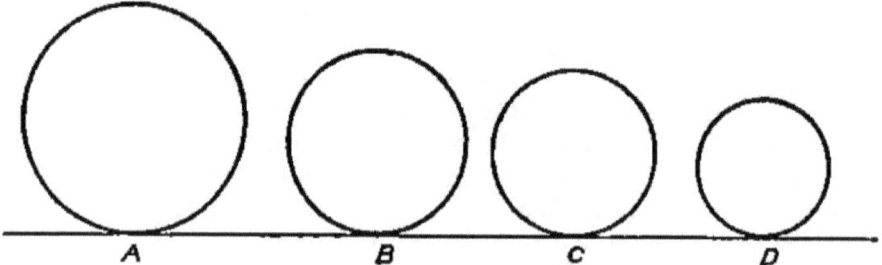

Grades of Agents by amount of Product of Uniform Quality

Complementary agents unite to form a product

3. *When two agents are necessary to secure a product, the value attributed to each is influenced by competing uses.* The thought of one agent independently producing a certain product is far too simple to correspond with reality. Two or more agents unite to produce a single product, and each agent at the same time can be used for acquiring other products. Complex as the problem appears, it is solved according to the principle of marginal utility at every moment in every market. The different

THE THEORY OF RENT

uses, figuratively speaking, bid for an agent, and thus its marginal utility is determined just as is the price of a good by the bidding of buyers. Indeed, it is the bidding of buyers, indirectly. The more urgent the use, the higher the bid. The felt importance is reflected from the consumption goods that are sought, to the agent that will aid to get them. Two or more agents that are mutually needed for the acquiring of a product are complementary goods. A complementary agent may be either other material agents or labor.

Complementary agents used intensively show diminishing returns

When labor is applied to an agent, either to improve the quality or to increase the quantity, it is subject to the law of diminishing returns. In the effort to increase the quantity of products, labor is applied first more intensively to the better agents. If it meets with resistance, if returns diminish, it is transferred to any of the poorer agents that have in them uses of as high grade as those still in the better agent. The superior effectiveness of the earlier over the later units of the added agent is called the "differential advantage" of the two fixed agents. The result of a day's labor applied to a field may be represented by 100, a second day's labor by 90 (it being only ninety per cent, as effectual), a third day's labor by 75; but it is more usual to say that the first field produces 10 more than the second and 25 more than the third, the second 15 more than the third. To the agent fixed in supply is attributed the difference in the effectiveness of the agent that is applied.

The rentless extensive margin of agents

4. *The marginal uses of indirect goods are free uses.* Here again is noted the close parallelism in the process of evaluating direct and indirect goods. There is an extensive margin in the use of an indirect agent, a point in the gradation from the better to the poorer agents where the materials and forces are left unused and have no value. Land beyond that point is free. Outworn goods in manifold forms, old pictures, old machines, having no longer charms even for a rummage sale, form a no-rent margin of wealth. On every hand a great multitude of things unused and worthless differ by only a shade from things that still are used and valued. Every rubbish-heap, rag-bag, junk-shop, and garret contains things once prized, now lingering on the margin of utilization.

There is also in agents an intensive margin, beyond which are certain unexploited uses in the things that we already have. This is a more subtle thought, but it has been already discussed in connection with diminishing returns. These potential uses in agents, uses which in the existing conditions lie outside the margin of utilization, of course have no value. We have noted that there is an equilibrium between these two margins. Rent is measured from a zero point of utility either in a good, or in other poorer grades of goods.

A corollary of this proposition is that there is a limit to the rental that anything can yield under any given condition. Below the present margin of utility of any goods there exist great quantities of free goods, unused goods, or unexploited uses. It is only uses above this margin that yield rent. Rent is the difference between the value of the better grades and the value of the free goods. It is therefore due to the limitation in the supply of indirect agents of the better quality, or to the scarcity of the more effective uses in those agents.

Restatement of rent, economic and contract
Economic rent is primary

5. *Rent may be redefined as the value of the scarce uses of wealth within a given period.* Rent is the felt importance of the usufructs of agents in securing gratification. It is measured by the marginal utility of any particular grade of agents in securing products. These definitions and the discussion throughout this chapter applies to economic rather than to contract rent. In fixing and agreeing on contract rent, men are seeking to estimate the importance of indirect goods, the importance that an agent will have in getting a product. They are bidding for the use of things, and what they bid is contract rent. Contract rent is based on the existence of economic rent. Economic rent does not depend on contract rent, but on the differences in the effectiveness of agents to secure a given product. If there were not differences in the product, and no limits to the supply of indirect agents, rent could not exist; it would be inconceivable. But these differences existing, economic rent inevitably arises, for men cannot keep from attaching value to the things that affect their desires. Contract rent in turn appears wherever the use of wealth becomes an object of exchange and agreement between men in a free society.

Chapter XI
Repair, Depreciation, and Destruction of Wealth: Relation to its Sale and Rent

§ I. Repair of Rent-Bearing Agents

The necessity of repairing nearly all economic agents

1. *The continued rent of indirect agents is dependent on the continual repair of certain parts necessary for their efficiency.* All earthly things wear out or decay. Whenever man's hand is withheld, nature takes possession of his work, regardless of his purposes. Dust gathers on unused clothes, and moths burrow in them. Shut up a house, and windows are shattered, roofs leak, and vermin swarm. To close a factory is to hasten the time when buildings and machinery will be piled upon the rubbish heap. The most magnificent and solid works of man have crumbled under the finger of time. The earth is strewn with ruins of gigantic engineering works, aqueducts, canals, temples, and monuments, whose restoration would be no less a task than was their first building. Everywhere vigilance and repairs are the conditions of continued uses of wealth. Some works of nature, such as waterfalls, may appear to have a continued use without repair, but they bear rent only when used with other things that must be constantly mended. A certain amount of labor on the banks of the mill-stream, and certain repairs on the dam, the water-wheel, and the gates are necessary. By a fiction in business contracts the waterfall may be dealt with apart from those conditions to its use, and may be rented, as a field is, with the agreement that the tenant keep up the repairs.

The efficiency of land as mere standing-room usually does not seem to be dependent on repairs. But here again the land yields rent in connection with other rent-bearing agents (such as houses and other agents above ground), which must be repaired. Standing-room on land is not a complete indirect agent; it is but one of the conditions for carrying on an industry, and even it often requires repairs to make it usable. Ranging from these extreme cases of stableness and durability, indirect agents vary to the extremes of fragility and ephemeralness.

The fertile lands of large regions have lost their usefulness

2. *Most of the qualities that contribute to make land fertile in agriculture being destructible, the constant repair of tilled land is necessary to its continued fertility.* If any things could be said to be indestructible, they would be some of the works of nature. In a sense, all matter is indestructible. Man cannot annihilate it, he can simply change its condition. But in economic discussion it is the value of things that is being considered, and from this point of view everything is in some degree destructible. The effects of bad husbandry are everywhere apparent, and in many regions fertile fields have been physically and economically destroyed. In Asia, lands that once supported millions, perhaps hundreds of millions, of population are now deserts. Egypt, for a time reduced to a semi-desert condition, has only in the past century been restored to a certain extent by the use of new methods and a return to the old ones. Many of the areas that were the granaries of Rome can now hardly support a sparse, half-starving population. The lands, or at any rate, the elements that gave them value, have been destroyed.

Wearing out of some American lands

Even in young America may be seen the effect of a failure to keep land in repair. As the new rich lands of the West were opened up, the old lands in the East were allowed to wear out, and many of them were abandoned. On the new lands in turn the same methods were followed, using up the first rich store of fertility with no attempt to keep up the quality of the soil. This may have been the best policy for the time; it would not have been economical to employ Old World methods of intensive husbandry when such rich extensive areas were being opened up. But the process was one destructive of natural resources. As settlement moved westward, great forests fell in ashes, and the soil was robbed of the fertile elements which it had taken centuries for nature to store up.

Wearing out of the parts the railroad

3. *The machinery and appliances used in transportation and manufacturing are all perishable in varying degrees.* Take as an example the great agency for transportation, the railway. The roadbed, which is but the natural soil excavated or filled to a better grade, is the most permanent part; yet every frost weakens, every rain undermines, a portion of it. Earthquake, landslide, and flood fill up the ditches, or tear down the embankments. Constant work is needed to keep it fit and safe for use. Above this is the track, slightly less permanent, more frequently changed. The ties rot, and even the rails of steel must be at times replaced. The rolling-stock is still less durable, and the different parts vary in length of life. It is said that the wheel-tires are renewed four times, the boiler three times, and the paint seven times, before a locomotive is entirely worn out. The oil used in the wheel, which is a necessary part of the running machine, has to be applied every day.

Depreciation of manufacturing appliances

There is a great difference in the length of life of manufacturing appliances.

REPAIR, DEPRECIATION, DESTRUCTION OF WEALTH

The building is fairly durable; yet an average depreciation-rate of one and one half per cent. a year must be allowed to offset a reduction in its value of over fifty per cent, in thirty years. Machinery differs greatly in durability; well-made, substantial machinery depreciates about five per cent. yearly. The engines and boilers depreciate more rapidly than the running gear; the loose tools have to be replaced every second to fourth year; while the materials consumed in the industry must be repaired and replaced at every repetition of the process of manufacture. If a factory is to be maintained in its efficiency in accordance with the terms of the renting contract, and is to continue its renting power, everything about it must be from time to time repaired and replaced.

Neglect of repairs often has evil effects

4. *Neglect or postponement of repairs must cause a falling off of the rent-earning power.* The neglect of repairs may have different results in the factory. The neglect of one kind simply reduces present rental while not preventing the future restoration of the plant to its full efficiency. If certain necessary tools wear out and are not replaced, the factory as a whole will be less efficient. Each part of the entire outfit being needed in due proportion, the loss in rental will correspond not merely to the lost efficiency of the missing tools, but to the crippled efficiency of the remaining appliances. Failure to apply seed to the land causes the land as a whole to be useless for that year's crop. In other cases, neglect of repairs increases the expenses of repairs and cuts off future rental. The adages, "A stitch in time saves nine," and "An ounce of prevention is worth a pound of cure," must be acted upon in every industry. The neglect to repair a roof causes damage to an amount many times the cost of a new roof. Failure to replace a bolt costing five cents may result in the rack and ruin of a machine worth many dollars. A handful of earth on a dike may save a whole country from destruction.

But sometimes is economical

Neglect of repairs may be economical, however, when outer conditions have first reduced the demand for the agent and consequently the rental. When the line of travel changes, it does not pay to keep an old hotel up to the same state of repair as when it had a great patronage. Old factories sometimes may better be allowed to depreciate while the price of repairs is invested in more prosperous industries. In a declining neighborhood the houses fall into decay, the owners seeing that "it would not pay" to keep them up.

§ II. Depreciation in Rent-earning Power of Agents Kept in Repair

Repairs cannot always prevent ultimate decay of agents

1. *Even where repairs are thoroughly kept up and present rent is undiminished, future*

rents may be decreasing because of natural decay. Changes go on in the substance of things which cannot be prevented by any attention to repairs. The wood in a framework will decay, the metals crystallize. There is also an unpreventable wear of parts that cannot be replaced without replacing the whole machine. It is the aim of the modern manufacturers to make machines like the wonderful one-horse shay, every part of equal durability. The development in America of the system of "interchangable parts" has greatly simplified and cheapened repairs, and has lengthened the working life of machines; nevertheless their lot is the scrap-heap at last. This general depreciation appears to be nearly avoided in large factories where there is serial replacement of the parts, but occasionally some invention or some improvement of process necessitates an almost completely new equipment. An old man once said to me: "I have lived in this house forty years: it was well built, has been repainted regularly, has never been allowed to leak a drop, and it is as good as it ever was. I see no reason why it could not be kept to eternity if always kept in repair." But the same could not be said of the house now. In general, there is finally a termination of the rent-earning power of wealth, and the whole has to be replaced.

Technical changes destroy the uses of agents

2. *A change in inventions and processes may reduce the rent of agents, independently of their material condition.* Rent is dependent on the indirect relation of things to wants; that relation may be changed if some other agent is found fitted to serve these wants more directly. Not only do the materials of houses change, but fashion and engineering skill change, making the old mansions cheerless and inconvenient, and affecting their rent-earning power. At every moment, in a progressive society, many rent-earning agents are being thrown out of use. The machinery in flour-mills has been almost completely changed, parts of it repeatedly, while the roller process has been substituted for the old millstones. Water-power, because of its uncertainty, has been replaced in many places by steam-power, and in many places steam-power in turn, has been rivaled by water-power since the improvements in the generation and transmission of electricity. A change in the process of making paper threw out of use much machinery that was only in part saved by its removal and adaptation to the making of coarser grades of paper. Many minor inventions in the iron industry, still more the invention of the Bessemer process, threw out of use great numbers of the old appliances.

Industrial circumstances affect the uses of agents

3. *A change in the outer conditions that give occasion to the use of agents may cause depreciation.* The exhaustion of materials on which machinery is employed may reduce its usefulness. A sawmill located in the midst of a forest has a high-earning power while the forest lasts, but when the forest is cut off the mill itself declines in value. Unless it can be removed to another forest and thus have its earning power renewed, it will have the value only of scrap-iron; it has become an indirect agent in the wrong place. Oil-boring machinery where a rich supply of oil is found has a high rental for a time, but when the oil-fields give out the machinery falls

in value, being worth more or less than the cost of transporting it according as the next oil-field is near or far. Changes in fashions, calling for different kinds of products, cause a depreciation in the value of the old agents. Coarse salt, evaporated by the sun, was used by our fathers, but the finer product of the steam process is driving out the product of the old solar plants. As homespun went out of use, much machinery still in good physical condition was cast aside. Changes in transportation work revolutions in industrial methods. Many prosperous small forges on the country roads of Pennsylvania became valueless after the building of the railroads. New forges were built at favored points where materials and products could be shipped by rail.

Various grades of efficiency in rent-bearers

4. *The agents employed in any industry range from the more efficient, high rent, down to the less efficient, low rent, grades in a more or less regular series.* It follows that as these changes are going on, the place of agents on the scale of efficiency is constantly shifting. The various agents represent all grades of efficiency. One depreciates, possibly is restored later and takes a high place, and again depreciates until finally it is thrown out of use. One loom embodies the latest improvements and corresponds to the most fertile field; another can still be made to yield a little rent; the use of a third results in certain loss. A great mass of no-rent agents lie just below the margin of utilization in every industry. Some of these are permanently abandoned; some will be taken back into use when business conditions improve. When the iron industry is dull, many forges are out of blast; but when iron is again in demand, there is a gradual taking up of the abandoned forges, factories, and machines as they are brought within the margin of profitable utilization. Many agents not actually earning a rent, may become rent-earning through a change in business conditions.

§ III. Destruction of Natural Stores of Materials

Destruction of the American forests

1. *A large part of industry is now conducted without regard to the preservation of the source of income.* A striking example of this is the use, or rather the destruction, of the American forests. In the last century the demand for lumber grew rapidly both on account of domestic needs and of the needs of the older countries. Great quantities of wood have been used and still greater quantities wasted, trees being girdled, the ground burned over, the timber destroyed in any way that would clear the soil—timber which to-day would be of far more value than is the cleared land on which it stood. Considering present needs and conditions, the labor seems to have been worse than wasted.

Effects on value of timber

The direct effect of this destruction of the supply has been the increase in the value of timber. To the settlers much of the timber was worse than useless; they paid and labored to get rid of it; now the supplies of lumber must be sought on the very margins of our territory: Florida, Maine, northern Michigan and Wisconsin, Washington, and Oregon. The supplies in Washington and Oregon are almost unavailable in the Eastern states on account of the cost of transportation. Professor Marsh, thirty years ago, strikingly characterized the policy that has been pursued: "We are breaking up the foundation timbers and the wainscoting of the house in which we live in order to boil our mess of pottage."

Physical effects

The indirect effects of these changes are fully as great as the direct ones. Forests greatly affect climate, temperature, and soil; they influence the humidity. They equalize the flow of streams, moderate floods, and by preventing the washing down of the rich soil, keep the mountain sides from becoming bare and sterile rocks. So, within the last two decades, the people in America have begun to think of forestry. Its purpose is to restore the forests to the condition of permanent rent-earners, to make the mountains yield not a temporary supply, but a perpetual crop of timber.

Possible exhaustion of the coal-supply

2. *The extraction of coal and other mineral deposits reduces for future generations a supply already limited.* The coal deposits in the earth have only recently been drawn upon. A small city like Ithaca probably uses to-day a greater quantity of coal than was used in all Europe two centuries ago. The large deposits of coal and their early development in England long gave a great advantage to English industry over that of other countries. In England, however, has first been felt the fear of the exhaustion of the coal-supply. Professor Jevons, in 1861, sounded the note of alarm; he prophesied that because the coal deposits of America were many times as great as those of England, industrial supremacy must inevitably pass to America. Already the supremacy in coal and iron production has passed to America, and that in textiles soon will come. In England the accessible supply of coal is limited, deeper shafts must be sunk, and the coal gotten with greater difficulty and at greater expense. Coal has risen in price in England within the last few years, and will continue to rise in the future. The coal deposits of America are thirty-seven times as great as those of England, but even these will soon be exhausted. And yet on the part of all except the coal trust, there appears in America a thoughtless disregard for the future. Supplies of copper, iron, and lead in favored positions are likewise limited, and are being rapidly centered in the hands of great companies. The increasing demand for these products insures a steadily rising income from their annual use. The value of the mines, being based on the series of incomes they will yield, may increase while their unused treasures dwindle in quantity.

Many natural resources are being rapidly exhausted

3. *The exhaustion of natural stores of material is due to civilization, but it threatens to put an end to industrial progress.* The savage does not go deep enough to use up permanently the world in which he lives. He uses the fruits that he finds, and those fruits are, almost without exception, renewed the next year. The only mines that were worked out in ancient times were gold and silver mines, while the mines of useful metals were touched but lightly. Within the last century the earth's crust has been exploited with startling rapidity. Scientific knowledge and mechanical improvement have combined to unlock the storehouses of the geologic ages. At the ever-increasing rate of their use, many important materials must be exhausted in the not far distant future. While it is probable that substitutes will be discovered for many of them, the outlook in some directions has little promise. To treat terminable incomes, exhaustible sources of supply, as permanent sources of income, leads alike to unsound theory and to reckless practice.

Chapter XII
Increase of Rent-bearers and of Rents

§ I. Efforts of Men to Increase Products and Rent-bearers

Desire for better agents impels men to improvements

1. *While man destroys some agents of production he multiplies many others.* We have noted many kinds of depreciation, destruction, and wearing out of wealth; but the normal thing in a healthy society is an increase, on the whole, of rent-bearers. The increase of rents is due to two causes: changes in the agents by which they become more efficient technically, or more numerous; and changes taking place outside of the agents, affecting the utility of the products. The first of these will be considered in this section.

The increase of the efficiency of agents is usually the aim of the individual producer, and thus is brought about an increase of the stock of wealth. In some cases, however, improvements such as the dredging of harbors or as the protecting of forests, are made by men collectively through the agency of governments. Somewhere, however, the desire for these changes must arise in the minds of individuals. Increase of most things involves "cost" or sacrifice, in the psychological sense; that is, man must strive, perhaps suffer, to get a certain result. This end, therefore, must be in itself desirable, and social organization must be such as to present a motive to the men to make the needed effort.

Improvements by adaptation of natural resources

2. *Rent-bearers may be increased in quantity and improved in quality by the adaptation of natural resources to man's purposes.* To get food, men use the tracts of land that under the conditions give the largest product. Other tracts less fertile, or for some reason less available, are ditched, tiled, and diked, and fertilizers are carried up steep hillsides to make a soil upon the very crags. In commerce and transportation, new ways are opened by canals, railroads, and tunnels. An isthmian canal will raise the efficiency of ships plying between New York and San Francisco, enabling them to carry a greater amount of freight within a year. The tolls will represent to the users an expenditure only partially offsetting the increased efficiency of the

INCREASE OF RENT-BEARERS AND OF RENTS

agents of transportation. By the building of wharves, the dredging of harbors, and by many other methods, indirect agents are constantly growing in number and efficiency.

Machinery is an adaptation of natural resources

3. *Rent-bearers may be increased by inventions and improvements that make machines stronger, quicker, and better.* This proposition is not logically different from the preceding. A machine is an arrangement of material things through which force may be indirectly applied to move matter. No fast line divides machinery as regards form, purpose, or cause of value, from the artificially improved natural agents that we have been discussing. Just as a field is drained, plowed, and cultivated to fit it better to yield a crop, so is the iron ore shaped into a form called a machine, better fitted to cut, carve, and weave as man wills. Machines are merely adaptations of natural resources.

Bettering quality of agents

Increase in machinery may be either in quality or quantity. The two causes have in most cases the same result. If the quality or efficiency of looms is doubled, it is as if their number had grown in like proportion. In its economic function the beast of burden may not illogically be classed with inanimate machines. The horses in America have been remarkably improved of recent years by the importation of thoroughbred stock from Europe. Ten or fifteen years ago the number of horses in the United States was found to have decreased, and there was much comment on this evidence of a declining industry. It was not at once recognized that there was embodied in horse-flesh more horse-power than ever before, as a single Norman horse has the strength of several Mexican mustangs. Numbers alone are not the measure of efficiency.

Increasing number and better grouping of agents

4. *The increase of wealth and the betterment of environment go on as well through the increase in the number of appliances and through their improved arrangement, as through changes in their kind.* A machine is an adjustment of various natural agents to each other so as to make a more efficient agent, and machines in turn may be adjusted as parts of a larger system of production. The ideal of the modern factory system is so to arrange the machinery that no bit of material will make an unnecessary motion. The log, once started through the mill, is carried automatically from one machine to another until it emerges as a roll of paper or as a box of tooth-picks, ready for use. In an American watch-factory one man tends twelve or fifteen automatic machines. A small brass rod is fed automatically to the machine; a piece is cut off, is picked up by a human-like metal hand; is put into a lathe, and shifted or held firmly while it goes through fifteen or twenty processes; and then is dropped into a box where it is ready for the "assembling" of the watch. As the machinery improves, factories making allied products are grouped to make a system still more efficient.

As the number of agents increases they are distributed so as to be where most useful to the owner. A man having two umbrellas keeps one at his office and the other at home; a student having two books of the same kind keeps one at his room and the other at the university; a farmer having two hoes keeps one at the barn and the other in a distant field, and by this distribution the agents are increased in efficiency.

A larger and better environment

The aim of a progressive society is to enlarge the environment, and constantly to adapt it better to the service of wants. This is done largely by mechanical agents, which capture the natural forces of the world, put them into the right place at the right time, and make them do the right thing, or which group and relate the materials of the world in the right ways. Some of the groupings in the chemical and physical world that do not fit man's purposes may be made to do so. The world in this way becomes more and more a great workshop, better and better adjusted to man's wants.

Increasing some rent-bearers reduces the rents of others

5. *The betterment of the environment of society in some directions reduces the rent of other parts.* The wish of the individual is to raise his own rent-bearers in efficiency, but in doing that he affects the agents owned and controlled by others. The ideal from a social standpoint is to increase not rent but the welfare of society, and this is not always the ideal of individuals seeking their own interest. However, as the efficiency of some agents rises, it becomes unnecessary and unprofitable to use the less fertile fields; they cease to be rent-bearers, and the rent of the richer fields falls under the influence of the new supply of products. Some inventions suddenly increase the efficiency of free goods to such a degree that the less efficient rented agents are thrown out of use, and the margin of utilization is moved to a higher plane than it was on before. Improved types of machinery more or less rapidly displace the older, less efficient types, which, therefore, more or less completely lose their rent-bearing power long before they are physically worn out. When improvements in agriculture that are applicable to a considerable area of land take place, and the product thus is increased and cheapened, the poorer land is abandoned. Inventions and improvements thus gradually becoming common property, increase the free goods and free uses not bearing rent and open to every one. One who improves the quality of a machine or the economy of a process may thus unintentionally injure some of the owners of low-rent agents, while unintentionally increasing the welfare of the mass of men for whom the margin of utilization is thus lifted.

§ II. Effects of Social Changes in Raising the Rents of Indirect Agents

Effect of decrease of the competing agents

1. *Changes in the number and kind of competing resources may raise the rents of particular agents.* Rents may increase without increase in the quantity or number of a particular group of agents or without change in their technical efficiency. As changes in the conditions of society may reduce rents, so other changes may increase them. Agents of the same kind may diminish in number, either absolutely or relatively. If some of the competing machines are destroyed, the rents of the machines that remain rise, while if new supplies are found, either in nature or by improved industrial processes, the rents of the older agents fall.

Effect of new uses for agents

2. *The discovery of new uses for agents or for their products raises their rents.* Farm land of the poorest kind often is found to contain valuable mineral deposits. Such a lucky find has lifted the mortgage from a farm in eastern Pennsylvania, from which, in two or three years, has been taken feldspar exceeding in value the agricultural products of the same land in the last fifty years. The discovery of building stone, coal, natural gas, or oil land may make the annual rent (or royalty) of land tenfold its former total value. Fitness to produce nettles is not ordinarily a virtue in land, but the discovery that certain fields produce a superior quality of the nettle used for heckling cloth, causes them to take on a new value. A mineral spring, because of the supposed or proved healing properties of its waters, may be as good as a mine to the owner. Peculiar fitness for the cultivation of celery may convert marsh land into a substantial source of income.

Social changes are constantly causing agents to shift from lower to higher uses. As population grows and groups about new industries, farm land is used for residence lots, and in turn for business purposes. Rents therefore rise, and this rise is reflected in the higher selling value of the land. If a new demand arises for the product of any machine, its rent rises, although it may continue to turn out the same product as measured by number or quantity. For, if consumers increase, a given supply of agents becomes relatively smaller than before.

Sudden variations in demand

3. *A rise in rents due to social changes may be relatively permanent or temporary.* Business conditions sometimes change quickly. An urgent demand for special machinery raises quickly its rent and value. It is said that lace machinery is sometimes thrown out of use for several years, until a sudden renewal of the demand for lace causes the rental to equal, in two years, more than the original cost. At such times the value of factories increases greatly, but after a few years of prosperity business again collapses. Such prosperous periods are the opportunity of the business man and of the promoter to sell the factory at its highest price. Machinery adapted only for a special product will not sell as readily when less

needed for its special use, as that which, like a turning-lathe, can be used for many purposes; but the more special the appliances needed for a certain product, the higher, more abnormal will be their temporary value when they are suddenly needed. Land near the site of an exposition takes on a very great value and again falls after the exposition is over. During the Boer War horses and mules rose in price in the United States on account of British purchases.

Cause efforts to increase the supply of agents

A rise in the value of any agent at once causes an attempt to duplicate it or to find a substitute for it; this attempt, if successful, puts a check or sets a limit to the rise. In this search for new devices the man who can see most quickly and clearly has a key to wealth. Some kinds of agents, as rare minerals or tools that can be produced only by highly skilled labor, cannot be increased rapidly in number and remain high in price for a long period; and favorably located building sites illustrate the same principle. In some cases, it is true, the demand may be due to some temporary cause, as in a period of unsound land speculation, but usually the growing value of location is due to a steady and abiding change in population or business.

Franchises guard the growing rents from the influence of substitution

4. *Such public utilities as are guarded from competition by franchises, often rise in rental with increase in population.* The leading classes of public utilities referred to are waterworks, gas-works, street-railways, ferries, and wharves. This evidently is only a special illustration of the principle just stated, where it is not easy to find a substitute for certain agents. Public franchises entitle the owners to special, sometimes exclusive, privileges, and protect them legally from competition. Not all franchises are valuable; many street-railways are unfortunate ventures, the earnings being insufficient to pay expenses, to say nothing of interest on the investment. But when they pay greatly, their high value is due to the impossibility of competition. The cars, mules, dynamos, steam-engines, and other agents combined to furnish transportation, have a special earning power because other similar agents are forbidden to be used in that market.

Various kinds of "unearned increments"

5. *Industry abounds with cases of unearned increments of value due to accidental and social causes raising the rents of wealth.* The term unearned increment may be defined as an increase in rents (or value) of agents, due to something other than the efforts or merits of the owner; in fact, it is that of which we have been speaking. In some cases powerful or wealthy men can bring about social changes in entirely legitimate ways. The owner of a large factory, moving it into the country, may buy up surrounding land and found a city, converting pasture lands and corn-fields into valuable building lots. Again, social changes are produced immorally, if not illegitimately, when wealthy men or influential politicians cause laws to be passed which inure to their advantage but which may ruin many other citizens.

INCREASE OF RENT-BEARERS AND OF RENTS

Also many chances of loss

In most cases, however, social changes are impersonally caused. The individual owner who profits by them is powerless to affect the result. He can only adapt his conduct in some measure so as to reap an advantage. He can strive to increase the number and quality and to get control of such agents as he foresees will yield higher rents. In making such a forecast there is chance of loss as well as of gain. The term "unearned increment" has been frequently used in recent years. It is often assumed to be a peculiar thing, sharply in contrast to other changes in value. The foregoing hasty review may serve to suggest how manifold and complex are the instances of it, and what an important part it plays in modern industry.

DIVISION C—CAPITALIZATION AND TIME-VALUE

Chapter XIII
Money as a Tool in Exchange

§ I. Origin of the Use of Money

The consideration of money can no longer be postponed

1. *The exchange of goods by barter is extremely difficult in most cases.* Thus far we have not considered the subject of money and have so far as possible avoided even the use of the term. Value in economics does not depend on money, and is not necessarily connected with it. Things can be compared in their utility, their importance to our welfare can be estimated, without the use of money. Many problems of economics can be discussed pretty thoroughly and solved without the use of the word money or any term of similar meaning. But to-day it is impossible to go very far in the discussion of economic questions without using the concept of money, which is interwoven with every practical and theoretical problem in economics. We have delayed to the farthest limit the formal recognition of the subject; but we are now approaching the question of capital and interest, and it is no longer possible to avoid a preliminary consideration of the money concept.

Exact measurement of utilities is not possible without some medium of exchange

In considering the problem of exchange of consumption goods, we have assumed that it is possible to weigh small differences in the marginal utility of goods, and that such differences have influence on exchange. Now in exchange by barter such a small estimate is impossible. In barter things are exchanged directly for each other in kind. If the two things do not chance to coincide in value, the exchange cannot be completed. An equivalent must be found, or a multiple, if the marginal utility of two goods is to be equalized for either party by exchange. As in most cases this adjustment must be very incomplete, many exchanges that otherwise would be advantageous cannot take place. In the earlier stages of development, this careful estimate of value is not found. Children do not make it. The typical trade of the small boy is a "trade even"; Johnny exchanges his gingerbread for Jimmie's jack-knife. It marks an epoch in the industrial development of the boy when he begins to keep store with pins, and no longer trades candy for apples, but both for pins, which have become the medium of exchange in his boy world. He then can express values in much more exact terms. In our society most children begin early to grow familiar with this conception; but travelers find some savage tribes still in the earlier childish stage of development, unable to grasp the thought of a general medium of exchange. When, through lack of a medium of exchange, there is a failure to adjust utilities, there is a loss of the possible advantage in each defeated exchange. There is a further waste of time and of vain efforts to find something that will be accepted in exchange, and the loss offsets a large part of the gain even when the barter is effected.

Money is found to serve as a general medium of exchange

2. *Some kind of enjoyable good in general use comes to be money, that is, to be accepted as a medium of exchange.* The difficulties just mentioned are met by the use of a medium of exchange. A medium of exchange is simply one kind of wealth which is taken, not for itself, but to pass along, in the belief that it will enable the taker to gratify his wants and distribute his purchasing power in a more effective way. Money is an "invention" in that it is a means of exchange that came into use independently in a great number of communities. It is not an invention in the sense of a mechanical device suddenly hit upon, but rather in the sense of a social custom that grows as its convenience is tested by practice. Money is used, in some degree, everywhere except in the most primitive tribes. Historically viewed, the money first used in any community is seen in every case to be a commodity capable of giving immediate gratification, a direct good in immediate use. It then gradually comes to be used as money, which is an indirect agent. Still later, when the money habit is well established, a kind of material having no utility except as a medium of exchange may come to be used.

Qualities of the primitive money

3. *Money in its origin is that good which best unites the qualities that make it easy to sell, to carry, to know, to keep, to divide, and unite.* It is evident that if some one commodity is gradually to take on this use as a medium of exchange there will be a choice; some things will be better fitted than others. First, this thing must have the quality of salability, or marketability. In the channels of exchange it is taken not because it is wanted for itself, but because it will help to get something else that is wanted. To be sure of a ready sale in a primitive community it must, however, be something that is generally desired. Food and clothing, which supply the fundamental physical needs, are the most generally used and desired of all goods. But they do not have the second quality of a good money material, that of great value in small bulk, transportability. Food is bulky. The carrying of a venison or of a bag of wheat on one's back a short distance requires an effort as great as that for the procuring of the food. Furs, however, have this quality in a high measure, united with other qualities of money, as is shown by their general use in the exchanges of northern tribes. Thirdly, a thing must be recognizable; counterfeits must be easily avoided, and the quality must be easy to test: this is the quality of cognizability. The love of ornament is universal in human societies,

and gives value to many materials combining in a high degree the qualities thus far named. Fourthly, the money material, when taken in exchange, must remain without loss of quality, perhaps for long periods, until it can be exchanged again. Food does not answer to this requirement, being organic and perishable. But some of the metals, having value in small bulk, salability, cognizability, and durability, step by step displaced other forms of money. Finally, money must be made of a material easy to divide and unite. It is a great convenience in small transactions to be able to represent a fractional value by a small coin. The money material thus, likewise, is easily shifted to and from its money use. It is a very poor money that has not this quality, yet a thing may serve for money in larger transactions without it. Cattle, slaves, and land have been thus used, although they answer in a very rough way these fundamental requirements of the money material.

Industrial changes affect the convenience of certain money forms

4. *The changing material and industrial conditions of society change the kind of money that is used.* The money use, as has just been shown, is a resultant of a number of different motives in men. Things that have the highest claim to fitness for money with a people at one stage of development would have a low claim at another. As each of these stages is passed, the thing used as money either increases or decreases in its fitness. The final choice depends on the resultant of all the advantages. The use of a material may become more general or less so. Shells used for ornament in poor communities cease to be so used in a higher state of advancement, and thus their salability ceases. Furs, used at some stage of development as money in all northern climes, cease to be generally marketable when the fur-bearing animals are nearly killed off and the fur trade declines. Tobacco was at one time in Virginia a great staple. Merchants were always ready to take it, and its market price was known by all; but as it ceased to be the almost exclusive product of the province, it lost the knowableness and marketability it had before. In agricultural and pastoral communities where every one had a share in the pasture, cattle were a fairly convenient form of money, but to-day would be a most inconvenient one; a city merchant exchanging goods for Poland China pigs and Texas steers would envy the proverbial owner of a white elephant.

The proved fitness of gold and silver as money

The value of the money material may fall so greatly as a result of greater production, as in the case of iron, tin, copper, that it becomes unsuitable. Again, as wealth grows, as exchanges increase, as the use of money develops, as commerce extends to more distant lands, the heavier, less precious metals fail to serve the money need, especially in the larger transactions. Thus, in a sense, different commodities compete, each trying to prove its fitness to be a medium of exchange; but only one, or two, or three at the most, can at one time hold such a place. Silver and gold, step by step, often making little progress in a century, have displaced other commodities, and are the staple and dominant forms of money in the world to-day. Every community has witnessed some stage of this evolution. Now nations are divided into two great groups, silver- and gold-using, in accordance with the metals they use as standards. The gold-using countries are the most advanced industrially, requiring the most valuable money metal. Many countries have passed in the last century from the silver to the gold standard, and in an intermediate period have tried to use both standards. The Asiatic and South American countries mainly use silver, while most of those in North America and Europe use gold.

While industrial changes thus affect the choice of money, in turn money reacts upon the other industrial conditions. If a new and more convenient material is found, or the value of the money metal changes to a degree that affects the generalness of its use, industry is greatly affected. The discovery of mines in America brought into Europe, in the sixteenth century, a great supply of the precious metals, and this change in the use of money reacted powerfully on industry. Money being itself one of the most important of the industrial conditions, is affected by and in turn affects all others.

§ II. Nature of the Use of Money

Money is an indirect agent, a tool to effect exchanges

1. *Money in all its money uses is an indirect agent, to be judged just as other indirect agents are.* The key to this section is the thought that the function of money is to serve as an indirect agent. Money is often, by a figure of speech, called a tool. Literally a tool is a bit of material which, taken in the hand, is used to apply force to other things, to shape them or move them. Figuratively, this is just what money does. A man takes it in his hand not to get enjoyment out of it, but to apply force, to move something, and that which he moves is the other commodity. Adam Smith aptly likened money to the road and wagons that transport goods, thus gratifying wants by putting things into a more convenient place. Money is only one of a multitude of forms of wealth. It is not even the most "valuable"; it has value just as other indirect agents have. The loss caused by taking away an indirect agent entirely is greater than the benefit usually attributed to it. Its utility in the extremest conditions is greater than its marginal utility under ordinary conditions. Food is not credited in the market with enormous value, but if starvation threatened, all else would be given for food. In a like manner, each individual values money according to the importance of the marginal service it renders, but the marginal service is far from measuring the loss that would be caused by the entire disuse of money. In a society without money, industrial processes would be very different, and exchange would be hampered in almost inconceivable ways. It is true, therefore, that money is an economic factor of high importance, but it is not so indispensable as many other factors to which far less value is attributed.

Why a poor community lacks money

A poor community has little money because it cannot afford more; it gets along with less money than is convenient just as it gets along with fewer indirect agents of every other kind than it could use. Pioneers in a poor community where the average wealth is low, cannot afford to keep a large number of wagons, plows, good roads, or school-houses. If the community were wealthy enough it would have more of these and of other things, and great as is the convenience of money, poorer communities have to do with little of it. It is, therefore, a confusion of cause and effect for poor communities to imagine that their poverty is due to lack of money.

The use of money as a common denominator

2. *Out of its use as a medium of exchange comes the use of money as a common denominator of values.* Money serves as a "common denominator," for, as all other things can be expressed in terms of money, through it the value of other things can be compared. The other things can be expressed in money because they are constantly exchanged for it. All things being compared with money, can in turn be compared with each other. Some consider this service as a common denominator to be the primary and most important function of money. Sometimes a money of account is found, which is not in use as a medium of exchange. Cattle and slaves have served as money of account while not used as a medium of exchange in larger transactions. Money of account is used, as the shilling in New York, which for a century has not been in use at all as a medium of exchange. It is, however, only apparently a denominator of value; the shilling represents five fourths of ten cents. The actual standard is the dollar; the shilling is only a habitual form of speech and is mentally reduced to terms of the money in use. A decimal system is a great convenience in the use of money as a common denominator, but not indispensable. It is a striking fact that England, until a few years ago the greatest industrial nation, still uses a money unit requiring cumbrous calculations.

Money used as a storehouse for saving.

3. *Other uses of money are as a storehouse of saving and as a standard of deferred payments. These uses grow out of those before mentioned.* The standard of deferred payments is the unit of value in which debts are agreed to be paid later. It is evidently most convenient, and therefore almost inevitable, that the common denominator in which all values are expressed from day to day should continue to be taken as the value unit when the completion of the exchange is delayed a day, a month, or a year. This will be more fully discussed at a later stage of our study.

The use of money as a storehouse of saving was more common formerly than it is now, when better ways than the hoarding of money are found for "laying up for a rainy day." In some measure, however, money is hourly serving this use, which is still an important one. Money kept to be used to-morrow or five years hence is a storehouse of value for twenty-four hours or for five years. In either case it is being kept to complete at a later time its use as a medium of exchange. A thing ceases to be money, logically viewed, the moment its owner keeps it without the purpose that it shall be spent ultimately. The typical miser is a man who has lost his reason as regards the money use. Money must be deemed, therefore, to perform the same essential service as a storehouse of saving that it does as a medium of exchange. In either case it is to be kept only to the moment when it will afford the maximum of pleasure.

§ III. The Value of Typical Money

The money use is added to other uses

1. *The money use, historically considered, is a new use added to a good, and increases the demand for that good.* The history of any particular kind of money may be traced back to a point where it was not money, since which the money use has been added gradually to the other uses. The value of the material later to become money is determined, as is that of any good, according to its marginal utility in all possible applications. No new theory is required to explain the value of this same commodity as it gradually acquires the added use of a medium of exchange. The new use influences demand for the thing just as do the other uses. What is here said must be understood as applying to typical money, which is at the same time a commodity having other uses. Other things that are not typical money come later to be used as money, under legal regulations.

The other uses continue, slightly modified by the money use

2. *A good that comes to be used as money continues to have a commodity use along with the money use.* When a thing is wanted for some quality that gives immediate gratification to the user, the explanation of its value is simple. Ornaments, shells, feathers, food can be seen to have a direct want-gratifying power. The money use is one that works no physical or visible change in goods, and to many minds it appears so different from other utilities that it remains quite mysterious and incomprehensible. To persons accustomed to thinking on problems of value, this case appears to be no more difficult than that of anything else having two or more uses. Cows are used for milk, for meat, and as beasts of burden. Each of these uses is logically independent as a cause of value, yet all are mutually related, the values of cattle being determined by the consideration of all their uses united into one scale of diminishing utility.

Money yields a series of rents which are the basis of its value

3. *The uses of money make it a rent-bearing form of wealth.* The rent that money yields is in the form of convenience and economy. This is sometimes rendered directly as psychic income, as in enabling the traveler to buy his dinner, for the money thus yields gratification just as does the carriage in which he rides. One may go for a day to the seashore without a parasol and suffer from heat, or without money and suffer from hunger. In every case where money is retained for a time in possession, there is expected from it a usufruct as great as, or greater than, can be secured from anything else for which it can be exchanged. This usufruct

is a net surplus, or income, yielded by a sum of money undiminished in amount up to the moment it is spent, but meantime increasing in the gratification it will help to secure. In many cases in practical business money yields gratification only indirectly, as the objective contract rent received as interest for borrowed money in business uses, or as economic rent when the use of money in business enables one to secure a larger income. Because money yields a rent men make the sacrifice involved in keeping a stock of it on hand. On this rent is based that part of the value of money that is derived from its money use. As the use of money as a standard of deferred payment, or basis of commercial obligations, does not require that it be owned by the parties writing the contract, this use of money is a free good, a sort of social by-product of the medium of exchange. When money is in use in a community, any person may draw up contracts in terms of money, borrowing and lending, buying and selling wealth, later to be repaid in other wealth or services expressed in the circulating medium.

The general use of money is characteristic of this age

4. *Money may be defined as a generally accepted material means of payment and medium of exchange.* This, its primary and essential function, may appear to be less important as new modes of balancing accounts of wealth are devised. But its functions as a common denominator of values and as a standard of deferred payment are increasingly important in an advancing society. It is this expression of the value of all other things in terms of money which may well be deemed the essential characteristic of the capitalistic age. In earlier periods wealth was thought of and expressed in concrete terms; now it is expressed in money. The general use of money affects men's ways of looking at wealth and speaking of it. Without appreciating the nature and function of money, it is impossible to grasp the significance of capital in modern industry, the consideration of which we are now to enter upon.

Chapter XIV
The Money Economy and the Concept of Capital

§ I. The Barter Economy and its Decline

Various points of view of the students regarding money

1. *The use of money prevails in very different degrees in various parts of the United States.* The members of this class, representing nearly every state and territory in the Union, have lived amid very diverse industrial conditions. Some know best the country where conditions are similar to those of a hundred years ago; some, the villages where may be seen the handicrafts and the small general store. Others know better the cities with their varied industries; while doubtless still others, through family relations, know of the methods of great wholesale business, perhaps even of the larger commerce and foreign trade. Methods differ in the different lines of business, and according as a man is a farmer, a merchant, or a banker, he has different ideas as to the use of money and of the part it plays in modern industry. You come to this study with different experiences and preconceptions; as a result every statement produces a somewhat different impression on each of you. This is true in general of the statements made in political economy; but it is most strikingly true in the discussions of money. A city boy rarely sees a case of barter; whereas in many parts of the West and Southwest, and in the mountainous districts of the East, a large part of the business is carried on in this way. Town and city in New York state differ in this respect, but hardly more than do the rural districts of the different sections of our country. Banks are very numerous in the East, are few in the Northwest, and still fewer in the South. Men can understand each other better in a discussion if they are conscious of the fact that they do not instinctively take the same point of view.

Countries differ in their use of money

2. *The extent to which, on an average, money is used in different countries of the world, differs widely.* Statements in political economy must be guarded; few of them

MONEY ECONOMY AND CONCEPT OF CAPITAL

can be taken as universally true. As the different parts of one country may be contrasted, so may the different countries. The use of money in Siberia would be much less than that in Moscow and St. Petersburg, and again the average use in Western Russia is doubtless less than that in Austria. In Austria the money use is less developed than in Germany. While there is now little difference between Germany and France in this respect, France for a long time was the more developed industrially and made greater use of money.

There is greater use of money in the cities of the outlying countries than in the rural districts. In the cities of Mexico banks and credit agencies are employed as in the American cities. The rural districts are more backward and make far less use of money than is the case in the United States. The great ports of China are provided with all the facilities of modern banking. In the great cities of India one can get a bank draft that will be paid in any part of the world. But go a very little way out of the cities of China and India, and conditions greatly change; money is far less used and principally as a storehouse of saving.

Slight use of money in the Middle Ages

3. *In a historical view the European nations are seen to begin with a barter economy and to pass through great changes as regards the use of money.* Here the view shifts from a comparison of different nations at the same moment to a comparison of the same nation through a period of centuries. To understand, even in a measure, what is about them men must know out of what it grows. In the early Middle Ages money was used chiefly in cities, and there only to a limited extent. Almost universally a "barter economy" prevailed, or, as it has been called, a "natural economy," a term taken from the German "Naturalien," which means natural products, enjoyable things, as opposed to money. Natural economy, therefore, means that condition of society in which things are exchanged in kind. In the Middle Ages land was the great and dominant form of wealth. The prince himself was dependent on land for his income. The conquering chief or invader took possession of the land and parceled it out to his followers, and they in turn to their vassals. The income of the rulers was in the form of "Naturalien" (wheat, chickens, eggs), the kind and amount of which was fixed by contract or by immemorial usage. The landlord had land as his wealth and income-getter; the tenant received the use of the land in payment for his labor.

Land, the main form of wealth, was rented without the use of money

The condition of the serf appears to have been, under these circumstances, inevitably connected with the "barter economy" as applied to the renting of land. A farm cannot be moved, and in medieval conditions its products mainly had to be used on the spot. If the serf was to use and enjoy the land, he had to stay upon it. Having no money he had to pay in labor or in products, for its usufruct. In those times the powerful man, politically, was also a wealthy man whose wealth consisted of landed estates. Between the landlord and the serf existed a lasting relation, inherited rather than voluntary, but similar in its conditions to the renting contract. The villein had the use of the stock, pastures, fields, woodlands, provided he kept them undiminished and undestroyed to transmit to his children. Under such conditions there was great fixity of economic relations. While in some respects this was a happy condition, it had its disadvantages. The renting contract, in connection with a fixed rotation of crops and some communal modes of cultivation, hindered improvements. The more intelligent cultivator could not change his methods for the better. It may be seen not only that the use of money on a medieval manor was slight, but that the conditions for the growth of the money habit were most unfavorable. The terms of agricultural contracts, the modes of speech, the habits and thought of the mass of the people, were therefore determined by the conditions of the barter economy. A change in these respects was slowly worked by forces originating outside, in a very different industrial environment.

Contrast between city wealth and feudal estates in the Middle Ages

4. *With the growth of cities developed a new class of wealthy men and a new view of wealth.* The student of history knows of the conflict that grew up during the Middle Ages between the cities and the landed aristocracy. It found its cause in economic conditions. There were obvious differences between the wealth of the feudal landlords, and the wealth that grew up in cities. One must be used mostly on the spot, the other can be moved. The fruits of one are perishable for the most part; the fruits of the other can be kept for a longer period. The methods of agriculture are exceptionally stable; production by handicraftsmen is dependent on the peculiar skill of the workman, giving greater room for invention and a premium on skill. The one industry may be carried on by servile labor; the other can be efficiently followed only by free workers having the ambition to excel.

Money thus more used in city trade

The use of money grew up in the city. The density of population made it easy, the growth of wealth made it possible, and the nature of the exchanges made it necessary. Whereas the relation of landlord and serf under the renting contract continues from year to year, the relation of the buyer and seller of shoes, hats, etc., in the city, is temporary, these things forming only a part of man's economic needs. Barter with a particular individual is much more inconvenient if exchange is only occasional than where the contract is a continuing one, and there is an annual balancing and settlement of accounts. So, as city industry and commerce grew the use of money increased, both in small neighborhood trade and in the larger transactions with distant countries; and thus the business methods of the cities grew into sharper contrast with those of the rural districts.

Money loaned and borrowed in cities

5. *The loan and hire of wealth in medieval cities came to be expressed as a money loan.* The loan of money and of other wealth expressed in terms of money, began in the cities. The use of money and the expression of the value of things in terms of money was common there throughout the Middle Ages. Moreover, as the

movable forms of wealth multiplied, the agreement to return borrowed wealth in kind became impossible in cities; the loan in terms of money became the only practicable thing. A merchant embarking on a trading expedition must have such a number and variety of goods, that he finds it both very difficult to rent them and wasteful in time to enumerate them and return them in like kind. It therefore became usual to make a loan either of the things expressed in terms of money, or of money with which to buy the things, thereby reducing to a single, simple, easily interpreted contract, the indebtedness which the borrowing of a thousand different things occasioned.

The medieval opposition to loans at interest

Such a contract differed not in economic purpose, but only in form and terms of obligation, from the renting of wealth. The church writers, however, got much confused in regard to the nature of money loans. They did not see that it was *things* which the merchant wished to borrow. They did not see that the money loan was simply a more convenient mode of transferring the use of wealth from one person to another. The moralists and lawmakers of that day said: Money is unfruitful, therefore taking interest for it is robbery. We cannot follow here the controversy as to the justice of interest on money which involved other ideas than those mentioned, but even to the present time traces of the old fallacy may be seen more or less plainly in the economic theory as well of conservative writers as of the socialistic opponents of interest. The principal sum expressed in the loan contract was called the capital sum, from *caput*, head, and the amount paid for its use was first called usury, money for the use. How the word interest came to take its place, and the word usury came to mean *excessive* interest is one of the most interesting chapters in economic history. The term capital then came to be connected with city wealth, with movable forms of wealth, with things supposed to be peculiarly "the product of labor"; and interest was assumed to be connected only with this capital. The term rent on the other hand was connected especially with the use of land. The connection was a historical accident, but it has had an important influence on economic theory.

Rivalry of the commercial and land-holding classes in Europe

6. *The owners of city wealth and of country landed estates often were opposed as well in social and political as in economic affairs.* The practical economic questions of the Middle Ages and the practical political questions largely turned on these two groups of interests. The men of wealth in the cities, the merchants and manufacturers, often were found opposed to the landed aristocracy. This social division between the commercial and agricultural classes doubtless helped to strengthen the prejudgment as to the nature of the two kinds of wealth. Indeed, in view of the situation, it may have been in a measure justifiable and expedient to contrast the thought of city wealth, which has come to be called capital, with that of landed wealth. But even if it were, it is now misleading and erroneous to continue the use of such concepts in a new country and in our modern conditions.

Land continues to be rented while city wealth is borrowed in money form

Indeed, for centuries the sharper features of the contrast have been steadily softened. The money economy of the city gradually spread to the rural districts, but never entirely displaced barter, which lingers everywhere. Important steps toward a money economy were the commuting of forced or customary labor of the serfs into a money payment to the lord, and at the same time the substitution of money payments for payments in kind (use of lands, specified goods, etc.) to the peasants. Thus arose a free peasant class receiving wages. But land continued to be rented and landed estates to be hereditary throughout Europe. As they did not pass from hand to hand as a commercial or marketable form of wealth, their value was rarely, if ever, expressed in terms of money and as a ratio to the rent they bore. The result was the fixing of the erroneous idea that agricultural wealth is essentially different in the character of its service and yield from wealth used in manufactures. One phase of the error was the idea held by the physiocratic writers and by Adam Smith that in agriculture "nature labors along with man," while in manufacture "nature does nothing, man does all." This view was corrected by later critics (Buchanan, Ricardo, and others), but the main portion of the fallacy persisted in the supposed contrast between the characters of the services performed by natural resources and by artificially produced wealth.

§ II. The Concept of Capital in Modern Business

Extension of the use of the money loan and of the capital concept

1. *The development of the use of money and credit has led to the expression of the value of all indirect agents, without distinction, in terms of money.* This is a capitalistic age. The development of a class of money-lenders has led to a transfer of all sorts of wealth from owners to users by means of money. As in medieval Europe city wealth was bought and sold, and measured and expressed, so in twentieth century America are the farm, the waterfall, and the mine. Every purchase with money owned or borrowed is to-day called an investment of capital. To invest means to clothe, and an investment of capital is clothing money in any kind of wealth, whether it be a ship, a factory, or a farm.

Interest on money is the contractual form in which more and more the use of wealth is paid for. The borrower does not ask the wealthy man to buy for him a factory and to rent it to him. It is not impossible for the transaction to take that form; but in practice it is inconvenient. The capital concept, the expression of wealth in the form of money, spreads over almost the whole face of the economic world. In promissory notes, mortgages, capital stock, bonds, and many other forms, are expressed the obligations of borrowers bound to pay regularly a sum called interest for the use of the multifarious wealth they have chosen to employ.

MONEY ECONOMY AND CONCEPT OF CAPITAL

Definition of capital

2. *Capital to-day may be defined as economic wealth expressed in terms of the general unit of value.* In economic discussion new conditions must be recognized and an attempt made to adapt definitions to the language and needs of practical life. By this definition, capital, at any given moment of time, includes all economic goods in existence, when they are thought of in terms of their value. But things have different durations, some are parts of the capital of the world only for an instant, others for a week, a month, or years. Most capital is composed of things durable in a large degree.

It has been seen above that there is no reason for keeping things unless they will increase in value, that is, unless a rental is logically attributable to them. Everything kept for a day, a month, a year, is kept because thus it will continually give off uses or by accumulating them it will become more useful. Hence, when interest is defined as the payment for the use of capital, it is connected with all wealth that is expressed in the capital form. In practical business and in theoretical discussion this is the idea of capital that alone can be consistently followed. Capital is the value equivalent of a sum of money "invested," "clothed" in forms of wealth purchased and exchanged. Wealth has become fluid in modern times; it was crystallized in medieval times. Under the new conditions, wealth, expressed in the mobile form of capital, flows into the most distant corners of the industrial world.

Distinction between money and capital

3. *Capital must not be identified with money although it is expressed in terms of money.* While money and capital are not identical, neither are they opposite or mutually contradictory. Money is but one species of the genus capital. It is a particularly durable form when industry as a whole is considered, a particularly fleeting form in the individual's possession, and a particularly important, though not necessarily the most important, form in its social significance. The things composing capital are concrete things, scarce forms of wealth, some of which are yielding gratification at the present moment, or are destined to do so at some future moment; others of which are not themselves giving direct gratification, but are indirect agents for the gratifying of wants. To this latter group belongs money.

The caution contained in this proposition may appear to some to be superfluous, but it is most needed. The mind is so prone to identify things that are expressed currently by the same words. The ease with which money and capital are thus confused has led to various popular fallacies on practical economic questions.

Contractual interest and rent involve a difference of business procedure

4. *Renting wealth and borrowing capital have the same economic purpose, but the capital contract presents certain peculiar features.* In the interest contract for the loan of capital the interest always is and must be expressed in money; the capital sum must be expressed as value; and the interest rate expresses the relation between these two values. In each of these features the interest contract is in contrast with the renting contract. While the rent itself may or may not be expressed in terms of

money, the value of the rented wealth is not so expressed, and there is no rent-rate expressing the relation between the two values.

The wealth concept and the capital concept contrasted

As here presented, the essence of the capital concept is in the mode or form of expression of wealth, not in the physical nature, the origin of its value, or any peculiarity in the kind of wealth; the content of the concept is limited only by man's thought of wealth, every good becoming capital when it is capitalized, that is, when the totality of its uses is expressed as a present sum of values. The difference between the wealth concept and the capital concept is therefore subjective, not objective; it is a difference in the mode of man's thought regarding wealth. The rent contract and the interest contract are modes of borrowing and lending which reflect this difference of conception. In their effort to express more exactly to themselves and to others the relative felt importance of their environment, men take in turn different points of view, and use different modes of expression. The most developed and exact of these devices for the social expression of valuations, which became possible only with a money economy and widened markets, is the capital concept, whose nature has been analyzed here.

The capital concept now prevalent

Summarizing the thought of this chapter, it may be said that the capital concept has gradually developed with industry, and is now the most widely prevailing mode of expressing the quantity of wealth. It is used in the discussion of all the most important problems of modern industry. The questions of income from wealth, of trusts and corporations, nearly all that is most notable in the development of modern industry, require the use of the capital concept. Yet (returning to the thought with which this chapter started) in many of the outlying districts other modes of looking upon wealth are employed. References to modern industry must be understood usually as applying to the most developed capitalistic conditions.

Chapter XV
The Capitalization of All Forms of Rent

§ I. The Purchase of Rent-charges as an Example of Capitalization

The nature and sale of rent-charges

1. *From the twelfth to the sixteenth centuries the sale and purchase of rent-charges was the most general form of borrowing and lending wealth.* A rent-charge in the Middle Ages was a definite income that was to be paid out of the rents of an estate, business house, manor, etc. The property was said to be "charged" with the payment of that income, and some estates were passed on for generations from father to son charged with a certain rent. It was thus possible for the owner of money to buy a rent-charge, either one that had been created a generation before, or a new one created by some landowner for the especial purpose of borrowing money to go on a crusade or of improving his estate or of investing in other business. The transaction took this form: the purchaser of the rent-charge paid a sum of money, called the capital sum, and obtained in return a rent-paper entitling him to receive permanently a given income. The house or land was security for the debt. The seller gave up the right to the rent as it came in year by year, and received in return a capital sum in hand. Generally he had the right to repay the sum whenever he wished and thus extinguish the rent-charge. Logically viewed, the purchaser bought an equitable part of the income, therefore an equitable part of that rent-bearing wealth. In effect it was just like a loan except that the purchaser of the rent-charge could not demand the repayment of his money. He could, however, sell the rent-charge when he wished to get his capital out. Gradually it became usual to sell and transfer rent-papers just as is done to-day with mortgages and bonds. Rent-papers thus came in the fifteenth century to be negotiable paper in somewhat general use. There was a rise and fall of the value of the rent-paper with changes in the demand for investment in rent-charges or with changes in the security.

Rent-charges were a convenient investment in medieval cities

2. *The sale of rent-charges grew out of an industrial need of the exchange of safe*

permanent incomes for larger sums of wealth. The custom of the purchase of rent-charges grew up in the cities. The increasing wealth of cities, the growth of commerce and enterprise, caused rent-charges to be sold by the owners of houses and real estate in the cities, and the custom spread to the country. It is an instance of the way income became more fluid in the cities during the Middle Ages. This kind of loan contrasted strikingly in the Middle Ages with those loans made commonly by reckless kings, prodigal nobles, and distressed peasants to secure consumption goods. Merchants needed large amounts of wealth for their growing enterprises, and they felt that if they could get a capital sum down they could make it earn more than the rent-charge. A perpetual income of one hundred units was therefore exchanged for a sum at the moment of twenty or twenty-five times that amount. As the wealth of the cities increased, there were some men who wished to retire from active business, and there were widows and children with property which they could not manage directly. Such persons either could not afford to take the risks of active business, or could not judge of them, and they formed a class of lenders or investors seeking some safe income. Between the two classes of active merchants and capitalist lenders, each of whom saw his own advantage and followed it, the practice of buying and selling rent-charges thus grew up.

Rent-charges were not forbidden by the church

The practice was allowed by the church, though interest and the lending of money were forbidden. The loan was substantially a loan of capital and the rent-charge was substantially interest, but in the eyes of the church moralists there was a marked difference, in that the obligation to the purchaser of the rent-charge was secured by a permanent and substantial form of wealth, and the contract usually was favorable to the borrowers. In its origin the practice was not merely an evasion of the law against usury, but a convenient form of contract. It doubtless came, however, to be used as a means of evading the law of the church against usury, and thus became an entering wedge for the general use of money loans.

The market value of rent-charges reflects the exchange ratio between present and future money incomes

3. *Rent-charges had a market-value, varying with time and place, and expressed as a number of years' purchase of the rent-charge.* The sellers of rent-charges were influenced by many motives: a lord wished to build a castle, or go on a crusade; a farmer wished to improve his estate; a merchant wished to embark on larger ventures. Opportunities thus opened in the cities for men of wealth to get a fixed income for a payment of ready money. In the cities, the buyers seeking a fixed income would bid down, or bid up, the value of the rent-charges, which thus came to have a quotable market value. In time, greater and greater amounts were paid by the investors in return for the guarantee of a given income. In rural districts the value of the charges was low, that is, the capital sum was but ten or twelve times the value of the annual rent-charge; while in the cities it rose to twenty and even twenty-five times the annual rent-charge.

A memento of this practice, probably, is the manner in which the price paid

THE CAPITALIZATION OF ALL FORMS OF RENT 91

for land is spoken of still in England and the continental countries in a phrase quite unfamiliar to American ears, as a certain number of "years' purchase." If an estate is sold for twenty times the annual net rental it is said to be sold at twenty "years' purchase." This does not mean that the rental for twenty years only is sold, but that the rental *in perpetuity* is sold for twenty times the annual rent; that is, the land is sold outright for twenty years' rent paid at once. The estate is looked upon primarily as yielding a fixed income; the value of the permanent possession of the estate is thought of as a certain number of times the value of the income secured. "Years' purchase" means, therefore, the length of time required for the income to amount to the purchasing price.

This attains the thought of the present value of the estate, or capital sum in it, though the capital sum is thought of as a multiple of the income, instead of the income being calculated as a percentage of the capital value. Now at the rate of "ten years' purchase" an investment of money in land affords an annual interest of ten per cent., as each year the rental is one tenth of the original investment; twelve years' purchase yields eight and one third per cent., twenty years' purchase, five per cent., and twenty-five years' purchase, four per cent. Increase in the number of years' purchase corresponds to a decrease in the rate of interest which the original investment of money, the capital sum, is expected to yield. This is equally true whether the investment be in the legal form of a purchase of the fee-simple of land, or in that of the purchase of a rent-charge. We are brought to this conclusion: that the present value of the rents in perpetuity, of any given wealth, is the capital value of the wealth; and that the reciprocal of the number of years' purchase is the rate of interest that an investment is expected to yield.

Purchase and sale of rent-charges gives way to more modern contracts

4. *The sale of rent-charges has gradually given place to the modern form of money loan.* The conditions of the contract in the sale of rent-charges were gradually changed for greater convenience. When the purchaser (the lender) was given the right to require repayment of the capital sum at the end of a specified time, the transaction was brought still closer to an ordinary loan. In this form, the sale of rent-charges is still found in southern Germany, but the greater simplicity of the money loan, and of the sale outright, has led to the almost total disuse of the older form of transaction.

The purchase of rent-charges was long looked upon as a very different thing from the loan of money, but to modern eyes it is not, and the old distinctions between the moralities of the two kinds of income appear now mainly quibbles, justified in a slight degree by certain social facts of the time. The rise of industry led to different ideas on the lending of money; the prejudice against it weakened in large classes of the population, especially in Protestant countries, and its use rapidly spread. Not until 1830 did a decision of Rome remove all disapproval on the part of the church. Rent-charges are instructive now as showing the mode in which rents began to be capitalized in earlier centuries.

§ II. Capitalization Involved in the Evaluating of Indirect Agents

The capital value of durable wealth is the sum of its expected rents

1. *The buying of any indirect agent is practically the purchasing of a "rent-charge."* To account rationally for the market value of anything, its importance must be traced back to "gratification." We have examined and accepted the proposition that if a good is not affording enjoyment at the present moment it is kept because it will yield a rent until it is used. If it is never to afford direct enjoyment, if it is never to mature physically into the class of enjoyable goods, the explanation for its value must be found in the fact that it is capable of yielding a series of rents of enjoyable goods. In the last analysis the value of anything must be found in its power of affording psychic income, a series of psychic rents. Now when such a durable income is bought outright, what is the basis on which its value is estimated? What other than the rents it will afford? Exactly as did the purchasers of a medieval rent-charge, the buyer of the durable wealth pays a definite sum in return for the right to enjoy a series of future rents. As was the case with rent-charges, however, the amount paid will be less than the full matured value of the rents. A long series, even a perpetual series, may be exchanged for no more than ten, twenty, or twenty-five annual rents. While therefore the selling value of the good is the sum of the values of the rents, it evidently is that sum discounted. Immediately, when we have reached this point in the reasoning, our proposition must suggest itself as self-evidently true in this form: the value of any good is the sum of the entire series of rents it contains, discounted, at *some* rate, to their present worth. What determines the rate of discount is a question that will call later for a fuller explanation.

Capital value is not primary

2. *There are two modes of approach to the problem of interest: one from the side of income (rents); the other, from the side of the bearer (capital).* The rate of interest expresses a relation between two values, the value of the income and the value of the sum loaned, whether it consists of money or of other wealth expressed in terms of money. But which of these values is primary in a study of the causes of value? Which is the base from which the other is derived by multiplying at the rate expressing their ratio? The answer to this question cannot be a matter of indifference to the economic theorist. Universally heretofore the study of interest has been approached from the side of capital. A capital sum was said to be invested and to earn a certain interest, that is, per cent., of that sum. The usage of speaking of the investment of capital as a sum given, and of "interest on capital" predisposes the mind to this view.

Expected rents are primary, and capital value is the "years' purchase"

But the approach from the side of income has been shown to be in some important cases the historical origin of the rate of interest, and we need but

THE CAPITALIZATION OF ALL FORMS OF RENT 93

reconsider reasoning that has gone before to see that this is the logical order in all cases. Rent, or income, is a link in the chain of value, connecting gratification or psychic income, consumption goods, rent or usufruct value, and finally capital value. To one keeping in mind the logical cause of value, it becomes inconceivable that capital value could precede income, a view possible only when a fragment of the problem is seen. This being true, the mere mention of a capital sum implies the interest problem, and assumes the interest rate. The capital is of that amount because the anticipated incomes, discounted at some rate, equal that sum. The capital sum is a certain number of years' purchase of the series of rents which can be secured by the use of wealth in various industries. The owner of a number of dollars (or of an amount of other wealth expressed in dollars) has open to him various investments. The value of any wealth is due to the possibility of deriving incomes from it. If, however, the expected income fails to be realized, the capital loses its value, or it is revalued on the basis of the new rents. The investment is then said to be a losing one. Thus, at each stage in the valuation of capital, before it is invested and at every moment thereafter when the valuation is readjusted to the rents realized or expected, rents are logically primary, the source from which the capital sum is derived.

The rate of capitalization of rents is not fixed merely in commerce

3. *The capitalization of comparatively safe permanent incomes from real estate contains within itself all the factors for the independent determination of the interest rate, and is not to be explained merely by reference to "the prevailing rate of interest" in other investments.* The value of land usually is explained simply as the capitalizing of its rents at "the prevailing rate of interest." The rate is assumed to be fixed by conditions in manufacturing and commerce, and if five per cent, can be gotten there the capitalist would never buy land unless investment in it were made equally attractive. The cause of the rate thus is supposed to rest outside the transaction itself, the exchange of land for other capital seeking investment. The economic student is safe in assuming always that explanations of this sort are fallacious. The cause of value in any one exchange or any one industry is not thus to be juggled and shifted into another industry. It is true that the values of goods are so wonderfully interrelated by substitution that as the price of fresh beef will affect that of salt mackerel, so the capitalization rate of machinery affects that of land; but the influence is not from one side only, it is mutual. When anything has value, it must have in itself an independent cause of value.

The exchange of any present and future rents results in a rate of time discount

It can not be otherwise in the particular problem of value called capitalization. The first task of scientific study is to state clearly the nature of the problem. In this case it is seen to be the exchange of a present sum of wealth for a series of future rents. Whenever there are income-bearers and buyers and sellers of them, there are the conditions required for the determination of the market rate at which those future incomes shall be discounted. Manufactures and commerce have no peculiar relation to this process. By a flight of scientific imagination we might assume that the stock of indirect agents in the world consisted only of natural food producers, and that this stock and its yield were absolutely unchangeable by man's will or efforts. Each man in such case would have to stand with hands tied, and take the fruits as they matured. Even in such a case there would be capitalization and a rate of discount on future rents. The fruit-tree (that is, the whole future series of fruits) would bear a certain relation to one year's yield; the field would bear a certain relation to its crop. Wherever there are buyers and sellers of more or less durable agents of it matters not what kind or origin, there are present the elements and causes for the fixing of a rate of time discount.

Capitalization of a perpetual uniform series of rents;

4. *In practical business may be seen innumerable instances of the capitalization of both permanent and limited series of incomes.* The simplest case is the capitalization of an unvarying and supposedly perpetual series of rents. Whatever the rate of time discount prevailing, rents infinitely distant become infinitesimally small when discount is compounded. The present rent is worth most, next year's less, and so on in a decreasing series.

Of a probably increasing series of rents;

But social changes alter rental values, and so far as these changes are foreseen, these anticipated or expected rents are made the basis for present capitalization. Investors and owners alike may foresee that a piece of land used only for agriculture will, within a few years, be taken up for city lots, or will be needed for a factory or as the site of a railroad station. The capitalized value would not in this case be based upon a series of uniform rents each of the amount yielded annually now, but on the progressive series expected. In some cases the physical output of an agent may decline while the price of the product increases. Modern foresters foresee that the selling price of the timber will be greater twenty-five years from now than it is to-day, and they therefore estimate the rental value of the forest on the basis of the future price, thus justifying expenditure that would be unwise if present prices were to continue.

And of a declining or fluctuating series of rents

Again the expected series of incomes may be declining, as the royalties (not typical rents) secured from mines. If the income is expected steadily to fall, and to disappear at the end of the twenty-fifth year, the value of the mine would be the capitalized sum of a limited and degressive series of incomes.

Mode of fixing the rate of time discount in practical business

Every exchange of a durable agent involves an estimate, rough and imperfect it may be, of that agent's future. The practical men, however, who are thus fixing the "capital value" of goods, are usually only dimly conscious of the logical nature of the process. In fact the process goes on in a way much less analytical and conscious, much more empirical, than this analysis would indicate. Most men simply buy as cheap as they can the agents which at the price they believe will add most to their income. The future changes are only roughly, not accurately estimated. The shrewd bargainer is the one who foresees more clearly than his fellows the complex changes to come. Other men blindly follow. The ability and the inability to foresee such changes make men rich and poor. In all this bidding for capital the logical basis of the value is the series of rents. When the agent is bought outright, the very concluding of the bargain fixes a relation between the expected value of the income and the value of the capital invested. In other words, the exchange of durable agents virtually wraps up in them a net income, which it is expected will unfold year by year when rents mature and are secured. At the moment of the investment, the expected rents are expressed as a percentage of the capital sum.

§ III. The Increasing Role of Capitalization in Modern Industry

As exchange increases capitalization of goods becomes more usual

1. *Where a system of exchange is highly developed, things are looked upon as capital yielding an objective income rather than as wealth yielding immediate means of enjoyment.* In the old organization of industry most men got most of their living from the things they raised or made. At the present time goods are gotten in the most indirect ways; men seek wealth because it will yield them an objective or money income, knowing that if they can get the income, they can get other things by exchange. In business to-day, wherever there is a rental, it is capitalized, has a market value, is bought and sold. Men compete in the purchase of income-yielding agents. There is a continual contest in judgment among investors to secure the largest rent for the smallest outlay. On the other hand, the owners of any rental strive to secure the largest capitalization for it that they can. In this market for capital it is money rents that are exchanged as an indirect means of arriving at gratifications.

Various kinds of corporation securities put expected incomes in saluble form

2. *The issue of capital stock is the putting of the incomes of wealth into marketable form.* Stock companies, or corporations, are business enterprises which issue stock, or certificates of a share in their wealth and income. Doubtless the convenience of the sale and transfer of invested capital by the use of stock, has been one of several reasons for the large increase of this form of organization during the past century. Originally the stock of a company taken collectively represented all the capital invested, and each share entitled the owner to a given portion of the total income earned. The shares were issued in regular denominations in terms of money, and this amount expressed on the face of the stock remained fixed. But as a business proves more or less profitable, the value of a share of its income rises and falls regardless of the original amount of stock issued. At once there is a divergence

between the nominal or face value and the market value of the stock. The nominal value is relatively permanent, the same year after year; it may increase by further issues, but rarely is it decreased. But when stock is the only form of claim on the earnings that is issued, the fluctuations of the market value of the stock record the real value of the business, that is, the capital value of the rents it is expected to yield. But in present practice there are several forms (of which stock is but one) in which an investor may buy a share in the earnings of a business. Bonds usually do not give their owner a vote in the management or make him in the technical legal sense a part owner in the business. Bonds representing money loaned to a company, and entitling their holder to regular interest payments, are nearest in form to the medieval rent-charge. Next stands preferred stock, which entitles the owners to share first in the dividends, if there are any; and finally the common stock, which gets a share only when the other claims are satisfied. By the multiplication and further variation of these readily salable claims on industrial incomes, the needs and desires of investors are met more fully and with greater precision.

Any continuing income can be capitalized

3. *Men seek to convert into marketable capital any increase of income in their wealth or business.* A man who invests a given capital sum in machines, buildings, and materials buys them, as others do, at prices that represent their usual, or market, earning power. If he succeeds exceptionally in his business, he makes the capital earn more than the rents on which it was capitalized. The same material wealth becomes worth more because of the reputation of his products, and therefore the trade-mark and good-will of the business can be capitalized. In this sense a good name can be sold, and is at least as much to be desired, even in a mercenary age, as great riches. Likewise, social changes, new needs, the growth of population, increase the net income of wealth, or the rents of a business. The basis of capital value is income, and whatever be its cause, political or economic, material income can and will be capitalized and added to the market value of the privilege, wealth, or industry on which the income is conditioned.

The capitalizing of franchises for public-service corporations

Notable cases of this sort arise in connection with public franchises. If a street-railway or a gas-company is given the exclusive right to operate in a given locality, any income above average interest on the investment is capitalized either in the higher price of the stock or in additional stock issued without the addition of any material to the plant. If the franchise is unlimited, the income may be capitalized as practically perpetual; if the franchise is limited, and is to expire in thirty or forty years, only the limited series of privileged incomes can ordinarily be capitalized. When, however, the managers are able to exert influence enough to have the franchise extended, and the investors believe in the skill of the managers and perhaps in their power to bribe the legislators, the value of the stock continues higher than it could usually be under a limited franchise. Such circumstances becloud the question whether the exceptional income arising under the franchise should go to the public or to the company. Granted, however, that the company is

THE CAPITALIZATION OF ALL FORMS OF RENT

entitled to the income, the burden of proof is on those who object to the capitalizing of the income as is done in every other business.

Some difficulties in the capitalization of corporate incomes

4. *The manipulation of dividends and the resulting changes in capitalization open up great opportunities for the dishonest increase of private fortunes.* A great change in the market value of stock is made by a comparatively small change in the income it regularly affords, for if the prevailing rate of interest on money loans is five per cent., each dollar of dividends is capitalized at $20. It might seem that the dividend would be declared if earned, otherwise not. The matter is not so simple and impersonal, however. The control of corporations is vested in the hands of a small group of directors who have both the opportunity and the temptation to withhold dividends when they are earned, to pay them with borrowed money if unearned, and in either case to keep the stockholders and the public in ignorance of the real condition and earning power of the business. The stocks can, by this manipulation of dividends, be made a lottery for the legitimate investor, a trap for the unwary, and a source of unrighteous gain by men recreant to their trusts.

In this way it may be seen that an earning power not known to bidders in the market does not enter into capitalization; a fictitious earning power, however, is capitalized so long as the investors continue to be deceived. Instances of this kind present problems not only of private morality, but of the preservation of free industrial institutions. The solution of these problems would perhaps be hastened if the economic nature of capitalization were more clearly understood. Capital value in modern industry is everywhere the expression of the serial rents of wealth, discounted at a prevailing rate of time discount.

Chapter XVI

Interest on Money Loans

§ I. Various Forms of Contract Interest

Distinction between contract interest and time-value

1. *Interest, the amount paid according to contract by one person to another for credit given in terms of money, is but one expression of a larger problem, that of the difference in present worth of goods at two periods of time.* This larger problem appears under several forms: first, as a difference in value, due to time, where there is no money expression (to be considered in the following chapter); second, in discount on a money loan for a short, definite time; third, in a long-time money loan at a fixed rate of interest; fourth, in a credit loan—that is, the sale of the thing on credit in terms of money.

The last three cases involve interest more or less clearly. Time-discount, as will be more fully explained, is the basis of interest. The interest may be greater or less than the time-discount in the goods, owing to miscalculation on the part of the borrower or to an unforeseen change in the conditions. Men bid for the use of wealth with the intention of repaying it at some future time, and the interest they agree to pay is based on their estimate of the discount of future rents, which they think is involved in the present valuations of the goods. Time-discount is involved in goods, however, in numberless cases where there is no contract interest. Even a Robinson Crusoe must recognize in his consumption goods and in his various indirect agents differences in value at different periods of time, of which he must take account.

Risk and expenses to the money-lender

2. *Gross interest must be distinguished from net interest.* The forms of wealth yielding incomes are so mutable, and are used under such complicated conditions, that both in theoretical discussion and in practice much care is needed to distinguish between the yield attributable to the income-bearer, and that attributable to other wealth or services used in connection with it. That the sum paid as interest on a loan contains other elements is recognized constantly in practice. As in the case of

INTEREST ON MONEY LOANS

contract-rent allowance must be made for repairs and depreciation, so in the case of contract-interest allowance must be made for risk, or the average loss occurring in the industry. Money loaned in hazardous ventures must yield a higher rate of interest. Likewise capital used by the owner in a hazardous venture must frequently earn very high returns (not all logically interest) to offset the losses that are likely to occur.

The lender must also, in estimating net interest, count the cost of placing, supervising, and collecting the loan. A pawnbroker lends only small sums and spends much time and effort to keep at interest a moderate capital. Five thousand dollars loaned in sums averaging ten dollars represents five hundred transactions, and yet if placed at five per cent, it yields but two hundred and fifty dollars a year. While, therefore, the borrower of a small sum estimates the economic interest (or anticipated gain in income) even higher than the oppressively high contract-interest he may be forced to pay, the lender must credit a large part of the gross interest to the labor he expends in carrying on the business.

Short-time loans by discounting of commercial paper

3. *The most usual form of short-time loan is that made by a bank or broker to business men on security of commercial paper.* By commercial paper is meant promissory notes given by customers of the merchants, bills of lading for goods that have been shipped to their customers, and various other evidences of indebtedness that may be offered the banks for discount. When goods have been sold on time (as thirty, sixty, or ninety days) the seller has the choice between letting the time expire and collecting the bills direct from the customers, and discounting the bills for ready money at the bank. According to the conditions and needs of the particular business, either method may be chosen. In most industries there is need for larger capital at the seasons when the product is put upon the market. The merchant or manufacturer plans his business in the expectation of an average rate of discount at such times, and if it chances that the discount rates are abnormally high, he has no choice but to go on borrowing and paying the high interest out of the expected profits of his business. This risk of a change in the interest rate is one of many chances he has to run.

Long-time loans by purchase of mortgages, bonds, and stocks

4. *Most debts in modern times are outstanding for a term of years and represent the lender's purchase of a claim on the earnings of some productive enterprise.* The simplest forms of long-time loans are those made on the security of real estate, which is mortgaged to the lender for the term of the debt. Usually the debtor is obliged to pay the interest either annually or semi-annually, and often, but not always, is permitted to reduce the principal by partial payments. These real-estate mortgages rest on the security of the particular mortgaged wealth, and, unlike most short-time loans in bank, are not personal obligations resting on the general credit of the borrower. Most other long-time debts share this character of being non-personal; if payment is defaulted, only the particular wealth can be sold for payment, not the general wealth of the borrower. Corporation bonds, issued by railroads and other

large stock companies, have increased greatly in number in recent years. They yield an income fixed in advance, and are secured usually by mortgage on the entire property of the corporation issuing them. The income of some special kinds of "preferred stocks" is so guaranteed as to make them for investors substantially the same as bonds. Another large class of long-time loans are those made by national, state, and local governments. Tens of billions of dollars of public debts are now outstanding, held by private investors in every walk of life.

The contract in the case of each kind of these loans provides for a fixed term after which the borrower must repay or renew, and for a fixed rate on the nominal or par value of the loan. Nearly all the securities (bonds, certificates, evidences of indebtedness) are salable at a market rate. It is therefore the income that is fixed, the selling price (or capital value) fluctuating above or below the nominal sum except just at the moment when it is payable. The long-time loan thus is very similar in its economic character to the old-time rent-charge.

The cost of credit to the improvident buyer

5. *The sale of goods on credit is a mode of lending and involves interest in a disguised form.* In some cases merchants will not sell cheaper for cash than for credit, for fear of offending their main body of credit customers; but this is exceptional, as there are good reasons why such a difference should be made. The credit sale usually involves interest, and often at a very high rate. In many stores there are two appreciably different prices, one for "slow pay," the other for "spot cash." If a bill paid at the end of the month is five per cent. more than the cash price, the difference is equal to sixty per cent. per annum for the privilege of postponing payment. Such a rate of interest is paid only by the improvident, but that is a large class ranging from factory workers to college students. The cash discounts allowed by merchants clearly express the time difference. On fifty to one hundred dollars of outstanding bills, many perfectly honest persons are paying interest at the rate of seventy-five per cent. per annum. The merchant is forced to make this difference because he must seek not only to earn interest on the capital thus invested, but to recover the costs of bookkeeping and collections, and the risk and loss of unpaid bills. The discounts allowed by manufacturers and wholesale houses measure in the same way the difference between cash and credit sales. Not unusual is a discount of "six per cent, in ten days, five per cent, in thirty, or sixty net." The buyer allowing his bills to run for two months (six per cent, for sixty days) pays thirty-six per cent, per annum for the use of that money. The difference is so great that it is impossible to carry on in this way a large business against strong competition. Such purchases on credit frequently are made, however, by dealers in small towns.

Evasion of legal rate of interest

6. *Interest is often concealed under other forms which increase the apparent rate.* This fact is well shown in the ways by which usury laws fixing the legal rate of interest are evaded. A simple method is for the lender to charge a commission for making the loan, or, if it is a bank, to charge for a pretended cost of exchange to bring the

money from some other city. Sometimes the borrower is required to keep larger deposits with the bank than he voluntarily would. Needing $5000, he is compelled to borrow $10,000 and to pay interest on twice as much as he is permitted to use. Again the borrower, in periods of unusual demand for money, is forced to make a long loan instead of a short one. When a one month's loan at ten per cent, would meet his need, he is forced to borrow for twelve months at six per cent., during ten months of which time four or five per cent, is the prevailing rate. In these and other ways the real rate, or burden of the loan, is made different from that which is expressed.

§ II. The Motive for Paying Interest

Money borrowed to buy consumption goods

1. *Interest for loans to obtain consumption goods is paid because they are felt to have greater importance at the moment than an equal amount (either of goods or of money) will have in the future.* A sudden stress of misfortune may impart to a thing at the moment far more than its usual value. One standing face to face with starvation cannot be worse off a year hence; often there is good ground to hope that if the present misfortune can be relieved, the future better fortune will make it possible to repay a loan with interest. In other cases, the object of a loan of consumption goods is to increase the future earning-power of the borrower. When the student borrows money that represents to him food, clothing, text-books, tuition, and other expenses incidental to a course in college, the expenditure is intended to increase the effectiveness of the worker. When he borrows he has little earning-power, but with that faith in himself which makes the young American so interesting, he pictures himself four years later, sheepskin in hand, drawing a munificent salary with which he can easily satisfy the most exacting Shylock. Such an expenditure is sometimes called "an investment of capital," but it should be called a consumption loan—nevertheless in many cases a loan wisely made. To call this an investment of capital is to confuse man, the end of production, with material means.

Sometimes this higher estimate of the present good is unwise, viewed in the light of wider experience. Goods that meet momentary desire make an exaggerated appeal to untrained minds. The child, the spendthrift, the savage, cannot properly estimate the relative values of present and future. The improvident sometimes lightly agree to pay an exorbitant interest for an immediate consumption loan, making a ruinous difference between present and future gratifications.

Money borrowed to buy indirect agents

2. *Interest on indirect agents is paid as a more or less indirect means of securing gratification.* This can be clearly seen when durable agents are hired that produce gratification directly. A carriage bought with borrowed capital and used for the pleasure of the borrower is expected to afford a utility greater than that to be gotten

by the amount of the interest in any other way. A spade bought with borrowed capital and used to cultivate the owner's garden is expected to add products of greater value than the interest.

But how is it in case the agent is used to gratify persons other than the owner? The music-teacher who buys a piano on credit expects to increase his earnings by a sum greater than the interest he has to pay. If the addition to his earnings exceeds the interest charge, it is because he has found a use for the borrowed capital greater than that on the basis of which it was capitalized in the market. The amount of the interest is secured through the pleasures and services the piano affords to the patrons of the teacher. In the most complex cases of the borrowing and use of indirect agents, there is ultimately this same basis for the interest: enjoyment afforded by the use of capital in the particular period. To the borrower, what the capital makes possible is an addition to his income as great as, or greater than, the prevailing interest. Most loans in our society are now of this sort. Money is borrowed to invest in business, to get better machinery or a larger stock; with this capital is secured a better or larger product, and the product finally being sold at a profit, the business man is at a point where he can satisfy his wants without encroaching on his capital. Logically, therefore, the consumer of the product pays the interest in the price, and the final consumer's enjoyment must be deemed the logical source of the money interest. The borrower's motive for paying interest on these indirect goods evidently is his hope of profit through realizing a greater money rent than he has contracted to pay for their use.

The special case of money borrowed to pay debts

3. *The money market in which short-time loans are made is peculiar in that the money frequently is borrowed to pay debts, not for investment.* In beginning the discussion of interest, it always is remarked that it is not money, but capital, that is borrowed and loaned. This caution against the superficial errors that so easily beset the popular discussion of interest is much needed, but it is well to note a peculiar case which is apparently in contradiction to this statement. The usual method by which money is loaned in the great industrial centers is called discount, which is the exchange of a certain sum of money for a note or other credit paper of a larger amount, the interest thus being taken out in advance. Much borrowing in the form of discount is for the same purpose as other borrowing—to acquire control of more productive agents, to embark on new enterprises. The peculiarity of the discount money-market is that an unusual number of loans are made to meet contracts that have already been made. There is always a great mass of outstanding obligations, and merchants are compelled to renew these loans on penalty of bankruptcy. This market for short-time loans is not connected closely with the general market for loanable capital. When the need is for ready money, other concrete capital cannot flow in to meet it. This special money demand, therefore, in time of greater or less stress, may fluctuate rapidly, and the interest rate be temporarily higher or lower than the rate on long-time loans. This case is similar to that where two markets, as a retail and a wholesale one, exist side by side, but slowly exerting a mutual influence.

Productive borrowers seek a profit on their investments

4. *In the long-time money loan the money generally is borrowed first merely as a medium of exchange to get control of indirect agents.* The borrower of a long-time money loan for productive purposes is always seeking to gain by investing the money in wealth that will yield an income larger than the interest he must pay. The borrower, therefore, invests in view of the rate of interest, of the market price of the goods in which he plans to invest, and of the probable chances for earning profits in the business. This case, where certain goods whose price is known are approximately selected before the money is borrowed for investment, is the type of loan to be kept most usually in mind in economic discussion.

Evidently the price of these goods, to control which is the real object of the loan, is merely the sum of the expected rents they will yield, capitalized at the prevailing rate of time-discount. The borrower expects either to make these particular goods earn rents larger than those on the basis of which they have been capitalized, or to transfer them to an economy where goods are capitalized at a higher rate than he is paying. The income yielded by these goods, if the borrower's expectation is fulfilled, is but the difference between present and future rents that has been wrapped up in their capitalization. As time elapses and the rents emerge in wisely chosen investments, the borrower has a surplus large enough to pay the contract interest. It appears, therefore, that the motive of the borrower is to get control of future rents at prices that already involve, in their capitalization, a rate of discount somewhat greater than the interest he contracts to pay.

The developed market for money loans

5. *The rate of contract interest on money loans is adjusted at each moment in the money market by the bidding for money loans.* This is a true statement only if it is understood in a somewhat superficial sense. No error connected with interest is, however, more crude than the view that the interest rate is in any broad sense due to the quantity of money. Some loans are made apart from the general market, by private agreement between borrower and lender; but in nearly every such case the rate agreed upon is seen to be closely related to that of the general market to which either borrower or lender can resort if he wishes. The greater number of borrowers and lenders of money have a range of choice in their bargaining. The interest rate in modern developed money markets is that rate which brings to equilibrium the demand for money loans and the money capital available within the period. If the ready, loanable money in private hands, in banks, in insurance-company reserves, &c., increases, a lower rate must be offered to borrowers; if the supply decreases, a higher rate will be quoted. In the one case, more men borrow; in the other, fewer borrow and more seek to lend. Thus a rate results, but a rate that is closely connected with a larger set of facts—those, indeed, which determine in the long run the rate of capitalization in the community.

Every person is a buyer or a seller of present goods

6. *The individual must adjust his business dealings to the market rate of interest.* The

market rate is fixed by the bidding of individuals, and every one has something to do with fixing it. In a multitude of minutely small ways, as present and future goods are compared by men, the rate of interest is affected positively or negatively. But for practical purposes the individual, counting for little in the midst of millions, must look upon the interest rate as beyond his influence. Therefore, while the rate is determined by each to some degree, all that any one does is to buy or sell present goods, borrow or lend capital, use up or save wealth, according as his own estimate of time-value is less or more than the market rate. In fact, the estimates of individuals diverge constantly from the market rate, but are brought into harmony by their actions with reference both to money loans and to the use and valuation of the various forms of wealth. A Robinson Crusoe working on his island and valuing future goods relatively to present goods higher than before, consumes less; or, valuing them lower, consumes more. The business man who values indirect agents above the market rate borrows, and if he miscalculates and fails to make them earn the expected rent, he loses. In this experimental way many other acts are influenced by the prevailing interest rate and in turn affect it, thus aiding to formulate society's estimate of the value of present as compared with future rents.

Chapter XVII
The Theory of Time-value

§ I. Definition and Scope of Time-value

The simplest cases of time-value

1. *Time-value is the difference between the values of things at different times.* Things differ in value according to form, place, quality of goods, and according to the feelings of men, and—not least important factor—according to time. The simplest and clearest case of time-value is the difference noticeable in the same thing at different moments. Is this good worth more now or next week? Shall this apple be eaten now or next winter? These questions can be answered only after comparing the marginal utilities which differ according to the varying conditions of the two periods.

All the other cases of time-value can, by the practical device of substituting other goods of equivalent value, be reduced to the typical case of comparison of the same thing at different times. The comparison may be between very similar things, the one consumed being replaced by a duplicate. An apple borrowed now may be returned next year in the form of one of the same size and quality. The essential thing in this comparison is not physical identity, but equivalence in size, sort, and quality at the two periods. This is borrowing under the renting contract.

Time-value in the case of different kinds of gratifications

But two or more quite different things may be expressed in terms of another thing and so be made comparable. Money becomes the value-unit through which different things may be reduced to the same terms for comparison. With this mode of expressing the value-equivalence of various goods, the interest contract first becomes possible, money (the standard of deferred payments) being the thing exchanged (possibly only in name) at two periods of time. What is really compared are various gratifications which may be produced by very different material things or services. In its last analysis comparison of values at different periods of time must be a comparison of psychic incomes, of two sums of gratification. The comparison of the value of a bushel of apples with that of a barrel of potatoes or a suit of clothes at the same moment appears simple enough. When all are expressed in terms of money, the comparison of each with its value-equivalent at a later date becomes easy. The simplicity and obviousness of time-value in the case of money loans at interest led men at first to recognize that phase of the problem exclusively, and later the term "interest," not without much confusion of thought, was given a wider significance. Let us now see how large a part of the whole problem of time-value is outside of the money loan.

Time-value is involved in capitalization of land

2. *The problem of time-value is quite separable from the concepts of money and capital, though usually connected with them in practice and theory.* It is true that the problem of time-value was first clearly recognized in connection with money and a formally expressed capital sum. Misled by this fact, and taking a very narrow view, writers seventy-five years ago recognized but dimly the problem of time-value in connection with the valuation of the incomes derived from land. It is true, as has been shown above, that the mere putting of an estimate on a durable good such as land involves the process of capitalization, which in turn implies a comparison of the values of the rents expected at different periods. Diminishing returns in the use of agents involves a loss of time to secure the usufructs emerging. The relation of these facts was not clearly seen until of late.

The phenomenon of time-value as above defined may be seen to be broader even than that of capitalization. The difference in the value of the successive rents of wealth must have been recognized and in some degree measured before there was any conscious calculation of capital value. Differences in value due to time are everywhere. The problem of time-value often is present where money is not even spoken of or thought of. Money no more causes this time-difference in value than balances cause weight.

Time-value is taken account of in the keeping up of repairs

3. *The problem of time-value is involved in repairs and depreciation, and in the use of consumption goods.* It is possible, as we have seen, to increase the sum available for present needs, and to encroach upon the future by postponing repairs on intermediate goods. The balancing of the cost of repairs against the future income is a never-ending task in practical business. One making repairs must purchase the needed materials and labor at a capitalization determined by their expected earning-power in other industries. If the repairs in question will not ensure an annual saving as great as this expected rent, they will not be made. When an industry is declining, it may, for the sake of putting the capital into a better business, be good policy to let the machinery fall into bad repair. The problem of time-value is involved in the application of one's energy to repairing one's own possessions. It is a thought of wide bearings that numberless minor decisions in every petty business involve, if they are correctly made, a measuring of the rate of capitalization.

THE THEORY OF TIME-VALUE

And in the choice of enjoyments

As will be more fully shown in discussing the relation of the prevailing rate of interest to saving, the recognition of time-value is implied in the use men make of consumption goods, in their postponement of enjoyment, in their storing of goods for future use. The varying gratifications yielded by consumption goods, and their values in different conditions cannot be explained without taking account of differences in time. Wherever there can be a choice in the time at which, and consequently in the conditions under which, a thing can be used, there is a choice presented between the different values. Time-value is present even in a period during which no goods continue to exist, as when a good is consumed at a moment of greater need, to be replaced at a time when less valuable. If an apple is borrowed on the promise to return an apple and a peach at the end of a year, the peach represents the time-difference in value but in the meantime there has been no apple in existence. It is only in a figurative sense that it may be said that interest is paid on that "capital." Interest is paid because of a difference in want-gratifying power, but during the interval there is no material capital.

Prodigality and vice involve a high discount of future happiness

4. *The problem of time-value is involved in much foolish pleasure, in prodigality, and in vice.* Economics touches frequently on the borders of ethics. If there were to be formulated an economics of personal conduct, it surely would give a large place to the comparison between present and future pleasures. Forethought, or prudence, is the virtue of recognizing not only future dangers to be avoided, but the greater future joys to be gained in exchange for present pleasures. The reckless and the prodigal underestimate the future and barter all to gratify the moment's impulse. The drinker exchanges the hopes of worthy life for the exhilaration of the spree. Indulgence in social pleasures, if secured at the price of lost sleep, weakened health, and debauched character, are loans from the future made by youthful prodigals at usurious interest. If no one ever paid more than a moderate rate of interest for the gratification of his present whims and impulses, most hospitals, drug-stores, and medical colleges would close, and half, if not all, the prisons would be empty.

Indeed, time difference in value is a universal phenomenon of life and conduct. Contract interest is but one phenomenal form of time-value, and this in turn is but one phase of value. This section may serve to suggest how much more varied and pervasive the fact of time-value is than has usually been recognized in popular or economic discussion of the subject of interest.

§ II. The Adjustment of the Rate of Time-discount

The exchange value of present and future goods

1. *The fixing of the discount on future goods is, in its essentials, like the fixing of the market price of consumption goods.* This problem appears to be one of the most

difficult in economic theory; but reduced to its simplest terms, it is an aspect of exchange value, and its ultimate explanation must be found in a comparison of psychic incomes. There must be noted the conditions of demand and supply, the interplay and final equilibrium of the two forces. The declining and marginal utility to the two parties to exchange must be carefully analyzed. One who can do these things is prepared to find the answer to the problem of time-value. Whenever a group of buyers and sellers meet, a ratio of exchange commonly will be arrived at. The ratio of exchange between buyers and sellers of present and future rents likewise is fixed at the estimates of a "marginal pair," at which point the amount offered and taken comes to equilibrium, for at that point no motive exists for any one to change sides.

The peculiar nature of the exchange in the case of time-value
Several reasons why this is not easily recognized

2. *Time-value as the premium rate on present goods is unlike the ordinary market price of goods only in the special nature of the utilities exchanged.* The one peculiar need in the theory of this subject is a clear understanding on this point. The goods exchanged, or compared, are direct and indirect goods, or present and future goods, or, more generally speaking, two goods or groups of goods unequally distant in time from present enjoyment. What are sold in a case such as capitalization, involving an estimate of time-value, are present goods or gratifications; what are bought are future gratifications, or indirect agents which stand for, typify, or make possible, future gratifications. Practically every man in a market acts on the knowledge of what the exchange of direct and indirect goods means; yet abstractly stated, the thought seems at first difficult. In valuing any durable good, the theory of time-value is implied. Every time a machine, a house, a book, a field, is bought, the distinction between direct and indirect goods is acted upon, for a choice has been made between present enjoyment and future provision. Anything that endures is an indirect good and implies in its valuation a premium rate on present goods.

The real nature of the exchange in time-valuation is made unclear by the uncertainty of life, leading men to work on to provide against possibility of mishaps; for the most part the world's treasures never afford to their temporary owners the gratification that they typify, or could give. The nature of this exchange is made unclear also by habit, under the influence of which the exchange in so many cases is not carefully thought out, is not the result of a close comparison of the utilities of goods in present and future moments. The real nature of this exchange is made unclear by the indirect, or induced, gratification derived from wealth. Wealth gives to its owner power, prestige, the esteem of his fellows, and pride in evidences of success and growing prosperity. Its very possession creates a new need and imparts to it another utility, that of insuring against the misery of a declining fortune one who has enjoyed wealth and power. Men make the greatest efforts up to the last moment of life to retain wealth that they will enjoy only in this subtle and indirect way. Thus every motive that leads men to postpone present enjoyment makes them bidders for indirect agents and for future goods, and helps to determine the market rate of premium on the present, and of discount on the

THE THEORY OF TIME-VALUE 109

future.

The scarcity of present gratifications

3. *There being a limited number of indirect agents, their limited powers in a given period limit the supply of present goods.* The principle is familiar that value is always connected with relative scarcity. Now the desire for the present goods is indefinitely large. If the right kind and quality could be had at will, an enormously greater amount of present goods would be used. But the present goods are dependent on indirect agents. The psychic income of a civilized community is dependent on a favorable and extremely refined environment: houses, libraries, theaters, the agencies of travel, as well as the sources supplying the more material needs. These indirect agents, even in the richest community, are limited in variety, in quality, and in number.

The total of future uses in vastly greater

But if indirect agents could produce an indefinitely large product at any given moment, the supply of present goods could be indefinitely increased. The supply of utilities, therefore, is limited by "diminishing returns" in the use of agents, making their maximum yield depend upon the lapse of time. The uses any given material can yield in a limited period have an absolute limit: an acre of land with the most perfect cultivation cannot feed the world; but remove the limit of time, wait an eternity, and the acre would yield an infinite crop. The economic return of a given agent in a given period is reached much sooner than the technical return. If agents are forced to yield more bountifully, it is at the sacrifice of utilities in other agents, and a point of maximum net yield is found in any given period. Here also the lapse of time is the condition of the increase of the net utilities derivable from limited agents.

The choice open to the investor of money

4. *The rate of capitalization of income and the rate of contract interest on money capital tend to unite into a single market rate.* A person wishing to exchange present goods or income for future goods may buy an income-bearer at its capitalized value, or he may create a new rent-bearer. Having saved a sum of money, either he may purchase a factory known to be profitable; or he may hire the services of men and unite them with materials and machinery to create a new industry or a new form of income-bearer; or he may loan his money to others to make either kind of purchase. In any one of the three cases it is evident that capitalization (that is, the discounting of future rents in goods) is the primary and important fact making possible the emergence of a surplus, or net yield, over and above the value of the capital. The expected uses contained not only in whole industrial establishments, but in the particular materials and agents united to form new agents, are purchased at their capitalized value; that is, the future uses have been discounted and have entered into the price of the goods as less than they will be when realized as actual rents. This is the crucial point in the theory either of contract interest or of time

value; for to explain the rate of interest as due to the process of "producing" capital agents out of other materials, is to beg the question involved. The surplus yielded by capital above its cost is but the realization of a net income made possible by the discounting of future rents.

The choice open to the borrower of wealth

A person wishing to make an exchange of the opposite kind to that described may sell his wealth for money; he may exchange for present enjoyable goods his income at its capitalized value; or he may use up what he has, let it depreciate, fail to make repairs, convert it to various consumption purposes, and thus invade his earning power. When the interest rate is five per cent., the sacrifice of any unit of regular income permits the spending of twenty times that amount for present enjoyment. The advantages of these various methods tend to equilibrium. If the owners of developed productive agents hold them at too high a capitalized value, investors will apply their efforts and savings to duplicating these forms of wealth. If, in turn, any of the minor factors, as materials or uses of goods, are overvalued (overcapitalized) it will appear ultimately in a check in the demand for them at these prices, and in a reduction in the demand for money loans. As it is possible for any investor and for any borrower to choose among these investments and loans, there is practically but one rate, the rate which expresses the general ratio of exchange between present and future income. Owners and investors take the line of least resistance, get the most they can for their money, and choose whatever form is most advantageous. The interrelations between the various interest rates are therefore close and constant. The market rate of interest thus extends over all forms of wealth and pervades every phase of business. The value of every durable agent is fixed with reference to a prevailing interest rate, through the discounting to their present worth of all the incomes it is believed to contain.

A sacrifice sale involves a high rate of interest

5. *Where goods are sold at forced sale or sacrifice, it is equivalent to a contract loan at a high rate of interest.* Market values being dependent upon market conditions, the offer of goods at a given moment may not find the usual or normal number of buyers or the usual demand. Just such conditions are most likely to exist at the times when business men feel an unusual need of money. Two courses are open to them in this emergency, either to borrow the money at a very high rate of interest, holding the goods for better prices, or to sell the goods under the unfavorable conditions. The end of both courses is the same—to get ready money; and the methods are not essentially unlike—the exchange of greater future values for present values. The sacrifice sale thus reveals the merchant's high estimate of the interest rate. The purchaser of some kinds of property in times of depression is securing them at a lower capitalization than they will later have. The rise in value may be foreseen as well by seller as by buyer, but the low capitalization reflects the high interest rate temporarily obtaining. A. T. Stewart is said to have laid the foundation of his fortune when, being out of debt himself, he bought up the bankrupt stocks of his competitors in a great financial panic. The high contract interest at such times is

THE THEORY OF TIME-VALUE 111

but the reflection of the high premium on present purchasing power. Here then is another mode in which the prevailing rate of interest on money loans is kept in close harmony with the rate of time valuation.

Interrelation of the money interest rate and of time-discount

6. *The rate of contract interest on safe long-time loans registers pretty nearly the prevailing rate of time-discount in the community.* There are of course different capital markets, and the estimates put upon next year's income as compared with this year's is very different in Montana, New York, and London. Because of the friction in the transfer of investments from one locality to another, these differences may persist indefinitely; but within each capital market the interest on any particular loan must, for reasons readily seen, tend to conform pretty closely to the prevailing rate. Various groups of men living in the same community have, however, varying estimates of time-value. The increase of safe long-time bonds issued by strong corporations and by wealthy nations as, for example, the New York Central Railroad, and the government of Great Britain, gives a large number of choice investments where the element of risk is almost entirely absent. Various agencies have developed for making the loans, that is, for bringing the borrower and lender together with the minimum of trouble and expense. Other efficient, but somewhat more costly, agencies for bringing together the owners of loanable capital and men wishing to use capital are savings-banks, building and loan associations, insurance companies issuing endowment policies, and mortgage-investment companies of many kinds. While on the one side of the bidding are thousands of lenders offering to exchange ready money for assured incomes, on the other are thousand of borrowers offering to exchange the promise of assured incomes for ready money. If either of these classes got far out of touch with the prevailing rate of capitalization, to which all the valuations are adjusted, that class would lose greatly.

Relations between the concepts of rent, interest, and time-value

7. *All the net usufructs actually yielded by wealth are rents; economic time-discount is never a realized income; it is merely a calculation form, or anticipation of the difference between present and future gratifications.* There has been much discussion as to what should be the relations in thought between rent and interest. Space permits here only an indication of the view on this question involved in the foregoing treatment. Rent, as the term is here applied, includes all the net productivity attributable to the ownership and use of capital, whether the yield be in economic form (in an increment of value) or in contractual form. Even contract money-interest must be looked upon as a species of the genus contract rent, the peculiarity in the money loan being merely that the thing which it is agreed to return is a certain number of units of the standard money.

The term "interest," first applied in the Middle Ages to a payment for the use of a money loan, came to be used more broadly by the earlier economists as the income attributable to those goods which generally were bought and sold in terms of money. In other words, interest was supposed (though erroneously) to be uniquely connected with the particular production instruments to which the term capital was narrowly and mistakenly confined. Still more to add to the confusion, the term interest was about this same time identified with the broad problem of time-value. The terminology has remained ever since in this stage of arrested development. Our suggestion is to retain the word interest in its original meaning, still almost universal in business circles, of a contractual payment on money loans, applying the term time-value (for lack of a better word) to the subtler economic problem.

Rent and time-value are essentially different phrases of the value problem

Time-value is here understood to be that all-pervading difference in the values of uses and gratifications of wealth at different points of time. A comparison of the value of momently appearing uses of wealth is the rent problem. Here are, therefore, very different aspects of the value problem. The rent conception is earlier grasped by men, is nearer in point of logic; the concept of time-value has only recently been clearly recognized. If men lived only in the moment, they would be concerned only with rent; living in the future also, they are constantly regulating their acts with reference to time-value.

Chapter XVIII
Relatively Fixed and Relatively Increasable Forms of Capital

§ I. How Various Forms of Capital May Be Increased

The older and the modern way of viewing wealth

1. *Men seek to increase income by increasing capital.* Men may strive to increase their rents without expressing the rent-bearer in terms of capital. Peasant owners and small proprietors, toiling fondly on their little estates, seeking steadily a larger crop, a larger income, accomplish wonders in bringing waste land to a high state of cultivation. Working on the soil that is at once their livelihood and their home, they do not consciously reckon the value of the labor they are putting upon it. No money can buy that which to them is beyond price. But, in our money economy, efforts are largely directed toward the increase of the capital sum. Investment takes the form of putting in a sum of money in the hope of getting an income bearing a certain relation to it. The first thought is of the value of the wealth invested, which has been carefully measured and expressed in dollars and cents. Wealth looked at in the older way was valued for what it did immediately for its owner, for its concrete fruits; looked at in the modern way, it is valued as a marketable income-bearer readily convertible into a multitude of other forms. Thus investments come to be thought of in terms of general purchasing power, from which it is expected to realize an income of a given percentage.

Free goods of unlimited supply

Beginning of scarcity of common materials

2. *There are some classes of goods that can be increased without any noticeable increase in difficulty.* The extremest examples are undiminished goods such as air, sea-water, the water of large rivers. These are free goods because, however much is used, the supply is immediately renewed. But they are undiminished only in a relative sense and in reference to present need. The water in the Western rivers long flowed on, undiminished by the uses made of it. But progressing civilization

required more water for cities, for mining, and for irrigation, and now states and corporations are going to law over these formerly undiminished free goods. Some kinds of goods are produced from such very common materials that it might seem possible, by the substitution of agents, to produce an unlimited supply. How can bricks be limited in number, being made as they are from one of the commonest materials on the earth's surface? But the largest clay banks are limited in size; a large proportion of the places where bricks are needed are not near a supply of clay of good quality; and after a brick-yard has been used for a time there is increasing difficulty in getting out the material. While, therefore, bricks are scarce and hard to get from the outset in some places, the scarcity grows more marked in many places at first well supplied. If materials are scarce in any degree, their continued use for one purpose increases their scarcity in all other uses. Economic goods are goods having value; value implies scarcity, and an increasing demand means inevitably a higher value at some point. This is true of clay, stone, water, and the commonest kinds of labor.

No scarce goods can be indefinitely increased

It has long been customary for economists to talk of economic goods that could be increased indefinitely (meaning infinitely or, in any event, without any limit ever appreciable to man) without any increase in the cost or scarcity. This class of goods was considered to be very large. There is no such class of economic goods; it is evidently impossible that there should be. If they are already "scarce," increasing demand must make them scarcer. There are, however, some goods that practically can be increased with so little difficulty that their limitation is not of great social importance. Progress, population, prosperity, are not primarily conditioned on their amount; limitation will be felt far earlier elsewhere. They are at one end of the scale; they are the relatively increasable goods.

The products of land are increased at a given time and place at increasing cost

3. *There is a large class of goods whose increase is seen to be gained with increasing difficulty.* This is seen most clearly in the diminishing returns from land. In the attempt to get some food-products in greater quantity from a given area at a given time, increasing difficulty is met with at once. This attempt continued for a series of years results in historical diminishing returns, as was strikingly illustrated in English experience during the Napoleonic wars, when wheat rose in value because of the greater difficulty of producing the larger supply needed. Some replenishing agents will restore themselves if given time; the forest will grow up if left untouched by man; the field will recover its fertile quality if allowed to lie fallow. But this self-replenishing of agents is a slow process, and time is costly. Man therefore tries in other ways to force more uses out of goods, until checked by the increasing difficulty. The goods subject to "the law of increasing cost," as it was called formerly, were considered to be a peculiar class comprising only a small portion of wealth. But it can now be seen that the law may apply ultimately, though in differing degrees, to every kind of economic goods. Indeed, the principle just discussed is no more than one phase of the law of economic

FIXED AND INCREASABLE FORMS OF CAPITAL 115

diminishing returns, which has a universal application to the realm of values.

Agents most nearly fixed in amount are somewhat increasable

4. *There is a class of goods, natural agents and stores of materials which appears to be relatively fixed in quantity or which is increasable only with much difficulty.* The first part of this proposition expresses mildly the thought that long obtained among economists: it was said that the supply of certain things was absolutely fixed, the chief of these being land used for agriculture. The idea as held by Malthus and Ricardo was modified by John Stuart Mill in somewhat inconsistent ways. Land, it was said, is a thing which "man cannot make," therefore its supply is fixed. The second part of the opening proposition expresses the view here held: the supply of no important class of goods is absolutely fixed, in any reasonable sense. Most, if not all, belong to the class that is increasable, although it may be with much difficulty. Even when the exact thing cannot be duplicated, as a bust by an ancient sculptor or an autograph of a dead author, many substitutes serving the same or closely related wants, affect and limit the demand, and thus increase the supply. Men cannot, it is true, increase the stores of copper in the earth, but they devise new processes to extract it from ores before worthless, and invent methods of procuring aluminium, which yields some of the same utilities as copper. Even the supply of land, as is shown elsewhere, is constantly changing. Thus all kinds of wealth can be increased in some degree; many kinds in the course of time are very greatly increased with little or no direct effort, but the supply of all alike can be secured in larger amount at any given moment only at the cost of increasing difficulty.

§ II. Social Significance of These Differences

Physical amount vs. economic supply

1. *Not the fixity of the physical amount of agents, but the economic supply is significant.* There is danger of confusion between these two ideas. The statement that "land" cannot be created and that therefore "the supply is fixed" involves a fallacy. The word supply means the amount that is available at the moment or during the period spoken of. The land in Greenland is not, and probably never can be, a part of the supply of land in England. The land in America for centuries was not, but now has become, for some purposes, a part of the supply in the same market as the land of England. The question of importance in economic discussion is not whether the physical material can be brought into existence, but whether the economic "supply" can be increased. The existence of coal-mines in Venus or Mars is of no economic importance to us, but coal-mines on the earth, yet undiscovered, present a potential supply that at any moment may be realized.

Discovery enlarges the supply of natural resources

2. *Discovery of new lands and of new natural deposits continually enlarges the economic supply of the agents most nearly fixed in physical amount.* This proposition states a historical fact. Any explanation of the economic occurrences of the last five centuries or of the immediate future, that ignores this fact of the increasing supply of many kinds of land and natural resources in the markets of the civilized world, must lead to false conclusions. The rate of this movement has been more rapid in the past century than theretofore, and perhaps more rapid than it will be henceforward; but that this development will continue in large measure and for a long period, is not open to question. Undeveloped areas will be opened to the world, and new geologic realms will be explored. Yet the notion criticized above is found in all the older text-books. The idea arose in England in the first quarter of the nineteenth century when land and food were rapidly rising in price, and it has vitiated a large part of both the economic theory and the practical conclusions on this subject.

The effective supply grows by invention

3. *Invention, including new modes of transportation and new processes, increases the economic supply of most scarce goods and provides substitutes for the others.* Some inventions increase economic supply by making available the uses in goods that were before unavailable. Subsoil ploughing annexes to agricultural land new layers of soil that are just as important as new acres added to the surface. If land could be used three times as deep, it would be as good for many purposes as if it were of three times the extent. New trade routes and new means of transportation add to the supplies available in the older countries as effectively as if their areas were increased. The building of railroads in western America had an effect on English rents identical in nature with that which would have been produced had an equal area of somewhat less fertile land touching England, risen out of the ocean. Every country in Europe has repeatedly felt the shock of these great economic changes which have compelled the recapitalization on a lower plane, of nearly all kinds of their landed wealth. Where the same agents have not been multiplied, substitutes have been found that are just as effective in meeting the economic need. It is the result, the gratification, that man seeks: any particular good is but the means to an end.

Production of land by physical change

4. *Increasing wealth and new labor make possible the increase of the agents that appear most nearly fixed in supply.* When the need arises men turn to new enterprises. The reclaiming of land in Holland is a striking but far from isolated example. Among the larger undertakings of this kind are the draining of the Haarlem Lake in 1840-58, by which 40,000 acres of rich land were made available, and the draining of the Zuyder Zee, which is adding 1,300,000 acres. Though there have been many minor undertakings of the kind, the area reclaimed is relatively small compared with the whole area of the land in the world used for agricultural purposes. There are still great areas of fens, swamps, and marshlands, such as those on the Jersey

FIXED AND INCREASABLE FORMS OF CAPITAL

coast in this country, which with moderate effort could be reclaimed. While the possibility must be recognized, the increase of the area of available agricultural land by means of such physical changes is relatively small.

And by the work of pioneers

The work of the pioneer, as a producer of a supply of land, is, however, of the greatest importance. The pioneer annexes new areas to the economic world and to the market in which he has lived. This is recognized of late by writers that perhaps do not fully mark its significance to economic theory. The work of the explorer and prospector is that of a producer of mineral resources, and daily market quotations reflect the changes in "the supply" of these natural stores.

Successive utilization of various grades of agents

5. *Limitation of the supply appears first in the better qualities, and efforts to increase wealth are then directed to making available the poorer grades.* Great quantities of the poorer grades of wealth, even of those things that are relatively fixed in supply, lie unused. Great areas on the edge of civilization still await the pioneer, the prospector, and the miner. Here is a source of wealth and a field for enterprise. The growth of society may cause some of the poorer agents in time to become the best. When men crossed the ocean to settle on Manhattan Island, it was a wilderness; but the growth of commerce has caused the land in New York city to become more valuable than that in London. Changes are still in progress, for of late the smaller ports to the south have increased their trade at a more rapid pace than New York has.

Goods ranged on a scale of increasableness

The difference in increasableness of the various forms of wealth is of importance in considering various social questions such as the effects of an increase of population, and the kinds of taxation most equitable and most favorable to the progress of society. Account must be taken of the fact that the number of bricks can be increased more easily than the amount of land; but there must not be overlooked the possibility of increase in any of these forms of wealth, nor the limits to the increase of any one of them. When one wishes to save or increase wealth, he turns to these great unappropriated fields, unused things or things imperfectly used, and tries to convert them into effective agents. The different forms of wealth may be ranged on a scale according to the ease with which they can be increased by effort. They may therefore be classed as relatively fixed and relatively increasable. Some natural resources belong at one end, and some at the other end of this scale. No hard and fast line divides the different kinds of goods, but the difference in degree of increasableness is a fact of great social importance, affecting the direction in which industry can and must progress.

Chapter XIX
Saving and Production as Affected by the Rate of Interest

§ I. Saving as Affected by the Interest Rate

The interest rate traces the division between present and future gratifications

1. *In the case of consumption goods, present marginal uses are often less than future uses as judged at the present.* The proposition that future goods sometimes have a greater instead of a less value than present goods may at first seem to deny the general fact of economic interest, which is a premium on present over future goods. The contradiction is only apparent, however, and the proposition is merely a proper interpretation of the theory of interest. The assertion that present goods have greater value than future goods, as we have accepted it, requires two explanations. First, it means that this difference exists when the two are judged and compared *at the present moment*. The future use when it matures may be much greater than the present use; indeed, the very existence of interest depends upon this surplus of value arising by the lapse of time in the future use. Secondly, the proposition does not mean that every concrete good, or every use of the goods, is worth more in the present than in the future; it means merely that the demand for present goods preponderates so that a market rate in favor of present possession prevails. In a great many cases a particular good may have a greater value to be kept for the future than to be used at present, in which case it is kept, or it is exchanged for something else having a higher value in the present. But this preference of the future over the present cannot pass a moderate limit without condemning the person to present misery, and at length to death. On the other hand the excessive preference of present over future would lead to the using up and wearing out of wealth, to the present enjoyment of every possible resource, on the penalty of future misery. Evidently somewhere between these two extremes there must be, in each economy, a ratio of exchange between present and future, which in fact is the interest rate. This rate applied to utilities traces through each good a line analagous to the isothermal line on the map, marking off a zone of utilities for the present and other zones for each period of the future. There is thus

SAVING AND PRODUCTION

a close relation between saving and the rate of time-discount.

The less necessary goods are the ones saved

Let us illustrate by the case of fruit stored in the cellar for future use. In the fall after the appetite for apples has been gratified up to a certain point, there still remains a large stock which affords less gratification if consumed at once than if kept for a time. Thus wood, food, and clothing are stored in the summer for the winter's need. Even the animals act on this principle. Squirrels, bees, and ants store up in the season of superfluity for the season of scarcity. The animals recognize with their feeble intelligence or by instinct, that a time will come when these consumption goods will represent greater importance to their welfare than they do at the moment. It results from the nature of wants and the principle of diminishing utility that in many cases some portion of a large supply of present goods must be worth less now than at a future time. This part, the marginal, less necessary part, will be left for a future time, and it is to this part that our opening proposition refers. This is roughly illustrated by the diagram.

Things that cannot be kept, perishable goods, do not permit of this comparison. But if goods that can be kept continue to be used after utility has fallen down the scale, their high value for the future is cast away. Man lives not alone in the present but, in a far greater measure than do any animals, he lives in the future also. His economic life and his economic judgment comprehend a great number of periods at once. With the aid of memory and imagination he forecasts the future, and compares it with the present. The diminishing utility of goods, therefore, is modified by this fact that a thing has want-gratifying power at different periods. Before man uses goods for an inferior purpose he will ask whether, if they are kept for the future, they will not gratify a greater want.

The less valuable rise in value with the lapse of time

2. *The gradual rise of a consumption good with the lapse of time from the lower to the higher degree of gratification is the rent it yields.* The difference in value of present and future rents is expressed by the discount of the future use when it is capitalized at any earlier moment, and emerges in the rise in value as the thing approaches to the time when it can render the later use. Next year the unit whose use is deferred will afford as much gratification as the earlier units do now, and more than if used at the present moment. The importance of any present utility is compared with its importance a year later, plus interest at a rate which expresses the limit to which future uses are discounted. Anything that makes men feel more the importance of future uses causes them to value those uses more. But the pressure of present want is such that a present use of a lower order competes with a future use of a higher order. Only goods of a lower order, nearer the margin, are reserved for the future. But just as the possibility of using a thing for several different purposes at present causes it to be valued more highly than if it had but one use, so the possibility of reserving to the future a portion of a stock imparts to every unit a higher marginal utility.

120 THE PRINCIPLES OF ECONOMICS

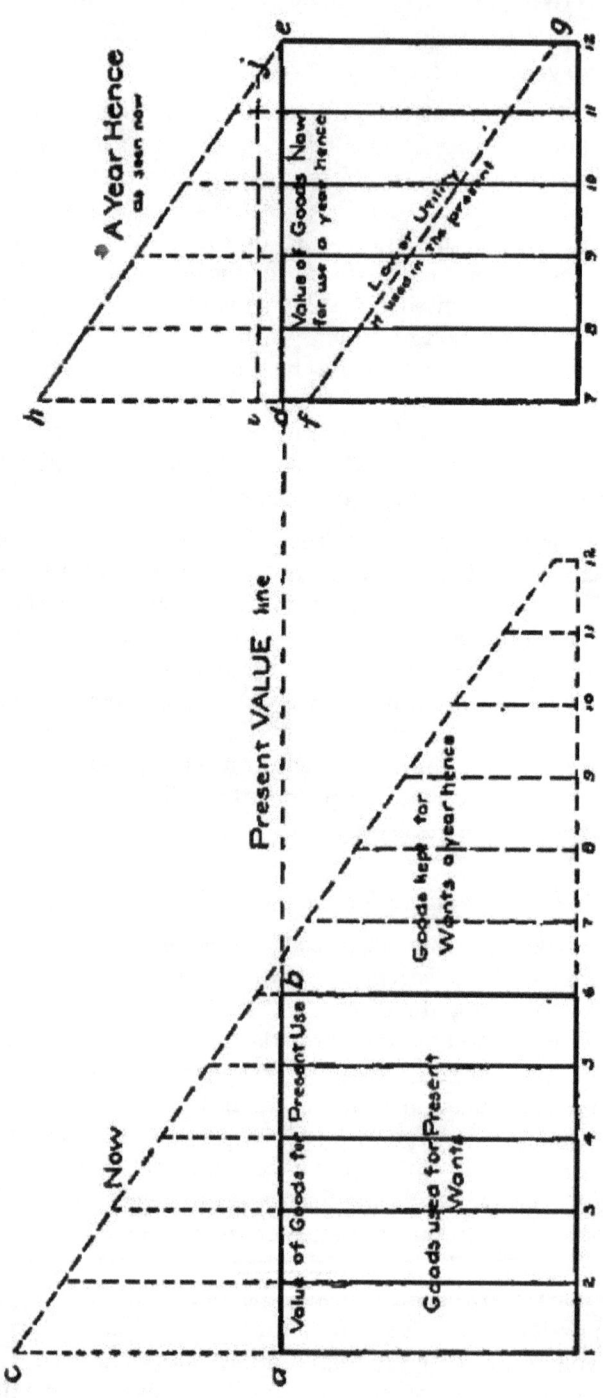

Present value line

SAVING AND PRODUCTION

Interest is the equalizer of time values

3. *The saving of present goods for future use is encouraged by the motive of gaining the interest.* Many consumption goods grow into higher uses in the hands of the owner, whether he uses them for himself or not. Ice may be stored in midwinter when it is all but a free good and a little labor serves to fill the ice-house. Kept until the summer months, the ice rises in value as the desire for it grows. Likewise the higher price secured by the owner of a thing kept for sale to others, reflects the change in utility, and affords practically a rent which is the motive for investing capital in that business. Any saver or abstainer puts aside present wants only when the future good, with the addition of time-value or of money interest, appears as large as the present good. Interest is therefore the equalizer of the value of things in different periods. Put into the scale of judgment when present and future are compared, it helps to balance the disparity in the gratifications given by economic goods in different periods of time.

Saving increases and improves economic agents

4. *The postponement of present wants results in bettering the economic environment for the future.* Economic environment means simply the economic conditions in which men live, the stock of wealth, the supply of useful things with which they are surrounded. This betterment may be only temporary, only for the immediate future. Like the busy bee or the prudent ant, one may in summer store the cellar with consumption goods to be consumed the following winter. But often there is a more lasting way of improving the economic environment by converting savings into durable indirect agents. The accumulation of wealth that will yield its fruits only after years of growth is the record, so to speak, of the successful competition of forethought with present desires. It means that the two periods have presented their respective claims and that men have decided in favor of the future. Saving thus lifts society from poverty to wealth by the progressive enlargement of the sources of future utilities.

The kinds of abstinence

5. *Abstinence is the faculty of mind that enables present wants to be subordinated to future wants.* Abstinence may be considered as a quality, or faculty, of the mind, or as an act resulting from that quality. There is little danger of confusion in this usage, but it is well to note the distinction and the fact that the former is the primary meaning. Abstinence expresses an act of the will, a choice made by man. It is the guardian of the future, so to speak, against the greediness of the present. For convenience we may speak of conservative abstinence as that which keeps men from using up or invading their present stock of resources, and of cumulative abstinence as that which impels them to add to that stock. There is no sharp dividing line, no abrupt break, between these two, yet on the whole they differ. There is a quality of mind very like the inertia or momentum of physical matter. The inertia of mind makes men resist stubbornly the reduction of wealth and of inherited social position; but it requires a more positive quality of mind to add to wealth at the cost of present sacrifice. Abstinence is embodied in individuals, never

elsewhere, and is found in most varying degrees of strength. Upon it depends the growth and betterment of man's environment.

§ II. Conditions Favorable to Saving

Political insecurity discourages saving

1. *Political security and domestic order are essential to the development of saving.* As saving results from a comparison of the future with the present, any lack of certainty regarding the future decreases the appeal it makes. Men employ roughly the theory of probabilities in this matter, and count a utility only half as much when there is but one chance in two of enjoying it. In countries where there are constant revolutions and border wars, as in Africa and South America, and in lands where brigandage is common, as in Italy, Macedonia, and Bulgaria, the motive for saving is cut in two. Oppressive and irregular taxation kills the motives of providence, and decreases the appeal made by the future. While the miserable subjects of the state live from hand to mouth, the very sources of the public revenue disappear. Improvidence grows upon such a people into a prevailing national custom; ambition is wanting; industry is the sport of chance; economic order and economic prosperity are impossible.

Influence of private property on saving

2. *Social institutions that give a motive to the individual are essential to saving.* Among these institutions the most important are the family and, closely connected with it, the institution of private property which, in its ideal manifestation, places the responsibility for economic welfare on the individual or the family. Through it the state says to men: "Save if you will; the wealth and its fruits shall be yours. But if you spend and consume all you can, you alone will suffer the consequences." It is true that the institution of private property never is found in an ideal form. Dishonest public officials weaken and defeat its benefits. Every propertyless family marks a failure in its purpose. Private property is a favorite object of attack by social reformers, but it never can be safely abolished in a civilized state until some other incentive is provided, equally effective to make men subordinate present desires to future welfare. Unless the mass of men can be greatly changed, property creates the only motive that can induce saving regularly and on a large scale. It diffuses responsibility for present consumption. It multiplies the motives for abstinence and thus increases the welfare of all economic society.

Safe and paying investments encourage saving

3. *Opportunity for the investment of small savings favors a spirit of abstinence.* The institution of small property, peasant proprietorship, worked powerfully in this direction in many parts of Europe, and the same effects have resulted in America from the wide diffusion of property in land. If the decline in the number of small

independent farmers has somewhat weakened this influence in America, in other ways other agencies are effectively performing the same functions. Savings-banks, penny banks, building and loan associations, penny-provident funds, and other convenient means of investing small sums, encourage men to reduce their tobacco bills, their candy bills, their saloon bills, and to lay aside for the winter's coal, for the children's education, for houses, for business investments, or for old age. Probably no one thing has given a greater stimulus to saving than has the development of insurance and the endowment policies in connection with it. While the great modern corporations have destroyed many of the small business enterprises into which so much of the saving of the past was put, at the same time the increase of negotiable paper, of loans, and of stock in joint-stock companies, has opened up other large fields for investors.

Changing interest rate in relation to saving

4. *Variations in the rate of discount of the future react upon the spirit of saving in various ways.* This very general proposition requires more detailed discussion. In general, a high rate of interest gives a large motive to save, for as the discount on the future is large, so is the reward for waiting. But this favoring motive may be offset by other unfavorable conditions, and is, in fact, wherever the high rate continues. In countries backward economically, where war, brigandage, and political oppression prevail, the rate of interest is frequently ten and twelve per cent. on the best secured loans. A high interest rate does not of itself insure a high degree of cumulative abstinence; it is only one of several factors. But in a new and favored country like America, a high rate of interest is a strong stimulus to saving. Again, interest may fall while saving continues at the same or a greater pace. Ordinarily a fall from six per cent. to five, giving men a smaller motive for abstinence, would be expected to cause less saving, yet this is not always the case. Custom and example help to fix a habit of saving in individuals and cause them to continue saving at a lower rate of interest. With the growth of wealth, the prevailing ideas as to the amount needed for a competence change, impelling to greater saving. The tendency, however, of a fall in the rate of interest is to weaken, and that of a rise of the rate, other things being equal, is to strengthen the motive to save. But the influence of the interest rate on saving is relative to the character of men.

§ III. Influence of the Interest Rate on Methods of Production

Saving permits improvement of agents

1. *The individual saver is enabled to improve the agents that he uses.* The simplest case is presented when means of enjoyment are improved and made more durable. If Crusoe on his island spends less time and fewer resources on gratifying his

immediate wants, he may improve the quality of his clothing and the convenience of his house and furniture. By thus putting his consumption goods into durable instead of temporary forms, he will increase eventually the sum of utilities enjoyed. Again, abstinence permits the tools of the laborer to be made more convenient. If the farmer spends less time in the garden and he and his family live on plainer food, while he makes a plow, mends a rake, and builds a shed, he will be enabled thereafter to gather a greater crop with less effort.

Saving of consumption goods for exchange

2. *Consumption goods, when saved, may be exchanged for services, and these may be used to create durable agents.* Various ways are open to one wishing to increase his stock of durable agents. He may forego seeking immediate enjoyments while he makes durable agents himself. Or he may make and save a stock of consumption goods, a surplus supply for the future, and exchange it for durable agents. Finally, one who has accumulated consumption goods can always exchange them for the services of those seeking subsistence and enjoyment; and thus in control of a labor force, he can direct it toward the production of new forms of productive agents.

Money savings are converted into other wealth

3. *In modern industry, saving frequently takes the form of money, which is then loaned to productive borrowers.* This is the typical form of saving in modern industry. As it is more and more the case that income takes first the form of money, saving most conveniently takes the money form. The clerk on a salary of $60 a month spends $50 and saves $10 which he lends to a neighbor or deposits in a savings-bank. The borrower is thus empowered to increase his stock of productive agents in the measure that the lender has limited his consumption. The complexity of the process by which money saving becomes embodied through a money loan in new productive agents should not blind to its real nature. The money is saved as a means to the exchange of present goods for future income. Money even in our day is occasionally stored away for future use under hearthstones or in old stockings and hollow trees, but this is a primitive and wasteful method, involving the loss of all the additional rents that its exchange and investment would yield.

If the money saved by the thrifty saver is loaned to a thriftless borrower, wealth is not increased, but merely changes hands. The prodigal mortgaging his wealth, spending the money, and living beyond his income, absorbs the savings of the other. One saves and adds to wealth, the other consumes it. There is no net increase of goods, but two individuals have shifted positions; each has gotten his reward of growing affluence or penury.

The "normal" end, however, of savings and loans is productive. The borrower, in getting control of purchasing power, aims to put a new machine where it will be useful, to remove obstacles, and to make economic agents more effective. Along the border-land of industry the active and alert borrower seeks out opportunities to make new agents earn a rental, and having found the opening, turns to the money market for the means to profit by it.

SAVING AND PRODUCTION

Lower interest means higher capitalization

4. *A fall in the rate of interest normally accompanies an increase in the mass, efficiency, and valuation of durable economic agents.* A lower rate of interest means a higher capitalization of all incomes. It is not that either can be called the cause of the other; rather both are aspects of the same thing, the interest rate merely registering the change in capitalization. If the rate of interest has been five per cent., an income of $100 has been capitalized at $2000. When the rate falls to four per cent. the income is recapitalized at $2500. All along the line of investment there is an increase in the value of the durable economic agents.

And more complex industrial processes

It encourages the increase of fixed charges to reduce cost of operation

Another phase of the change is the greater complexity of the processes of industry. Production becomes technically more complex when interest falls. Rental, product, and present goods, bear a smaller ratio to the value of capital, and therefore it becomes advantageous to apply newly formed capital to uses which before did not justify the investment. Where formerly the utility of a second tool did not justify its making, now it can be made to earn the smaller rental needed to balance its capital value. One form, therefore, which the change takes, is a multiplication of the tools already used. Things are placed wherever most convenient. Another form this change takes is the putting of new links into the chain of technical production. Cost of operation constantly is compared with fixed charges, the interest with the capital investment. Expensive improvements on railroads, the straightening of curves, the tunneling of mountains, the reducing of grades, the replacement of lighter by heavier rails, have been made possible by a fall in the rate of interest. A fall in the rate of interest disturbs the equilibrium that has been arrived at, between the cost of operation, the amount paid for wages, coal, etc., and the income on permanent investment. If the rate of interest has been five per cent. and falls to four per cent. many permanent improvements before unwise become economical. One thousand dollars paid annually in wages then balanced an interest charge on a capital investment of $20,000; now it balances the interest charge on $25,000. It becomes a paying thing for the railroad to abandon or throw aside an enormous capital represented by the old, less perfect roadbed, and build a new one alongside of it. The changes of this kind one sees in traveling on the great and progressive railroads, reflect in part the growth of traffic, but in part also a change of the interest rate, making it a net saving to increase the capital investment in order to reduce the cost of operation per unit of traffic.

Diffused benefits of saving

The benefits of saving viewed broadly are not confined to the owner of the wealth saved, but are diffused throughout society, in the degree that they increase and improve the industrial environment, and thus raise the efficiency of production. Such a change works the same results as would a magical increase in the fertility of the soil, an improvement in the richness and accessibility of natural mineral stores, or in the quantity and quality of artificial appliances.

PART II
THE VALUE OF HUMAN SERVICES

DIVISION A—LABOR AND WAGES

Chapter XX
Labor and Classes of Laborers

§ I.   Relation of Labor to Wealth

Work and play defined and distinguished

1. *Labor is any human effort having an aim or purpose outside of itself.* It is difficult to define satisfactorily the term labor. No definition will quite mark off all the cases. The efforts put forth by men may be classified according as they are pleasant in themselves, and according as they have separable useful results. These two factors combine to form four groups of actions.

Effort	Objective result sought	Name of action
1. Pleasurable	Not useful	Play
2. Pleasurable	Useful	Labor
3. Painful	Useful	Labor
4. Painful	Not useful	No special name

The fourth combination is not found in rational life, for no motive exists to do a painful act for a useless result. Let us consider the other three.

Play

The first group comprises most of the sports, games, and pastimes found in every land and time. In the mere putting forth of the powers of mind and muscle there is a joy felt by children and men of all races, and this is heightened by companionship, emulation, and even by a spice of danger. Play is not dependent on a useful objective result later to be enjoyed, but, like beauty, is its own excuse for being. The tired student goes out-of-doors to bat the tennis-ball, making no change in the material world, except to wear out his shoes and to lose the ball, but finding that hour rich in the joy of life. If properly chosen, play strengthens and vivifies both soul and body, leaving an afterglow of health and happiness. The choice of sports and temperance in their pursuit are among the surest tests of wisdom in men and in societies. A love of vigorous play no less than the power of sustained work, marks the dominant and progressive peoples of the earth.

Labor as pleasure

Acts in the second group give pleasure and at the same time leave an objective result. The hunter gets more pleasure if he returns with well-filled bags of game, but the distinction between the sportsman and the "pot-hunter" is not hard to find. The one has his joy in the sport, the other in the material results of the sport. This kind of action presents some puzzling cases, but in general must be classed as labor, since labor is to be judged by the objective economic results rather than by the pleasure of the act itself.

Labor as sacrifice

In a third class are the acts that are painful in themselves, that are done unwillingly, but that leave a pleasurable result. Unfortunately a large part of the actions of men are of this class, which to most minds is the typical labor.

Joy in work is the ideal

There is thus labor that is pleasurable in itself and labor that is painful though it leads to a desirable result. The social ideal clearly is that all human labor should be made pleasurable. Social dreamers love to picture a day when all shall find for effort a full reward in the mere doing,—the reward of the artist, of the scholar, of the saint, in addition to the objective result in economic wealth. Probably we are slowly nearing this ideal. Not only in the professions and in the esthetic arts, but in commerce, in mechanics, and in the humblest walks of life are found men free from envy, rejoicing in their daily tasks. Such is the normal feeling of the healthy optimist. And yet in every serious occupation there are numberless moments and occasions when the spirit flags and only hard necessity holds men to their tasks. The dilettante does not go far or long or steadily; the real tasks of the world are done by men that labor, now with joy, now wearily.

The distinction between men and things

2. *The agents of production compose two great species, material goods and human services.* Our discussion of consumption goods, rent, and interest has been an analysis of the nature and uses of material goods. We now come to the other great species, human services, which comprise those acts of men (one's own or other's) that minister to the gratification of wants. There are also misdirected efforts, and evil deeds which are "disutilities" to all but the doer.

The distinction between men and things is fundamental in modern economic discussion where each man is looked upon as free. It is not so clear where slavery exists and the master looks in the same way upon the services of his cattle, of his chattel slaves, and of his land. Even in the freest society, man's services are compared purely as to their utility, with the uses of other parts of the material world. It is said that the price of mules at the Pennsylvania mines has been affected by immigration, because a man and a mule sometimes represent interchangeable services. But in the study of political economy the distinction between men and other material things must never be lost sight of; they are the two fundamental classes of economic agents, the one being solely a means to an end, the other being an end in itself.

Rent and wages mutually affect each other

3. *Labor and material wealth are complementary and indispensable to each other in most of their uses.* The discussion of material wealth and its value apart from the subject of labor, of the problem of rent and interest apart from that of wages, does not imply that this material wealth would have the same value in real life if labor were absent. As one field affects the value of another field, and one good, by substitution, the value of another good, so does labor affect material wealth. Some material wealth can be used apart from labor, but most of it must be used in combination with some labor. Rent, therefore, is not determined in concrete cases apart from men and their services. It is allowable, however, in abstract analysis, to simplify the question by leaving out a difficult complication, and thus to set forth more clearly the logical bearing and effect of a certain factor.

Certain shares of the product are logically attributed to each

Each of two kinds of agents used together affects the utility of the other, and the value of the product. If neither can be credited with the whole value, how is any distribution to be made between them? It is not possible to measure their technical services in the product, but it usually is possible to gage their marginal utility under particular conditions. Flour, water, and labor are needed to make biscuits; but water being a free agent, does not enter into the combination with any marginal utility. A match also is almost indispensable to start the fire (and who has not seen the time when he would give far more for a match than for a bucket of coal), but as things usually are, the match is credited with a value of a very small fraction of a cent. Again, how is to be measured the economic service of the tree and of the labor needed for gathering its fruits? There is here suggested the superficial aspect of what is known as the problem of complementary values. Where two or more things are indispensable to a product, how much shall be credited to each?

Labor gratifies directly and indirectly

4. *Human service has the same general relation to wants that material goods have, affording gratification either directly or indirectly.* It is axiomatic that to be "economic goods" human efforts like material goods must afford utilities whose importance is felt. Many services give pleasure directly and are immediately consumed. A tropical potentate has an attendant to fan him, and another to carry an umbrella; a humble citizen is shaved, doctored, sung to, and played for. The gratification in such cases is directly produced in personal comfort, in the consciousness of heightened beauty, in the feeling of self-esteem. Value is thus created and

consumed immediately, taking no material form apart from the consumer.

Labor embodied for a time in material form

But the results of most human services may be seen to rest, at least temporarily, in some material form. Effort is put upon a material thing to be used later. The work of the waiter in spreading and arranging the table is not an immediate service, for it is embodied in material form an hour or two before the meal. The service of cook no less than that of gardener and butcher, is put into material form before it comes to the consumer. The woodman fells, cuts up and splits a tree, and piles it at the door, putting his labor into a utility to be consumed months afterward. The old economists used to class labor as productive and unproductive according as it was or was not embodied in material form. The classing of the services of cook, waiter, valet, etc., as unproductive seems, even from the old point of view, to have been inconsistent, and the attempt to distinguish services by any such test is now wholly given up. Whether the service rests in material form for a week, a month, a year, or as often happens, for a much longer period, is not essential. The test of the productiveness of services is not their embodiment in material form, but their appearance as psychic income, their ministry to wants. The most varied kinds of human activity may be unified by this thought in the concept of economic labor.

§ II. Varieties of Talents and of Abilities in Men

Grades of labor are analogous to grades of wealth

1. *As material things differ in their fitness to gratify wants, so do men differ in their powers of labor.* The fields, hammers, plows, tools, and machinery of different kinds and qualities have been seen to grade off from the best to the poorest. The poorest, discarded or just about to be discarded, are no-rent agents. The utility felt and recognized in the better qualities is expressed in the rents they yield. Recognizing the variety and inequality of human talent, some economists of late speak of the "rent" of ability, meaning that, like land rent, the greater utility (and corresponding reward) of some labor as compared with others, reflects the difference in the quality of agents. But this expression, though often met in contemporary economic writings, is one to be avoided because it tends to blur the essential distinction between human and other agents. Pursuing the same analogy some economists have talked of capitalizing the worker,—expressing in a lump sum the value of the man as the present worth of the series of incomes which he may be expected to earn in his working life. This, also, is to be avoided, for while possibly it is suggestive in studying some problems, it is on the whole a misleading analogy, dimming the distinction between free-workers and owned and exchangeable wealth.

Physical differences among men

2. *The physical strength of workers differs according to age, individual, race, and sex.*

Differences due to age are the most obvious. The child, at first weak, grows toward his maximum of physical strength, which he attains before his fullest intellectual capacity. The period of maximum physical working power lasts fifteen to twenty-five years according to the individual, and then gradually declines as the old worker approaches again the inefficiency of the child. Mental efficiency develops more slowly and longer, the highest qualities of judgment and wisdom being the fruits only of a life rich in experiences. Families and strains of stock differ notably in physical and mental powers; one excels in stature, another in development of muscle. The differences within families are inexplicable, sometimes one brother excelling in one thing, the other in another. The physically perfect man is a rare product. Among three thousand students are but two score endowed with the remarkable combination of lungs, heart, muscle, nerve, and character, that makes possible the finest athletes. The national and racial differences in working power, even in the simplest tasks, are marked but difficult to explain, as so many influences of customs, habits of life, and varieties of diet modify the result. We cannot tell how much of the Englishman's great superiority over the East Indiaman is due to individual, native differences of mind and body, how much to the social environment in which they have lived. Certainly, though, the difference is not mainly one in size; in the Chinese War the little brown men of Japan outmarched all the others. Certainly fiber counts for more than bulk, and character for more than muscle.

Comparative strength of men and women

A difference in the physical strength of the sexes is found in some degree throughout the world, but it would appear to be far more marked in civilized than in savage communities. Compare the records at the Vassar field-games with that of the men in any leading college: in the hundred-yard dash, fifteen seconds as against ten and a fraction; in the high jump, forty-eight inches as against six feet and over. The muscular force of American college women as tested in the Yale and the Oberlin gymnasiums is but one third that of men, that is, taking all the students, the weaklings and the little men along with the athletes, and the women large and small. As to strength of back the average for men is 154 kilograms, for women 54 kilograms; legs, average for men 186, average for women 76.5; right forearm, average for men 56, average for women 21.4. This is an abnormal difference. The natural and possible strength is more nearly attained by men than by women under our social conditions. Women escape the physical toil which strengthens, but not the mental strain which kills. Men carry more of the wood, but the women not less of the worries. A fairer test is applied among peasants in field-work in France and Germany, where the strength of women is found to be about two thirds that of men. American women should do and will do more to attain their natural strength when we attain sounder ideas of education and saner modes of living.

Talent and training as factors of efficiency

3. *Differences in intelligence are a resultant of native talent and acquired ability.* It is

difficult to distinguish these two factors sharply. Two men sitting side by side in an examination, get the same grade; one of them has had excellent preparation from childhood, and all the opportunities that money, travel, and cultured associates can give; the other, under great difficulties, has prepared in a country district school with a little coaching now and then, and struggling against great odds, has at last entered college. The same grade does not mean that their natural ability or even their efficiency in this particular class, is equal. Yet the grade is the best expression to be had of their efficiency in the particular work. Native intelligence shortens the time needed for preparation in any calling; hastens new methods; decreases the cost of supervision; saves materials, tools, and time; diminishes loss from breakage; makes possible the use of finer machinery and better appliances, and imparts those subtler qualities that distinguish the best from the mediocre products. Education and native talent are in a degree interchangeable; one supplements the other. Education increases adaptability; the trained mind will outstrip the untrained mind of greater power. It makes direction easier, fits for higher tasks, and decreases the difficulty of coöperation. Any ability may be helped by education in the broad and true sense, though a fool cannot be made wise by training, and though many a potential genius doubtless has been dwarfed in dusty school-rooms by stupid teachers.

The moral qualities required in industry

4. *The moral qualities of the worker are increasingly important as society grows more complex.* The need of a particular moral quality is relative to the special task in hand. Honesty is needed in the bank teller, but he need not spoil a good story. The champion broncho-buster of Arizona is not a Sunday-school superintendent. So, discipline, obedience, self-control, regularity, and punctuality are needed, for more and more in these days business is run by the watch; confidence, patience, good temper, in fact all the virtues in the calendar are necessary at some time and place, and most of them are needed all the time in business. Places may be found in our developed society for those who are deficient in these qualities (it is fortunate that it is so), but these are the poorer places. Many men fail to examine the qualities necessary for success, and do not understand the causes of their own failure. Blind to their own faults, they are dropped down one notch after another in the scale of industry, and, equally blind to the virtues of their successful rivals, they rail against the unjust fates.

The union of many qualities needed

5. *Skill and capacity in industrial tasks is a resultant of many qualities.* The simplest task calls for a combination of force and judgment,—even the digging of a ditch, the raising of a window, or the fitting of a stovepipe. For most industrial tasks rarer combinations of qualities are required. The retail clerk must be neat, punctual, polite, and long suffering. A confidential clerk must have discretion, judgment, and other moral qualities in an unusual combination. The substitution of qualities is possible within limits; a rare quality may make amends for the lack of a commoner one, and a man may, because of peculiar fitness in some regards, continue to hold

a position for which in other ways he is little fitted. The rarest and most valued worker is one uniting many good qualities and fitted to deal with emergencies. The economic efficiency of the worker often is no stronger than its weakest link. A strong motive for training is offered by the fact that supplying some one lacking quality may raise the total efficiency in a remarkable degree.

Inequality of talents shown by biologic studies

6. *Biologic studies have of late made clearer the existence and continuation of the inequality of talents.* The political philosophy of the eighteenth century was based on the idea of natural rights and natural equality. Adam Smith, accepting the prevailing view, discussed wages on the assumption that all men had equal natural ability. It is still a favorite assumption of radical social reformers that the natural ability of all men is equal, and that all the differences in success result from political injustice. The study of biology of late has made patent the unending differences that prevail throughout the animate world. No two members of the same family or species are just alike; no two pigeons have wings of just the same length. Nature by numberless devices is experimenting constantly with variations on either side of the established mean. The accepted fact of biologic evolution rests on the foundation of inequality in structure and powers, making possible selection and adaptation. Men in all their qualities of mind and body display this kaleidescopic variety. In all life there is inequality, and the whole drama of human history as well as that of biologic evolution must be meaningless or illusory to the man who does not see this truth. Accustomed now to this point of view, we as inevitably think of the natural inequalities in men as did Adam Smith of their equality.

This fact does not force to the conclusion that industrial inequality as it exists to-day, the great disparity of incomes, correctly or justly reflects the degree of difference in men's qualities, either native or acquired. It does not follow that a thousand-dollar income represents ten times the ability of a hundred dollar one — far from it. But to those who ignore the inequality of men, the whole problem of industrial remuneration must remain a mystery. A crude socialism is possible only to those who are blind to the enormous differences in human capacity.

Scarcity of labor is essential to wages
Unlimited demand for labor

7. *The scarcity of human services, relative to wants, is the fundamental fact in the problem of wages.* It is clearly seen that some qualities of service are scarce. Most women will confess that they cannot warble as Patti could, most men will admit that they have not the mercantile ability of John Wanamaker. The man of mediocre capacity recognizes even through the fog of his self-esteem that there is a reason for the high value of certain rare services. But it must also be recognized that the commonest services have value only because they are scarce. There are many things to be done if there were labor enough to do them. There is no need to "make work," in the popular sense; it is here, but labor is lacking to do it. It is true there

may be a temporary superfluity of human labor at a time of an industrial crisis. There is at all times a superfluity of "useless" human agents whose qualities are such that they have no net utility. The ignorant, insane, feeble-minded, vicious, drunken, and debauched, can give to the world only negative utilities. But services that are in any degree useful are nearly always in demand, and the higher services are so rare that they are in great demand. The proverb, "There's always room at the top," is seen to be true when conditions are thus analyzed. There is a large, though limited, supply of the commoner kinds of services at the bottom of the scale, but in every branch of human effort there is a never-ending lack of that higher qualification and training required for the best results.

Chapter XXI
The Supply of Labor

§ I. What is a Doctrine of Population?

The employer's and the social view of supply of labor

1. *The supply of labor means here not the number of workers available in any one industry, but the number available in the whole field of industry.* The individual employer thinks of the supply of labor as consisting of the men seeking employment in his special industry. In this view it is the demand by the employers that apportions the workers among the various occupations. The social view of the supply of labor, however, looks at the whole field. The demand for labor is then seen to be represented not by human employers, but by resources and agents presenting opportunities and demanding labor to employ them. The rich acre, the tool, the machine, all material wealth needing the human touch to give it a higher utility, represent a demand for labor in this broad sense. The thought of a supply of labor is therefore relative to that of the demand embodied in resources. A million men are a great or a small supply of labor according as they occupy a little island or a large continent, according as they are equipped with a small or a large supply of agents.

Population in relation to resources

2. *"Supply of labor," as an economic problem, presents a large and complex case of diminishing returns.* The population of different countries and of different sections of a country is seen to bear a general relation to their resources. An unintelligent race with little wealth and poor machinery is doomed to remain few in numbers. Mountains, districts poorly watered, the frozen regions of the North, are sparsely populated because natural resources are lacking. If food production alone is thought of there are apparent exceptions to this statement, but there are no absolute contradictions of it. A favored harbor may make possible a flourishing commerce on a rocky coast; an unfertile soil may support a large population when great deposits of coal or iron insure by exchange great food-supplies. Productivity must be measured under modern conditions by the purchasing power that is possible

in the environment. The connection of wealth and resources with the extent of the population is in itself a recognition of diminishing returns, of an objective limit to the number of men that can occupy a certain area and employ a given stock of agents.

Equilibrium between numbers of animals of different species

3. *Each species of the lower animals is seen to have a relatively fixed habitat limited by its food-supply and by its enemies.* The rocks tell a story of a slow and steady change that has gone on in the earth and in the species of animals that inhabit it. History records some rapid changes due to convulsions of nature or to interference by man with the natural conditions. But the usual condition is an equilibrium of numbers, long maintained, though each species appears to have in itself a capacity for unlimited increase. Why this contradiction? The limit set by the food-supply is seen in a simple case when herbivorous animals are placed on an island from which they cannot escape, and where there are no dogs, wolves, weasels, or foxes. Substantially this experiment was unintentionally tried on an enormous scale with the rabbit in Australia. This peculiar and long-isolated continent contained none of the rabbit's ancient enemies. The rabbits became a pest, devastated great areas, were hunted, trapped, poisoned, and great numbers of them died of starvation outside the fences erected to stop their advance. In the imaginary island they would increase up to the point where starvation would bring about an equilibrium between the number of animals and the food supply. The destruction of one kind of animal by another limits numbers in another way. The number of lions is limited by the number of their prey in the region where they roam. The number of deer, therefore, is limited in two ways, by the amount of their food and by the number of lions which catch the deer. The more numerous the lions, the fewer the deer; the fewer the deer, the greater the supply of vegetable food; as the pressure increases on one side, it decreases on the other, until an equilibrium is reached.

The surplus of life germs

Throughout nature each species of animal keeps its customary place, changing little despite its efforts to increase and to crowd into the habitat of other species. Even the slow-breeding elephant, with a period of gestation of three years, and producing one calf at a birth, would cover the entire earth and leave no standing-room in a few centuries if every calf born could live to full age. The myriads of frogs born every spring, the swarms of insects, the countless plants, are struggling to find a foothold on the crowded earth. Of the vastly greater number of seeds and embryos, only one in a multitude ever comes or could come to maturity. Here are the undisputed facts on which rests a biologic "doctrine of population," so to speak, for the vegetable and lower animal world. Because of the limited powers of the soil, no form of life, animal or vegetable, can continue to increase even for a single generation, without meeting enormous forces of opposition, which destroy great numbers and set a limit to the increase of the species.

These facts related to the doctrine of population

4. *A doctrine of human population is a reasoned explanation of the causes determining the number of people in the world.* Man in his economic life is constantly struggling with the problem of the scarcity of goods. If in any given environment men continue long to increase, they must, like the lower animals, meet limits in the capacities of the resources they use. The supply of labor force which is thus brought to be combined with the material agents must meet with diminishing returns unless these agents also continue to increase at a like rate. The relation of population to resources thus presents probably the most fundamental problem in the realm of economics. It is a problem of great complexity, bristling with difficulties, and incapable of exact mathematical treatment; but it is capable of rational study. There is a great difference between a purely fatalistic view of this question and the view that is to be reached by a consideration of the motives, causes, and physical influences at work. It is possible to find some principles in the chaos of prejudices and contradictions that the subject presents. The fruit of a century of discussion of the economic, social, and biologic factors involved, is a rational, if not a final, doctrine of population.

§ II. Population in Human Society

The biologic stage of human population

1. *In the earlier stages of human history, population is limited mainly by biologic factors.* The biologic stage continues so long as there are no artificial restraints put on the birth-rate, and no deliberate destruction of offspring for the purposes of limiting the size of the family. There the limits are all objective; they are found in scantiness of the food-supply, or in destruction by enemies, animal or human. Each species has an average or normal birth-rate, great or small. Just why this varies, why the rabbit produces a score of young in a year, and the elephant but one in three years, is a question capable of a rational answer, but it is one for the natural scientist rather than for the economist. Each species is impelled by instinct to realize this birth-rate, to bring into existence as many young as possible.

No human society known to us is so primitive that it has not passed this stage, but many societies have risen but little above it. In most savage tribes, where starvation, disease, and war are constantly at work, the difficult task is to maintain the population. Few of those born arrive at maturity. The custom of the adoption of captives from hostile tribes is widespread, because the efficiency and even the survival of the tribe depends upon keeping up its number of warriors.

War among primitive societies

2. *War for the possession of limited resources is the first rude social remedy for an excess of population.* War is the normal condition of most primitive tribes. Its cause usually appears to be standing feuds and ancient enmities, but the deeper and

abiding cause is the struggle for hunting-grounds, for pasturage, for natural resources. The rude industry and economy of hunting, fishing, or pastoral peoples, or of those in the earlier stages of agriculture, requires a large area for a small population. Distant excursions and frequent forays, when food fails, develop rival claims to favored districts, and war is the only settlement. Fighting under these conditions is an activity of such economic importance that much of the energy of the tribe must be strenuously given to it. The ceaseless loss of life in savage wars is almost incredible to modern minds. The invasion of the Roman Empire by the Teutonic tribes, the later successive inundations of medieval Europe by the fierce pastoral tribes from central Asia, are more recent and familiar examples of the economic and political effects of the increase of population and of the outgrowing of resources by barbarian peoples. When the custom arises of capturing enemies and reducing them to slavery instead of killing them, forces are set into operation to reorganize society and to create new checks on the growth of population.

Crude beginnings of volitional control

3. *Volitional control of population begins by the destruction of offspring before or after birth.* The population problem ceases to be simply biologic, and takes on its sociological aspect, when the awakening intelligence of man first grasps the mystery of birth, and when the first attempts are made in any way to regulate family relations or to interfere with the growth of numbers. The student of primitive peoples finds in the methods applied to prevent the birth of children an almost inconceivable brutality. The same methods to a large degree persist in savage communities to-day. Infanticide was generally practiced in ancient times among peoples of advanced civilization, as, for example, in Sparta and Rome, where not only deformed and weak children, but unwelcome ones, commonly were destroyed. The practice, if not legalized, is at least permitted even to-day by public opinion in great portions of India, China, and other densely populated districts of the world. It is one of the dark spots on our own civilization.

Private property limits population

The problem a psychic one

4. *The pressure of increase of numbers on resources is confined by individual industry and by private property to special portions of the population.* A condition of communism, where all the members of the tribe or family share equally, means that all enjoy together when food and wealth are abundant, and all starve together when it becomes scarce. Along with a fierce enmity for other tribes, is found in many early societies a close approximation to tribal communism. Private property alters the nature of the struggle for subsistence and of the motives for limiting population. Society divides into a number of partially independent classes or family groups, each holding its share of wealth apart, not in common with the tribe. A society with private property is like a ship divided into a number of water-tight compartments. In communistic conditions if population increases, all sink together into want. The self-interest of those having private property keeps them from dividing their property, and starvation is confined to the propertyless members. This acts in two

ways: it increases the motive for the production of wealth; it gives a motive for the limitation of the consumers of the wealth. A smaller family with larger resources means a wider margin between numbers and misery. This converts the problem of population from a material one of a balance of food and physical needs, to a psychic one of a balance of motives in the minds of men. When this stage is reached, the extreme objective limit of the birth-rate or of increase of population is no longer attained in the well-to-do classes, although it may still continue to be in the less provident.

Social classes differ in volitional control

5. *Volitional control is effective in very different degrees in different families and industrial classes.* The possession of property is both a sign of forethought and an incentive to it. Concern for the welfare of children is one of the most powerful motives, especially after social distinctions become marked. It may become abnormally strong, leading parents to sacrifice their own welfare or their own lives foolishly for their children, as is done often in the accumulation of property. Among the classes with property the provision for the children depends not only upon the amount of wealth, but upon the number among whom it is to be divided. It is simple division: wealth the dividend, number of children the divisor.

Among the poorer classes very different motives operate. After the first few years the parents' income is increased by the earnings of the children, both on the farm and in the factory districts if the laws do not prohibit child labor. Moreover, when the children are grown, their wages will depend on the general labor market, not upon the number of their brothers and sisters. So, according as the family income is from rents or from wages, the motives of the parents differ.

Motives in volitional control

Postponement of marriage must be classed as a mode of volitional control of population. The average age of marriage, both of men and women, is higher in the classes of greater wealth and ambition than in the poorer classes. The contrast in this regard between civilized and savage peoples is likewise noteworthy. The failure to marry, from whatever cause, is, in the social view of the question, volitional control. It is rare that the motive is directly and immediately the wish to avoid parenthood; now it is religious zeal, again it is disappointed sentiment; here it is conflicting duty, and there it is the individual selfish wish to retain an undivided income for one's own enjoyment. By countless strands of motive in the form of sentiments, social institutions, and interests, the primitive impulses of humanity are firmly bound; and in varying degrees, in different classes, the enormous possibilities of reproduction are controlled by human volition.

§ III. Current Aspect of the Population Problem

The many motives controlling population

1. *Changes in population are resultants of many forces: those favoring a high birth-rate and low death-rate, and those limiting births or survival.* Whether the population on the whole shall grow, stand still, or diminish, depends upon the relative strength of contending forces making for life or death. But this control may lose its cruder aspect and may be waged in the realm of motive. More and more it is volition that controls in human society the growth of population; less and less it is the objective limit of the food-supply. Dire need resulting in ill-health and even in starvation, is still acting in some portions of society, but less to-day than ever before. The growth of population in this stage is not "fatalistic," as there is no inevitable tendency to increase or to decrease. It depends on the interaction of a number of forces, clearly distinguishable, by which population actually is kept far within the limits of food resources. Volitional control is not by a central and unified despotism determining human action, but it is by motives of the most complex sort, diffused throughout society and acting upon every member of it.

The standard of life in Asiatic countries

2. *The desire to maintain and raise the standard of life is the most effective motive limiting population in our society.* The phrase "standard of life" expresses the complex thought of that measure of necessities, comforts, and luxuries considered by any individual to be indispensable for himself and his children; that measure which he will make great sacrifices to secure. This standard differs from land to land, and from time to time. In the Asiatic countries it is so low that it touches in large classes the minimum of subsistence. Despite adverse influences and the uninterrupted series of famines, the population of India in the last century under English rule increased from two hundred millions to three hundred millions. Such a population "lets out all the slack" of income, and never takes up any. The great public works of irrigation, forestry, and transportation, and the development of industry under English rule, gave an opportunity for a higher standard of living; but it was used instead to permit the existence of a greater number of men in the same old misery. These facts have a bearing upon the question of Oriental immigration to America. The emigration of millions of Chinese from their native land would leave no void in their numbers. Peopling their own land constantly down to their own standard of living, they have the power, if they are tempted hither in great numbers, to people this continent also to the same density.

The American standard

The American standard of living, while it differs in different classes, is on the whole the highest found anywhere in the world. The increasing appeal to individual selfishness in the last twenty-five years, the greater ease of travel and taste for it, the multiplied and costly pleasures and pastimes, make children a greater and greater burden. The abnormal conditions of city life increase the sacrifice required to support children, and take away a large part of the value of their services in the home. In the greater cities are whole areas larger than the city of Ithaca where children are not admitted to the apartment houses, where no one who has a child can rent rooms. Despite the increasing incomes of the masses of the population, the number of childless homes is increasing, and while the standard of comfort grows, the size of the average family dwindles.

The decreasing death-rate

3. *Great improvements in medical and in sanitary science are decreasing the death-rate and thus partly neutralizing the effects of a lower birth-rate.* The death-rate in a community is a fairly good index of its general welfare. The death of a large proportion of the children before they arrive at maturity indicates poverty or ignorance. The death-rate in the Middle Ages, especially in cities, was tremendously high, but during the last hundred years has steadily decreased. The race of man which, ever since the beginnings of volitional control, probably has had a smaller death-rate relative to the total number of individuals coming into existence than has any other species of living creatures, has to-day a far lower rate than ever before. Even in the most miserable industrial population where one half the children die before they are five years old, the death-rate is much less than among the young of the lion or the eagle.

The quality of population counts

4. *Volitional control is acting with the greatest force in the more capable classes and thus threatens to reduce the quality of the population.* The quality of population is of more import than its quantity, alike in its economic, its social, and its ethical results. The productive force of a population is not measured merely by numbers. "Who" make up the population at any moment is no more a matter of indifference than "how many." One new-born child represents a negative addition to society, unintelligent, incapable, foredoomed to become a burden; another, with energy, thrift, inventive genius, comes to enrich and uplift his fellow-men. Quality counts for much.

Change in the American birth-rate

The average number of children reaching maturity in the families of the American colonists was six; the average number to-day in families of American descent is about two. Since many of these do not live to maturity, and of those who do survive many do not marry, the stock does not maintain itself in numbers. Much larger families are found among the poor whites of the mountains, the foreign population, the negroes, and, in general, in the lower ranks of labor. Forces are at work to sterilize or reduce in number the more intelligent elements of the population. The "new woman" movement, tempting into "careers," takes away from family life many of the women most worthy to become the mothers of succeeding generations, Self-interest is at war with the social interest. The individual asks, "Am I bound to sacrifice my comfort and happiness to the general good?" If this continues, the result must be a steady decline in the proportion of the population born of the successful strains of stock, and a steady increase of the descendants of the mediocre and duller-witted elements.

Rate of increase in the nineteenth century

5. *Population increased at an unprecedented rate throughout Christendom in the nineteenth century, but the pace is now slackening.* The nineteenth century saw a great increase in the food-supplies available for Europe. The resources of the American continent were hardly touched until the great Western movement of population began and new agencies of transportation brought American fields thousands of miles nearer to European markets. The improvement of machinery and of other economic equipment in Europe likewise aided to increase production rapidly. Population followed, though not with equal step. Europe had a population of 200,000,000 in 1800, nearly 400,000,000 in 1900. The increase in England was from 12 to 18 per cent, each decade; it had 8,000,000 in 1800 and 30,000,000 in 1900. The United States had 5,000,000 at the beginning of the century and 75,000,000 at the close, an increase of over 30 per cent, each decade. Recently there has been a notable decline in the rate of increase in all the countries of Europe. France is already at the stationary stage, and England probably will have reached it by the middle of the century. The rate of increase by decades has fallen in America from thirty-three to twenty-four since the Civil War. Though the movement of the population is still upward, large classes are stationary or declining in numbers.

Conclusion

Population should increase more slowly than wealth and resources if progress is to go on. It has done so in the past century, and there is no probability of a too rapid increase in Christendom in the near future. A stationary or declining population, while not desirable, is not an impossibility. But this does not destroy the significance of the fact that there is inherent in humanity a great potential power of increase, the realization of which would be disastrous, the control of which is an important and ever-present condition of the social welfare.

Chapter XXII
Conditions for Efficient Labor

§ I. Objective Physical Conditions

Subjective and objective factors of efficiency

1. *The efficiency of labor, in its broadest sense, is its ability to render services or produce things that minister to welfare.* The efficiency of labor is a resultant of many influences. In part it depends on the physical and mental powers of men; in part on things outside of the worker that either stimulate and strengthen him, or give him more favorable conditions in which to work. These are respectively the subjective and the objective factors of efficiency. In its broader sense, therefore, the phrase "efficiency of labor" implies any and every influence that makes for a larger and better supply of goods.

Bounty and goodness of productive agents affect the output of labor

2. *The efficiency of labor is limited objectively by the abundance and quality of material resources.* Material resources include both those called natural (as the field and its fertile qualities), and those called artificial (as improvements and machinery). According as these resources are more or less developed, as labor is employed in a fertile or a barren field, with a sharp tool or a dull one, with a highly developed machine or a poor one, the product is more or less. If resources were much more abundant than at present, many goods now scarce would become almost, or quite, free. In the last chapter it was shown that an increase of the labor in a limited area or with a limited supply of indirect agents results in a decline in the relative bounty of the environment. A certain part of the result is thought of as due to material agents, a certain part to labor. "Efficiency of labor" is thought of in the narrower sense as the part of the product that is logically attributable to labor,—the laborer's contribution to the value of the product,—as apart from rent, the part attributable to material resources.

CONDITIONS FOR EFFICIENT LABOR 145

Causal relation of wages and efficiency; food

3. *The laborer's efficiency is greatly affected by the quality of his food, clothing, and shelter.* Usually workmen that are getting good wages enjoy abundant food and creature comforts; poorly paid workers go scantily fed. The question arises: which is cause, which effect? Some maintain that all that is needed to make workmen more efficient is to feed them well. In some cases this is probably true. The Porto Ricans enlisted in the American regular army are reported to have increased at once in strength, weight, and vigor; the Filipino recruits, thanks to the American army rations, soon outgrew their uniforms. Some employers in Europe pay their workmen an extra sum on condition that it is spent for meat. But if wages increase, it is by no means certain that more or better food will be bought or if it is that the workmen's powers will be increased. There is a limit to the benefits of increasing food. There is some reason to believe that in America great numbers of our people, perhaps even many manual laborers, would be better off if they bought simpler and less costly food. The maximum of health and vigor may be attained with moderate outlay, and beyond that point richer food doubtless does more harm than good. Poor judgment in the selection of food is shown in many workers' families, and there is no appreciation of its influence on health.

An experiment in feeding

A few years ago an experiment in the feeding of pigs was tried on the Cornell farm. Four groups of six pigs each were put in four different pens and fed four different rations. Though alike in breed and age; the groups began at once to differ in character. One group squealed more; another scratched more; another waxed fat faster. Every week they were weighed, and finally were butchered, hung up, and photographed. At that same time, at the Elmira Reformatory Mr. Brockway was experimenting on some criminals of the lower class. They were given daily baths, special physical exercises, and were fed on a specially bountiful diet. Scientific philanthropy stopped there, but photographs "before and after," reproduced in the printed reports, show the great physical improvement that resulted, and a marked change occurred likewise in disposition and intelligence. Many laboratory experiments have been made of late to test the chemical nature and the physiological effects of foods. It is becoming more fully recognized that the quality and quantity of food, and the cooking of it, have a great influence on the economic quality of the worker.

Clothing

The effect of the quality and amount of clothing, while of course varying with the climate, is in general of less practical importance. Loss of heat and energy, dulling the powers, stiffening the muscles, causing illness with many trains of evils, make ill-clad workmen inefficient. The cost of clothing enough for comfort is, however, comparatively small, the amount spent for ornament is comparatively high. Even more important in its effects on efficiency is housing. The conditions in the factory and in the home make for health or for disease.

Physical conditions surrounding labor grow worse or better

4. *The growth of society is, for the average man, making some of the conditions of efficiency more difficult, others more easy, to secure.* In agricultural and sparse populations fresh air, sunshine, good water, and unbounded natural playgrounds for children, where they can grow into strong and efficient manhood, are free goods. As population grows more dense, these things become more difficult to secure; men are brought into unnatural conditions, the evils of slum and factory life develop, and the housing problem appears.

The character of the housing and working places could well be left to individuals in early times. If the individual chose to live and work in unsuitable places and under unsanitary conditions, it was usually his own fault and he bore the consequences. When the unsanitary conditions about each family are visited upon its neighbors, society must deal with them. Engineering, sanitary science, and medicine must be directed against the evils; factory and tenement-house legislation must seek to make possible a decent life in the cities, the factories, and the homes. Indeed, in many places the development in these and other directions has enabled the mass of the workers to enjoy blessings impossible to the most favored in the past.

§ II. Social Conditions Favoring Efficiency

Government to insure the reward to labor

1. *The first social condition for the workers' efficiency is political security.* For the same reason that this condition is favorable to the growth of capital, it is essential if men are to labor in the present and for the future. As the framers of the Constitution expressed it, the function of government is to insure domestic tranquillity, provide for the common defense, and insure the blessings of liberty to the citizen. Directness and certainty of reward are more essential than mere size of reward in insuring action and effort. There must be a close relation between work and the fruits of work. Political insecurity weakens this relation and makes the reward dependent on chance.

Common honesty as a condition to efficient labor

2. *The prevalence of standards of honesty in private and public business is a condition to high efficiency.* Corruption in government has the same effect as political insecurity; in fact, it is but another form of it. We are accustomed to the thought that in an Asiatic despotism a worker beginning a task is uncertain whether he will reap the reward, as public officials may at any moment seize upon the fruits of his labor. But in our own country similar evils are not entirely lacking. Assessments often are unfair, and justice sometimes is bought. Men in high executive positions are able to make or mar the fortunes of their followers. Sometimes a legislator from a country town goes to the state capital poor and returns rich. Such things becoming

generally known tend to break down the motives to industry. They breed the notion that wealth is more dependent on chance or jobbery than on efficient service. Dishonesty in private business means the use of energy not to produce wealth, not to add to the sum for all to enjoy, but to get it from some one else. Public corruption and commercial dishonesty alike entail on the industrious not only the immediate loss, but the far greater cost of weakened character, relaxed energy, and decreased efficiency of labor.

Effect of caste on efficiency of lower and upper classes

3. *Custom and social ideals that raise or depress hope and ambition, affect efficiency.* The institution called caste, which fixes the place of the worker and makes it impossible to rise out of the social position in which he is born, and disgraceful to do any work reserved to other castes, is deadening to energy. It exists in some form throughout the world, and where it is not called by that name, the same caste spirit is at work. The European peasants in the Middle Ages lived under the shadow of it. Where slavery exists the master class at times feels its hardships. "It is not so hard to live," says the hungry Creole daughter in "The Grandissimes," "but it is hard to be ladies.... We are compelled not to make a living. Look at me: I can cook, but I must not cook; I am skilful with the needle, but I must not take in sewing; I could keep accounts; I could nurse the sick; but I must not." Nowhere in the world is there less caste than in America, but it is here. The negro's low measure of industrial virtues is partly the cause of the prejudice against him, but in turn doubtless inherited class feeling is in some measure the cause of his inefficiency. To close to a worker all but the menial occupations is to take from him the most powerful motives for effort. The thought is paralyzing. The race problem in America is in part one of caste sentiment, whatever can or cannot be done about it.

American democracy and the efficiency of labor

Democracy makes for the efficiency of American industry not less than do the great natural resources. If America is to surpass the world in all the great industrial lines, it will be largely because of her ideas and institutions. They lead to greater energy and to a faster working pace in all grades of labor than is found anywhere else in the world. There is danger that as the West is closed to settlement something of the spirit of enterprise will be lost. To Western eyes already the young men in the older East seem to be trammeled by social conventions. In an older community there is less of hopeful ambition; one's position depends more on what his fathers achieved; in the new community, more on what he does himself. If it is true, as wise students declare, that the frontier has been the nursery of our democratic ideas, we may well ask what effect the closing of the frontier will have on our national sentiment and on our material prosperity.

The balance of advantage between work and leisure

4. *Custom and national temperament affect the efficiency of labor by determining the*

normal period of labor time. After the bare necessities of life are provided for, the worker has a wide or narrow margin of productive energy to use as he pleases. If four hours' work a day would enable him to live, will he work longer or will he stop? The answer is determined by the balance of utility and disutility. Will additional hours of labor yield more gratification than idleness yields? Does the pain of toil repel more than its fruits attract? The use made of spare time differs according to climate, race, and temperament. In the tropics the margin is converted usually into loafing, in the temperate zones largely into objective forms of enjoyment. Individual differences are plainly seen when each man labors on his own field. The prudent man, in the old maxims, makes hay while the sun shines and ploughs deep while sluggards sleep. In the modern larger organization of industry, working hours are much the same for all workers in the establishment. Individual preferences are still expressed, however, in irregularity of employment. In the South some manufacturers have found that on an average the negroes will work in a factory not more than five or six hours a day, working ten hours for four days and lying off two days a week. Such a standard of working hours is the mark of the primitive stage of wants and industrial qualities, although a shortening of the hours of manual labor, as incomes increase above bare subsistence, is in accord with a rational valuation of leisure. A moderate change in that direction cannot but increase rather than diminish the efficiency of labor.

§ III. Division of Labor

Division and exchange of labor

1. *Division of labor is a term expressing that complex arrangement of industrial society whereby individual workers are enabled to apply themselves to the production of certain kinds of goods, securing others by exchange.* The term "division of labor" is simple, but the thought is a complex one. Its full discussion would cover the whole field of political economy, but only its most essential aspects can here be touched upon. Division of labor and exchange are counterparts and mutually determine each other. Division of labor depends on the extent of the market, and in turn widens its limits. The number of articles that any one would care to produce at one time and place depends upon the opportunity to exchange them. These two aspects of industry thus are inseparable in thought and practice. The worker finds division of labor existing as a social institution and, according as he adapts himself to it wisely or foolishly, it increases more or less his efficiency.

Division of labor between trades and territories

2. *Division of labor is primarily between individuals, but appears between trades, territories, and nations.* In division of labor between trades, each worker applies himself to the production of some product or group of products and secures other goods by exchange. A special form of this is territorial division of labor, arising out of differences in soil, climate, and natural products, when each community

CONDITIONS FOR EFFICIENT LABOR

develops in a high degree some one class of products to exchange in distant or foreign trade. Division of labor beginning because of such natural differences, becomes fixed by habit and training, by the advantage of a larger and regular labor supply, by the economy of nearness to related and tributary industries, and by the use of waste products where industry is conducted on a large scale. The natural advantages in another district must be large to enable it to start successfully against these acquired economies, and territorial division of labor thus tends to continue for long periods when once established.

Advantages of division of labor

3. *Division of labor increases efficiency by: (a) increasing skill; (b) saving time; (c) saving tools and materials; (d) improving quality; (e) increasing knowledge; (f) stimulating invention; (g) encouraging enterprise; (h) economizing talent.* There is a tradition that an ingenious lecturer in one of our universities was accustomed to give to his class eighty reasons why division of labor was of advantage. It is none too many, as every reason for the modern, as contrasted with the primitive, organization of industry should be included. The phrase division of labor is but a synonym for specialization, a word that expresses all that is most characteristic of our complex industrial society. The headings just given may serve, however, to suggest the leading phases of the subject. Repetition of the same task trains the muscles, forms a mental habit, and gives the swiftness and deftness of touch called *skill*. Specialization *saves time* by making unnecessary the physical change of place for the worker, the frequent shifting of tools, and the mental readjustment required for the undertaking of a new task. Specialization *saves tools* for, either each kind of work must be most ineffectively done, or there must be provided for each worker a complete set of tools which thus will be used rarely and will rust out rather than wear out. If a few tools are thoroughly used, they yield a larger income on the investment, and require less care and repairs in proportion to their uses. In fact this fuller economic use of machinery and plant where a large product is turned out at one place, is a prime factor in the advantages of large production, a subject to be treated elsewhere much more fully than is here possible. By specialization is made possible a *quality* of goods never to be secured by the less skilled efforts of the Jack-of-all trades. The specialist steadily grows in *knowledge* of his materials and of the best processes, and he gains a power of delicate observation and facility in meeting new difficulties that are impossible when attention is divided among a number of tasks. By dividing and simplifying processes, specialization *stimulates invention*. The most complex machines have been developed gradually by combinations and adaptations of simple tools, and the more a process is subdivided, the greater is the chance of hitting upon a device to repeat mechanically the few simple movements. Division of labor increases the motives of emulation and *enterprise*, by making possible the more exact comparison of results. It *economizes talent* by giving to each the highest task of which he is capable, while fitting the less efficient workers into the minor places made possible by subdivision. In an American wagon-factory, a one-armed man operating a machine is turning out as large a product and earning as high wages as any other employee. The same advantages of specialization

are found with modifying conditions in educational and professional lines. The marvelous progress of science in recent years has been made possible by each worker's doing a few things and doing them well.

Best adjustment of talent and occupation

Choice of a life career

4. *The individual worker, to attain his highest economic efficiency, must select from the occupations made possible by division of labor the one for which his talents are best fitted.* It seems unnecessary to state this almost axiomatic truth, yet the slight reflection given to the choice of an occupation by most young people gives to this statement a very practical bearing. The world is filled with industrial misfits, "round men in square holes," good carpenters spoiled to make poor doctors. It so often happens that the natural aptitude of the youth is the thing last or, in any event, least considered. Unreasoning imitation, family traditions, parental wishes, class pride, social prejudice, childish whim, are often decisive of the life career. Happily in some cases, before too late, the man "finds himself," but too often the poverty of the family and the obstacles to education preclude the exercise of intelligent choice. It is of importance to society as well as to the individual that talent should be discovered in time, that tasks should be fitted to aptitudes, that each member of society should attain to his highest efficiency. The approach to this ideal, made possible by popular education, the decline of caste, the spread of genuine democracy, the progress of social justice, will increase not only the workers' efficiency, but society's abiding welfare.

Chapter XXIII
The Law of Wages

§ I.   Nature of Wages and the Wages Problem

Wages and rent compared and contrasted

1. *Wage in the broad sense is the income due to labor, in distinction from that due to the control of material agents.* The uses of material agents, studied under the subject of rent, are sometimes called "material services." The adjective refers to the source or bearer of the use, and does not imply that the service is to be thought of as a material thing. In its last analysis a service is never a material thing, but a psychic effect on men and their wants. Material services and human services are merely specific kinds of the genus services (or utilities), and it would doubtless be a better usage to speak of labor's services and wealth's uses. Wages bear the same relation to man's services that rent does to the material uses of wealth. Wages are more like rent than like interest in that neither wages nor rent are expressed as a percentage. While rent is the value of the uses of things, wages is the value of the services of men. In discussing interest, wealth is capitalized; but, in discussing wages, men are thought of as affording utilities for a time, as is wealth under the renting contract. The resemblance thus is very close between rent and wages, but not so close between wages and interest.

Despite this interesting analogy, it is not well to speak, as some do, of "the rent of labor"—as well might one speak of the wages of wealth. Such a usage only beclouds the distinction between two concepts, suggesting identity where there are important differences. The aim of scientific classification is missed when contrasts are thus concealed under a single term.

Nature of the law of wages

2. *A law of wages is a statement of the relation of the general causes of value to the value of human services.* In real life no one agent is valued independently of other goods. The felt importance of a good depends on the degree to which other wants are gratified. If men are starving, they attach less importance to ornaments; if cold, more importance to clothing and fuel, being willing to part even with some needed

food to secure them. That is, man's desire for each thing is affected by his general condition and by the existence of other goods and wants. A similar relation exists between the values of indirect agents, and must exist between wages and rent.

We are to discuss the law of wages. An economic law does not state a command; it is not a political law; it states merely an observed relation. Things do not need to happen actually according to any law of wages that can be formulated, but they will happen in the measure that the assumed conditions exist. The law states a tendency of wages, just as the law of gravitation states a tendency and does not predict positively whether a given object will fall at a given moment. The "law of wages," therefore, is to be understood as a hypothetical statement of the value that will be attributed to labor under a given set of conditions.

Economic wages and contract wages

3. *Economic wages are the value of human services in the broad sense; contract wages are the goods paid by one man to another according to an agreement.* In discussing rent and interest, we have become familiar with this important distinction between economic and contract values. Economic wages are fundamental, the primary subject of theoretical study. Contract wages are the wages paid by one man to another in accordance with an agreement, and may not at this moment coincide with economic wages. When the contract was made, one party may have been ignorant or helpless, and have failed to get all he now could; or meantime the conditions may have changed. But contract wages are based on economic wages and tend to conform to them. If one person performs services for another without expecting to receive economic goods or services in return, it is a gift, not wages. A workman can get as contract wages the amount of his economic wage if free competition exists and he acts intelligently. Of course, these are important conditions.

Real and nominal wages must be distinguished: real wages are the reward of labor as measured in goods and enjoyments; nominal wages are the reward expressed in terms of money, whose purchasing power varies from time to time and from place to place.

Scarce services gratify wants

4. *Human services, being one of the conditions of psychic income, bear the same relation to wants that material goods bear.* As the material agents that are fitted to gratify wants are scarce, labor is applied to the outer world to change and adapt it, thus making it answer desire better. Labor, thus, in many of its applications merely supplements the bounty of nature. Men have a use to and for each other; they have a relation to other men's welfare similar to that borne by material things. The different human actions have all grades of relation to gratification, from harmful to helpful, just as things have. According to their relation to this scale services therefore become ranked either high or low in the estimation of men. Some acts are negative services, to use the term service in a paradoxical sense; they are things to be avoided and escaped. Value then is attributed to the services of men according

THE LAW OF WAGES

to their rank in this scale, just as it is to the uses of agents in the case of rent.

Scarcity is the condition of value in labor, as it is of value in any good; but scarcity is a relative term. The commonest kinds of labor would not ordinarily be called scarce, but compared with their possible desirable uses, they are scarce, and this fact is the key to a large part of the wage problem. The question is: how and in what degree does this scarcity cause value to attach to labor?

§ II. The Different Modes of Earning Wages

The simplest case of economic wages

1. *The self-employed laborer earns wages in the broad economic sense.* In this sense the isolated workman, Robinson Crusoe on his island, earns wages, but these wages could not be measured at all exactly. They are a part of an indivisible income, and there is no way to determine how much should be attributed to the uses of the wealth employed and how much to the labor. The independent farmer, producing on his own farm nearly everything he consumes, may be said to earn wages in the broad sense. These can, moreover, be estimated, because they can be compared with what he could get by working for some one else. The farmer, therefore, attributes a certain part of his income to the farm as rent and a certain part to his own labor as wages.

Wages of the self-employed exchanging worker

2. *The wages of self-employed labor are often simply the value of the material product it secures by exchange.* Labor has value indirectly because embodied in products. The value of these products is reflected to the labor which secures them. The wages of the fisherman day by day, as he follows his vocation, are simply the market value of the fish he catches day by day. The gold-miner, working with simple tools in the days of placer-mining, earned wages exactly expressed by the gold he washed out.

The independent worker with few tools does not think of attributing any considerable part of his income to his tools. The umbrella-mender's "kit" is so small that his true wage is little less than his total receipts. The tinker, the shoemaker, and the tailor, who went from house to house in the old days, thought only in the vaguest way of marking off from their incomes a part to be counted as the rent of their little outfit of tools. Until very recent times the capital invested in tools commonly was small, and usually was owned by the handworker who thus received an undivided income, of which wages were by far the larger part. It was inevitable, therefore, that labor alone should have been thought of as the cause of the value of goods produced by the artisans in the towns and cities. This error, small at first, was magnified as the capital investment of modern industry grew, and it persists in many fallacious notions that still taint modern economic theory.

Both impersonal and personal causes of contract wages

3. *Contract wages, paid by an employer, rest on the same cause of value, the direct or indirect effect of labor in the gratifying of wants.* When contract wages come to be spoken of, the personal element of bargaining between man and man comes in to obscure somewhat the impersonal causes that are operating. If the fisher and the miner bring their products to the general markets, the impersonal part of the problem is uppermost and the wages are recognized to be the market value of the material products. But if an employer hires a number of workmen, and the labor of each becomes merged and lost to view in a complex product, the uncritical mind stops, loses all hold on a guiding principle of value, and sees only the superficial fact of a personal bargain between employer and workman. Such a view overlooks the logical cause of value, and the network of impersonal forces which enwraps and binds the personal acts.

A single direct personal service

To begin with the simplest case: workers often are temporarily employed to produce for others means of gratification at once consumed. The barber shaves his patron, the ferryman takes the traveler across the river, the boy carries a message, the surgeon sets a broken bone. Each performs a useful service, but produces no long-abiding material result outside of the beneficiary, and no separable, salable material good. When each is paid according to the value of the gratification afforded, the first step is taken toward the regular contract-wage relation between man and man.

The continued wage contract for personal services

In ordinary domestic service the only condition not present in the cases just given is the more abiding character of the contract relation. The employer does not hire a coachman each time he wishes to take a ride, but having summed up the advantages of a coachman's services, he buys them by the month or the year. The price is determined in the market for coachmen of the needed ability, qualities ranging from stupid to bright, from weak to strong, and from drunk to sober. Instead of buying flowers from day to day, a wealthy man hires a gardener to cultivate them in a conservatory. The average market price of flowers influences the wages paid to the gardener, his wages being but the sum of the values (or of his contribution to the values) of flowers, well-kept lawn, and garden products. According to the conditions of each household and of the general market, the one or the other mode of buying these utilities is the more advantageous.

Labor employed on products exchanged

4. *The payment of the laborer to produce goods for exchange is the most common modern case of wages.* The relation of wages to the value of the product is in this case more complex, for the employer is directing the labor to gratifying the wants of others, not his own wants. It is the desire of prospective customers for the product, and the chance of exchanging it, that will eventually enable the employer

THE LAW OF WAGES

to recover the amounts paid to laborers. Labor is only one of the elements entering into the product. Within limits it may be substituted for the other elements, fewer machines being used and more laborers, or vice versa. No more will be given for any labor than it is expected to add to the value of the product. As employers test by experience the contribution of the marginal labor to the value of the product, labor is constantly compared with the value of other things.

When industry becomes complex, the connection between the wages and the value ultimately realized in the product may be broken for a time, but rarely for a very long time. Because of miscalculations, labor is employed on things that prove to be quite valueless, and on other things that have a much greater value than was expected. When months or years intervene before the value of the labor is realized in the sale of the product, the employer must forecast the outcome as best he can, and employ labor only when the wages promise to be recovered. These are complicating facts, but in any logical view they do not falsify the principle that wages are determined by their prospective contribution to the utility of goods.

Various methods of remuneration, but one general rule

5. *The wages paid by the various methods of remuneration—as, by time, by the piece, by premium for output—all conform in a general way to the economic value of the service.* Many methods are employed to measure the services of wage workers. If time is used, a general or average output is assumed, and the workman must come up to that standard if he is to hold his place. If payment is by the piece, the price per piece must be enough to make possible the prevailing time-wage to workers of that grade if the supply is to be maintained in that industry. The convenience of the different methods of payment varies from industry to industry, and even from task to task within the same factory, so that now one, now another method is followed. In any case, however, the aim is to find some convenient measurement of the rate of labor, and of its contribution to the value of the product.

§ III. Wages as Exemplifying the General Law of Value

Ratio of exchange of services adjusted to their marginal utility

1. *Each grade of labor is a potential supply of desirable things and its wage is determined in essentially the same way as if it were an actual supply.* If all the various psychic goods that labor produces were spread out before men in visible form, some would be in great demand, some would exchange in a very unfavorable ratio with others. The exchange would come to equilibrium at a point where each buyer had adjusted his supply of enjoyments in the most favorable way, had so distributed his purchasing power as to get those kinds and amounts of services which afford him the highest possible sum of enjoyment.

Differences in wages persist

In this situation the real wages of some being so much more than those of others, the low-paid workers will have a motive to change their occupations. But the various laborers have limited abilities and cannot change at will and, despite the unfavorable ratio, they may be compelled to continue at the same work. Just as apples cannot become peaches or sheep become horses when there is a change in their price, so the unskilled workman cannot become skilled quickly, if he ever can, and the possibility of changing occupations within any reasonable period is very small indeed. Labor is constantly trying to adjust itself, to get into the better-paid industries. It moves, it emigrates, it seeks training and education. Especially the workers between the ages of fifteen and twenty-five choose the callings that promise the highest reward. Within limits an adjustment is possible, but these limits are not wide and not quickly shifted, and the wages of labor continue diverse in different occupations for an indefinite time.

Various grades of labor and rates of wages

2. *The term general rate of wages can be used only of a certain grade of labor and of the rate for the average worker.* Every grade and kind of ability has its rate of wages. To be sure, it is sometimes convenient to speak in a broad but inexact way of "a general rate of wages," when comparing different countries and periods. When it is said that the rate of wages is higher in America than in England, in England than in France, in France than in India, the comparison is between men of the same occupation in the different countries; *e.g.*, the unskilled laborer or the mechanic gets more here than the same grade of laborer gets in England. There is no such thing as a general rate of wages extending throughout all industries.

The different grades of ability differ more markedly in wages than do industries compared as wholes. In the manufacture of cloth all grades of ability are required, from the highly paid artist and engineer, down to the roustabout in the yard. The industries of manufacturing, commerce, and education alike require the coöperation of bookkeepers, janitors, carpenters, and superintendents. It is easy in most cases to pass from any grade of occupation in one industry to a corresponding grade in another industry; but it is difficult to pass from a lower grade to a higher grade in the same or another industry.

Equilibrium of services and wages

Abstractly considered, that is, wherever free competition exists, there is a constant tendency toward a state of equilibrium; each workman is moving into the industry where he earns the highest possible amount, and where he receives just what his fellow-men estimate his importance to be, judged by the service he performs. Each man's place is determined by his specific gravity, just as the place of liquids poured into a glass is determined by their density. There is much reason to believe that this condition is approached actually in a far greater degree than is thought by those who come to the question with preconceived notions of what ought to be, or of what they would like to see. This principle of the economic wage does not preclude the questioning of the justice of existing institutions, but it is a guide in the discussion of all practical problems of wages.

Wages follow the law of marginal valuation

3. *The law of wages may be stated thus: in any state of the labor market the wages of any labor or class of labor is equal to its marginal contribution—that is, to the value of its products.* Each agent in industry, whether it be a plough, a horse, or a man, is valued in connection with other agents, never apart or isolated. It is not the total service any one of them performs that can be got at; all that can be got at is the utility attributed to the last unit of supply. Their marginal contribution determines their importance. Each agent is considered in combination with other things at a given moment under existing conditions of supply.

Wages exemplify the general law of value

This statement of the law of wages is broad, and appears to be modified in many ways in practice: by changes in industry, by ignorance on the part of the worker, by unequal skill in bargaining; but the law of wages just stated allows for these modifications, and is a guide amid the complexity of facts, for it gives a place to the influence of trade unions, caste, and everything else that affects the labor-supply. The law of wages is but the general law of value, working itself out amid the special conditions accompanying the gratification of wants by human effort.

Chapter XXIV
The Relation of Labor to Value

§ I.   Relation of Rent to Wages

Concrete conditions of industry must be studied with wages

1. *The law of wages must be considered in connection with other far-reaching influences.* One may use the sentence, "the marginal productivity of labor determines wages," without having a true understanding of its meaning. Memorizing a definition is only the first step toward economic reasoning. Till that definition becomes a real thing in the student's thought it helps him but little. The law of wages is an abstract statement of the logical relation of wages to utility; it is not a concrete statement of the industrial conditions in which labor works, yet these are more nearly in the nature of true causes of value. The marginal utility is itself determined by forces and conditions outside of labor that are constantly changing. The more thorough is the student's knowledge of the actual conditions of industry, the more correctly he can apprehend the relations of wages to other incomes, and the more wisely he will apply the abstract law to practical life.

Productivity of labor and diminishing returns of natural agents

2. *The marginal productivity of labor is affected by the relative abundance and efficiency of natural resources.* If land suddenly becomes more abundant through the opening up of new continents, the lower grades of agents are sooner or later abandoned. Labor having more of a choice as to the place where it is to be used, spreads itself over the better grades and takes on a greater marginal productivity. The marginal unit of labor working on better soil than before produces more, and wages expressed in produce are higher. Ground rent, on the other hand, is less under these conditions. If, however, the land is fixed in area, and population increases, no other change taking place, the principle of diminishing returns applies. The marginal laborers (the last arrivals or the growing generation) being compelled to work with less efficient resources on a poorer quality of land, produce less than was the rule before, and a smaller product therefore is attributed to all the laborers of that grade. They get lower wages and more goes as rent to the owners of the

THE RELATION OF LABOR TO VALUE 159

land. By shifting of occupations this reduction may be somewhat moderated and equalized among the workers in other industries. In both these cases, wages vary more than does the physical amount of the total product. In the first case, wages are a larger proportion of a larger product; in the second case, the product is larger (there being more laborers) but wages are a smaller proportion of it.

The iron law of wages

3. *The unwarranted assumption that a disproportionate increase in population is sure to occur, gave rise to the subsistence theory, or iron law of wages.* This assumption is now seen not to correspond with what is occurring in the civilized world. A hundred years ago, however, when the poorer classes of Europe appeared to be increasing with little restraint, it was not strange that thinkers should look upon this increase as inevitable. According to the subsistence theory, the question of population was simply a question of food; it was believed that men surely would multiply up to the point where they could not further increase their numbers, and starvation wages would be the rule. It was this way of looking at things that gave to political economy the name of the dismal science. When population is limited in large measure by volitional means instead of by war, starvation, and other material means, the problem changes and the error in such a theory of wages becomes clear.

The standard of living, and wages

The "standard of living" theory of wages is a refined form of the subsistence theory. This theory is that wages must rise to meet the cost of any standard that the laborers may set, and below which they will refuse to multiply. This is probably a fragmentary truth, but is quite inadequate as a theory. A high standard of living and all the social institutions and customs that aid in keeping the population from too rapid increase, are factors in determining ultimately the marginal productivity of labor and, hence, the height of wages. If these restraining influences suddenly were withdrawn, a reduction of wages would follow slowly because of the diminishing returns of material agents. But the standard of living is merely a partial and negative factor. No limitation of the number of workers can raise wages above their productive contribution and, in the present state of industry, a considerable falling off in population might be expected to result in a loss of enterprise, of coöperation, and of capital. The positive factor in wages is productivity.

If labor increases faster than wealth, wages fall

4. *An increase of population more rapid than that of the artificial industrial agents would reduce marginal productivity.* Labor makes use of many kinds of agents besides the so-called natural resources. If population is stationary while tools are allowed to wear out or if an increasing population, while opening up a proportionate supply of land for food, fails to accumulate a proportionate stock of other tools, the marginal productivity of labor must diminish. Labor would be more imperfectly equipped with spades, hoes, wagons, horses, cattle, machinery.

These artificial agents help in getting not only manufactured products, but food products. The equipment of labor must keep pace with the number of workers or they will be forced to the lower, or less effective, uses in the tools. On the other hand, the growth of science and invention, and the growth of wealth faster than the population, equipping labor as it does with more efficient implements, cause the marginal productivity of labor to rise, and hence also the wages.

The wage-fund theory explained

5. *The "wage-fund theory" was an imperfect perception of this truth that wages are influenced by the efficiency of the industrial equipment.* As the subsistence theory took a partial view, looking at agricultural land alone as the determinant of wages, so the wage-fund theory looked alone at a portion of the capital in the hands of employers which was the fund from which wages were paid. The large part played in discussion by this doctrine and the strong hold it had on thought is somewhat puzzling now; for if one begins to doubt its entire truth it is difficult to be quite just to its merits or to state it in a form that is plausible. The theory was that wages depended on the amount of capital that, in some way not clearly seen, was set apart by employers for the payment of wages. The capital making up the fund out of which wages were supposed to be paid, was only a very small part of all capital, even in the narrow sense in which that term was then used. It was assumed that this wage fund, once set aside, was necessarily paid out to laborers, wages being therefore determined by simple division: laborers were the divisor, the wage fund the dividend, and the average wage the result. When the theory is thus baldly expressed, it appears to begin and end on the surface of the facts; and the wage fund appears to be rather the arithmetic sum of variously determined payments than, in any sense, the cause of wages.

The wage-fund theory a partial truth

The abler wage-fund theorists did not fail at times to see, though too dimly, as the determining causes behind the employers' action, certain other things, such as the material facilities, the desires of consumers, the capabilities of the workers, and the resulting value of the labor. The element of truth which still should be recognized in this theory is that the relation of labor to its equipment influences its efficiency, and determines the part of the product to be set aside for wages. In that sense, wages are related to the abstinence of capitalists and to the supply of "capital," but capital understood not as a special fund of the employers, but, in a broader sense, as labor's entire environment of indirect agents.

§ II. Relation of Time-value to Wages

Labor may be near or far, in time, from gratifications

1. *The services of labor, whether for one's self or others, have a more or less immediate*

THE RELATION OF LABOR TO VALUE

relation in time to the gratifying of wants. While all human efforts to which the term services is applied have a relation to wants, there is much diversity in their nearness to the gratification for which they are destined. The process may be technically roundabout, to use the language of recent economists. One may break a stick from a tree, pick up a stone and drill a hole in it, catch an animal, cut thongs, tie the handle to the stone, and use it as a weapon to kill other animals for food, the first step being taken with the last object in view. But a still more essential relation we have seen to be the relation in time. Some things, some goods, are used at once, some after a long interval; some are durable, others perishable. Labor produces a song or a glass of lemonade to be consumed on the instant; it is employed on bridges, monuments, railroads, or interoceanic canals lasting for centuries. In all these cases the general object sought is the same though very different intervals of time must elapse before the gratification matures.

All future products of labor are discounted to their present value

2. *As different periods of time must elapse before services are enjoyed, the expected value of all products but those immediately available is discounted in advance.* The services that afford gratification immediately, and those that afford gratification at a later time, are judged and compared at one and the same moment. All economic life centers in the present. This difference in the time of services surely cannot be ignored. If Robinson Crusoe, at work on his island with his limited supply of energy, continues to provide for next year's enjoyment, neglecting the present, present goods become scarce and their utility rises as compared with the future goods the same labor secures. To escape inconvenience, and in the extremest case to escape starvation, Crusoe would be compelled to restore the equilibrium between the wants of the two periods by shifting his labor back to the present. So in each little economic group and in our complex society there is constant rivalry of present and future wants, competing for the limited present supply of labor. The present says, "Give me your labor and I will give you the fullest enjoyment." The future says, "I will give you a greater gratification, but you must wait for it." A given labor force thus making possible a wide range of choice among present and future services, labor is distributed according to the prevailing rate of time-value, which, as we have seen, is approximately expressed by the rate of interest. If the rate of interest is high, it means that the present is urgent and will not easily yield to the future. If the rate is low, it implies that the present is comparatively well provided for, and that future wants are given more consideration.

The employer adjusts his labor force to the interest rate

3. *The employer in hiring labor and producing goods takes account of these time differences.* In the preceding paragraph has been noted the influence of time differences in the simplest problem of economic wages. Interest is likewise taken account of in the bargains between workman and employer, by which contract wages are fixed. The employer of labor works subject to a prevailing rate of interest. If he ignores it he must lose. He should direct a given amount of labor to products that mature next year only when their expected selling price is greater

than that of products that can be marketed this year. This difference due to time can no more be ignored than can any other difference in the cost of products. If the employer keeps the future goods to sell later, they will normally increase in value as they approach maturity; if he markets the goods at once, he normally must pass on to the purchaser the benefit of the discount he has made on their future value. That is to say, it is not the employer of labor, the purchaser of labor as such, who gains by discounting the future value of labor; it is the investor of capital (whether employer or later purchaser) who secures the rent as it matures.

The discount of the future value of services is inevitable

4. *Hence all wages paid for help on products that are remote are based on the present worth, or discounted value, of the future gratification to which the labor contributes.* The idea is held in one form or another by all radical socialistic writers, that the laborer does not get the full value of his products. In the sense that is here discussed, he does not. He does not get what the product will sell for in the future. He gets the probable future value at its present worth, discounted at the prevailing rate. That part of the employer's gains corresponding to this discount on labor is economic time-value.

Nor is this discount of future services dependent on a political system or on private property or on the wage system, as some have assumed. It is a universal truth. It is in the nature of wants that present and future should differ. A communistic or socialistic state would have to take account of this difference, else the whole social economy would be irrational and there would be no principle by which to apportion in time the productive forces of the community. Contracts to pay interest and contracts to pay wages might be forbidden and made criminal by formal law, but time-value would persist.

Relations of wages, rent, and time-value

5. *Wages and rent are coördinate species of the value problem; time-value is a different kind of problem, bearing to both the other problems a similar relation.* A close examination of the problems of rent and wages serves to bring out the close parallelism of these two forms of income as here defined. Rent is the value of the usufruct of wealth, wages are the value of the usufruct of labor. The bearer of the use in one case is material goods, in the other is human agents. Different in the source of use, they are in large measure alike in the form of contract, or nature of the calculation. Together rent and wages comprise the value of all currently arising uses; they are the two coördinate species of the genus "value of uses." The two groups of uses are closely interrelated in practice, each acting and reacting on the value of the other.

Time-value is a different genus of the value problem. Having to do with time differences, it must be found in connection with every use that is not immediate, whatever be the bearer of that use. Its application to rent is more frequent and obvious, as only the uses of material agents are capitalized, that is, sold in perpetuity. Moreover any service of labor that is not at once consumed is fixed

§ III. The Relation of Labor to Value

Several conditions of value

1. *Labor is a cause, but only one of the causes of value.* A cause is some one condition which is seen to be necessary to the existence of a thing, and usually that condition which brings the thing about, other things being assumed. In what sense ought a cause of value be spoken of? In one sense it is in the minds of men—it is their wants; again, looked at objectively it is in the nature of the good—it is the quality that fits it to gratify the want. But if both these causes are operative, and labor is applied to fit goods better to gratify wants, labor appears as the cause of value. Personal causes are so much more evident, an explanation through personal causation is so much more satisfying in the earlier stages of scientific inquiry, that labor long continued to be looked upon as the one source of value. This erroneous view has never quite ceased to influence economic thought, and a great deal of effort has been directed to formulating theories of value based upon it. The cruder form of the error has now almost disappeared, but in various little recognized ways it still persists.

Two phases of economic production

2. *Economic production is the origin, or genesis, of value finding its source either in objective things or in services.* The writers of fifty years ago defined economic production as the application of labor to the creation of wealth. But as there are two factors in production, man and material things, so there are two productive sources of value. In some cases the origin of value is attributable to man's action; in other cases scarce uses arise in objective things without man's action. Broad as is this definition of production, it does not include the enjoyment of free goods, as in the case of the care-free darky basking in the sun. Anything that, causing a feeling of greater importance to attach to a thing, changes it from a free good to a scarce good or makes it more scarce, is a cause of its value. A large rainfall causing a greater crop of grain may be thought of as producing utility. The regular surplus of value attributable to the waterfall or to the railroad, is the product of the material services of wealth. Production through human action is the more obvious and is the more usually thought of; the part of material agents must be recognized if the fallacies of the labor theory of value are to be avoided.

Labor applied to creating utility

3. *Human activity is directed to shaping and arranging things so as to increase their want-gratifying power.* Human and non-human agents are combined in different proportions in various products. In one thing more land and machinery are used,

in another more labor is used. But either of these two great classes of agents may touch the vanishing point in the production of value. While it is true that man's part is the most striking aspect of production, yet there may be value without labor. The study of rent puts this abstractly, but in a clear light. In actual life, however, a part of the value is usually attributable to rent, a part to labor.

Value of labor derived from its products

But in what sense is even this part attributable? Not in the sense that the labor is the original source of value which imparts that value to its products. The usufruct of wealth is the basis of rent; the need to pay rent is not the cause of value in the product. Likewise, product is the basis of wages, labor is not the origin of value. Labor, like the forces and qualities of wealth, is the cause of technical changes. These changes, if favorable, cause the goods to take on a higher value which is reflected back to the labor. The labor itself has not a predetermined, ascertainable value, but only a resultant, derived value. An exception to this statement appears on a superficial view of the value of labor hired under the wage contract to make a particular product. The labor having a market value because of a large number of well-known alternate uses, can be diverted to a particular use only on condition of a definite payment. Labor here, as viewed by the employer, appears to have an original value; products, a derived value. But in the logical view, labor is seen to impart technical qualities to the goods; in turn, the goods to impart value to the labor. Man hunts throughout industry for those things to which his labor can be applied usefully. He foresees in them the changes that will increase the value. It is only as he has judged rightly that the value taken on by the things is reflected back to the labor attributed to it.

No unit of labor to serve as a standard of value

4. *Labor being of many qualities and receiving many rates of pay, there is no unit of labor that can be used as a measure of value.* The idea of finding in a "unit of labor" an objective standard of value to which the value of all other things could be reduced has been a very attractive one. This fallacious hope animates every one beginning to think of the value problem. The thought was so plausibly formulated by Ricardo that it continued for a long time to be the generally accepted doctrine of value. Although most writers reject the formal statement of the labor theory of value, use is frequently made, even now, of the phrase "unit of labor," suggesting the thought that labor is the standard by which the value of all goods may be measured. This unit of labor of the text-books may be seen to be either labor arbitrarily assumed to be of uniform quality and quantity, as a day of unskilled labor (in that form quite incomparable as to amount with other qualities), or a given amount of money invested in labor of different grades at its market value. It is only by expressing labor in terms of its value that the various grades of skilled and unskilled labor can be reduced to a homogeneous unit, which is but a unit of money wages. This should not deceive us into the belief that in any peculiar sense labor can be used as a unit of value. It is equally valid and convenient to speak of units of machinery and of units of land. In terms of capital a factory site can be expressed as a multiple

THE RELATION OF LABOR TO VALUE   165

of a potato patch not less perfectly than can a sculptor's labor as a multiple of a ditch-digger's.

Scarcity and utility of labor

Scarcity of things desired is the one objective condition of value. The things that labor can produce and the labor to produce them being scarce, labor takes on a value. All things at last become comparable in terms of psychic income in each individual's judgment, but as yet neither in this comparison nor in the market values that are fixed in exchange, has any absolute standard been found by which the utility of all goods or the welfare of all men can be measured.

Chapter XXV
The Wage System and its Results

§ I. Systems of Labor

The wage system defined

Never the exclusive form of organization

1. *The wage system is the organization of industry wherein some men, owning and directing capital, buy at their competitive value the services of men without capital.* The wage system is a method of organization never found completely realized. A community made up entirely of independent small farmers, living each on his little patch of ground, does not have any essential feature of the wage system. So long as they continue to be independent small farmers, owners of small capital, self-employing workers, the wage system does not exist in complete form. Some men with capital in every community are working for wages, while others, as independent producers, are their own employers. Society is not sharply divided into two classes, one controlling all the working capital, the other quite without resources. The wage system may be spoken of as prevailing to-day not as the exclusive, but as the typical, or dominant, form, while side by side or along with it is found independent production. It is clear that the wages here spoken of are contract wages. The wage system implies a money contract between employer and employed. The relation or bond between them is that of a wage payment.

The wage system cannot be judged properly apart from questions to be later considered, such as private property and the enterpriser's part in industry; but some consideration of the subject properly belongs here. The wage system has become of recent years in America the dominant form of industry. The theory of wages is applied most frequently in the discussion of contract wages, and there are certain practical relations between the results of the wage system and the theory of wages.

Workers subordinate in early societies

2. *The wage system, historically considered, is seen not to have displaced a system*

of independent labor. This question should be viewed in historical perspective. As far back as history can be traced, the masses of workers have been subordinate. Civilization began with direction, with obedience to superiors on the part of the mass of men. Within the family, in the rudest tribes, the women and children were subject to the will of the stronger, the head of the family. Among the Aryan races the family system was widened, and the patriarch of the tribe secured personal obedience and economic service from all members of the community. Chattel slavery, the typical form of industrial organization in early tropical civilization, seems to have been one of the necessary steps to progress from rude conditions; students to-day incline to view it as an essential stage in the history of the race. But as conditions changed with industrial development, chattel slavery became a hindrance to progress, a disadvantage to higher industry.

Place of the workers in the Middle Ages

3. *Serfdom for rural labor and many limitations on the workman's freedom in the towns, were the prevailing conditions in medieval Europe.* Serfdom was both a political and an economic relation. The serf was bound to the soil; the lord could command and control him; but the serf's obligations were pretty well defined. He had to give services, but in return for them he got something definite in the form of protection and the use of land. Between the lord and the serf continued a lifelong contract, which passed by inheritance from father to son, in the case both of the master and of the serf. In the towns conditions were better for the skilled workmen, but many things bore heavily on the mass of the workers shut out from special privileges. There were strict rules of apprenticeship; gild regulations forbidding the free choice of a trade or a residence; laws against immigration; settlement laws making it impossible for poor men to remove from one place to another; arbitrary regulation of wages, either by the gilds in the towns or by national councils and parliaments, forbidding the workmen to take the competitive wages that economic conditions forced the employers to pay; combination laws forbidding laborers to combine in their own interest. It is not an attractive picture, but, as far as is possible in a few words, it is a truthful picture of the conditions that existed before the coming of the modern system.

The wage system not the main cause of present evils

4. *Many continuing limitations on the freedom of the worker are not the results of the wage system or a part of it, but are opposed to its complete workings.* The worker's ignorance is a limitation, preventing the choice of an occupation for which he might naturally be fitted. Neglect of children by parents is a limitation, preventing industrial training and the development of qualities that would make it possible for the child to excel. The faults of human nature cannot be attributed to any "system"; and if they are remediable, it is by education and better social opportunity. Trade unions often forbid boys to become apprentices, and forbid the choice of a trade except under conditions so exacting that to many they are impossible. Such limitations are made by the privileged few in their own interest, but they are annoying and opposed to the interests of the many. The typical wage

system would be one in which all such hindrances were lacking, in which there were no social or political limitations on free competition except such as would help in educating and training the worker. The wage system should be judged by what it is, not by things directly opposed to its spirit.

§ II. The Wage System as it Is

Merits and faults of the definite wage payment

1. *Under the wage contract the worker gets in a definite sum at once the market value of his services.* Under the wage contract the employer takes the risk as to the future selling price of the product. That he is the one best prepared to assume the risk will be made clearer in the discussion of the employer's function. Wage payment, therefore, is a form of insurance to the workingman; he gets something definite instead of taking chances he is ill prepared to take. Wage payment is a form of credit to the laborer whose labor has not yet produced the distant gratification. The employer advances to the workman the value of the future gratification, discounting it at the prevailing rate of interest. The darker side of the wage bargain is that the "cash nexus," as Carlyle expressed it, is too often the only bond between the parties. When the wages are paid, the employer considers his obligations discharged. There is a lack of fellowship and sympathy in it all. Work should be a bond of communion between men, but as it is, the laborers in some great factories and their employers live in entirely different worlds. The great inequality of their condition makes mutual understanding difficult. They are master and man, "boss" and hireling, not co-workers, each with a worthy part in the noble tasks of industry.

Strength and weakness of the worker in competition

2. *The wage-earner gets the competitive value of his services, securing in most cases much more than a bare subsistence.* At the present time competition is in a large measure active among employed as well as among employers. A believer in the subsistence theory of wages must, under these conditions, expect wages to fall to the starvation level. But according to the law of wages here presented, it is to be expected that wages can and will remain indefinitely above that level, falling or rising as conditions change. The increase in material wealth of itself tends to increase the wages of the workman. The laborer, though without resources and even though not contributing to the increase of capital by saving, thus shares in the benefit of increasing capital. It is true that under some conditions the workman is at a disadvantage in making the wage contract; labor must be applied from day to day or it is lost, and the laborer must work to live. While this does not determine the rate of wages in the long run in any occupation nor to any great extent except among the lowest grades of labor, it does give an advantage for the moment to the employer, and enables him to exercise at times a harsh power over the workmen in his immediate neighborhood. A single workman is thus very

often at a disadvantage, but it must not be overlooked that in a large degree the competition for good workmen is effective between employers in different trades and in distant localities.

Wages as affecting the ambition of the worker

3. *Increase of efficiency due to the sacrifice of parents or to personal exertion, goes to the individual worker.* The most essential practical feature in any industrial system is the appeal to the ambition of each man. This appeal is made where a premium is placed on increasing efficiency, by insuring to it a higher return. This result is possible and in large measure is attained under the wage system. Little less important is the appeal to family affection to make possible by its sacrifices each worker's best preparation.

An offsetting disadvantage appears in the loss to the laborer in the decline of his powers. As he gains in wages if he increases in efficiency, so he loses if his strength fails from accident or in the course of years. This loss falls upon him, not, as is sometimes said to have been the case under serfdom or slavery, upon his owner (as if that secured to the slave immunity from suffering). It is true that in general under the wage system the worker has no guarantee against loss of work or, what is equally important, against sudden changes in industry. He may be, and often is, a victim of invention and of changes in machinery or industrial processes, by which the masses of men are the gainers.

Large liberty of the wage-worker

4. *Liberty of the worker in his choice of work and outside of working hours makes for happiness, character, and progress.* Opinion is almost a unit as to the truth of this statement. The present wage system is the freest condition for the mass of men that ever has existed. Their religious, political, and personal convictions, are for the most part inviolate. There is a true but much misused maxim that liberty has its dangers. Freedom means freedom to make mistakes. Intelligence and strong industrial virtues are required to exercise properly a freedom newly acquired. Thus it is the lowest class of labor that reaps the smallest advantage from free conditions, and that suffers most from their misuse.

Limits to the worker's liberty

The main evil in the wage system is certainly not that the liberty of the worker is too great, but that it is too small. The sale of labor involves the obeying of orders during certain hours specified in the contract. Here again the evil is greatest in the lowest grades of work, while the great majority of wage-earners are left a large measure of choice in the time and manner of their work. Where labor is severe and without joy to the worker, it appears to be little better than a form of slavery. Contrast the condition of the section hand, cursed and beaten by a brutal foreman, with that of the wage-earner in the locomotive-cab, self-respecting, self-directing, and trusted with the safety of property and lives. The wage system is manifold, it is adaptable. If it holds a portion of the laborers with a harsh hand, it gives to all a wide measure of opportunity, and to most a great degree of independence in their lives. A hasty resort to indiscriminating analogy, as in calling wage-work "slavery," does not further truth or social justice.

§ III. Progress of the Masses under the Wage System

The rise of money wages

1. *The nineteenth century was a period of great progress for the masses in America, England, and throughout Europe.* There are differences of opinion as to the extent of this progress, the way in which it is to be measured, and the degree to which it is an occasion for congratulation. There is no longer any dispute as to the actual fact that it has taken place. Many lines of evidence converge to confirm this one conclusion. The average money wages in the United States may be represented in 1840 by 87.7, in 1860 by 100, and in 1891 by 161.2. This was the high mark for a time and a decline followed. Again wages rose from 1897 on, and in 1899 had reached 163.2. They have continued to rise since and in 1903 attained the highest point in the history of our country and therefore in the history of the world. Another temporary decline undoubtedly will occur when industrial conditions become less prosperous.

Changes in real wages

Real wages, also, the power to purchase goods with labor, are greater than ever before so far as this can be measured in the price of leading commodities. The offsetting loss of the free health-giving pleasures of country life cannot easily be expressed. In England likewise the rise in money wages has been great. In 1860 it is represented by 100, in 1870 by 113, in 1880 by 125, in 1891 by 140, in the intervals some decline occurring. For a century in all civilized lands wages have moved in an ever-rising series of waves. The purchasing power of wages in England increased ninety per cent, in the thirty years between 1860 and 1891. Throughout Europe the same general change is seen, going always hand in hand with new industrial methods and the displacing of the old agricultural system by the wage system. As the hours of labor have at the same time been shortened, the workers have gained doubly.

Need of a broad explanation of rising wages

2. *This progress is mainly due to the opening up of rich natural resources and to the development of industrial processes.* Recognized in some measure by every one, this progress is attributed by different observers to different causes: in America, by many to the protective tariff; in England, by many to the freer trade introduced about 1840; throughout the continent of Europe, to the spread of constitutional government and free institutions; by trade-unions everywhere, to the organization of labor. There is, doubtless, under certain conditions, some portion of truth in

THE WAGE SYSTEM AND ITS RESULTS 171

each of these claims. But, either separately or altogether, they fall short of a broad, reasonable, and sufficient explanation. The two-fold proposition just presented, the justification for which has been given in preceding chapters, points to a general and adequate cause.

The gloomy view as to the wage system was mistaken

Seventy-five years ago it was thought that, with the increase of machinery, of factories, of the concentrated control of wealth, and especially with the wage system, there must go a steady depression in the welfare of the workingman. This idea was connected with the iron law of wages. It was believed by some that, whatever the causes of advancing social income might be, the wage system would rob the wage-earners of all share in progress. In view of the facts, if it cannot now be asserted positively that the wage system is the cause of all the gain, it can be asserted negatively that it is not inconsistent with great progress on the part of the laboring classes. It might be possible to go further and to maintain that the organization of industry, under the wage system and competitive conditions, by its encouragement of enterprise, energy, and economy, has been an indispensable condition in the industrial progress which has in turn made possible the rising wages of labor.

More workers now in better-paid callings

3. *The increased proportion of workers in the higher occupations means a further rise in the average condition of the masses.* A smaller proportion of workers is now engaged in the low-paid industries than fifty years ago, and a correspondingly larger proportion is in the better, or highly paid, industries. Decade by decade the proportion shifts toward the upper part of the scale. Both in America and in England (doubtless also in other countries) more men are now engaged in the higher professions and skilled occupations, a smaller proportion in the lower occupations. This would raise the average of wages even if the wages of particular occupations had not risen.

The masses gain by general social advance

4. *The diffused advantages of progress mean relatively more to the masses than to the rich.* In the olden days the poor man was bound to the spot where he lived, the rich man had his carriage; to-day poor and rich ride side by side in the trolley car. The introduction of these cheap methods of enjoyment means relatively more to the poor. Better medical care, better sanitation, more abundant food, clothing, comfort, free schools, and libraries have all a part in this movement. The enormous possibilities in these lines are just beginning to be realized. The achievements of the last twenty years read like a story from fairy-land. It tells the leveling up of the conditions enjoyed by the common man.

Better social conditions must grow out of the wage system
Improvement in the wage system

5. *Any sound method of improving social conditions must grow out of experience, not break with it.* Even if things were on the downward instead of the upward road there would be no excuse for wild speculation. The only rational way is to find what is good in what is, and build upon it. There can be no excuse for suggesting a method from imagination. Projects of social change must be tried by successful experiment, and gradually fitted to present needs. It is in this way that the higher forms of life have developed; it is in this way that social and political institutions have come into being. Things that work successfully first in a small way are worthy of trial on a larger scale. The wage system is a favorite object of attack for radical social reformers. It has many unlovely features and there are many individual cases of hardship. It may well be asked, What method shall be pursued to reform it? Its retention, however, is not inconsistent with very great changes in the present political and economic arrangements. The impersonal economic forces are working for improvement; but further, there is a growth of sentiment, an increase in sympathy, a feeling among men that the "cash nexus" is not the only bond that should unite different classes, and this sympathy is becoming an economic force, softening and improving many of the most unlovely features of the modern wage system.

Chapter XXVI
Machinery and Labor

§ I. Extent of the Use of Machinery

Tools, machines, and power

1. *A machine is a mechanical device by which power is applied in an automatically repeated manner, to change the place or form of things.* It is not easy, perhaps not important, to distinguish the machine from the tool in every case. Tools are portions of matter, such as bone, wood, iron, which man guides and directs in applying his energy to things. A machine may be used by the foot, but the hand is the great tool-using member. In many cases there is a clearly marked distinction between tool and machine. A simple, single piece that can be taken into the hand, as a spade, a hammer, a knife, is a tool; a combination of wheels, levers, pulleys, etc., is a machine. The simplest machine is but a slight adaptation of the tool, by which power may be applied in an automatically repeated manner. The drag develops into the cart, a simple machine. The spinning-stick, a tool used in ancient times, developed into the Saxon spinning-wheel of the sixteenth century, the form used when America was colonized. The use of power derived from nature, as that of wind and water and steam, while not the essential mark of machines, is the most characteristic feature of their modern development. Hand-machines, such as the hand-press and the type-writer, have had important industrial results, but it is the use of power leading to the concentration of industry and the ownership of machinery by the employers that has the greatest significance in the modern economic problem.

Machinery brought in an industrial revolution

2. *Machinery of many sorts has long been used, but the "age of machinery" begins with the eighteenth century.* Inventions, new machines, and new processes, though not frequent, were not unknown in the Middle Ages; but no one class of machines took possession of a whole field of industry and gave rise to a great economic problem by the displacing of labor. The great industrial changes in the Middle Ages generally grew out of political changes, or of changes of routes of trade

whereby large industries were disturbed, or of changes in the use of land through new methods and the bringing into use of land in other places. The industrial changes in England at the end of the eighteenth century on the contrary were due mainly to great mechanical inventions. The development of the textile machines for cotton and wool spinning and weaving mark the beginning of the movement. Here for the first time were inventions in such numbers, of such a nature, and under such conditions, that they were rapidly and widely applied, affecting the lives of a great number of workers. The steam-engine at the same time opened up the long line of mechanical inventions by which wood and iron are shaped and wrought, and the iron industry underwent notable developments. Since that time, have taken place in all Western countries that rapid expansion in the use of machines and those notable changes in industrial organization which distinguish our era from all others.

Increased use of power

3. *Machinery is applicable in very different degrees to the different processes and industries.* Machinery can save much labor in some directions, little or none in others. It is especially adapted to the application of power. In the United States, in 1870, in manufactures alone, two and one third million horse-power were used; in 1900, eleven and one third million, the increase being five-fold. It is said that in the world, in 1870, three and one half million horse-power was furnished by stationary engines, ten millions by locomotives. Probably to-day the total is four-fold as great.

Machines can best be used in manufactures

Machinery is applicable with especial advantage to industries that change the form of materials easily transported and widely used. There must be a large output to justify the use of machinery. In 1840 a man's work in spinning cotton was three hundred and twenty times as effective as in 1769, in 1855 it was seven hundred times; and though the rate of improvement is diminishing, to-day the productivity of such labor is still greater. Similar examples are found in the manufacture of shoes, and in all varieties of wood- and iron-work. Machinery is most applicable where there is a compact plant; not so easily where the power has to be distributed over a wide area, unless a special track can be provided.

Not to so great an extent in agriculture

Machinery, therefore, has affected manufactures much more immediately and greatly than it has agriculture. It has not as yet, for example, been found practicable to apply steam to ploughing to any great extent. As the profitable use of most farm machinery requires a level surface and a large area given to a single crop, it cannot be used as well east of the Alleghany Mountains as in the Mississippi Valley, and it is still uneconomical in large portions of the civilized world. Despite this difficulty the methods of the farmer of to-day contrast strongly with those of one hundred or fifty years ago. Planters and seeders, reapers, harvesters, corn-shellers, hay-loaders, automatic unloading-forks, elevators, water-power-, steam-, and gasoline-engines allow great economies. The labor needed to produce food for one hundred people is a fraction of what it was one hundred years ago. In many other industries machines are usable only in a slight measure, indirectly, or not at all. They are of the least assistance in the personal services, and in the work of the thinker, the teacher, the speaker, and the artist.

§ II. Effect of Machinery on the Welfare and Wages of the Masses

Evil of sudden introduction of machinery

1. *The immediate effect of improved machinery, if suddenly introduced, is almost always to throw some men out of employment.* Any sudden change in industry injures men who have become adapted to the work that is affected. A well-mastered trade, a wage-earning though intangible possession, may be made suddenly valueless. Men cannot quickly change their methods of working or their place of work. This is as true of change brought about by new trade routes or by scientific discoveries (where machinery does not enter in) as in the case of labor-saving machines. If machines displace labor rapidly, men who cannot adjust themselves to the new conditions suffer, and there are always some who cannot adjust themselves, always some who suffer. It is rarely possible for a man past middle life to shift over into a new trade where his efficiency will be as great and his pay as high as in the old. New methods of puddling iron sent many old men into the poorhouses of Pennsylvania only a few years ago. Even where the total employment increases, the individual sometimes suffers. The increased demand resulting from the cheapening of a product may call for more workers than were employed before the new machinery came in, and yet some of the former workmen may be thrown out of employment. The introduction of the linotype is said to have displaced a large number of hand type-setters, but to have increased greatly the amount of printing. As the machines are expensive and cannot be worked properly by men not highly expert, men past thirty-five years of age have not been allowed to learn their use.

Loss falls on the less efficient workers

The least efficient men in any trade always suffer most. The change crushes hardest the man at the margin of employment. The more skilled workman can hasten his pace and still earn a living wage in competition with a machine, while the less skilled can but drop out entirely, innocent victims of an economic change, sacrifices to the cause of industrial progress. Happily such pathetic incidents are relatively not numerous. Most machinery is introduced in commercial centers, and gradually spreads to other factories in such a way that most men can adapt themselves to the change. The effect of machinery must not be judged by the extreme cases. It was found that there were more hand-looms in use in England in 1850 than fifty years before, though in the meantime power-looms had displaced the hand-looms in all the great factories.

Error of the "lump of labor" notion

2. *After time for adjustment, the total sum of employment is as great as before, but the labor is differently distributed.* The "lump of labor" idea, as it is called, is widely held, especially among workingmen. The notion is that there is exactly so much labor predetermined to be done; therefore, if machines are introduced, there is that much less for men to do. The logical conclusion easily drawn is that every machine reduces wages. Few, however, would go on to the further conclusion that in the aggregate the existing machinery, like an enormous vampire, is sucking the life-blood of the working-people,—though traces of such a notion frequently appear.

Effect of machinery varies in different industries

If extreme examples are taken, it may be made to appear either that an increase or that a decrease of employment results from machinery. Industries grade off from those that are capable of developing a greater and greater demand, to those at the other extreme that are capable of a very slight increase, as a result of a lowering of the price. There seems to be practically no limit to the consumption of textiles, provided their price falls; the demand for dress alone is indefinitely expansible. Queen Elizabeth, who had a different dress for every day in the year, has many potential imitators. There is a constant increase relatively, as well as absolutely, in the number employed in transportation, as each census shows; there are more railroad men relatively than there were stage-drivers and teamsters before the day of railroads. The number of people now engaged in printing books and papers is larger by far than in the days when all the books of the world were written by the old monks in their cloisters. The proportion of workers in agriculture, on the other hand, is less than it formerly was. In part this is a change in appearance only, for the farmer once made a large part of his tools which are now made by workers employed in manufactures, yet who in a very real way are aiding in agriculture. In part the change is, however, the effect of the use of machinery and other improvements in agricultural processes. The amount of raw-food products required for each hundred persons is quite inelastic. As it becomes possible to expend more for food, the change is made in quality, variety, flavor, rather than in quantity. The greater part of the saving in the cost of food is, however, expended in other products, and the labor saved in agriculture finds employment in supplying these rising wants. In other cases also, new industries are made possible as machines liberate energy from the production of the more necessary goods. At each census it is necessary to change the schedule of occupations, because men have adopted callings unknown before.

Abnormal effect of the new machinery in England

3. *In some cases the introduction of new machines injures particular workmen.* The

only reason for the use of machinery is to improve the quality or to lower the price of products. If the workers can do nothing but blindly pursue the same tasks, it is to be expected that the wages of hand-labor will fall in a particular trade into which machinery is suddenly introduced. When, as sometimes happens, employers introduce machines for the immediate purpose of breaking a strike, the workmen are convinced that machinery is the enemy of labor.

Because the extensive introduction of machinery in England was at first accompanied by the unhappy result of a lengthening of the hours of labor in factories, this result was deemed to be necessary in all other cases. It was in fact quite abnormal, and has not been seen elsewhere. The owners of factories wished to keep their machines employed as many hours as possible; the laboring classes of England, being at the same time demoralized and depressed by industrial and social influences that had no logical connection with machinery, had no power to resist this movement. In all other countries of Europe and in America, where the introduction of machinery has been more gradual and normal, it has been followed immediately by a shortening of working hours, as eventually it was in England also.

Higher wages logically result from the use of machinery

4. *Indeed, the economic effect of improved appliances is logically and inevitably to raise wages.* It has been shown above, in the discussion of wages, that if the efficiency of machines increases faster than does the number of workers who use them, the marginal application of labor stops at the higher uses or services of agents and is not forced to the lower. The more perfect the economic environment, the higher the incomes even of those who own no part of the machinery. A part of this benefit may appear in the form of higher money wages received, a part in the form of the lower price of things bought. Real wages are the essential thing, and as a consumer the laborer shares with every other member of society in the benefits of improved machinery. The benefits resulting from greater abundance are diffused, and as goods are brought from the high, or scarcity, end of the scale of value down toward the level of free goods, everybody gains by the abundance and cheapness.

Some grades gain more than others

The general, or average, gain is not to be judged by comparing the conditions of the lowest grade of society with those of fifty years ago, for while that grade may have been bettered only a little, it has been possible for large numbers to rise to higher grades because of the use of machinery. The physical tasks are to-day much lighter than ever before, and a larger proportion of society is engaged in industries that require skill and thought rather than physical labor. That portion of the work is being more and more shifted upon machines. It is important, though, to distinguish between classes of workers in judging of the benefits and evils of machines. A machine is "an iron man," it has been said, and comes into competition with other men to lower their wages by outworking and underbidding them. But this iron man can do only automatic tasks; it is not capable of exercising judgment. Every intelligent laborer who can adjust, adapt, fit himself for more intelligent action will rise above the machine and profit by its presence. But the crude physical labor which can compete only on the plane of automatic machines, must find its field of employment more and more hedged in. If the wages of unskilled labor are not depressed, it is because of the enterprise of others who rise to more skilled employments and thus reduce the competitors of the lowest rank.

The growth of factories

5. *The early effects of the factory system on the health, intelligence, and morals of the workers often have been bad; but not necessarily the abiding effects.* Some kinds of machines can be more profitably used when they are grouped in great factories, and, where this is common, it is spoken of as the factory system. In the ideal modern factory (realized in few cases) each smaller machine is a part of a larger organization of machinery, so perfect that the material goes in at one end of the building and out at the other without the loss of a single motion. Factories compel great numbers of laborers to live near each other and to work together. The sudden crowding together of people into new social relations is usually bad for morals. Men are moral under the eyes of their neighbors, acquaintances, and families; habits become adjusted to right standards, and the temptations in new conditions are always great. Until of late, engineering science has not been able to deal with the problems that arise where population is densely crowded, and the early factories with their surroundings were most unsanitary. Under the degrading conditions that resulted in some places, especially in England, the effect of machinery on the intelligence of the workers was bad. Whether this is its natural result is debatable, but the factory worker in general does not appear to be less intelligent than the agricultural worker. The alertness of the city dweller is due doubtless to social contact more than to the immediate work he does. This work may or may not be less thought-awakening than work with simple tools. There is a general improvement along all the lines of intelligence, morals, and health. The conditions in the cities as regards health and morals are approaching those of agricultural communities. While many factory districts are forlorn, there may be seen around many factories more happy conditions, better buildings, better sanitation, increased leisure for workers, workmen's clubs, educational agencies, and many other evidences of civic and social progress.

Problems of large industry

6. *The great social consequences flowing from the concentration of industry and wealth are the most serious problems in the relation of machinery to labor.* The ownership of tools was widely diffused in medieval times. It is not yet evident how many can own a share in great factories, but the control drifts into few hands. It is not yet clear what social effects great corporations will have on our democratic institutions. Many problems of large industry remain to be solved in the near future. The question in the old form, as to the effect of machinery on labor, is no longer open. It has been clearly answered by experience and explained by theory: the economic effect of machinery is to lift the productiveness and efficiency of the average man. The benefits are unequally distributed, but nearly all share in them

to some degree. The question which the future will have to answer is, What will be the social and political effects of the great fortunes that have been made possible by the enormous development of machinery?

Chapter XXVII
Trade-unions

§ I. The Objects of Trade-unions

Definition and purposes of trade-unions

1. *A trade-union is an association of wage-workers for purposes of mutual information, mutual help, and for the raising of wages.* The term trade-union is used in a general sense both of combinations of workers in the same trade, and of men in different trades, though usually the latter are called *labor*-unions. The "Knights of Labor" is a good example of the labor-union, the "American Federation of Labor" of a combination of trade-unions. The Knights of Labor is composed of local branches to which workers of every class except lawyers and saloon-keepers are admitted. The Federation of Labor, however, is composed of chapters, or lodges, that are homogeneous, all the men of each lodge being in the same trade.

The definition given is broad enough to include the various degrees of help given and the various methods adopted by trade-unions to accomplish their objects. Trade-unions are mutual-benefit associations: insurance against accident, sickness, death, or lack of employment, forms an important part, and in some cases almost the whole of their work. All unions in a measure serve their members as employment bureaus, while in some unions this is a most important feature. Through trade-papers, correspondence, and personal meetings, information is exchanged regarding trade conditions, and great mutual service is thus rendered. But a great deal of the help given is in the more impersonal economic ways: help to get from the employers better wages, to secure shorter hours, to improve in various ways the conditions of employment.

Lack of personal touch between employers and workmen

2. *The organization of workers has resulted from the separation of the economic and personal interests of employers and workmen.* The control of industry has become more concentrated during the age of machinery, and this has reduced the feeling of economic unity among the different ranks of industry. There is now to the average workman no possibility of becoming a master, an employer. The largeness

of industry forbids, moreover, the meeting and personal acquaintance of employer and workman which were before possible. Misunderstandings grow when men cannot talk over their differences. The social chasm has widened between the workmen and the responsible director of industry. As a result of these changes, the attitude of the employer very often has become that of the buyer of labor as a mere ware. He has with the mass of his employees no personal relations whatever. Under these conditions, when the employer feels the presence of competition, he is more likely to force the lowest wage that is possible. It is not unusual for the immediate direction of factories to be intrusted to paid managers, who are responsible to the stockholders and whose work is judged only by the dividends they succeed in earning. Many examples might be found where the managers or the resident owners have wished to pursue a more liberal policy than the absentee shareholders would permit.

Lack of personal acquaintance among workers

3. *The need of organization of labor has grown with the growth of factories and with the loss of personal touch among the workers.* This is another aspect of the point just mentioned. The smaller the number of employers, the easier is it by an understanding to suppress competition on their side. If there is only one factory of a kind in a town or city, the employer is able to drive a harder bargain with the worker. Especially in times of industrial depression is a change of employment difficult for the laborer; it involves much risk, and loss of time and money in moving. In the long run competition must be felt even in such cases. The unfair employer will find his workmen drifting away, his force reduced in number and quality, and his evil reputation going abroad among workmen. But there is a great deal of friction in this adjustment and the loss falls largely upon the workman. In a large industry, especially, the workers have no personal acquaintance with each other, nothing to give them a sense of unity and power. In the old-fashioned shop, with its close association and its interchange of views, could grow up a strong public opinion; but in the wilderness of a modern factory the worker may be unknown in name and character to the man who touches elbows with him. Moreover, in America differences in nationality and in speech among immigrant workers is often an effective factor in preventing the assertion of their interests. There is an analogy (though it is only an analogy) between these conditions and the political conditions that have led pure democracies to give way to representative governments. So long as a community is small and men know each other personally, there may be popular government, but when the number becomes larger the only way in which public opinion can be concentrated and made effective is by delegating the functions of government to representatives.

Main objects of trade-unions to-day

4. *The main objects of labor-unions to-day are to improve conditions in their working places, to maintain or increase wages, and to shorten working hours.* Better conditions of safety and sanitation in their work were not the first thought of the unions. The workers, as a result of habit and ignorance, were strangely unconcerned about this

matter. Reforms in this direction at the outset had to come largely from sympathetic observers. But since better ideals have been developed, organized laborers strive to improve the sanitary, moral, and other conditions in the places of work. Their main object, however, was for a long time to raise wages, or to resist any decrease. Shorter hours have been a prime object of recent years, and almost coördinate with that of higher wages. The eight-hour movement has declined somewhat of late, but a few years ago it seemed possible that the eight-hour day would become the rule. This aim has never been lost sight of, however, and now and then another step is taken toward it. Labor leaders have repeatedly asserted in recent years, when the two demands have been made together, that shorter hours were more desirable than increased wages.

§ II. The Methods of Trade-unions

Organized labor seeks to prevent competition among workers

1. *The union's first aim is to get control of all the labor force in the market, and to minimize competition among workers.* Every labor federation aims to extend its control to every branch of its trade. A sense of wrong is one of the strongest forces to bring the workers into the organization. The appeal to a common interest is effective in times of great grievance, as it was effective in the dangerous times of the American Revolution, though failing during the Confederation. The unwilling are first persuaded, then coerced by threats, by petty persecutions, by the most cruel of all peaceful weapons, social ostracism, and finally by personal violence. The "public opinion" and class feeling fostered among workers by their organization are analogous to the sense of patriotism and loyalty in the country at large, and at times displace it, as is seen in the opposition to the militia and to the maintenance of public order at times of strikes. The individual who declines to enter the union is denounced as a traitor and made to feel the scorn of his associates. When all these measures fail, pressure is brought to bear upon the employer to get him to force the unwilling workers into the union.

The union seeks to secure the full competitive wage

And as much more as possible

2. *Its next aim is to use collective in the place of individual bargaining, to force as much as the competitive wage, and more if possible.* The term collective bargaining has been much used to describe bargaining between a group of labor leaders, the delegated representatives of the workingmen, and a group of employers or directors. It is sometimes claimed that all the trade-union seeks is to put the workman on an equality with the employer in bargaining, enabling him to get all he would if competition were free on both sides. It is said that organized labor simply prevents the employer from following the maxim of Napoleon to "divide and conquer," from meeting his employees one by one and forcing his own terms upon them.

But the most effective argument in organizing the trade-union is that it forces a higher wage, more than the market would warrant. It is sometimes assumed by labor leaders that competitive wages would be very low, almost starvation wages, and anything above that level is credited to the work of the union; while in other cases where the wages are already large, the purpose frankly avowed is to limit the labor supply in the particular trade and to force a monopoly wage by any means possible. One's opinion of trade-unions is likely to differ according as they work in one or the other of these ways. The impartial onlooker sympathizes with the efforts of the trade-unions in so far as they serve merely to put the workers on an equality with the employers in bargaining. The public wants to see "fair play," and up to a certain point the union is merely a device to get fair play. But if the union is a device to defeat competition, to force artificially high wages, it will be judged differently. The public readily sees that if the unions force more than a fair and open market affords, it is rarely at the expense of the employer; that in the long run it is at the expense of the purchasing public itself, including the unprivileged workmen shut out from the monopoly of labor.

The issue of the closed shop vs. the open shop

3. *In order to accomplish their ends, the trade-unions seek to control their employers' business in various ways.* They demand, first, that no non-union men shall be employed even at union wages; they demand that the employer shall help them to force his employees into the unions. In this very usual demand for the "closed shop" or "union shop" the public can see very little justice. On this point, nearly always, unions forfeit in a strike the sympathy of the public; yet the unions assert that it is almost absolutely necessary to gain this point in order to carry out their objects. If a union and a non-union man work side by side there are many ways in which the employer may make the union man suffer. If business slackens, it is likely to be the union man that is discharged; if any preference is given, it is to the non-union man. Certainly all will agree that if the unions are to get the strength to enforce *all* their demands it is essential that they make good this claim which leaves the employer almost helpless. Yet it certainly is not essential to the accomplishing of valuable services for the members of the union. The educational and mutual-benefit features are attained without this means; and much experience shows that, if their cause is strong, the organized men can carry with them a large proportion of the workers and the sympathy of the public in a contest for higher wages. It never has seemed to any considerable portion of the public any more desirable that organized labor through its officers should be able to dictate to employees, than that employers should crush the workmen. It is by just this assumption that union advocates beg the question of the "union shop."

Other limitations put upon industry by unions

Further, the unions direct and control the employment of labor, often limit the number of apprentices in a trade, and assume to determine who shall enjoy the privilege of learning it. They limit the output, fix the maximum amount, and forbid the use of labor-saving machinery. Whenever the unions are charged with these acts, labor leaders either deny the facts or avoid giving a direct answer, but there is no doubt that the charge is true in many ways and in many cases. The requirement that each special kind of work shall be controlled by a special trade, and disputes between rival trades, for which their jealousies are responsible, give rise to great annoyance, expense, and loss to employers and to the entire public.

The strike and the boycott

4. *The strike is a threat and a mode of attack to enforce the demands of the union.* To most newly organized laborers the union appeals mainly as an instrument for striking, for threatening the employer or for making him suffer. When a new union is formed, it is nearly always dedicated by a strike, which is the simultaneous stopping of work by a number of workers. A strike is intended to force the employer to grant the wages and conditions demanded. Its effectiveness lies in the injury which it occasions or threatens in the stopping of machinery, the ruin of material, the loss of custom, and the failure to complete contracts undertaken. Its success being dependent on the inability of the employer to fill the places of the strikers, their energies are bent on persuading or coercing other workers from taking employment. There are many ways of coercing workers without personal violence. Public opinion does much, and probably the severest of all coercive measures is the social ostracism of the worker. What may be called the endless-chain boycott is an excommunication, without measure or limit, of the non-union worker and of every one in any way befriending him or the employer. So far as in their power lies, the enraged strikers dissolve the very bonds of society, brother casts off brother, and mother disowns son. The unhappy conditions in the coal regions in 1902 rivaled the tragedies of civil war. A reasonable use of the boycott, refusal to maintain social relations with the person who offends one, is doubtless a part of personal liberty; but the boycott, as experience shows, has moral limits, and it should have strict legal limits. Its use beyond the moderate limit of the first degree of personal relations is anti-social to the degree of criminality, whether it be used as the weapon of organized workers or of organized wealth.

Violence in strikes is mob law

When peaceable means fail, often there is a recourse to violence both against the employer and his property and against the non-union men. The evils of violence in strikes often are tardily recognized by the public, whose sympathy up to a certain point is with the striker as "the under dog." It is slow to realize that strike violence is mob-law. Whenever men of one group assume the right to coerce forcibly and to wreak their hatred against one of their fellow-workers, it is a blow at political liberty. No free society can safely go the first step in permitting one group of men to usurp control over others in this way.

Costliness of strikes

5. *The great losses caused by strikes are the penalty of an unsolved industrial problem.* The losses to workers in wages, to employers and to investors in income and

property, and to the public in interruption of business, aggregate an enormous sum. It is, however, impossible to estimate it at all exactly, as the losses are in many cases indirect and intangible. The strikers are concerned not with the balance of total losses and total gains to society as a whole, but with the net gain that in the long run accrues to them. It is true that there are indirect gains not easily calculable, as the advance of wages made to avoid a strike while the lesson of the consequences is still fresh. Opinion among workingmen is not a unit as to the value of strikes. A few years ago it seemed safe to say that strikes were declining as compared with the period of the early eighties. It is probably true, as is often said, that as laborers become educated they put less faith in strikes. The epidemic of labor troubles, marking the years from 1899 to 1903, gave no evidence of a decrease in the use of strikes, yet many of these were due to the recent organization in various trades. The coal strike of 1902, though doubtless due to real grievances, was opposed by the officers of the union, an unusually capable set of men, but the more violent and discordant elements overruled the more pacific counsels. The public is perhaps as favorable as it has ever been to the cause of labor, but it appears to have less patience with strikes than it had fifteen years ago, and strikes usually fail if not backed by public opinion. The public has not as yet thought out consistent conclusions on the question of the rights of the union. It is just now much impressed with the value of arbitration. As experience destroys the unsound sentiments, and divides the wise from the unwise measures, a peaceable solution of industrial differences must and will be found.

§ III. Combination and Wages

Wages are raised by a labor monopoly

1. *Wages in particular industries often are maintained above the competitive rate.* The older economic writers were somewhat unsympathetic with trade-unions, and were even inclined to deny that organization could be helpful in any way in raising wages. This view, it must now be recognized, was mistaken, and overlooked the hindrances to competition and the effective economic forces that organization can bring into play. The sympathies of most men favor the wage-earner so strongly that they hesitate to express an opinion in any way unfavorable to his efforts to raise wages. But the view of the economic theorist as to the services of the union cannot be as roseate as is that of the union labor leader. The general proposition, however, is applicable, that wherever it is possible to limit supply, prices may be raised. If men fitted to do a certain work are not permitted to do it, labor in the special industry becomes more scarce and consequently more highly valued. This involves the result that some men are forced to remain where they get lower wages than they could earn if free to act. The temporary need of the employer may enable the union to force from him a division of his profits. If the trade-union watches its opportunity and takes occasion to strike when a failure to fill orders would cause him great loss, it may compel him to pay for a time more than the normal value

of the labor. It may well be doubted whether such action on the part of labor is generous, fair, honest, or in the long run wise; but that it may be immediately effective cannot be denied. By the principle of complementary goods an essential kind of labor can be given an artificially high value, if its supply can be controlled. If only the labor that is ready and willing to come in to take the place of the strikers can for a time be kept out, wages may be fixed practically according to monopoly principles, later to be discussed in connection with capitalistic organization.

Exaggerated claims made for trade-unions

2. *Trade-unions can, in various but limited ways, set in motion economic forces to increase the productiveness of labor.* It is difficult to take a moderate view of trade-unions; it is easier to go to one extreme or the other. In a book by Trant, reprinted from the English edition and circulated by the American Federation of Labor as representing its theory and claims, all the advances in wages that have been made are said to be due to the trade-unions. This claim is believed by many besides the members of trade-unions. The thought is sometimes expressed even by social students that but for the trade-unions wages in America would be the same as in 1850. Many well-known facts should cause such an opinion to be accepted with hesitation, to say the least. Only about one tenth of the workers in England are unionists and of the twenty-two million workers in the United States, far less than ten per cent. are organized. Can it be maintained that one tenth of the labor supply fixes the value of all? In many lines where labor is not organized, as in teaching, clerical positions, professional and domestic service, wages have risen even more than in organized trade. The evidence advanced to support the extreme claim is that wages are higher in some organized trades than in other unorganized trades requiring the same grade of laborers. Trant says that "where there are no unions wages should be lower. This is exactly the case"; and he quotes: "Wherever we find union principles ignored, a low rate of wages prevails and the reverse where organization is perfect." But he later explains in part this difference: "The union men are the best workmen and often employers pay a man more than union wages. This is not surprising as no man can be a union carpenter unless he be in good health, have worked a certain number of years at his trade, be a good workman, of steady habits and good moral character."

Certain unquestionable reasons why union wages should be higher

If this be true, it is in accordance with strict competitive principles that, as the elite of the trade, they should get higher wages than those outside. Moreover the unions exist mainly in the more populated places where cost of living, wages, and all prices range higher than in the towns. A much higher standard of work prevails in the cities, both among union and non-union men, and the old men and the inefficient drift away to the smaller towns and the places where wages are lower. Many of the differences are explicable without taking any account of the union. So far as unions tend toward intelligence, education, sobriety, efficiency, fuller and fairer competition, they are economic factors in all branches of industry, and it cannot be doubted that they do work in some measure in all these ways.

So far also as they strengthen the bargaining power of the laborers, or as they can enforce a monopoly of labor in a particular trade and locality, they can secure the full competitive or even a monopoly price.

Labor organizations a minor factor in lifting the mass of the workers
The chief factors determining wages

3. *Wages viewed in general industry, and in the long run, are determined mainly by impersonal economic forces.* That implies the converse, that they are not determined mainly by the trade-unions. This statement, in fact, is admitted in calmer moments by the extreme partisans of the unions. Even the book before quoted says somewhat vaguely that "it is an error to think that the trade-union seeks to determine the rate of wages. It cannot do that. It can do no more than affect them." Again it says: "Capital is increasing faster than population.... It seems therefore merely in obedience to natural laws that wages should rise." Men can easily see personal and immediate results. They cannot follow out the impersonal and ultimate workings of economic forces. The leaders make exaggerated claims; laborers believe them and pay their dues more readily; the public believes them and is the more inclined to pardon the excesses of so important an institution. That wages in a number of special trades are raised in a considerable degree cannot be questioned. The open or secret use of violence and other anti-social forces make much of this boasted service to some of the workers, an injury to others, and an occasion of reproach from the citizen who condemns the spirit of lawlessness thus encouraged. The chief factors tending to raise the general standard of wages are the productiveness of industry, peace, order, and security to wealth, honesty in man and master, in lawmaker and in judge, the efficiency and intelligence of the workers, and an earnest effort on their part to get the share that competition would accord them. Chiefly, though not exclusively, because of their bearing on this last factor, trade-unions have a useful, even though subordinate, part in the regulating of wages over the whole field of employment.

DIVISION B—
ENTERPRISE AND PROFITS

Chapter XXVIII
Production and the Combination of the Factors

§ I. The Nature of Production

Man's active intervention in production here to be studied

1. *The aim of industrial effort is the increase of the quantity and quality of scarce goods; this is economic production.* The thought has become familiar to the student that the supply of economic resources of whatever sort is limited, while the wants are practically unlimited. A supply of consumption goods meets a perennial stream of wants, the result being that value is attributed to things. The aim of production is to add to scarce things, to make the supply of goods as large as possible. There is occasion here to recall the thought of the two aspects of production noticed in Chapter 24. Man's part in production is passive when goods come into existence without his effort. One can imagine the indolent savage of the tropics, lying under the banana-tree, letting the fruit drop into his mouth. One can conceive of a tribe living upon manna, where every day the people awoke to discover a certain amount of food provided to each person's hand. Though no effort could increase that amount, still, if the food differed in flavor and the better qualities were rare, value would come into existence and exchange would arise. Now there is something very analogous to that in daily experience. There are some goods which effort can do little to increase. Usually, however, there is a possibility of change and adaptation to make them better suited to needs, and there is required the use of intelligence to choose among the goods and to employ them in the best way. Further, man can intervene and direct the course of industry; he does not merely gather what is provided. It is this active intervention and effort that is here to be considered.

The four essential characteristics of value

2. *To have value, a thing must be of the right stuff, in the right form, at the right time, and at the right place to gratify wants.* A distinction is sometimes made between elemental, form, time, and place value. It is a mistake to say that the value of anything is due to any one of these features, for to have value all must be

united in a single thing. But the distinction is useful in emphasizing the missing characteristics, which if supplied, cause value to emerge. Ice may be considered to have form value when produced artificially by a machine, time value when stored from winter to summer, and place value when brought from the north to the south. But not less essential is the psychological condition of a hungry and thirsty population ready to consume the ice. Any act or agent is said to be productive which works in any one of these respects: puts things in better form, or in a more fitting place, or provides them at a more fitting time to serve human wants.

Economic vs. technical changes in goods

3. *Economic production (in contrast with technical or merely formal production) is such a change in goods as is attended by an increase in value.* It is often well to contrast form, appearance, imitation, with the thing itself, the reality. Men sometimes go through the forms of study when their eyes and thoughts are wandering; through the form of getting a college education when they are simply having a good time. Likewise in production there is the form and the reality. The young lady just out of boarding-school rarely produces a masterpiece with the tubes and brushes that Raphael might have used. The justification for amateur work is to be found in the doing and not in the market value of the result. Blue rosebuds, painted with loving if unskilled touch on red velvet slippers, may bloom into a romance and happiness; but to the economist this appears to be a consumption of good pigment for amusement, not a creation of value. The difference between the form and value of productive effort becomes, in the study of business organization, a most essential question. The significance of leadership and control of industry is found in this fact that economic goods may be united to produce results having either a less or a greater value than the materials that are used.

Acquisition vs. social production

4. *Individual acquisition may be contrasted with social production in cases where the individual increases his wealth at the expense of others, without adding to value.* Most economic efforts increase the income of the individual and the income of society at the same time. The fruits of the field and the uses of machines are net additions to current income; they are not merely subtracted from the income of one and added to that of another. The increase of products by labor may depress somewhat the exchange value of competing labor, but the general welfare is furthered by the greater abundance. With very slight qualification it is true that in these cases the good of each is the good of all. But in some forms of human effort, social and individual interests clash. When two men bet, one gains and the other loses. The gambler's gain is a loss not only directly to his beaten opponent but indirectly to society. Certain forms of speculation approach dangerously near to the appropriation of the goods of others, and others become outright stealing, or cheating so nearly like stealing that it would be treated as a crime if discovered. But many a man prowls along the border-line of crime all his life and succeeds in making large gains without falling into the clutches of the law. Cheating that can be detected, and outright stealing, are prohibited by the law not because the burglar

is an idler; he loses sleep; he has his trials too. The pursuit of burglary requires courage, effort, and ingenuity, but society does not reward these as virtues nor recognize as production the transfer of wealth from the bank-vault to the pocket of the burglar. It is the aim of social institutions to harmonize individual and social interests in the pursuit of wealth, to force men into lines of action where individual acquisition adds to the sum of social utilities. But there are many marginal cases where human justice discriminates only in a bungling way, and many controverted questions arise at the meeting-point of ethics, economics, and law.

Industries are socially more or less productive

5. *In this sense, productive industries may be distinguished from unproductive ones.* The old distinction between productive and unproductive labor rested on the idea that production must be embodied in material and lasting form. We have rejected this for the thought that the tests of production are to be found in feeling, not in outward things. The distinction, therefore, between productive and unproductive labor must now be of a very different kind. Viewed from the social standpoint, the efforts of men may be seen to be directed along more or less productive lines. Enterprise and effort shade off from the more to the less productive, from the extreme where the value is a net addition to wealth, through other cases where one's gain is partly at the cost of others, to fraud and crime where there is merely a transfer of ownership.

§ II. Combination of the Factors

The factors of production defined

1. *The various parts, materials, and agents that unite to form products are called the factors of production.* In a general sense every separate thing that enters into industry is a factor; as, in agriculture, for example, the seed, plows, fields, fences, barns, cattle, labor. But usually in economic discussion, these numerous factors are grouped in large classes. The main factors are two, variously named as man and nature, or labor and material agents, or humanity and wealth. Rejecting, as we have, the old view as to the nature of consumption goods and as to the nature and possibility of the distinction between "land" and artificial capital, we class under wealth all material economic agents whatsoever. The discussion of labor and wages has broadly laid down the principles that apply to the value of human effort, but the factor of directing energy presents in modern society so many important features that it calls for special and fuller consideration.

Progressive stages of control over natural conditions

2. *The economic progress of society has been marked by decreasing dependence on the bounties and chances of nature and by increasing control of natural forces by man.* Various stages of progress in human history have been recognized. First is the stage of

appropriation—the stage of hunting, or of fishing, or of gathering fruits. Man in this stage is still an animal in his economic methods, not guiding and controlling nature, but merely gathering what nature chances to bring forth. The limitations to man's powers in this stage are marked. There is excess of supply and waste at one season, scarcity and great suffering at another. With such crude utilization of the bounties of nature, a vast area will support but a small population. When sheep and cattle have been domesticated, and where there is a large area for grazing, industry rises to the *pastoral* stage. While still dependent on nature's bounties for the feeding of his cattle, man is hourly intervening to increase, regulate, and improve the supply of food and materials. Famines are more rare, economic welfare is greater, a greater population is nourished on the same area. The *agricultural* stage begins whenever man plants seeds, trims, tends, and increases by his care the supply of vegetable food. This is a still greater intervention in the course of nature. Man anticipates the future, directs forces, and groups materials to his purpose of getting a regular food-supply. He is thus himself forced into settled life, begins hand-production, and makes the first steps in commerce. Then gradually comes the *industrial* stage, in which control over nature grows, supplies increase, machinery and motive forces are utilized, and humanity is in the full tide of industrial development. These are not sharply marked changes, but throughout all there is a growth of security, of certainty, and of productivity. With man's increasing power and foresight, chance is lessened, for directing energy takes its place.

Increasing importance of skilled organization and direction

The source of American enterprise

3. *For a high efficiency of production, as a whole, conditions must favor the best organization and direction of industry.* Industry is dependent primarily upon natural resources. Climate, rainfall, iron deposits, fuel, supply of wood or coal, predetermine in large measure the limits within, and the direction in which, the industry of any community can move. The progress of production depends also on an increasing efficiency of labor as embodied in individual men, and upon social and political conditions making possible an increase of capital. But—a condition as important as any of these—production is dependent also on a wise combination of the factors. Social, political, and economic conditions must be such as to call forth the factor of direction and control of industry, to make possible industrial progress. This is one of the greatest sources of America's superiority to-day. It has been strikingly said that it is now no longer "young America and old Europe," but "old America and young Europe." America is older in industrial experience; Europe, with undeveloped resources, awaits the touch of American methods and machinery. There are dynamic forces in American society not present in equal degree in any other. It is therefore not alone the great resources of coal and iron,— equal resources may be found in unexplored parts of the world,—it is the dynamic social forces, invention, enterprise, and organization, which have brought America to the forefront in industry. Her natural resources have thus yielded an incentive and a premium to enterprise as a sort of by-product. Absence of caste, political liberty, the democracy following the spread of the frontier, have not made it

possible for every one to succeed, but they have made it possible, as nowhere else in the world, for real ability to scale the barriers of birth, poverty, and hardship. A conservative population never can equal a progressive population in industrial efficiency. It has been remarked that America has little to fear from Oriental competition so long as the avenues of education and enterprise are open to her young men, insuring her the highest capacity in the organization and direction of industry.

Growing specialization of industry

4. *A high efficiency of industry is dependent on many social causes making possible a great specialization.* It was said in another connection that division of labor is dependent upon the size of the market. With a large population massed at one spot, so that the demand for even the less important products is large, there may be a high specialization of industry. An increase of transportation, such as railways and telegraphs, is equivalent for many economic purposes to growth of population on one spot. In colonial days it took ten days to go from Boston to Philadelphia, and two weeks to go to Washington. San Francisco is now for many economic purposes but one fourth as far from Boston as Washington was at that time. California and the eastern states are distant only thirty minutes by telegraph and three days and a fraction by railroad, and are thus in many respects in the same market. The great development during the past century in the means of communication and of carriage has made possible, as never before, the massing of population to secure the advantages of division of labor in most lines, without meeting the hitherto insurmountable difficulty in the securing of food for such large numbers in a limited space. The population draws its food from the whole vast area; whereas it is massed at the points more favorable for other products and can make use of the most highly specialized machinery. These several conditions thus have favored the growth of large industry under a single control and direction, on a scale never before approached. These changes have brought in their train social problems connected with the concentration of economic power. It remains to be seen whether the unquestioned economies of this new organization can be retained and improved while it is divested of its evils.

Growing importance of directive ability

5. *With the growing division of labor, grows the need of the highest ability for the directing of industry.* Ability may be judged by various standards. From one point of view, the scientific mind, grouping facts in the cold light of reason to arrive at truth, is the highest type. But supreme, each in his own sphere, are also the artist expressing, through painting, poetry, dramatic action, and music, the subtleties and complexities of feeling, the moral philosopher, the prophet, the preacher, in the best sense of the term the teacher, all aiding to guide the spiritual forces of humanity along lines that make for social welfare. Not least is the business enterpriser, whose function is to direct the economic forces for production. It is vain to assign a mean place to the organizing intelligence and its social work. Its importance grows apace with the growing magnitude and complexity of industry.

Misjudgment now will destroy more wealth, and wise judgment can produce larger results, than ever before. The captain of industry also may work as an artist or as a gambler; he may, by the methods he pursues, uplift the moral plane of his society or he may help to corrupt and degrade it. No citizen is in control of more potent influence for good or ill than the successful business organizer. On the attitude of society toward him, and on the standards to which he is held, depend in large measure the use that will be made of his exceptional powers.

Chapter XXIX
Business Organization and the Enterpriser's Function

§ I. The Direction of Industry

Judgment and self-direction as elements in personal skill

1. *In the simplest kinds of individual production the value of the results depends largely on intelligent choice.* Even for the solitary worker the choice of the right time to do work is most important. The first thing Robinson Crusoe did was to turn to the ship to save as much as possible of the cargo before it was dashed in pieces by the waves. If he had begun first to till the soil to provide a future supply of food it would have shown one kind of foresight, but it would have shown very poor judgment. Every moment of delay in recovering the cargo of the wrecked vessel cost him many useful materials. The humblest farmer has a great range of choice and a need of good judgment in fixing the time to sow, to reap, to do each simple task. There is the same need to-day for the small shopkeepers, for the blacksmiths, for the small producers of all kinds to make wise choice of time in the use of their own labor. There is also a wide range of choice in the distributing and combining of labor, agents, and materials. A limited supply of agents can be used to secure a variety of goods, more or less desirable. There are many chances for mistake, but in the long run it is judgment, not chance, that determines the success of one man as compared with another. There is a choice in ways and methods by which a thing can be done. There are many wrong ways, there is but one best way, at any stage of industrial progress. While most work is done in customary ways and little independent judgment is required, yet in every business from time to time new problems arise and call for an exercise of choice as to methods. Moral qualities are continually called for, such as control of impulse, and the giving up of the comfort of the moment. The wisdom of our fathers is embodied in a multitude of proverbs that suggest the wise course. Men must "make hay while the sun shines," not lie in the shade. But virtue fails less often from lack of knowledge than from lack of will. As men differ in judgment, character, and will-power, their products differ, even in the simplest circumstances. The ability to choose and to do wisely is an

element in personal skill.

Direction of a group of workers

2. *When men work in an associated group, the direction of effort becomes relatively more important.* The first and simplest advantage of association is working in unison. Men unite their muscular efforts for a single task, and accomplish what is impossible to them working singly. But when many work in unison, the right selection of time and way is of greater importance; a mistake will waste more materials and agents. If association is to yield its advantages, there must be division of labor; hence harmony of effort, hence agreement or direction. While the gain of well-directed association is large, the waste of ill-directed effort is greater, when specialization has taken place, than with isolated workers. Most communal societies have failed because of the lack of a good head. The few exceptional successes have been due to the presence of a man of superior ability, such as George Rapp of the Harmonist Community, who, had he lived in this day, could have become easily the head of a great business corporation.

Direction of interrelated groups

3. *Where various industrial groups are associated, direction becomes still more important.* In the single group it is an internal harmony alone that is needed. The work of a dozen men must be so arranged that each is in his fitting place. But as this group comes into contact with others, the relationship becomes two-fold, and there must be both internal and external harmony. The more complex the economic organization of society, the more the chance of mistake and the more injurious are the mistakes to a wide range of interests. Large amounts of capital and labor can be rapidly lost through lack of wise direction of associated groups.

Greatest need now of capable direction of industry

4. *The increased efficiency of industry has been accompanied by the specialization of control.* The crude, early methods of enforcing harmony in industry were slavery and political subordination. Under division of labor, with free workmen, industry is ruled by impersonal economic forces that bring the less capable under the direction of the more capable. This work is rudely done, no doubt, but the penalties of bad direction of labor and capital are so great that blundering cannot be permitted. The man who shovels dirt must do it at the right time and place if, in this complex society, it counts for something and gives the effort value. If he cannot choose well for himself, he comes under direction. The average man cannot decide nearly as well here as he could on a desert island where and when to put in his spade. There it would be to raise food for the current year; here it may be to dig a canal or a tunnel whose uses will not become actual for many years. The more distant the end sought, the more difficult is the choice. To every worker, according to his personal skill, is left some degree of choice in the method of his work, but in a large part of industry the range of choice is very narrow. The man with the shovel and the man with the hoe come under direction.

§ II. Qualities of a Business Organizer

Technical knowledge and skill

1. *The organizer and director of industry must first have technical knowledge of methods, processes, and materials.* The qualities required in the direction of industry are implied in the foregoing section, but they may be more specifically enumerated. Knowledge of technical processes is relatively more important in the direction of industry in the earlier stage. In the single independent producer it is the quality most desirable. He must know the quality of the materials with which he works and the best modes of combining them. But, as industrial organization becomes more complex, only a broad knowledge and ability to judge of the results of different processes and to compare plans are necessary in the organizer. He can hire the technical knowledge of details required in the larger management of business. Draftsmen, engineers, pattern-makers, men with far more education and capacity in certain lines than the business manager, work under his direction.

Judgment of men

2. *The organizer requires ability to judge men and tact in relations with them.* In the small group, ability to get on well in personal contact with workmen is of great importance. Especially rare is the genial manner that wins the confidence and even the affection of the men. A sense of humor and the ability to turn a joke are said to have obviated many a strike and thus to have prevented losses both to the employer and to the men. In large affairs much of this managing tact can be hired in good foremen; but the organizer must still have a knowledge of men, ability to judge of human nature, to select his subordinates, and to animate them with his own purposes and plans. Mr. Carnegie has said that an appropriate epitaph for himself would be, "He was a man who knew how to surround himself with men abler than he was himself." That seems too modest; but in a sense it is not, because he claims for himself, and justly, the highest of all industrial qualities. A great administrator in political or industrial affairs can dispense with everything else rather than with this, the supreme quality of the great organizer.

Foresight in commercial affairs

3. *The organizer must have unusual foresight and the ability to form a large commercial policy.* This proposition is to be interpreted relatively to the task before the organizer, and to the size of the business. Modern industry anticipates demand far more than did primitive industry. Large amounts of materials and energy are embarked in directions from which they cannot be recalled. With the progress of electrical engineering it soon may become possible to recall at any moment a cargo embarked for a distant port. But no wireless telegraphy is able to recall the great masses of capital that are embarked on distant and definite journeys in modern business. The organizer anticipates future demand, and prepares for it. The process has been figuratively expressed somewhat as follows: the enterpriser throws into the crucible great quantities of material; they melt, and an industrial result is secured, but whether the deposit is greater in value than the material is

a question that cannot be answered for years. The need of anticipating demand is greater to-day than ever before, and this requires large investments months and even years in advance. The losses are proportionally large if there is miscalculation of demand. A large commercial policy is one that takes into account the more distant factors, and anticipates the new conditions. The rare ability to do this is rightly called statemanship in economic affairs.

Command of financial resources

4. *The organizer need not himself have great wealth, but he must have ability to command financial resources.* Business to-day is done in many cases with borrowed capital. Even a subscription to stock is frequently as much in the nature of a loan, made in reliance on the reputation of the organizer, as an investment for profits. There are many temporary needs that require sudden loans. The confidence of investors, whether banks, trust companies, individual shareholders or investors in bonds, must be secured by the organizer. Good judgment of the money market often is as vital as judgment of the market for the particular product. In some of the largest corporate enterprises this quality becomes the most essential.

Scarcity of great organizing ability
The industrial leaders

5. *Organizing ability of the highest order is rarely found.* This is almost a superfluous statement after the foregoing. According to the theory of chances, such a combination and balancing of qualities is likely to occur in very few cases. Even where it exists, it may not be discovered or developed. The man may not find his opportunity, nor the task the man. There are many misfits in the world. On the occasion of the visit of Prince Henry of Prussia to America, in 1902, he was entertained at luncheon in New York with one hundred of the leaders in invention, finance, and industry, wherein have been the most characteristic achievements of America. In jocular reference to the French Academy, whose members are the forty most noted literary men of France, the newspapers called this the meeting of America's one hundred immortals. There were J. P. Morgan, the great financier; Vanderbilt, Hill, and Harriman, the railroad kings; Carnegie, the iron magnate; Irving Scott, "the man who built the Oregon"—nearly all the company deserving a place at the table mainly by reason of excellence as business organizers. Such a gathering has a dramatic interest as presenting the greatest leaders of industry, but about other tables might be gathered thousands of other less notable figures worthy to be accounted captains of industry in their several fields. One may well ask, How did they come into the important places they occupy?

§ III. The Selection of Ability

Various roads to industrial leadership

1. *The men actually in control of industry have been selected in manifold ways.* Skill develops a small industry into a large one. A small factory owner gradually adds machine to machine, building to building, till he finds himself at the head of a great industry. Or an employee develops ability and becomes an employer. Who does not know of some one who, as a small boy, went into a store to do chores, worked up to a clerkship and, enlisting the confidence of men of wealth, was enabled to establish a business of his own and become an employer? Others have won promotion from the ranks to the head of a large industry in which they secured at last a controlling interest. Employees that have proved their ability may be selected by the directors of a stock company. Men that have worked their way up from the ranks may bequeath their business positions to their sons and grandsons, as in the case of the Vanderbilts and the Goulds. And finally, but rarely, there may be selection by fellow-workmen in the case of coöperative business.

Success as the evidence of ability

2. *There is a constant selective process: dropping out the weak and advancing the efficient organizer.* There is, to be sure, an element of chance in this selection. The process in general is a rude one. Accidents and unforeseen changes, industrial crises, failure of health at a critical moment, fraud and crime, may defeat men of ability and they may never regain their foothold. Lack of experience may lead to disaster a naturally able but youthful heir, too suddenly burdened with the responsibilities of a fortune. On the other hand, men of limited ability may inherit fortunes and preserve them by caution, without enterprise. It is not always true, even in America, that "It is but three generations from shirt-sleeves to shirt-sleeves," although many fortunes slip away from the sons of rich fathers. In general, success in retaining the control of a business is an evidence of considerable ability. By loss of fortune unwisely risked, through unforeseen changes in methods, and after manifold blunders, the less capable drop out. Thus, by the ceaseless working of competition, the higher places are taken by those most capable of filling them, and the efficiency both of the employers and of the workmen is increased.

Various modes of business organization

3. *In the various kinds of business organization the merits of men and of methods are tested.* The independent producer working entirely alone, directing his own industry, is analogous to the animal organism of a single cell. More complex is the family partnership found often in early stages of industry but more rarely now, where the father directs the work of his children and all share in common. The simplest form of the wage system is the single employer with a few assistants. When the employer is in danger of losing valuable assistants, he sometimes gives them a share in the business. In the ordinary partnership, two or more men divide the ownership and duties, agreeing as to the division of control. Coöperation among workmen, though rare, gives an unusual opportunity for the discovery

of special talent. The dominant form of organization to-day is that of the stock company, or corporation, the ownership of which is divided among the holders of shares of stock, or of certificates of membership.

Many chances to try ability

This variety of organization affords opportunity for a two-fold test: that of the ability of men and of the merits, in varying circumstances, of the different forms of organization. Methods of organization are constantly tested by their results. Men having money to invest are asking whether they would be better off to go into business by themselves, or to join with a partner, or to buy stock in some large corporation. Each of these forms of organization has its peculiar advantages. A stock company can better enlist large amounts of capital, while the individual employer is generally more free from dictation and can adapt his business more quickly to changing conditions. At the same time this variety of organization offers better opportunities for managing ability to show its metal. On the watch towers of industry are many observers sweeping the horizon for the appearance of men of business talent. Some characters develop better under direction; others prove that nowhere does native ability count for more, and mere book-schooling for less, than in business administration. There is some ground for the belief that a college education does not increase executive capacity in business. Such ability often seems to be a freak of nature and a product of practical experience, rather than the result of college training.

Chapter XXX
Cost of Production

§ I. Cost of Production from the Enterpriser's Point of View

The enterpriser's cost

1. *The task of the enterpriser is to get together the essential factors to secure valuable products.* The enterpriser must first decide what product he will endeavor to secure, and the kind, the place, the time, the quantity, and the quality. He must then select in the right proportion the materials, labor, plant, and machinery necessary for that product. He must purchase these factors in the market at the lowest price he can, unite them and sell the product to recover the expenses in the selling price. A thousand items enter into the cost and perhaps a single product emerges. What the business man thus pays out, expressed in money form, are the costs that are here to be considered.

Several meanings of cost

2. *The term cost of production is used in several senses, the chief of which are money cost, psychic cost, and alternative cost.* The ambiguity of this term is a source of much confusion. *Psychic cost* is the pain, fatigue, irksomeness of labor. This is not definitely measured except at rare points. When the pain of work more than offsets the value of the product, the worker who is free to determine the length of his own working-day, stops. At that point the psychic cost and the utility of the marginal unit are almost equal in intensity—the one as a positive, the other as a negative quantity. But the value of the product as a whole cannot be related to the psychic cost or sacrifice, and therefore it cannot serve as a measure of cost in every-day business. *Alternative cost* is any good or gratification that must be given up when any other good is chosen. One may stay at home and read a book or go on a picnic; the pleasure of reading the book will cost the pleasure of the picnic. A good dress may cost a happy vacation that must be given up for it. In this sense, each thing is a cost of every other thing that might be chosen in the place of it. Alternative cost is therefore manifold and indefinite. The thought is significant at the moment of a

choice, but it is not constantly measurable for practical purposes. The *money cost* is the practical cost generally implied in the term cost of production. It expresses not the pain of the laborer in doing the work, not the sacrifice of the owner of the capital in saving the money, but merely the sum of money paid out by the producer. There is frequent confusion of these ideas in economic discussion, few even of the leading economists of the nineteenth century having quite escaped it.

The cost of the factors is their market price

3. *The enterpriser, looking upon the cost of most of the factors as fixed, seeks to combine them as economically as possible.* Whether the enterpriser is running a factory or a farm, is engaged in a retail or a wholesale store, is conducting a school or a railroad, he has to solve much the same problem. By close attention, good judgment, skilful bargaining, he may be able to buy slightly cheaper than his competitors, and thus have an advantage over them at the outset. When he does this, it is usually by searching out a better market in which to buy, buying at a better time, and judging better than his competitors the quality of goods. If, in a given market at a given time, goods are sold to one more cheaply than to others, it is an act of generosity. Even the best buyers pay nearly the prevailing market price for agents. The most successful enterprisers are not found to be those paying lower wages or lower ground-rent than their competitors. It must not be forgotten that the main forces fixing the prices of agents are impersonal, and can be only slightly modified in most cases by a particular buyer. He looks therefore upon the cost of the elements as an ultimate fact which he can change little, if at all, and he shows his judgment chiefly in the selection of quality. Cost determines and limits the extent of his business and determines the price at which he sells.

The right proportioning of the factors

4. *The right proportioning and skilful substitution of the factors is a delicate technical task for the enterpriser.* Good buying and good selling must precede and follow the central part of the enterpriser's task, that is, the combining of the various factors. Each factor is applied, subject to diminishing returns, up to a point where its addition will not secure the value attributed to it in its cost. The enterpriser is constantly studying the question whether the application of another unit of any one factor at the price will add to the value of the product as much or more than the cost. This calculation is made for every one of the minor factors entering into the business, and for the business as a whole. The proper proportion varies at different prices, or costs. If wages rise, "it pays" to get machinery; if wages fall, it pays to let the machinery deteriorate and to do more by hand-labor. Likewise there is constant substitution of the various materials. The right proportions change constantly with inventions. A model factory is so proportioned that the buildings hold the right number of machines, with the right amount of space for the workmen, and the right amount of power. If there is more of a single factor than the ideal proportion, it is an unnecessary cost. Even the model factory begins to be out of date almost as soon as the walls are dry, and the latest method is to build as nearly as possible on the unit system, so that new parts may be added

COST OF PRODUCTION

without the loss of harmony and proportion.

Pressure of price toward cost at certain points

The enterpriser in contact with costs

5. *The enterpriser's costs determine the lowest price at which he can continue to sell, but if successful he may have a wide margin of profits.* New factories are constantly arising with new and better adjustments. In industries of competing products, also, the processes are changing. Hence there is always a pressure of competition on some enterprisers who constantly complain that they must sell below the cost of production. The organizers of a trust always declare, some no doubt truly, that they have been selling below the cost of production. Business men say that competition is destructive, and it certainly does destroy the less favorably situated enterprises. Each enterpriser's price is the highest he can get in the market for his product; it may far exceed his costs; it may even fall below them, but only temporarily, for if sales continue to encroach on capital, the sheriff soon closes the doors. Successful competitors are constantly pressing upon the marginal enterpriser, fixing a price that leaves themselves a profit, but is below his cost. Even the most successful enterpriser comes into contact with cost, and seems to be compelled by it. He reaches out for trade, and sells some (not all) goods at a price which leaves him no profit. He enlarges his factory and ships goods farther, paying the freight, which means a lower price at the factory. The expanding business, therefore, comes at length to the point where it cannot go farther at the prevailing prices. Hence the business man's view of the costs is that they determine value. It is true in the sense that the supply of a particular product in any market is at last limited by cost of marginal producers or of marginal portions of supply. But it is not true of all the units of product that costs determine, or equal, market price. There is a margin above costs to the successful enterpriser on a large portion of his output. The margin may be narrow or wide, according to the business. The margin is "profit," or the gain of the enterpriser.

§ II. Cost of Production from the Economist's Standpoint

Money cost not the ultimate explanation of value

1. *The economist should view money cost as an intermediate and not as an ultimate explanation of value.* The value of all things must be traced back to gratification, to the relation of goods with psychic income. This being true, the value of the factors which the enterpriser uses must be derived from the value of the products, and not the reverse. This does not mean that the business man is deceived into the belief that he has in cost of production a final explanation of value. He simply is not interested in that question. He knows that there are many influences determining the cost of the factors he buys, but they are distant; he cannot influence them, and in the single stage of his production they seem to fix the price. In some purchases,

and on the stock exchange, a marvelous recognition and analysis of the most distant influences is necessary; but in general a superficial view of value is taken in business; it does not pay to do other. The logical treatment, however, must go deeper into the question and trace the cost of agents back to the ultimate cause of value, that is, to want-gratifying power. To say that the price of a product is determined by the money cost, or price, of the factors is simply to postpone the answer to the question of value; one has still to ask, What determines the money cost, or price, of those factors themselves?

The cost of agents is fixed by their marginal utility in alternative uses

2. *The demand for any factor entering into products is reflected, in an increased price, to its cost in all competing products.* Figuratively speaking, products compete with each other for the factors that enter into them. According to location, quality of the soil, and improvements, a certain area of land has various rival uses. These uses bid for the land, or put in an economic claim for it. Products of a higher value outbid and exclude those of a lower. If fine wine can be raised on a piece of land, potatoes ordinarily will not be planted in it. But if there is such a supply of that quality of land that it continues to be used side by side for both products, it will have the same value and yield the same rental in both uses. The least utility yielded by any portion of the supply fixes the value of all the units. Machines are usually made for some product determined in advance, but often they are only partially specialized and within limits they can be adapted. Sewing-machine factories were readily turned to the making of bicycles at the time of greatest demand, and bicycle factories later were used for the making of automobiles. Thus, in general, machinery is used for the product to which it contributes the most value. Any enterpriser seeking it for any other use finds its "cost" affected by its various alternative uses. The same is true of all the materials and of all the grades of labor entering into products. The enterpriser's *cost* is therefore the reflection of the want-gratifying power of the productive agent in all its other uses as well as in the particular product he desires. To the enterpriser, cost seems the cause of the value of a product. To the economist it should be clear that the utility found in the various products is the basis of value in the factors, *i. e.*, of the costs.

A single source of a single product

3. *The genealogy of value may thus be traced through the various intermediate products to consumption goods.* A single product having a single source of supply shows most clearly the reflection of value directly from the product. The discovery of a mineral spring or of a good quality of building-stone on worthless land, will cause a value to attach at once to the source of supply. When a great singer like Adelina Patti commands several thousand dollars for each appearance in concert, the source is the magical throat of the singer, and the salary reflects the utility of the music in the minds of delighted hearers.

One source of several products

When the one source of supply yields several different kinds of products there is just one new condition which confuses the thought and suggests the error that value begins in the source (with costs therefore) and not in the product. Looking at the products severally, no one of them explains the value of the source, and, on the contrary, each one is seen to have a value independent of the particular use to which it is put. To make the illustration most simple: a savage finds in a wreck on the coast a number of bars of iron. His fellows wish them for various purposes: to make arrow heads, spears, knives, hatchets, hoes, ornaments, nails, needles, etc. Value is in this case derived in part, through the source, from the alternate uses. Taken jointly and considered as one sum, the value of the various products accounts as completely and exclusively for the value of the source as if they were merged into one product. The source (S) is distributed to each of the products in accordance with their marginal utility, and therefore the value of the various products from any source of supply constantly tends to equality. Any unit of product sought for any purpose must be paid for according to a marginal utility determined in all the applications. The genesis of the value is in the utility of the product; the value of the source is derived.

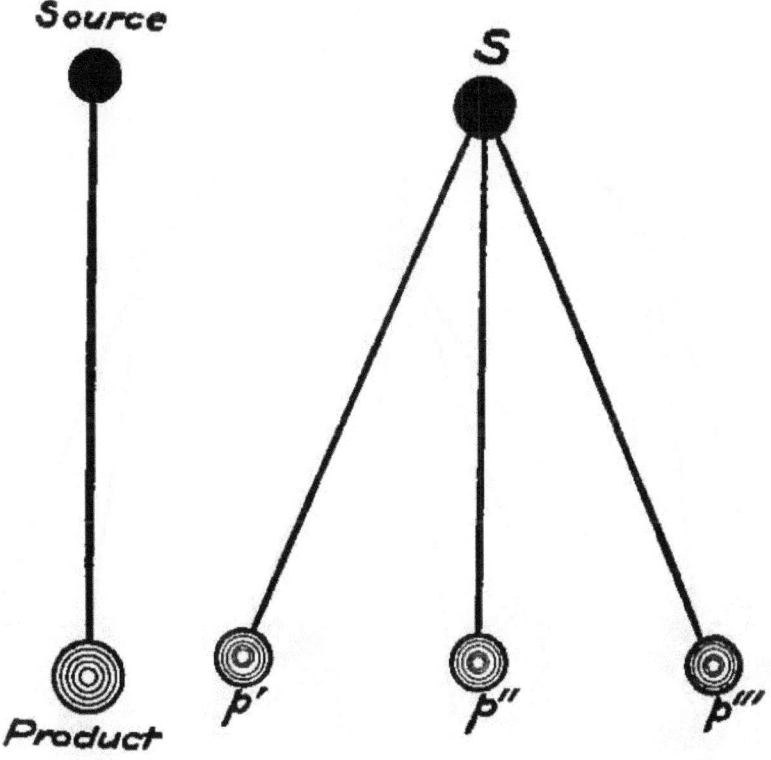

1. A single Product
2. Several Products from one Source

Complex conditions with intermediate products

In actual life the problem is far more complex, and yet, through its settlement runs just the same principle. There is constant bidding for materials, and through their price the claims of rival products are adjusted. A point is reached where it does not pay to use any more of an agent in a certain industry; the production of another unit results in a loss. There is a most complex relation among many different industries using the same factors, the value of a unit of product (at *a*) being reflected up to the source, and through successive links to the most distant product (*z*). The effect of this is to reduce the sale (of *z*) and correspondingly the use made of the agent in question. A higher price of leather, due to the increased use of shoes, raises the value of hides and cattle (this increasing the extent of cattle raising) and raises thus the cost of carriage-trimmings, pocket-books, foot-balls, leather belts, and every other leather product. As the price rises, substitutes for leather, and imitations of it, are used for such of the products as cannot bear the increased cost of leather.

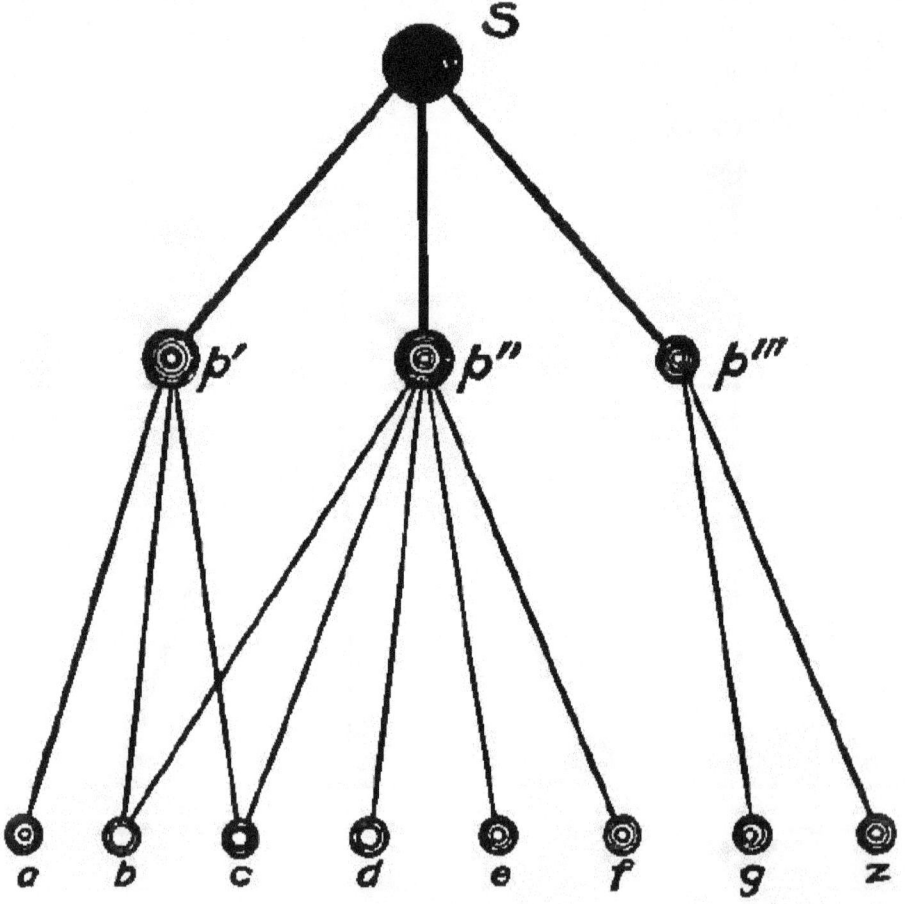

3. Complex Relations through Intermediate Products

COST OF PRODUCTION

The enterpriser the medium of price movements

Costs are an expression of consumers' estimates

4. *The enterpriser does not fix the value of products or of agents, but is the medium through which consumers express their estimates.* The enterpriser who anticipates aright and satisfies the public taste is the good medium. He readily transmits and accurately focuses the rays of public judgment. One that misjudges is a poor medium. The enterpriser is himself the servant of costs. Laborers sometimes assume that the employer can dictate wages, prices, and markets, can rule things with a lordly hand. With rare exceptions the ultimate control in these matters by business men is very slight. In the main the enterpriser masters the situation only by bowing to it, just as the scientist and the engineer gain mastery over nature because they know when to bend and how to obey. The consumer, by deciding to buy this or that product, sets in motion waves of value. The consumers of products are the true purchasers of labor, materials, and uses of agents. The enterpriser must conform closely to cost, to the price prevailing for the moment, or his competitors in this day of narrow margins will seize the opportunity. The enterpriser is merely the distributor or equalizer of cost among all the different products for which different agents can be used. If he acts efficiently, profits arise.

Chapter XXXI
The Law of Profits

§ I. Meaning of Terms

Broadest use of the term profit

1. *The term profit is popularly used as any gain or advantage secured by any means in business.* The terms used in economics, being taken from popular language, vary in meaning according to the context. It is necessary to clear thinking to reject some words entirely and when using others to define them more strictly. The broad usage of the term profits just noted includes every kind of return to industry: such as interest on capital, and wages or services of the man owning the industry. Precise thinking requires its use in a much narrower sense.

Used of gross gains on sales

2. *A common meaning of profits in retail business is the gross gain on a given sale.* Buying an article for one dollar and selling it for two dollars, is said by the merchant to be selling at one hundred per cent. profit, jocularly called, "The Dutchman's one per cent." The cost price is considered to be that paid to the manufacturer or wholesaler. In different lines of goods there is added regularly to this cost twenty, thirty, or fifty per cent., as the case may be, as the merchant's profit on the sale. This is of course a gross profit, and not net, or true profit. It leaves out of account rent, interest on capital, clerk hire, freight, and many other minor items that enter into the cost of running a store. It often happens that the Dutchman's way of reckoning is nearer the truth, and that the gross profit of one hundred per cent. proves at the end of the year to be only a net profit of one per cent. This evidently is a loose meaning, impossible in the discussion of theoretical questions. This meaning is sometimes developed, making profits the sum of all the gross profits on separate sales within a year, or the difference between the wholesale and retail prices of goods sold within the year.

Another meaning given to the term is gross profit (as above) compared with the capital invested. The "profit" in this case varies partly with the rate of the turnover. To illustrate: if the amount invested in a printing-office is $100,000, and

THE LAW OF PROFITS

the annual business done is $300,000, the capital is said to be turned over three times; if the gross profits on sales averaged twenty per cent., they would be sixty per cent. on the investment; but, if the capital had been turned over four times, the gross profit would have been eighty per cent. on the investment.

Of net gains as a percentage of invested capital

3. *Another meaning of profits is the annual net gain of the business, as compared with the average investment of capital.* This is a long step toward greater definiteness. If at the end of a year it were found that after paying all outside expenses there were $10,000 to set aside, this would be accounted a profit of ten per cent. on $100,000 invested. But confusion still reigns because of wide variation in the methods of estimating costs before fixing net profits. In one case the enterpriser rents lands and buildings, in another he owns them; in one case he has borrowed money and counts interest as a cost, in another he is free from debt; in one case he counts as a part of cost an estimated fair salary for himself and his partners, in another (usually in a small business) no such allowance is made Such a variation in business usage is most perplexing. In all these cases one must have the exact conditions in mind before it is possible to make any comparisons and draw any conclusions as to the relative profits of different industries.

Profits in economic theory

4. *In the narrower and exacter sense profits are the net gain of the enterpriser after counting the rent of material agents and contract wages of employees at the prevailing rates.* Into the practical problem of cost and profit many factors enter, and the theoretical problem is to determine just how much ought to be attributed to each. In a large business usually the practical bookkeeping problem is not unlike that of economic analysis. A stock company counts as cost, as a part of fixed charges, interest on capital borrowed either from banks or bondholders. Its managers are paid salaries, counted as a part of cost. The net balance, after deducting these and all other expenses, is counted profits and paid in dividends to stock-holders. The economic student is not attempting to get a theory of profits that is in contrast with practice. Rather, he is trying to analyze profits generally, just as they are analyzed in the few cases where the books are properly kept. In economic theory, therefore, profits are the part of the gain of any business that is logically attributable to fortunate investment and good management; profits are the income attributable to the enterpriser's services.

Profits a species of wages

5. *Typical economic profits are thus a species of wages but are marked by peculiar features.* In some of the older treatises on political economy, profits are treated merely as a combination of "wages of management," and of interest on capital invested. A man hired at a fixed sum to manage a business is receiving simply contract wages. Economic profits are not *contract* wages, not being paid by agreement, but being yielded impersonally by the industry. Profits are, however,

economic wages or the earnings of services. As business has developed, it has been seen that the enterpriser's work has its peculiar character and deserves special attention. The old English word "enterpriser," used of the "adventurer" who embarked in foreign trade, may fittingly apply to the organizer and director of business to-day. Foreign trade then, more often than now, was most uncertain, and there were many chances that the ship would be lost, or the venture prove a losing one. In the simplest business to-day there is this element of enterprise, or undertaking, combined with ordinary capital and labor. As industry develops, this special service stands out more clearly. In the corner-grocer and in the manager of the little news-stand, the elements of enterprise and labor are not apart. In the large wholesale house, the enterpriser is seen to be not merely an abstractly thinkable function, but a separate and concrete person. The typical enterpriser is the man who gives his time and energies to the launching and guiding of business.

§ II. The Typical Enterpriser's Services Reviewed

The enterpriser's skilful use of capital

1. *The enterpriser guarantees to the capitalist-lender a fixed return.* Agents will yield the highest economic rent of which they are capable only in the hands of those who can use them with exceptional skill. Owners of capital who for any reason, such as youth, inexperience, ill health, incapacity, or conflicting duties, are not able to make agents yield the average rent, seek out, or are sought out by, those who in general can make the agents yield more than the average. The interest contract between them is one of mutual advantage, in that the enterpriser pays a definite sum to the investor unable himself to apply his productive agents. Immense sums of capital are now put into the hands of small enterprisers, such as Western farmers improving their lands, builders of city homes and business blocks, and small manufacturers. But stocks and bonds of corporations give a wide variety of investments which shade off from the safer or capitalistic type, to the more uncertain, or enterpriser's type. First-mortgage bonds, being a first claim on the income and property, have the highest security and yield generally the lowest interest. Even national bonds are not absolutely safe, and for that reason as well as because of their fluctuation in price, even their purchase has something of the nature of an enterprise. Stocks are the enterpriser's type of investment, the dividends being more uncertain, but giving the chance of a higher return than the average. It is because some stand ready to assume the risk of making goods yield average returns or more, that others can sit and enjoy a fixed income with little effort and in comparative security.

The enterpriser's insurance of the lender's capital

2. *The enterpriser gives up the certain income to be got by lending his own capital, and, becoming a borrower, offers his capital as insurance to the lender.* Every business has an element of uncertainty in it, and some one must meet the risk. A man with marked

ability as an organizer of industry is rarely found long without capital of his own. But even a penniless man who can gain the confidence of investors is able to get backing and to secure the necessary funds to engage in business. The lenders in such a case, however, run a greater risk than when the enterpriser is a man of some means, and they therefore ask a higher rate of interest than if they were loaning to a wealthy man or to a wealthy company. They are in part the enterprisers. When, as usually, the enterpriser invests some of his own capital, it is a guarantee of his good faith, a sort of insurance reserve to protect the lender from loss. The first loss falls on the enterpriser, and the chance of loss to the lender is in large part, though not entirely, eliminated. It is characteristic of modern loans that the borrower may be rich, not poor,—often richer than the lender. The mortgage on real estate and the creditor's claim on a merchant's property usually give security of far greater value than the loan.

The enterpriser's insurance of the laborer's production

3. *The enterpriser gives to other workers a definite amount for services applied to distant ends.* In discussing the wage system it was pointed out that most labor at the present time is put upon future goods. It is not known what they will be worth a month or a year later when they mature as consumption goods; their present worth can merely be estimated. If they prove to be worth little, the profits may be nothing or less than nothing. The enterpriser, however, buys the services for ready money, embodies them in goods, and assumes the risk; the goods may sell for more or less than the wages. It is sometimes said with a certain irony that if the enterpriser assumes the risk he is very careful to pay so little for labor that he does not lose. In this naive view the enterpriser is so independent of the market that he can pay much or little as he pleases. In fact in many cases he gains little, and in many he loses and loses largely.

The risk of the enterpriser's services

4. *The enterpriser risks his own services and accepts an indefinite chance instead of a definite amount for them.* Assuming the risk for the right conduct of industry, he backs himself, expresses his faith in himself as a manager who can make labor earn more than the prevailing wages and make capital yield more than the prevailing rate of interest. If it were otherwise, he would loan what capital he has instead of borrowing more; instead of employing others, he would himself seek employment in some other industry. Men are constantly shifting from the class of hired workers to that of enterprisers. It is a rude and often tragic process of adjustment and selection that enables men having ability as enterprisers to continue in that work, and forces others into the class of employees.

The enterpriser the intermediary in industry

5. *The enterpriser is the economic buffer; economic forces are transmitted through him.* In a more primitive industry each man is wage-earner, capitalist, and enterpriser combined in one. As industry develops, some of the factors of cost become

distinguishable, and relatively stable and calculable. A low rate of interest, ranging from three to four per cent., can be secured with practical certainty by putting one's money into good corporation securities, into the savings-bank, or into national bonds. Contract wages in each class of labor also are fixed by competition at a point where they are a medium or average of gains and losses. The enterpriser is the most movable element. As the specialized risk-taker, he is the spring or buffer, which takes up and distributes the strain of industry. He feels first the influence of changing conditions. If the prices of his products fall, the first loss comes upon him, and he avoids further loss as best he can by paying less for materials and labor. At such times the wage-earners look upon him as their evil genius, and usually blame him for lowering their wages, not the public for refusing to buy the product at the former high prices. Again, if prices rise, he gains from the increased value of the stock in his hand that has been produced at low cost. If the employer often appears to be a hard man, his disposition is the result of "natural selection." He is placed between the powerful, selfish forces of competition, and his economic survival is conditioned on vigilance, strength, and self-assertion. Weak generosity cannot endure.

Fluctuation of profits

6. *Profits therefore fluctuate more from industry to industry and from man to man than do other incomes.* As a somewhat exceptional case, small employers in industries such as baking and tailoring, may for long periods get less for their work than their employees get in wages. The pride in being an employer and occasional chances of greater gains perhaps explain the fact. The fluctuations of the market may sweep away from the enterpriser not only all his "profits," but all his accumulated wealth. As a consequence, profits may be at other times very high, for men will not take the risk of great losses unless there is a chance of large gains. While the income of the salaried man is occasionally advanced, and then for long periods remains unchanged, the profits of enterprise come in waves. In seasons of prosperity the income of the employer swells with a dramatic swiftness while rents and wages move tardily upward. But for years again the employer earns a return hardly exceeding a low interest on the capital invested in the enterprise, or runs the business for a time at a loss. Profits of this kind should not be spoken of as a percentage. Greater or less, they are the net result attributable to the enterpriser's skill, and bear no fixed or calculable relation to any capital investment.

§ III. Statement of the Law of Profits

Anti-social or pseudo-profits

1. *Some apparent profits are due to anti-social or criminal acts.* Cheating, lying, breaking of contracts, bribery of public officials, and many similar acts may greatly increase individual incomes. These are not profits, as the term is here understood, but they are hard to distinguish from profits in practical life. One man gains a

THE LAW OF PROFITS

temporary success by acts that are later punished as crimes; another, guilty of like deeds, escapes conviction for lack of evidence or on technicalities, and enjoys ill-gotten wealth. More fortunes, however, are due to actions on the border-line of ethics, which society is not yet honest enough to condemn or wise enough to prevent. No code of laws can be framed that will make possible the punishment of all anti-social acts. Any law that would catch all the guilty would injure many of the innocent. Economic analysis may exclude from the concept of profits the gains made by such means, but only omniscience could distinguish them in every actual case from "swag and boodle."

Chance profits

2. *Some profits are the result of pure chance or luck.* What is luck? A result that is not calculable, coming to pass in conditions where a rational choice is not possible, is called luck, for lack of another name. Now pure luck often brings temporary profit to the individual, but chance does not in the least account for the average and abiding profits. There is bad luck as well as good luck. According to the law of chance, in the tossing of a coin for "heads and tails," one side is as likely to come up as the other, and in the long run the number of heads and tails will be equal. Where cases are numerous, losses and gains distribute themselves about a general average, and may be eliminated by insurance, as that against fire, flood, lightning, against sickness of the employer, which would cripple the business, or against his death, which would check it. But many factors evade all attempts to reduce them to rule, and chance remains a considerable factor in the success of many individuals. It still sometimes appears better to be born lucky than rich.

Profits due to a union of chance and choice

3. *Some profits are temporary gains from happy but not entirely accidental choice of the best course.* Many cases of profit said to be due to chance are found on closer knowledge to be due to superior judgment. A slight advantage in choice will give now and then apparently chance gains. The adventurer who, on the discovery of gold, goes at once to California or to Alaska, may stumble upon a gold-mine. It is luck; but if he stays at home it is more likely, according to the theory of chances, that he will stumble over an ash-heap. In places where gold-mines are comparatively plentiful, one takes chances between a load of lead and a bag of money. Throughout life there is constant opportunity, but it must be sought. One who has the good judgment to be ever at the right time at the place where he has the best chance of stumbling upon a good thing, usually gets the advantage, and men call it luck. The more the causes of success in general are studied, the larger is found the element of choice, the smaller that of luck. Some writers make these temporary gains the essence of profits. Considering that profits are always due to the introduction of new and better methods, and not to the continued use of better ones, they argue that as the knowledge of these becomes common property profits will disappear. But this in our view is a partial truth.

Skill the essential condition of continuing profits

4. *Continuing profits arise from the continued exercise of superior judgment.* After all the chance elements are taken into account, there remain differences in the abilities of men, and a continued and ever-renewed need of organizing power. Profits, being recognized as due to these differences in the abilities just as rent is due to differences in the fertility and efficiency of goods, have therefore been called differential gains. There would be no objection to the term were it not intended to emphasize a supposed difference between profits and rents on the one hand and interest and wages on the other.

Risk of loss reduced by skill

Some writers have so magnified the thought that the enterpriser's function is to assume risk, as to make it a denial of the view that profits are the earnings of ability. The risks of business are not those of the throwing of dice in which (if it is fair) skill plays no part, and gains in the long run offset losses. Business risks are rather those of the rope-walker in crossing Niagara; the task is easily undertaken by the skilful Blondin, it is fatally dangerous to the man of unsteady nerve and limb. Profits are due not to risks, but to superior skill in taking risks. They are not subtracted from the gains of labor but are earned, in the same sense in which the wages of skilled labor are earned. So long as some men have better organizing ability than others, have better judgment, are better able to take the risks, there is reason to believe that profits will continue.

Profits are the share, or income, of the enterpriser for his skill in directing industry and in assuming the risks. Despite the complex influences, they are determined by his contribution to industry essentially as is the value of any skilled service.

Chapter XXXII
Profit-sharing, Producers' and Consumers' Coöperation

§ I. Profit-sharing

Nature and definition of profit-sharing

1. *Profit-sharing is rewarding labor with a share of the profits in addition to contract wages.* The essential mark of profit-sharing is that the additional payment depends on the net profits of the whole business at the end of the year. It is not to be confused with a free gift, or with special privileges granted by the employer, such as lunchrooms, bathrooms or houses at a low rent. Profit-sharing is a contract made in advance, not a free gift. Nor is it the same as a bonus or premium for a larger output, made contingent on the physical product, on the increased number of pieces turned out by the workmen, individually or in groups. Premium for output is given for something directly under the influence of the worker. The amount of profits is affected by the amount of output, but also by a number of other things that are quite outside the control of the workmen.

The possibilities of profit-sharing

2. *The purpose of the employer in adopting profit-sharing is to stimulate the industry of the workers, thus reducing waste and cost of labor and supervision.* The employer adopting the plan does not intend to lose by it; he believes that if he can get his workmen to take an interest in the business his costs will be reduced. He offers to divide with them the resulting savings. There is, in every factory, greater or less waste of materials, destruction of tools, and loss of time, that no rules or penalties can prevent. If the worker can be made to take a strong enough personal interest he will use care when the eye of the foreman is not upon him. The product also can be slightly increased in many ways by the workmen's exertions or suggestions. In some cases the quality of the work cannot be insured by the closest inspection as well as it can be by a small degree of personal interest. Either responsibility for the fault cannot be fixed, or the defect is one not measurable by any easily

applied standard. Strikes are averted, good feeling is promoted, and contentment is furthered if the interest of the worker can be made to approach, and actually to be in harmony with, that of the employer. The economic result of the plan, if it can be made to work, must be to reduce the costs of these establishments below what they are. The crucial question is whether this alone insures that the costs will be less than those of competitors, thus giving a source out of which an increased amount, really a wage, can be paid to the laborer. This additional wage is made conditional on the employer's success in gaining a net profit on the year's business.

Its successes and failures

3. *The profit-sharing plan is now successfully working in over one hundred firms in America and Europe.* The plan was first tried in Paris by Leclaire, a house-painter. In house-painting there is often a great waste of materials and time by men working singly or in small groups in different parts of the city. By this new method Leclaire enlisted the aid of the workmen, reduced the costs, and increased the profits. It is a remarkable fact that the plan has been continued successfully by the same firm to the present time. The most important examples of profit-sharing in the United States are the Pillsbury Mills in Minneapolis, Procter and Gamble's soap-factories at Ivorydale, O., and the Nelson Mfg. Co. at Leclaire, Ill. In some cases both manufacturer and workman value the system highly. N. P. Gilman, the author of "Profit Sharing," puts the ratio of successes very high. Others declare that the failures are mostly lost sight of and are very many. The proportion of business done in this way is not large. One hundred firms is a very small fraction of one per cent. of the total number of firms in Germany, France, England, and America. A still more important fact is that this method of remuneration did not spread in the ten years preceding 1900.

Objections to and difficulties in profit-sharing in practice

4. *The failure of profit-sharing to grow is due to objections on the side both of the employer and of the workman.* On the side of the workman there is the bookkeeping difficulty. He is suspicious, and he lacks knowledge of the business. If at the end of the year the books show no profits, the workman loses confidence, considers the plan to be mere deception, and rejects it. Moreover, the plan puts a limitation upon the workman's freedom to compete for better wages by changing his place of work. It is almost indispensable to make length of service a condition to the sharing of profits. Workmen coming and going, working only a few months, cannot be allowed to share; the percentage given to the others increases with length of employment. Whenever men are thus practically subject to a fine (equal to the amount of shared profits) if they accept a better position, there is danger of a covert lowering of wages. The plan tends to break up the trade-unions, which is one of the reasons that the employers like it, and is the reason that organized labor opposes it. The employer on his part objects to the interference with his management, the troublesome inspection of the books, and the constant grumbling and complaint of the workmen. It makes known the amount of his profits; if they are large, the advertising of his success invites competition; if they are small, publicity injures

his credit and depresses the value of his property. In view of all these difficulties it is not surprising that while the plan often starts promisingly, it usually loses its efficiency after a short trial. Business methods are severely subject to the principle of the survival of the fittest. Through competition and the survival of the firms that adopt improvements, better methods must eventually supplant poorer ones. If a method fails to spread when it has been tried for fifty years and all are free to adopt it, there must be some defects inherent in it. That must be our conclusion as to profit-sharing.

Defective character of profit-sharing

5. *It is usually better to make wages depend on the worker's efficiency rather than on the profits of the whole business.* The strongest motive to efficiency is present when reward is connected immediately and directly with effort, not with some result only slightly under the worker's control. In profit-sharing the added share is only partially due to increased effort of the worker. Labor is but one of the groups of costs. Profits are the net result of many influences. Chief among these is the wisdom of the enterpriser in planning and conducting the business. The "profits" may be nothing, though the worker may be exerting himself to the utmost. The plan is, therefore, reactionary, not in accord with the general progress of the wage system, which is tending constantly to centralize responsibility, to put the risk into the hands of competent managers, and to secure to the worker a definite amount in advance, as high as conditions make possible. The system of premiums, or bonus payments, for output, gives in most cases better results and is rapidly spreading. It is sounder in conception and works better in practice. This premium depends on the increase by the laborer of the output of his particular machine or process as compared with a standard based on the experience of some definite period.

§ II. Producers' Coöperation

Purpose of producers' coöperation

1. *Producers' coöperation is the union of workers in a self-employing group to do away with any other enterpriser than themselves, and to secure for themselves the profits.* Its object is not to do away with any return on the capital investment. Capital may be borrowed either from outsiders or from the individual coöperators, and is paid a stipulated interest apart from the profits. The source of the gain is to be found in the saving of what the worker looks upon as the needless drain of profits into the pockets of the employer. The hope is that the enterpriser's function (if it is admitted that he has any useful function) will be performed by the workers collectively or through their representatives. They undertake to furnish brain as well as muscle, management as well as hand-work. The hope is even to increase the profits through increasing the stimulus to the workers and by saving in friction, disputes, and strikes.

218   THE PRINCIPLES OF ECONOMICS

Its limited success

2. *Practically the plan has been made to work in a comparatively few simple industries.* The most notable examples of successful coöperation in America have been the cooper-shops in Minneapolis. There were a simple problem of costs, few and uniform materials, patterns, and qualities of product, few machines and much hand-labor, simple well-known processes, a sure local market. Mr. Lloyd, in a recent book, describes many successful societies in England, but they are all of a simple sort of industry, as agriculture and dairy-farming. Within the whole field of industry, this method of organization makes little if any progress. Most experiments have failed and the successful ones often become ordinary stock companies with the most able men in control. Therefore, whether losing or making money, they nearly all cease to exist as coöperative enterprises. This result has disappointed the prophecies of many wise men of seventy-five years ago. In the time of John Stuart Mill, great expectations were entertained of the future of productive coöperation, which was thought to be a solution of the whole social problem.

Its main difficulty

3. *The main difficulty in productive coöperation is to secure managing ability of a high order.* There is no touchstone for business talent, no way of selecting it with any certainty in advance of trial. This selection is made hard in coöperative shops by the jealousies and rivalries, and by the politics among the workmen. A man thus selected by his fellows finds it almost impossible to enforce discipline. In coöperation there is occasionally developed good business ability that might have remained dormant under the wage system; some workmen showing unusual capacity cease to be handicraftsmen. But the unwillingness on the part of the workers to pay high salaries results in the loss of able managers. Having demonstrated their ability, the leaders go to competing industries where their function is not in such bad repute, and where higher salaries can be earned; or they go into business independently, being able easily to get control of the necessary capital.

Coöperators under-value the enterpriser's function

4. *Most coöperative schemes have suffered from a lack of good theory, an inability of the workers to see the importance of the enterpriser's service.* Most men make a very imperfect analysis of the productive process. They see that a large part of the product does not go to the workmen; they see the gross amount going to the enterpriser, and they ignore the fact that this contains the cost of materials, interest on capital, and incidental expenses. They ignore further that the enterpriser's function is a productive and essential one. The theory of exploitation, or robbery, as explaining the employer's profits, is very commonly held in a more or less vague way by workmen. With a body of intelligent and thoroughly honest workmen, keenly alive to the truth, the dangers, and the risks of the enterprise, coöperation would be possible in many industries where now it is not. The producers' coöperative schemes usually stumble into an unsuspected pitfall. When a heedless and over-confident army ventures into an enemy's country without a knowledge of its geography, without a map, and without leaders that have been tested on the field

of battle, the result can easily be foreseen.

§ III. Consumers' Coöperation

Nature and kinds of consumers' coöperation

1. *Consumers' coöperation is the union of a number of buyers to save for themselves the profits of the merchants or agents.* There are many classes of consumers' coöperation, but the chief ones are: (1) to sell goods (retail stores); (2) to provide insurance (coöperative insurance companies); (3) to provide credit or capital (coöperative banks). These are also productive enterprises, for the merchant's work adds value to the goods, the insurance company and its agent do a real service, the profits of the small bank are, ordinarily, earned fairly under existing conditions. The terms producers' and consumers' coöperation merely set in contrast the part of the productive process that is undertaken. Producers' coöperation is concerned with the earlier steps, usually stopping when the product is disposed of to wholesale or retail merchants. Consumers' coöperation (often called distributive coöperation) is concerned with the later steps, the placing of a consumption good (rarely also productive agents) into the hands of the final user. It imparts the same value to goods that the retail merchant does. The one thing this class of coöperators is sure of when they begin is a number of consumers to make use of the service or products they purpose to supply; hence the name.

Costliness of competitive mercantile business

2. *The waste of competitive mercantile business is the source from which it is expected that the savings of the coöperative enterprise will come.* It is a great expense to the retail dealer to secure a body of customers. Rent of store-room, clerk hire, interest on invested capital are fixed charges, which can be met only on condition of a regular and frequent turnover of the stock. To attract customers the dealer must have a well-located store, must advertise, keep open long hours, and pay idle clerks. Frequently he must give credit, raising the price enough to cover the expense of bookkeeping, collection, bad accounts, and loss of interest. The public's likings, whims, lack of judgment, and lack of business analysis make these charges necessary. There are many communities where it would be impossible to carry on a cash business even at considerably lower prices. Customers are exacting and require the costly delivery of small packages; two horses and a driver must travel two miles to deliver a spool of thread or a half-dozen oranges. Frequent changes of fashion and the shifting of customers from one store to another keep the merchant always insecure in his trade. A number of buyers mutually agreeing to pay cash, to buy at certain times, to place all their orders with one store, to go to a cheaper location, down an alley or into a basement, can save much of this cost on one condition: that the management approaches in its efficiency that of ordinary competitive business. In spite of all these advantages, if there is inefficient management the final cost will be no less than that of ordinary business.

The more successful coöperative stores

3. *Despite the possibilities of saving, most coöperative stores fail through a lack of good management.* Note first the greater successes. Since 1842, from which time it dates, the coöperative-store movement has progressed steadily in England, where the scores of retail societies are federated and own large wholesale stores. The long experience has developed good methods and a conservatism almost inconceivable to an American mind. They are practically great stock companies in which one can buy a share at a small cost and become a purchaser at usual prices, receiving a dividend later according to the amount of his purchases. Coöperative stores in American universities are generally successful, apparently because they don't coöperate. Some get into politics and go the way of the wicked. The survivors gravitate into the hands of a committee of the faculty, which tries to employ an efficient manager, and administers the business as a public trust without private profit. The wastefulness of multiplying orders for text-books to be used by a class whose number is definitely known in advance, and the comparatively uniform character of the supplies, make economy peculiarly easy in this case. A large part of the services of the coöperative store, however, are indirect; it reduces and regulates the charges in the stores near by.

The failures and their causes

Nearly all the Granger stores, started thirty years ago in great numbers, and most of the coöperative stores among American workmen, have failed. The failure is easily explained by the ignorance of danger, by lack of harmony, by credit sales, and by inefficient management. The wastes of competitive business are partly a tax imposed upon men (taken collectively) by their lack of business method; the community is not intelligent enough, honest enough, or self-sacrificing enough to do business in the most economical way. Partly they are the price paid for variety and change, and for the cherished American right "to kick"—something difficult for the members of a coöperative store to do without hurting themselves.

Profit-sharing and coöperation in relation to the enterpriser

Continued need of the enterpriser

4. *The experience with these plans verifies the analysis of the enterpriser's function: pure profits are the earnings of a productive service.* Comparing these three plans, they are seen to be alike in seeking to make workers share some of the profits, to change the destination to which profits would go. The first would create profits by the effort of the workers, and give them a part of the saving. The second would have collective workers perform the enterpriser's work in the factory and get his reward. The third would have collective buyers do the work of the merchant and save his profits and other costs. The last is the easiest to do. Profit-sharing is next in difficulty, and producers' coöperation is the hardest of all to put into practice. In some cases, under some conditions, the enterpriser's services may be more economically performed than at present, for the waste is great. But taking men as they are and things as they are, in most places the enterpriser's service is necessary

and must be paid for. His contribution to the success of the industry depends on his nature and ability, and it can be distinguished theoretically and practically from the contribution made by the workmen. Nothing but changes in human nature, in education, and in morality can diminish the necessity for his service.

Chapter XXXIII
Monopoly Profits

§ I. Nature of Monopoly

Difficulty of fixing the meaning of monopoly

1. *The term monopoly is used loosely and in many senses.* In popular discussion monopoly means almost any wealthy corporation or the power the corporation possesses, a power which is usually thought of as oppressive. Even economists have held the vaguest ideas regarding monopoly. The recent rise of trusts and monopolies has given a large new body of facts bearing upon the subject, but all the resulting discussion by the public and by economists has not brought agreement upon a definition entirely satisfactory. When usage has not settled upon any one meaning, the selection of a definition is in a measure arbitrary, though it may be guided by logic and considerations of expediency. Let us state the various meanings and indicate the one adopted in this discussion.

Monopoly is not merely scarcity

2. *Monopoly should not be used as synonymous with scarcity.* Scarcity is the essential condition of all value. The simplest things—bricks, sand, the commonest unskilled labor—would have no value were there not a degree of scarcity relative to the wants that may be gratified. "Monopoly," whatever else it means, always conveys the idea of some exceptional kind of scarcity, scarcity due in part to some source or cause not ordinarily present. It is a bad practice in definition to apply two words to one idea, leaving the other idea unnamed, as is done when monopoly is made synonymous with scarcity. Both words are needed. Such a usage unfortunately is common in economic literature. Many economic writers, for example, have called landownership monopoly, saying that land being the work of nature cannot be increased by men, and therefore must always be scarce. Even if it were true that in the economic sense land could be produced by man, there still would be confusion here between a general class of goods and a special thing. The fact that a particular field cannot be duplicated does not make a monopoly of land as a whole, any more than the existence of desert land in Arizona makes land valueless or a free

good. Nor is a land-owner a monopolist any more than is the owner of a valuable machine. The owner of forty acres of land worth four hundred dollars, or the owner of a village lot worth a hundred dollars, can hardly be called a monopolist. It leads to absurdity to use the word monopoly with reference to landownership indiscriminately. Neither mere scarcity nor the limitation of natural stores should be called monopoly when ownership is scattered and combination between owners does not exist.

Monopoly is not merely superior economic power

3. *The ability of superior material agents and of skilled workers to secure higher returns than do poor ones does not constitute monopoly.* The free competition assumed in abstract discussions of value, does not mean equal capacity or efficiency, but the legal freedom and personal willingness to move a productive agent into the highest industrial place it is capable of holding. The rocky field does not compete with the fertile one in the sense that it can yield the same uses. The field fit only for potatoes does not compete with those rare and favored localities that can raise the best wines. The gardener earning two dollars a day does not compete with the skilled physician with an income of twenty thousand dollars a year, for he has not the economic capacity to do so; but he is *free* to compete (as is the owner of the rocky field) unless law, caste, class legislation, social prejudice, or some other objective factor forbids. Anything, however, that prevents the labor or capital of buyers or sellers from application for which they are fitted, defeats free competition. To use the term monopoly of any and every limitation of economic ability is to extend it to every case of value. To use it of the high wages of skilled workmen, where no union to suppress competition exists among them, is to make it a colorless synonym of scarcity. It should be confined to a narrower and more exclusive use. Some special kinds of limitation should be connected with the idea of monopoly.

Monopoly consists in unified control

4. *The limitation connected with monopoly is not that of economic capacity but that of ownership and control.* The derivation of the word from the Greek points to the general thought: *monos*, alone, and *poléo*, to sell, a single seller, the sole source of supply in a given market. The term was first used in England of special grants or patents of monopoly from the crown to make or deal in specified articles, such as soap, candles, etc. The political power of the state created and defended the monopoly. This policy is pursued in a limited degree to-day for the encouragement of invention, in the granting of patents and copyrights. In the current definition, "The exclusive right, power, or privilege of dealing in some article or trading in some market," the term "dealing in" is well chosen, for it is broad enough to cover cases of buying as well as selling, and includes power derived from political as well as from other sources. But the term "exclusive" is too absolute, allows of no gradations, and makes the definition applicable only in the rarest cases.

Definition of monopoly

Monopoly limits supply

5. *Monopoly is such a degree of control over the supply of goods in a given market that a net gain will result to the seller if a portion is withheld.* Every producer has control over some agents and some portion of the supply of products; but ordinarily the portion controlled by any one is so small that withholding it entirely from sale would not cause the market price to rise in any appreciable degree. The producer in such a case regulates his action as if the market price were fixed beyond his control, and he uses his productive agents fully up to the point where costs equal price on the marginal unit of product. A skilled worker getting five dollars a day loses that sum every day he is idle. A landowner whose land can command a competitive rent of ten dollars an acre must take that sum or less, or nothing; he cannot get more. How can a net gain ever result from a smaller sale? As a reduction of supply results in a higher price, it is possible, as is seen in the paradox of value, for a situation to arise in the case of some goods, where a smaller number of units yield a larger sum in the market than a larger number of units. But the seller's interest lies not in the increase of total sales, but in that of net gains. Net gains, being the product of the number of units sold multiplied by the gain on each unit, increase at a much faster rate than do total sales. The existence of monopoly power in any degree depends therefore on several factors: the effect of contraction of supply in raising prices, the effect on costs, the number of units remaining in the ownership of the one contracting supply, and the possibility of preventing others from increasing supply later to profit by the higher prices.

§ II. Kinds of Monopoly

The sources of monopoly power

Political monopoly

1. *Monopoly gets its power from political, economic, and commercial sources.* A political monopoly derives its power of control from a special grant from the government, forbidding others to engage in that business. The typical political monopoly is that conferred by a crown patent bestowing the exclusive right to carry on a certain business. A second kind is that conferred by a patent for invention, or the copyright on books, the object of which is to stimulate invention, research, and writing by giving the full control and protection of the government to the inventor and writer or their assignees. In this case the privilege is socially earned by the monopolist; it is not gotten for nothing. Moreover, the patent is limited in time, expires and becomes a social possession. A third kind is a government monopoly for purposes of revenue. In France, the government controls the tobacco trade, and the high price charged for tobacco makes the monopoly yield a large income. A fourth kind are public franchises for public service, as street-railways, lights, gas, waterworks, etc. These are granted to private capitalists to induce them to invest

capital in something which has public utility.

Economic monopoly

Economic monopoly arises when the ownership of scarce natural agents, as mines, land, water-power, comes under the control of one man or one group of men who agree on a price. Economic monopoly is a result of private property that is undesigned by the government or by society. It is exceptional, considering the whole range of private property, but it is important. The oil-wells embracing the main sources of the world's supply have come under one control. One corporation may control so many of the richest iron-mines of the country as to be able to fix a price different from that which would result under competition. Coal-mines, especially those of some peculiar and limited kind, such as anthracite, appear to become easily an object of monopolization. Economic monopoly merges into political monopolies, such as patents and franchises. Private property is a political institution designed to further social welfare, and only rarely is any particular property a monopoly. Private control of great natural resources doubtless would have been prohibited had it been foreseen.

Commercial monopoly

Commercial monopoly, variously called contractual, organized, or capitalistic monopoly, arises where men unite their wealth to control a market, to overpower or intimidate opposition, and to keep out or limit competition by the mere magnitude of their wealth. These various kinds so merge into each other that they cannot always be distinguished in practice. A patent may help a capitalistic monopoly in getting control of a market; great wealth may enable a company to get control of rare natural resources.

Special classes of monopoly

2. *Monopolies may, for special purposes, be classified also as selling and buying, producing and trading, lasting and temporary, general and local.* The terms selling and buying monopoly explain themselves, though the latter conflicts with the etymology. Under conditions of barter the selling and the buying monopoly would be the same thing in two aspects. A selling monopoly is by far the more common, but a buying monopoly may be connected with it. A large oil-refining corporation that sells most of the product may by various methods succeed in driving out the competitors who would buy the crude oil. It thus becomes practically the only outlet for the oil product, and the owners of the land thus must share their ownership with the buying monopoly by accepting, within certain limits, the price it fixes. The Hudson Bay Company, dealing in furs, had practically this sort of power in North America. Many instances can be found, yet, relatively to the selling monopolies, those of the buying kind are rare. A producing monopoly is one controlling the manufacture or the source of supply of an article; a trading monopoly is one controlling the avenues of commerce between the source and the consumers. Monopolies are lasting or temporary, according to the duration

of control. By far the larger number are of the temporary sort, because high prices strongly stimulate efforts to develop other sources of supply. Yet the average profits of a monopoly may be large throughout a succession of periods of high and low prices. Monopolies are general or local, according to the extent of territory where their power is felt. At its maximum where transportation and other costs most effectually shut out competition, monopoly power shades off to zero on the border-line of competitive territory.

Relativity of monopoly

The test of monopoly

3. *Degrees of power to affect price result from varying extent of control; monopoly is a relative term.* The term monopoly by its derivation has reference to a single seller; but there are other thoughts in the concept. Monopoly has reference also to the amount of the supply controlled. The frequent use of the adjectives partial, limited, and virtual are implied but usually superfluous recognitions of the relative character of monopoly. Ownership of a particular knife, pencil, book, makes one the unique seller of it, but confers no monopoly power, as the power of substitution is practically absolute; the welfare of no one depends in any appreciable measure on that particular pencil. Ownership of an important fraction of an entire species of goods gives more power to affect value. One owning a large part of the desirable building sites or houses in town may gain by occasionally letting one stand vacant in order to drive better bargains with tenants. A trade-union may control most of the labor-supply of one kind in a town. But the test of monopoly is that a gain results from a higher price and fewer sales. It begins at the point where there is a motive to limit the supply in accordance with the paradox of value. The control of an entire species of goods gives price-fixing power, limited only by substitution of goods. Even though one person controlled all the coal and wood in any market, their prices still would be limited. If there were but one possible source of meat-supply, most people could live without meat. The monopoly of great species of goods can thus be seen gradually to merge from one grade into another. It is a matter of quality as well as quantity. There is more or less of it in the different industries, and, as noted in the preceding paragraph, it varies over time and territory.

§ III. The Fixing of a Monopoly Price

Forces governing competitive prices

1. *A competitive producer gets the highest price that will permit him to dispose of his product.* The enterpriser seeks to get the highest price for his product that the market will afford. His ability to continue making a profit at a lower price does not induce him to reduce the price unless the reduction is to his interest. The ordinary competing manufacturer is limited in his price by two things: first, his customers

MONOPOLY PROFITS

may cease to buy such articles entirely and may substitute other goods if the price is too high; secondly, they may buy of other sellers. Between his wish to keep the price up, and the customer's wish to buy as cheaply as he can, the price is fixed at a point where there is no inducement for others to come in and reduce his sales, or for him to seek a better market. There may be under these conditions a potential but very limited monopoly power. The sole druggist in a small town might occasionally get extortionate prices from particular customers in times of dire need, but he would thus drive away much of his custom, and would tempt a fairer and less grasping competitor to come in. Thus, when men and capital are free to come and go, there results an average or normal return for ability and agents of a certain grade. Prices come to equilibrium where each is selling his total product.

Monopoly's greater control of price

2. *Where a monopoly exists to a greater or less degree, there is less reason to fear loss of custom to competitors.* The degree of control determines the fear of competitors. If the control is slight, a very small rise of price will bring in competitors. The monopoly profits in this case either must be very small or they will be very brief. Those outside, controlling a large supply, will be tempted by large profits to market it at once and to increase it as fast as possible. Even where a large part of the supply is under one control, the fear of substitution puts a limit on the price demanded. If the control were extended to all wealth, the monopolist would be the absolute despot of the lives of his fellows. But as things are, the monopolist aims, just as the competitor does, to get the price that gives the maximum gain. The monopolist, however, is in a more or less favored position, as he can raise his price considerably before losing the most of his customers. Much depends on whether the costs increase or decrease as output grows. Where a large increase in output greatly decreases the cost, lower price may leave a larger margin between the cost and the selling price. A general monopoly price is therefore not an unlimited price. It is higher than the competitive price if the same cost of production is maintained. It may conceivably be lower than the former competitive price if the economies of combination greatly reduce the cost and justify a large increase of the output.

Discriminating monopoly rates

3. *A monopoly often seeks to avoid a general market price, and it adjusts its charge in each small market separately.* This is a most important aspect of the monopoly problem and a most important modification of the principle just stated. A market price is the expression of the least urgent demand that aids in carrying off a given supply. It is a maxim that there can be but one price at a time in a given market. The baker ordinarily sells the loaf at the same price to every one buying a given quantity. If he had a monopoly of the bread-supply, however, he might deal with each customer separately, ascertain, by personal inquiry into the lives of the citizens and by the aid of a force of detectives, just how much each could or would pay rather than do without bread. The policy of varying prices is thus followed by monopolies, though usually in a less inquisitorial way, to enable them to get the

highest possible returns. Under the name of "charging what the traffic will bear," it is practiced by the railroads as local and personal discrimination. The endurance of some communities and of some individuals being greater than that of others, the burden is adjusted to the back, being made not as light but as heavy as each can be forced to bear.

Low rates to destroy competitors

Large monopolies dealing in commodities use an adaptation of this method to kill off small competitors who, within a certain district, sell at less than the monopoly price. Prices are suddenly reduced in that community below cost until, the small competitor being ruined, the monopoly rate is reëstablished perhaps higher than before. Fear of suffering a like fate prevents others from attempting competition even when prices offer a great attraction and give a high monopoly profit.

The source of monopolistic profits

The profits of monopoly can be explained by the ordinary laws of value, yet evidently they form a peculiar economic and social problem. They appear to be due not to the services of the enterpriser in increasing production, but to his success in limiting it. There is, therefore, an anti-social element in them not found in the profits of ordinary industry. This deserves further and closer study.

Chapter XXXIV

Growth of Trusts and Combinations in the United States

§ I. Growth of Large Industry in the United States

Distinction between large capital

Large production

And monopoly

1. *In the discussion of the so-called trust problem three things must be distinguished: large individual capital, large production, and monopoly power.* Capital, in the sense of valuable agents, is found in the smallest as well as the largest industry, and every owner, from the small shop-keeper to the wealthiest bondholder, is a capitalist. In popular discussion, however, the word frequently implies great wealth in a single hand, though this wealth may be invested in a large number of small industries. Large production is the concentration of capital into large units of industry. The capital may be the same as before, the ownership may or may not be widely diffused, but the control and management are unified. Large factories may or may not have monopoly power; as factories grow in size, competition among them often becomes more, not less, complete and severe. On the contrary, monopoly, as before defined, may exist where the industry is small, as the waterworks in a small town, or a small factory for making patented articles. In periods of depression a business with a capital of ten thousand dollars may go on and prosper, while one with millions may be forced into bankruptcy. These three ideas—great individual wealth, large industry, and monopoly power—are often hopelessly confused in the discussion of present-day questions.

Stages of tools and household industries

Of simple machines

And of large industry

2. *Three industrial stages may be broadly distinguished: that of tools, that of machines*

and small factories, and that of large production. Men are prone to forget that all the world is not doing just as they are. Over two thirds of the people on the globe are still in the first industrial stage. One billion people use only tools, and have no better source and means of power than domestic animals. This is true in the most of Asia and Africa, in the greater part of South America, and in many portions of North America. About two hundred million people live in the stage of simple machines and small factories. These are found in eastern and southern Europe, small portions of South America, some parts even of the United States. In this stage there is not enough manufacturing power in the community to supply much more than its own needs. About two hundred million people in the United States and western Europe have reached the third and highest industrial plane, where the highest mechanical devices are employed and industry becomes highly specialized. These differences are broadly stated; there are contrasts within every nation. Three hundred miles from here, in the Alleghanies, people still can be found spinning and weaving and wearing homespun as in colonial days. In a trip of twenty miles in Tyrol or Switzerland one can observe every one of these industrial stages. The most striking development, if not the typical form, in America to-day is large or concentrated industry.

Household industry in America

Recent changes in number of factories

3. *In the last half century the unit of organization in leading industries has tended to grow larger.* Seventy-five years ago a tool-using household industry, on farms and in homes where the greater part of the things used were produced in the family, was still the typical organization in the United States. The early factories growing out of the household industry were small. A family specialized in producing cloth and exchanged with its neighbors; so with shoes, candles, soap, canned goods, cured meats, etc. Since that time two counter forces have been at work to affect the ratio of manufacturing establishments to population. The number of establishments has been increased by specialization of farming which has called for many industries to produce the things once made on farms, and by increasing wealth and invention, which has made possible many small industries supplying things before almost unknown. The number of establishments has been diminished as the staple products that can be transported have come to be made in larger factories. The resultant of these movements during the thirty years ending in 1900 is somewhat surprising: the ratio of factories (with an output worth five hundred dollars) to population has somewhat increased. In 1870 there were two hundred and fifty-two thousand establishments; in 1890, three hundred and fifty-five thousand, and in 1900, five hundred and twelve thousand, a ratio to population of one to one hundred and sixty-two, one hundred and seventy-seven, and one hundred forty-four respectively. The last date was one of great industrial prosperity, and doubtless many ephemeral enterprises had been called into existence, thus giving a somewhat abnormal result. Moreover, there has been a large increase in the number of things made in factories which were formerly made in the homes, and which then did not appear at all in the census of manufactures.

GROWTH OF TRUSTS

Large production in some industries

In cotton-weaving, however, the unit of industry is growing, factories in 1870 numbering nine hundred and fifty-six; in 1890, nine hundred and five; in 1900, one thousand and fifty-five, the later increase being due to the fact that many new factories in the South have been started in the last decade. The population meantime doubled. This movement has been going on for seventy years, there being about the same number of mills in 1900 as in 1830, though population had multiplied six-fold. Iron- and steel-mills numbered one thousand three hundred in 1880, one thousand in 1890, and nine hundred and sixty-five in 1900. In industries having local markets and sources of supply for materials, the change has been less rapid. There were twenty-four thousand grist-mills in 1880, eighteen thousand in 1890, and twenty-five thousand in 1900, a change of ratio from two thousand one hundred to three thousand population per grist-mill. There were twenty-six thousand sawmills in 1880, twenty-two thousand in 1890, and thirty-three thousand in 1900, a change from about one thousand nine hundred and twenty to two thousand two hundred and seventy persons per sawmill.

But while the number of establishments in these staple industries was decreasing, the number of employees per establishment in most cases was increasing. The average in all industries, in 1870, was eight; in 1890, twelve; in 1900, ten and four tenths. In cotton-mills, in 1870, the average was one hundred and eighty-four; in 1890, two hundred and forty-four; in 1900, two hundred and eighty-seven. The grist-mills, in 1880, had two and four tenths persons per establishment; in 1890, three and four tenths. The sawmills, in 1880, averaged six employees each; in 1890, fourteen; iron- and steel-mills in 1880, one hundred and twenty-one each; in 1890, one hundred and ninety-six.

Growing concentration of capital into large industries

4. *The amount of capital per establishment is tending to increase in the leading lines of industry.* The amount of capital is not so easy to determine as the number of employees, and it is recognized that the census figures on this subject are only approximately correct. We are told that in cotton-mills, in 1830, the average capital invested was fifty thousand dollars; in 1890, nearly four hundred thousand dollars; in 1900, four hundred and forty thousand dollars. It is easy to observe the large increase in investment of capital in flouring-mills since the new processes came into use. The average capital of all industries does not grow as in the staple ones, for many smaller industries have come into existence. In 1880, the average capital was eleven thousand dollars; in 1900, it was eighteen thousand dollars.

Recent formation of combinations

The years between 1890 and 1900 saw the rapid formation of trusts and combinations, and of larger industries. Consolidation took place on a great scale in railroads and in manufactures. Much of this has been of such a kind that it does not appear at all in the figures showing the number of establishments and of employees. Many discrepancies appear in the data regarding this movement given by different authorities, as there is no generally accepted rule by which to determine the selection of the companies to be included in the lists, and as the conditions are changing from day to day. A competent financial authority[1] gives the following figures regarding the "industrial" trusts (manufacturing and commercial) and gas trusts, organized in the United States between 1860 and 1899, not including combinations in such businesses as banking, shipping, railroad transportation, etc. The figures refer to the reorganization and consolidation of industries into larger units, some of which have much and others little or no monopoly power.

Decade	Number Organized	Total Nominal Capital
1860-69	2	$13,000,000
1870-79	4	135,000,000
1880-89	18	288,000,000
1890-99	157	3,150,000,000
Total, 40 years	181	$3,586,000,000

The number organized and the capital represented by this movement in the last of these decades are eight times as great as in the thirty years preceding. In the last ten years can be traced the influence of general industrial conditions.

Year	Number Organized	Total Nominal Capital
1890	6	$82,000,000
1891	13	168,000,000
1892	13	140,000,000
1893	5	226,000,000
1894	2	35,000,000
1895	7	104,000,000
1896	3	40,000,000
1897	6	93,000,000
1898	22	574,000,000
1899	80	1,688,000,000
Total, 10 years	157	$3,150,000,000

The first three years enjoyed great prosperity and the number of combinations were six, thirteen, thirteen. In 1893, the number was less, but the total nominal capital (preferred and common stocks and bonds) was still the greatest it had ever been in any year. Then came the period of depression, 1894-97, when both the numbers and the capital were comparatively small. Then followed the period of the greatest formation of trust companies the world has ever seen, which extended from 1898 to 1901, and ended in 1902.

---

[1] Compiled from data given by "The Journal of Commerce and Commercial Bulletin," reprinted in "The Commercial Year Book," Vol. V, 1900, pp. 564-569.

Trust statistics for 1904

In a list recently revised by another authority[2] it appears that the data for all "industrial trusts" (nearly, but not quite, comparable with the foregoing figures), are in round numbers as follows:

Date	Number	Number of Plants Acquired or Controlled	Total Nominal Capital
Jan. 1, 1904	318	5288	$7,246,000,000

These figures would indicate that the industrial trusts more than doubled within four years, most of the growth being within three years. The same authority, in a more comprehensive list, classifies in six groups all so-called "trusts" of the United States, at the date of January 1, 1904, as follows (the figures just given above are the totals of the first three groups):

Groups	Number	Number of Plants Acquired or Controlled	Total Nominal Capital
1. Greater industrial trusts	7	1528	$2,660,000,000
2. Lesser industrial trusts	298	3426	4,055,000,000
3. Other industrial trusts in process of reorganization or readjustment	13	334	528,000,000
4. Franchise trusts	111	1336	3,735,000,000
5. Great steam railroad groups	6	790	9,017,000,000
6. Allied independent railroad groups	10	250	380,000,000
Total,	445	8664	$20,000,000,000

§ II. Advantages of Large Production

Economical use of machinery in large production

1. *A great technical advantage of large production is the better and fuller use of machinery.* A large factory with a large output can keep a special machine adjusted for each pattern and process, whereas in a small factory much time and energy are wasted in adjusting one machine for various processes. The machinery in a large factory is thus more fully utilized. Compare the machinery used in a large ax-factory with that used in twenty-five small ax-factories having the same total output: the one hundred and fifty workmen in twenty-five small factories would use twenty-five shears, one hundred trip-hammers, fifty grindstone-pits, fifty

---

[2] John Moody, "The Truth About the Trusts," 1904.

polishing-frames, a total of two hundred and twenty-five machines; the same one hundred and fifty men in one large factory would require three shears, a saving of twenty-two; twenty trip-hammers, a saving of eighty; thirty-seven grindstone-pits, a saving of thirteen; thirty polishing-frames, a saving of twenty; a total of ninety machines, a saving of one hundred and thirty-five machines. The difference in cost due to machinery is not so great as these figures indicate, as the unused machines last longer; but in the small factory there is more depreciation from rust and decay, and a larger proportionate investment of capital for which interest must be earned. The average amount of stock and materials required in a large factory is not so great in proportion to the output.

Economy in labor power

2. *In a large factory the division of labor may be more complete and effective.* The technical economies of the division of labor can be realized in large measure only when a number of men work together. Partly because of the advantages in the use of machinery, but partly from other causes, labor in a large group is proportionately more effective than in a small group, especially in producing form-value. In making plows, nine men working separately will average sixty-six plows each per year, while one hundred and eighty men working together will average one hundred and ten each per year, the output per man being increased sixty-six and two thirds per cent. In a rifle-factory with a daily output of fifty, eight men are needed for the same product that can be supplied by three men in a factory with an output of one thousand daily.

Miscellaneous economies

3. *In the larger industry the costs of management, supervision, and marketing are relatively less.* Division of labor decreases the difficulty of supervision in larger factories, where the processes are divided, systematized, and made a matter of routine. The necessary inspection of the results is more rapid and easy. The advertising of certain kinds of goods involves a large and inevitable outlay, which is relatively less for a larger business, as the greater the output the smaller the burden on each unit of the product. Combination effects a great saving in the number of commercial travelers, a result partly due to the decrease in competition, but partly also to better organization. Each of twenty different factories must send its drummers into every part of the country to seek business. In combination they can divide the territory, visit every merchant and get larger orders at smaller cost. Supplies can be purchased more cheaply in large amounts, and shipments in car-load and train-load lots make possible special (sometimes illegal) concessions from railroads and from carriers on waterways.

Limits to the growth of a single factory

4. *There are some disadvantages in a large industry which put a limit to the growth of a single local establishment.* There is practically a limit to the advantages of size in a factory. When each man is working on the smallest possible subdivision of the

product, doubling the number of employees will not increase his skill. When the finest machinery can be kept constantly in use, economy in its use has reached the maximum. As large factories tend to create cities around them, land rises in value and higher wages must be paid the workmen. Small factories are constantly seeking out lower rents, taxes, wages, salaries, cheaper local sources of materials, cheap though limited sources of power, and thus they compete successfully in many markets. The point is reached in the growth of establishments where oversight cannot be as perfect and complete; the eye of the master cannot be over all. The market that can be reached by one factory is limited by distance, as the cost of transportation finally offsets all the other advantages of large industry.

Do not necessarily limit consolidation

It is evident that most of these reasons apply to a single local factory with far greater force than to a federation of locally scattered plants. It was once believed that the growing disadvantages of large industry would set an early limit to consolidation. While there is a truth in this thought not to be overlooked, the effects must now be recognized to be more distant than was supposed. The limits to the advantages of combination have been removed by the application of the federative plan which makes possible under one management the maximum of advantages with the minimum of the disadvantages in large industry. That was the discovery of the early promoters of the trust movement.

§ III. Causes of Industrial Combinations

Trusts in the legal and the popular sense

1. *Trusts are large combinations of capital with some degree of monopoly power.* The original, legal meaning of the term trust does not include the idea of monopoly. The old legal idea of a trust is the confidence imposed in a trustee. The method that was adopted by the early combinations was the trust method, that is, they made use of this legal device: the stock of the separate companies was put into the hands of a board of trustees to whom was thus given the right to control. As it has been found possible to accomplish the same end without the use of this legal method, the popular meaning of the word trust, as applied to a monopoly, no longer agrees with the legal meaning. The word trust is popularly used of any large industry, though usually there is connected with it the idea of some evil power to raise prices to the consumers. A large number of the corporations called trusts have, however, little monopoly power, and some have none at all. They are simply large establishments.

Economies of combination

2. *A strong reason for combination of competing plants is found in the legitimate economies of large production.* The economies that are possible within a single factory

may be still greater in a number of combined or federated industries. The cost of management, amount of stock carried, advertising, cost of selling the product, may all be smaller per unit of product. A large aggregation can control credit better and escape loss from bad debts. By regulating and equalizing the output in the different localities, it can run more nearly full time. Being acquainted with the entire situation, it can reduce the friction. A strong combination has advantages in shipment. It can have a clearing-house for orders and ship from the nearest source of supply. The least efficient factories can be first closed when demand falls off. Factories can be specialized to produce that for which each is best fitted. The magnitude of the industry and its presence in different localities strengthens its influence with the railroads. Its political as well as its economic power is increased.

Integration of industry

A recent phase of corporate growth is the "integration of industry," that is, the grouping under one control of a whole series of industries. One company may carry the iron ore through all the processes from the mine to the finished product. A railroad line across the continent owns its own steamers for shipping goods to Asia or Europe. Large wholesale houses own or control the output of entire factories. The possibilities in this direction have only begun to be realized.

Combination prevents competition

3. *The men uniting to form a trust always declare that its formation is the necessary result of excessive competition.* The statement is often true in the sense that a hard fight and lower prices have preceded the formation of the trust. But as this excessive competition usually is for the very purpose of forcing the combination, this explanation is a begging of the question. It is fallacious also in that it ignores the marginal principle in the problem of profits. Profits are never homogeneous from factory to factory, and to those that are on the margin competition may appear excessive. It is generally the largest and strongest factories, in the more favored situations, that, in order to get rid of troublesome competitors, force the smaller, weaker, industries to come into the trust. When, therefore, it is said that competition is destructive, it may be a partial truth, but more likely it is a pleasantry reflecting the happy humor of the prosperous promoters of the combination.

Financial gains of combination

4. *Another strong motive for the combination is the profit to promoters and organizers.* There are indirect as well as direct gains to the managers of a large business. There is the gain from the production and sale of goods to consumers, and there is the gain from the financial management, from the rise and fall in the value of stock. The promoters of a combination often expect to make from sales to the investing public far more than from sales to the consumer of the product. A season of prosperity and confidence, when trusts and their enormous profits are constantly discussed, has an effect on the public mind like that of the discovery of a new El Dorado, a California, or a Klondike. Then is the time for the wily promoter to offer

GROWTH OF TRUSTS

shares without limit to investors.

These considerations show that the trust is not simple in its cause, nor in its nature. In a sense the most artificial of industrial arrangements, in another sense it is a natural evolution of industry. More and more it is being recognized that though it has in it something of evil, it has as well something of good, and certainly much of the inevitable.

Chapter XXXV
Effect of Trusts on Prices

§ I. How Trusts Might Affect Prices

Economics of the trust problem

1. *The economist's task, strictly confined, is to explain the relation of trusts to prices, not to solve the problem of their political control.* The question of trusts is such a large one that its discussion here must be confined to those aspects having close relation to the central subject of economic study,—the laws of value. These laws were by the older economists thought to be true only within the limits of free competition. Seeing that in various ways this freedom is interfered with not only by caste, custom, organized labor, but by patents, political privileges, and the power of large aggregations of capital (in short by all things that check the flow of ability and of agents from one industry to another), the question occurs: Are the abstract laws of rents, profits, and wages of any significance or of any help in discussing the great practical questions of to-day? Are not prices determined by the personal whim of industrial despots who can bid defiance to the laws of price? The control of trusts by legislative action is largely a political problem, but it must be guided by a correct economic analysis. Proposed legislative measures often assume or imply that in no way, directly or indirectly, is competition found in the problem. It should be the aim of economic study to make clear the true bearing and force of monopoly power in practical problems of value.

Limited power of trusts

Monopoly and supply

2. *The fundamental principles of market value cannot be changed by a trust; a selling monopoly can affect price only as it affects supply or demand.* The strongest "trust" yet seen has not been omnipotent. Many careless expressions on the subject are heard even from ordinarily careful writers and speakers: "The trust can fix its own prices," "has unlimited control," "can determine what it will pay and for what it will sell." This implies that trusts are benevolent, seeing that the prices they charge are usually not far in excess of competitive prices in the past. Such a view overlooks

EFFECT OF TRUSTS ON PRICES

the forces that limit the price a monopoly can charge. The law according to which the value of products on the market is determined, is as valid where there is a trust as anywhere else. The marginal utility of goods to the consumer determines the price of any given supply. If the supply remains the same, no trust can make the price go higher. What it gets in exchange are the services or the wealth of the rest of the public. At what rate can it exchange its products for the products of others (including other trusts)? The monopoly usually directs its efforts to affecting the supply, leaving the price to adjust itself. (This is the case of the selling monopoly; the statement must be adjusted where it is a buying monopoly.) It can affect the supply either by lessening its own output or by intimidating and forcing out its competitors. It is true that this logical order is not always the order of events. The trust does not first limit the supply, and then wait for prices to adjust themselves; it first raises its prices, but unless it is prepared to limit the supply in accordance with the new resulting conditions of demand, such action would be vain. The control of the sources of supply is the logical explanation of the higher price, even though the limitation of supply is effected later by successive acts found necessary to maintain the higher price.

Monopoly price is therefore a rational thing, not a mystery entirely out of harmony with the simple law of value laid down for consumption goods. The trust works as the magician does, not as was thought of old, in defiance of natural laws, but in harmony with them and by their aid. The view the public took of the trusts was at first medieval. That should not be the view to-day.

Monopolistic gains from successful combination

3. *The economies of large production after a successful combination may be divided in varying proportions among monopolists, workmen, and consumers.* If the great economies of large production are effected by a new combination which makes no attempt to fix a higher price and limit production, where will the fruits of these economies go? They will go first to the owners of the trust, because, unless inspired by motives of philanthropy, they have no need to lower prices. Though they are in possession of special facilities, they will try to secure as high a price as before. A wider margin permits greater profits on each unit without limiting the output or the sales. They may retain this so long as they do not yield to the temptation to increase the output in proportion to their new facilities.

Gains to workmen

These economies, may, however, at times inure to the benefit of the workmen in higher wages if they succeed by any means whatever in squeezing the employers at this time of exceptional gains. The suggestion has even come from employers that in order to allay labor troubles there should be a union of capital and labor to squeeze the consumer, by doing away with all competition in fixing prices. This proposition to divide the plunder of monopoly has been viewed approvingly by some leaders of organized labor, but it does not look especially alluring to the general public, to which is assigned the humble part of paying the bill.

Gains to consumers

Part of the advantages will go to the consumer whenever there is a motive on the part of the large establishment to increase supply in order to get a larger profit or to forestall new competition. As the improvements become matters of public knowledge, most of the new economic methods can and will be adopted by new enterprisers, and other large aggregations of capital will be induced to come in to reap the benefits. The effect, of course, is an increase in supply and a lowering of prices. The fiat of the trust to prices to remain fixed while supply increases is as vain as a mortal's commands to the waves to be still. The undesigned result of the economies of large production, therefore, where control is not great, is to lower the prices and to diffuse the benefits among the public.

Social burden of monopoly profits

4. *If the trust succeeds in raising its prices it gains at the expense of the community.* If a producer has some monopoly power, recognizes and uses it, his gain does not correspond with an increase in production. It is taken from those who buy these products, it is deducted from the psychic incomes of other members of society. This raising of prices actually reduces technical production, for the output is limited in order to secure the higher price. The probably less urgent wants of the receivers of monopoly incomes are gratified in place of the probably more urgent wants of the average purchaser. The result is a decreased social income, with an increase of the inequality of distribution. There is an analogy here with the effects of trade-unions. If the trade-union succeeds in forcing prices higher than the competitive prices, it gains at the expense of the other portion of the community. But while its gains appear to be more largely at the expense of the richer elements of society, the gains of the trust are more likely at the expense of the poorer elements. If the success of organized labor means to some extent a leveling up of income, the success of the trust means a still further inequality. Hence a difference in public sympathy in the two cases.

The praise and blame for trust prices

5. *The responsibility for either the rise or the decline of trust prices cannot always be determined.* Prices are changing constantly under competitive conditions. In this active, moving world, changes of demand, the exhaustion of sources of supply, new processes, expiration of patents, opening up of new lines of transportation, affect prices in a multitude of ways entirely independent of organization. Trust-controlled industries are open to all these influences. Economic forces cannot be isolated as can elements in a chemical laboratory, and, therefore, trusts claim the credit for all the reductions of price that have occurred. By such a calculation the trusts usually make a showing of progress, as, until 1896, for twenty years the tendency of prices in most lines was downward. Always getting the highest price they can under the market conditions, they yet pose as benefactors. They would claim that the economies possible only under trust organization cause even a monopoly price to be less than a competitive price would be. Critics of the trusts, on the other hand, charge them with causing all the increase that occurs, and with

EFFECT OF TRUSTS ON PRICES

checking the decline in prices. The critics compare the percentages of decline in price during the decades before and after the combination was formed, and as it is impossible for a geometric rate of decrease in price, as a result of improvements, to be long maintained, this showing is very unfavorable to the trusts. A method has been found, however, of testing, in the case of a few leading industries, the effects they have had on the price of their portion of the productive process.

§ II. How Trusts Have Affected Prices

Trusts raise prices

The oil trust

1. *Examination of the course of prices in the case of some notable trusts shows that, wherever effective, they raise prices above the competitive rate possible to smaller production.* The most instructive study in the subject is that undertaken by J. W. Jenks a number of years ago, and later developed by him when working with the Industrial Commission from 1898 to 1900. Its results are embodied in a series of charts. It appears that the price of refined petroleum, in 1871, was twenty-five and seven tenths cents per gallon; in 1880, eight and six tenths cents; in 1887, seven and eight tenths cents; in 1900, seven and eight tenths cents. A writer in the "North American Review" claims that this decline was due to the economies accomplished by the Standard Oil Trust. It will be noticed, however, that prices fell most rapidly (from twenty-five and seven tenths cents to eight and six tenths cents) between 1871 to 1880, a period of intense competition, when the industry was new, and when the independent companies, fighting for their existence, introduced many improvements and began the construction of the pipe-lines that were later secured by the Standard Oil Co. Despite this rapid decline, the smaller companies still could have maintained a profitable business had it not been for the ruinous discrimination of the railroads against them. Because of this, the Standard Oil Co., in 1880, obtained almost complete control. The price twenty years later than that date was less than a cent cheaper. In the meantime the price for a time continued to fall. Competition was never quite stilled. The small competitor, wherever he saw a chance, has nibbled off a bit of the tempting profits. The rise from 1898 to 1900 was in accord with that occurring in other lines. A much lower cost of production is now possible to the great monopoly with its larger sales and more economical methods. The by-products, unknown at the beginning of the period, now yield large sums, yet the price remains much the same as a quarter of a century ago. The trust has succeeded in retaining a large part of the increasing margin of price over cost.

The sugar trust

The influence of the sugar trust may be studied by what is known as the method of differentials. The differential in sugar is the difference between the cost of the raw sugar and the refined granulated sugar. Raw sugar is the main material and the principal fluctuating item of cost beyond the control of the trust. Changes in the differential reflect the changes in profits except as modified by a cheapening of the process. The period from 1880 to 1887 was one of great competition. In 1880, the differential was one and ninety-two hundredths cents on each pound of refined sugar, but it fell steadily till, in 1887, it had reached sixty-four hundredths cents. In the fall of that year the trust was formed; and the next year the differential had risen to one and twenty-five hundredths cents, in 1889 to one and thirty-two hundredths cents. Tempted by the enormous profits, the rival refineries of Claus Spreckel were started, and with competition the differential fell, in 1890, to seventy hundredths cents. The rival factories were then bought up and under the new combination the differential went sailing up to one and three hundredths in 1892, and to one and fifteen hundredths in 1893. Rival factories again arose and competition grew stronger, reducing the differential to ninety-four hundredths in 1894. It was in that year that the firm of Arbuckle Brothers and Claus Doscher each opened a great refinery, and in the next year the differential fell to fifty hundredths cents. In 1900, some agreement, the terms of which were unknown to the public, was entered into by the rivals and the differential had risen, in March, 1901, to ninety-five hundredths cents. In every case the differential fell when competition was effective and went up when monopoly power was regained.

The nail trust

The differential of steel-wire nails is the difference between the cost of the steel billets and the price of the wire. Between 1890 and 1895 there was a steady decline in the differential. In 1895 was formed the nail pool, an agreement to share the profits, a form of combination. A rapid advance took place, both in the price and in the differential. In the fall of 1896 the pool was broken and then occurred a fall in prices and in the differential during 1896-97. In January, 1899, the nail trust was formed, controlling sixty-five to ninety-five per cent. of the output of wire nails, and a rapid advance occurred in the price and also in the differential.

The tin-plate trust

The tin-plate industry practically had its origin in the United States, in 1892, under the McKinley tariff. As competition increased, prices and the differential fluctuated and declined. At the end of 1898 the tin-plate company was formed and prices at once started upward with a rapid increase in the differential. Cause may, in a measure, be mistaken here for effect. In these cases the part of the rise in price due to the rise of materials is not brought about by the trust. The differential represents its part of the productive process and its source of profits. The power to make the differential high is due in part to the general conditions of business in the last three years considered. The profits of all industries in those years increased. While prices may have risen partly because the trust was formed, it may have been possible to form the trust because prices were rising. The general conclusion is that trust prices are always raised when, and to the extent that, control is secured. They are lowered below normal prices when competition becomes troublesome.

EFFECT OF TRUSTS ON PRICES

Fluctuation of prices probably has been more rapid and more spasmodic under trusts than it has been under ordinary competitive conditions.

Effective trusts injure various producers

2. *A large degree of monopoly control may lower the incomes of producers of materials, the value of competitive plants, and prices in special local markets.* A strong selling monopoly tends to become also a buying monopoly. A great industry using great quantities of materials may either own the sources or purchase from small producers. The steel trust owns mines, and ships and railroads to bring the ore to the furnaces; but the tobacco trust buys from the farmers. If the packing, refining, and marketing of a product is monopolized, the sellers of the raw or partly finished product are subject to one-sided competition. The small producers of tobacco, of crude oil, and of anthracite coal claim that the effect of the trusts is to give them lower prices for their products. Some have been severely punished by the monopolies for refusing to take the first offer made. Monopoly is thus likewise able to purchase competing plants at ridiculously small sums, by first making them valueless through fierce price-cutting, or by threats of it. "Rich" is often a relative term, and it is said that many a small millionaire producer has anxiously waited to see whether the great trust would next turn its attention to him.

The persistence of competition reducing prices

3. *Competition of less capable producers works in most cases to prevent the great or continued rise of trust prices.* Early trusts overestimated their power. The persistence of competition in industries where the trusts have had great advantages in position and resources has been astonishing. The wall-paper trust, though for many years it kept prices above competitive rates, was repeatedly undermined by competition. The whisky trust, while it frequently raised prices, was as often forced by the growth of small distilleries to lower them below competitive rates. Competition in the oil industry has persisted under the greatest difficulties. The smaller companies have hauled the product by wagon when the trust was moving it by pipe-lines. The continuance of high prices by a trust depends on a high degree of control of supply. A recognition of the limits of their power has led trusts in some cases to a policy of moderate prices, affording a good profit, but not encouraging competition.

Supply as the condition of low prices

The limits of the power of the trust to control prices are strikingly shown by the fact that it cannot even insure low prices if the market conditions do not justify them. The steel trust, in 1902-3, declared that it would not advance the price of steel rails above twenty-eight dollars, and this was hailed as a beneficent effect of trust control, which, by equalizing production, could prevent excessive fluctuations of price. But the trust's declaration was a bit of inexpensive humor on the part of the managers; the trust had nothing to sell at the price quoted, as its entire product had been sold out months in advance. While, therefore, the trust continued calmly to quote steel rails at twenty-eight dollars, competition raised the market price to thirty-three dollars a ton; twenty-eight dollars or more was paid for second-hand rails, and a proportionate price for other iron products. Such exceptional conditions, raising prices to abnormal levels, are followed by a decline disastrous not only to the small producer, but to the trusts as well.

Modes of controlling trusts

4. *The control of the trusts must be sought in the direction of maintaining potential competition through fair and free conditions of industry.* Many of the remedies suggested are reactionary and would give up the benefits of large production. Measures must be sought in harmony with the economic principles of price. Since many of the trusts have grown wealthy by special shipping privileges from the great quasi-public corporations, the railroads, and by special favors from public or corporation officers, who have been false to their duties, the solution must be a political and moral one; it must be sought in the development of honest citizenship and of a more efficient social regulation of quasi-public industries. The conditions of competition may be made fairer by requiring publicity of accounts, and by making it impossible for great corporations to strangle their local competitors by special and temporary prices. The state here has the same duty to perform that it has to protect the weak man from personal violence at the hands of the strong. This will not prevent competition, but it will determine the ways in which the rivalries of men can be manifested. Any measures for controlling the great combinations must start from a right understanding of the law of value, neither underestimating nor overestimating their economic power. Public sentiment toward the trust question has changed somewhat in recent years, because the nature of trusts and the extent of their power are better understood. There is now less fear of them, and more confidence that they can be tamed and made to serve the welfare of society.

Chapter XXXVI
Gambling, Speculation, and Promoters' Profits

§ I.   Gambling vs. Insurance

Unavoidable chances

1. *Many forms of chance are inseparable from the individual enterprise.* There are what may be called natural chances chances, arising from the uncertainties of the seasons, from rainfall, heat, hail, storm, flood, lightning, land-slides. Such chances must be taken both by the small enterpriser and by the large. In an earlier condition of society natural chance almost dominated industry, and it still remains and must always remain an important factor to deal with. There are political chances, as war and riot; as legislation on money, tariffs, credit, and business relations. These are caused, it is true, by the action of men, but it is a collective action out of the control, to a greater or less degree, of the individual—absolutely out of the control of most individuals. Men of greater political influence can to some extent control these chances, possibly in their own favor. There are chances of carelessness causing fire, explosions, wrecks on misplaced switches, and involving penalties and losses that must be met. There is the chance of physical or mental collapse, as the sudden insanity or the sudden death, unforeseen and unpreventable, of one performing responsible duties. Sickness often wrecks the plans and the fortune of a whole family. There are economic changes, such as those in methods of production, in machinery, in methods of transportation; such as the growth of fashions or the growth of population changing demand in some directions and for some materials.

Average of chances in each industry

Some of these chances are more connected with money-lending, others with manufacturing; some with agriculture, others with commerce; but all are present in some degree in every industry. In the broadest view they are not chances, for on the basis of experience it can be foretold that they will occur to some one; but no individual can tell when and how they will occur to him. A general average of chances in different lines of business causes some to be called safe, others extra-hazardous. The chance is averaged and added to the profit or gain of that industry, for an extra-hazardous industry must in general afford a higher average of profit in order to induce men to engage in it. It is folly to take a risk without ascertaining its degree, so far as general experience enables one to choose. But inasmuch and in as far as the gains and losses fall unequally upon different individuals, income depends on chance.

Other chances artificial and avoidable

2. *The essence of gambling is the attempt to gain by taking chances that are not the unavoidable incidents of productive enterprise.* The chances just enumerated are not sought, but avoided as far as possible; yet they must be borne by some one, and the burden must be distributed throughout society. There are unquestionably many kinds of chance-taking which differ from these in economic, and therefore in moral quality; but it has taxed the ingenuity of philosophers to lay down an abstract definition of gambling that would permit ready and certain distinction in practice between gambling and legitimate chance-taking. Typical gambling is the transfer of wealth on the outcome of events absolutely unpredictable, so far as the two gamblers are concerned. Examples are the shaking of unloaded dice or the honest dealing of a pack of cards. There can be no doubt of the entire lack of a productive economic basis in the betting on prices carried on in so-called bucket-shops by ignorant persons having no connection with the market of real things, and seeking to get something for nothing as a result of mere chance.

Cheating and gambling

Cheating is not a necessary mark of gambling, although the cruder kinds of dishonesty, such as the loading of dice or the collusion of horse-owners or of horse-jockeys to deceive the betting public, are so common that they seem often to be its essential feature. Gamblers recognize fair as opposed to unfair methods. Fair gambling is a kind of minor morality within the immoral field of gambling, like the honor found among thieves. Gambling bears somewhat the same relation to legitimate chance-taking that play does to labor. The chance-taking in gambling has no useful purpose or result outside itself. The gamblers constitute themselves a little fictitious economic circle, and they transfer gains and losses on the turn of events that have no practical objective result within their circle except to determine the direction of the transfer.

Various cases of a mixed nature; partisan bets

3. *Legitimate forms of chance, or risk-taking, shade off into illegitimate forms, or gambling.* Ranging between the extremes of legitimate risk-taking and of gambling are a number of cases of a mixed nature. The bets made on college games, races, and contests differ from ordinary bets only in the added feature of so-called college loyalty (a travesty on the real sentiment). These college gambling contracts are supposed (according to a mode of reasoning found also among primitive peoples) to exercise a subtle and irresistible influence upon the result. A crew that enters the race with the odds against it is unnerved and undone, thinks the patriotic

GAMBLING, SPECULATION, AND PROFITS

collegian.

Knowledge and skill affecting the result

In nearly all wagers, judgment in some degree influences the choice of sides. One man bets on a horse whose pedigree and performances he knows thoroughly; another judges by the horse's appearance as it comes upon the track. The professional book-makers have the latest possible and most exact information on which to base their bids.

In the bets made on one's own prowess, as on speed in running or rowing, or in playing cards (wherein also the element of pure chance is mingled) the chance-taking is still far over on the uneconomic side of the border-line. The running is for the sake of the wager, not for a useful purpose. A premium won by a runner for speed in delivering a message of economic importance is in striking contrast to the winnings in a wager.

Finally, the very border-line of difficulty is reached in the purchase and sale of goods in the market with a view of profiting by chance changes in price. Land speculation, the purchasing and holding of lumber, grain, cattle, and other tangible and useful things, must be judged liberally. The quality of gambling depends somewhat on the motive as well as on the ability of the actor. The enterpriser dealing with real wealth, and fitted to take the risks, both because of his resources and of his exceptional knowledge, needs the motive of gain, and in a sense can be said to earn socially what he gets. The motive of the uninformed must be a blind trust in luck, and a hope to gain from a rise in prices which they are quite unable to foresee or rationally to explain.

Gambling an economic loss to society

4. *In its relation to value, a bet, or wager, is the exchange of the chance of loss for the chance of gain, involving a social loss.* Even when fairest, the average results of such an exchange must be unfavorable to society. One person loses a part of his income that gratifies relatively urgent wants; another gains something that gratifies only less urgent wants than were represented by the sum he risked. The area that is subtracted from the loser's psychic income is larger than the area added to the winner's psychic income. The result would be different on the impossible condition that it were always the poorer man that gained and the richer one that lost. Betting, then, does not produce wealth; it merely transfers ownership in a way that reduces the total want-gratifying power of wealth.

The effects that gambling and betting have upon character are still more important and dangerous than their effects upon income. Motives of economic activity are reduced; energy is diverted from productive enterprise; society is demoralized through dishonesty of men intoxicated by gambling; speculation and embezzlement occur; and there is a reduction both of production and of enjoyment in society. These things can be reasoned out with mathematical certainty by means of the law of marginal utility.

Insurance as a wager

5. *Insurance is, in outer form, a bet; but its essential purpose is the useful one of equalizing and eliminating chance.* In its early form insurance was a bet made by a ship-owner to protect his cargo from loss. The chance of loss in shipping was even greater in the Middle Ages than now, and it became customary for the ship-owner to bet with a wealthy man that the ship would not return. If it did come back, the owner could afford to pay the bet; if it did not, he won his bet and thus recovered a part of his loss. It was what is called to-day "a hedge," that is, one bet made to neutralize, or offset, another. This gave to the smaller merchant the advantage of distributing his losses over a number of voyages, as was done by the owner of many vessels. Antonio, the wealthy merchant, is made thus to express his security:

> "My ventures are not in one bottom trusted
> Nor to one place; nor is my whole estate
> Upon the fortune of this present year.
> Therefore my merchandise makes me not sad."

Gradually there came about a specialization of risk-taking by the men most able to bear it. They could tell by experience about what was the degree of uncertainty, and could lay their wagers accordingly. When several insurers were in the same business, competition forced them to insure the vessel and cargo of the ordinary trader for something near the percentage of risk involved. The insurance thus tended to become a mutual protection to the ship-owners; what had to be paid in premiums to cover risk came to be counted as part of the cost of carrying on that business.

Insurance as mutual protection

Modern insurance is mutual in nearly every case: the total premiums equal the total losses plus operating expenses, the interest on the reserve of premiums counting as part of the premium. Each one gets protection for the loss of his property in return for the payment of a sum that will cover the losses on others' property. Such an exchange is a profitable one. The premium comes from marginal income; the loss of house or property would fall upon the parts of income having higher marginal utility. The less urgent wants of the present are sacrificed in order to protect the income that gratifies the more urgent wants of the future. In insurance each party gives a smaller utility for a greater; each has a margin of advantage; while the greater certainty in business stimulates effort and rewards it. This is quite the opposite of the working of betting and gambling.

Conditions of sound insurance

6. *To be economically sound, insurance must have to do with real productive agents, and with somewhat regular, ascertainable events beyond the control of the insured.* The difficulties that arise in case of fire-insurance are due largely to the failure to meet these requirements. When the insured sets fire to his own buildings, fire insurance ceases to be a legitimate thing. Constant efforts are made by insurance companies to guard against these "moral risks," the least calculable of any. Merchants whose

GAMBLING, SPECULATION, AND PROFITS

stocks have been mysteriously burned two or three times find difficulty in getting insured. In life-insurance it was the custom formerly to refuse to pay death-losses in case of suicide; but now that condition is attached only for the first two or three years. It being reasonable to suppose that no man would plan suicide years in advance, death by one's own hand some years after taking life-insurance is regarded as coming under the ordinary rule of chance.

§ II. The Speculator as a Risk-taker

An element of speculation in all business

1. *Every enterpriser is to some extent specializing as a risk-taker.* This familiar idea may be taken as a starting point in discussing speculation. In its broadest sense speculation means to look into things, to examine attentively, study deeply, contemplate, meditate. In a business sense the speculator is one who studies carefully the conditions and the chances of a change of prices; hence arises the thought that speculation is connected with chance. The enterpriser can estimate these chances better than most men. He stands on a hilltop sweeping the horizon, and can see farther than the workingman can. He relieves the other agents of part of the risk, and he insures both laborer and capitalist against future fluctuations of prices. Some of the profits of successful enterprise in countries where no system of regular insurance has grown up, and in certain lines here where no insurance is possible, are speculative gains of this sort. Offsetting them, however, in large measure, are the speculative losses, by which in many cases the investment has been swept away altogether. The cautious business man tries to reduce chance as much as possible by insurance, and to confine his thought and worry to the parts of the productive process where his ability counts in the result. The wise have found out that it is better to shift the risk to some specialist who can take it better than they. For a man who has his thought and effort concentrated on running a flour-mill, it is foolish to take the risks of fire, of loss in shipment, of a rise in the price of grain needed to fill outstanding orders—it is as foolish as it would be for him to make his own machinery. Insurance being the economical way to cover risk, the reckless will, in the long run, be eliminated from the ranks of enterprisers.

Specialization of risk taking

2. *In some lines the risk of marketing and carrying large stocks becomes highly specialized, so that ordinary enterprisers shift it to a small group of risk-takers.* In buying and selling large quantities of produce there is required the closest and most exclusive attention of a small group of men. The marketing of some staple products requires the most minute acquaintance with world conditions. To foretell the price of wheat one must know the rainfall in India, the condition of the crop in Argentina, must be in touch as nearly as possible with every unit of supply that will come into the market. Such knowledge is sought by the great produce speculators in the central markets. If all means of communication—telegraph, cables, mails—

are open to all, competition among these speculators becomes intense, and the result is the extremest efficiency. Their survival depends on the development of acute insight into market conditions. It is the testimony of expert witnesses and of writers in the report of the Industrial Commission that the margin at which farm produce is sold has fallen greatly in the last few years. These products are marketed along the lines of the least resistance, that is, of the greatest economy. The function of the commercial specialists is to foresee the markets, and to ship to the best place, at the right time, in the right quantities. If a product shipped to Liverpool will, by the time it arrives there, be worth more in Hamburg, there is a loss. Such difficult decisions can be made best by a small group of men selected by competition. When handling actual products they perform a real economic service.

Produce speculators as insurers

Source of legitimate speculators' gain

3. *Even some mere speculators on the produce markets may and do at times perform a productive service as risk-takers.* Many of the speculators in staples, wheat, corn, wool, rarely handle the material things, the real products. They make it their business to study the world conditions, to foresee prices, and in a sense to bet upon them. Regular merchants buy and sell fictitious products of these men. When a miller buys ten thousand bushels of wheat that will remain in the mill three months before they are marketed as actual flour, he at the same time sells that number of bushels to a speculator for future delivery; or selling flour for future delivery the miller buys a future in wheat. In either case he cancels the chance of loss or gain, giving up the chance of profit in the rise of wheat in exchange for protection from the loss of the product on his hands. To him this is legitimate insurance, for he is striving not to create an artificial risk, but like the medieval ship-owners, to neutralize one that is inseparable from the ordinary conditions of his business.

One may ask, How, if the miller in the long run benefits, can the speculator gain? He does not intend to perform this service for nothing. Yet as the sales in the whole market equal the purchases, some say that there can be no profits to the speculator. There are unsuccessful speculators and at any rate their losses go to the successful as a sort of gambling profit. Speculators do not dine entirely on "lambs"; they are anthropophagous. But, further, the sales to legitimate purchasers should net a gain to the abler speculator. In proportion as his estimates are correct, there will remain a regular slight margin of profit to him. If he agrees to sell wheat at eighty-five cents to be delivered in three months, he expects it to be a little less at that time. In the long run the ablest speculator probably buys at a little less and sells at a little more than the price really proves to be. This means that the merchants in the long run pay something for protection against changes in prices, just as they pay something for insurance. And yet this is the cheapest way to eliminate risk, and a man engaged on a large scale in milling is, it is said, at a disadvantage if he neglects this method of marginal buying.

Ignorant and dishonest speculation

4. *The buying of margins by the "lambs" is simple betting, and much manipulation of the market is dishonest.* What has just been described is the more legitimate phase of marginal buying, not its darker aspect. One who, having no special opportunities to know the market, buys or sells wheat, or other commodities or securities, on margin, is called a lamb. He is simply betting. He has no unusual skill; he cannot foresee the result. The commission paid to brokers "loads the dice" slightly; the opportunities of the larger dealer of anticipating information load the dice heavily against the lambs. Secret combinations and all kinds of false rumors cause fluctuations large enough to use up the margins of the small speculator. At times a number of powerful dealers unite to cause an artificially high or low price, a situation called "a corner." But this is little other than gambling between betters. The general public gains and loses little if any by these operations, except in the evil effects they entail socially.

§ III. Promoter's and Trustee's Profits

The promoter's service to the owners

1. *The promoter of trusts performs in some ways a substantial economic service.* A promoter is one who undertakes to convert a number of unrelated factories, or establishments, into a trust, or combination. He gets options on different factories, that is, the right to buy them at an agreed price within certain time limits. He gets some banking house to underwrite the combination, that is, to agree to dispose of a number of shares to the investing public. A certain number of shares go to the owners, a certain number to the banking house for its services in underwriting, and a substantial number, it may be ten or twenty per cent, of the enormous capitalization, to the promoter himself. This is payment for his ability to water the stock successfully, to capitalize it for more than its former value. Evidently the owners think he earns the money or they would not pay him. So far as there are economic advantages in large production, and inasmuch as there is always friction in the forming of new industrial arrangements, there is a real social service performed by the promoter. The gains of the promoter are in part the legitimate price of progress.

The loss of the investors

2. *A large part of the profits of promoter and of owners is unfairly taken from the investor.* The larger modern business is less and less attached to particular neighborhoods. A much smaller proportion of investments is made in industries which the investor himself can control or even see in operation. Business, therefore, in these days is done largely on faith in other men. Especially the investor takes great chances. The prospectus announcing a reorganization is frequently misleading. It frequently misrepresents the sources of income and the probable dividends, conceals essential

facts, and makes misleading statements. The capitalization often is absurdly high, compared with the value of the different establishments. In one case eight million dollars of stock were issued to represent factories whose combined value had been five hundred thousand dollars. So far as the capitalization is based on the increased profits due to the monopoly power, the profits of reorganization are taken out of the pockets of the public. But in fact even monopoly earnings cannot support such valuations, and from the outset if fair dividends are paid, they are falsely paid out of capital, not out of earnings. With the approach of bad times there must be a suspension of dividends, a fall in the value of securities, and a loss falling upon the investors. Such practices are a serious evil, for the stability of industry depends on the opening up of opportunities for safe investment to the average man.

The speculating trustee

3. *Corporation officers and trustees, speculating in the stocks of their own companies, are reaping illegitimate gains.* It is recognized by public sentiment and in law that for public officials to let contracts to themselves is bad morals and bad public policy. It is the duty of legislators not to make laws for companies in which they are interested. One of the greatest scandals in American public life, "the Credit Mobilier affair," was caused by the acceptance by members of Congress, virtually as a gift, of shares in a company that was seeking favoring legislation. Such action must be looked upon as a sort of industrial treason, comparable to the old form of political treason. Corporation officers are in a position of public trust toward the investors quite comparable to that of government officers toward the citizens. The power of directors and of other officers to manipulate earnings and dividends, and thus to affect the market value of the stock, leaves the investing public helpless. The practice by officials in great corporations of speculating in their own stocks, whose prices they can manipulate, is so common as scarcely to attract comment. Large fortunes result from this betrayal of the trust imposed by the shareholders. This is not legitimate speculation; it is like loading the dice, pulling the horse, drugging the pugilist—things despised and condemned even in gambling and sporting circles.

Two types of speculation

It appears, therefore, that in the complex conditions of modern business there is a legitimate concentration of risk in the more capable hands, but also a growth of opportunities for illegitimate speculation and for large dishonest gains that were not possible before. These two types of speculation should be distinguished, as far as possible, in thought and in practice; but this it not easy in concrete instances, which vary almost indistinguishably from the clear case of honest earnings to the other extreme of illegitimate gains.

Chapter XXXVII
Crises and Industrial Depressions

§ I. Definition and Description of Crises

Broader definition of a crisis

1. *In a broad sense, a crisis is a decisive moment or turning point; hence, in industry, a collapse of prosperity.* In the course of a fever the crisis is the point where there is a turn for the better or for the worse. The figure of speech as applied to industrial conditions would seem to fail, in that what precedes is apparently exuberant health, not disease. Business conditions do not move along uniformly. There are waves of prosperity. Profits are apparently great, then may be suddenly swept away. The profits of the prosperous time are partly illusory, or exist only on paper. The situation has all the unhealthiness of the fever-patient. Men trade in promises and when the crisis comes, they have only promises for profits. The discussion of business management and profits is not complete without a consideration of this rhythmic movement of confidence and prices.

A crisis in the business affairs of an individual, in the sense of a collapse of prosperity, may occur from many mischances. A local crisis may be felt in some one neighborhood as a result of flood, of fire, or of other accidents. Such a case was that which occurred in 1864, in Manchester, England, when the cotton factories were compelled to close because the supply of cotton was cut off by the blockade of the ports of the South in the Civil War. Such a local crisis sometimes results from a change of transportation, throwing a town out of the line of trade. These have been mentioned in discussing chance and risk; but the phenomenon known generally as an industrial crisis is of wider extent and of a more peculiar nature.

Various types of crises

2. *In a more special sense a financial crisis is the confusion and loss that mark the end of a period of rising prices; an industrial depression is the period of hard times that follows.* The word crisis suggests a brief period, a moment, something that is severe, sudden, and soon over. The term financial panic is frequently used as a synonym for financial crisis. A crisis in the narrower sense has to do with prices—

is always connected with money in some way. While, therefore, crises may be divided into industrial, speculative, and financial, according to their immediate occasion, all of them are financial in the sense that they have to do with a change in the general price level. A crisis is a jolt to prices which shatters the credit of some banks, brokers, merchants, and manufacturers. Crises are thus peculiar to the money economy and to a developed industry. Not every business misfortune is to be called an industrial crisis, but only those where prices and credit are generally depressed. A long period of hard times is sometimes called a crisis, but it is better to distinguish it by the term industrial depression.

Industrial conditions preceding a crisis

3. *The period leading up to a crisis is one of general prosperity.* Industry in successive decades does not pass through an unvarying series of changes, but history repeats itself with sufficient regularity to justify the view that a certain series of changes is typical in modern industry. When prices are at the lowest point many factories are closed, and much labor is unemployed. Conditions are worse in some industries than in others. General economy and great caution prevail; few new enterprises are undertaken. To those having available money this is a good time to buy, and property begins to change hands. Then hoarded money begins to come out of its hiding-places. Money flows in from other countries, particularly if business conditions are better abroad than here, for low prices make a country a good place in which to buy. At the same time that the money in circulation thus increases, there is a general return of confidence that increases credit. Not only are there more dollars, but each does more work. Then old enterprises are resumed and new ones are undertaken. The purchase of materials in larger quantities causes a rise in prices and an increase in costs. The surplus labor on the margin of efficiency gets employment, and wages begin to increase. The only classes not sharing in this improvement are the receivers of fixed incomes. As prices rise, the purchasing power of their incomes gradually falls.

The crisis and its results

4. *The crisis is a moment of widespread loss, which is followed by a long period of small profits to most enterprises, and of enforced economy.* As prices cease to go up rapidly, the question arises in many minds whether the movement can continue, and if not, when it will cease. Men wish to hold on for the last profits, and are willing to risk something to gain them. When foreign prices do not rise in as great proportion as domestic prices, foreign imports are stimulated and the quantity of exports falls. This disturbs the equilibrium of money and requires at length large and continued exportation of specie. This checks prices, and, reducing the specie reserves of the banks, compels them to be more cautious. The fall in the value of many stocks and securities held by the banks forces many brokers and speculators to convert their resources into ready money. This is the moment of danger; weak enterprises find their foundations crumbling, and there are many failures. The falling prices, the shattered credit, and the financial losses force many factories to close; many workmen are thrown out of employment, and business must again enter upon a

period of retrenchment, for it has completed the cycle of changing prices.

§ II. Crises in the Nineteenth Century

No financial crises in the Middle Ages

1. *The periods of industrial hardship in the Middle Ages were connected with adverse conditions of production, not with the collapse of prices.* Periods of exceptional hardship in medieval times were mostly due to political oppression, famine, wars, pestilence, and scourges of nature. There being very little of the money economy, there was no development of credit and of credit prices. The money economy began, as has been noted, in the cities. As the use of money spread, as larger commercial enterprises were undertaken, as borrowing and the payment of interest became common, there began to appear in city trading circles, on a small scale, the phenomena of the modern crisis.

European crises of the eighteenth and nineteenth centuries

2. *In Europe general industrial crises date from 1763 and have occurred at more or less regular intervals since.* It frequently is said that the cycle, or period, of crises is ten years, but it takes an elastic imagination to find support for this in history. The crises of the eighteenth century occurred in 1763, 1783, 1793, these dates marking the close of wars of some magnitude. The crises were not widespread or general, but were more marked in England, which was most developed industrially and in its money economy. Likewise in the nineteenth century, the crises were of unequal force in the various countries, usually being severer in England. The English crises may be roughly dated 1803, 1825, 1838, 1847, 1857, 1864, 1875, 1890. These were attributed to various causes; that of 1825 to over-trading abroad; that of 1847 to railroad-building; that of 1864 to the interruption of the cotton trade and of commerce, as a result of the Civil War in America. While in many parts of England the crisis of 1864 was unusually severe, in other countries it was of little moment. Germany, after several years of great speculative prosperity, had a most severe crisis in 1875; while France (a somewhat significant fact), although prostrated by the war of 1870-71, losing a large amount of wealth, and paying a thousand millions of dollars to Germany as a war indemnity, escaped a commercial crisis almost entirely at that time.

Crises in the United States

3. *In the United States there have been five marked crises: the first in 1817, the last in 1893.* These crises were of date 1817-20, 1837-39, 1857, 1873, 1893. Major crises thus occurred about twenty years apart, and minor crises in several instances alternated with them, notably in 1866, 1884, and we might add, 1903. These crises were the culmination of different kinds of speculation, usually spoken of as their causes. The crisis of 1817 was due to over-trading and to the immense importation

following the war of 1812 and the resumption of commerce with Europe in 1816. In 1837-39 came in quick succession two crises, not quite distinct from each other, the second similar to the relapse of a fever patient. The immediate occasions were over-speculation in lands, a great issue of bank money, national expansion, and over-confidence, possibly in some degree the heedless financial measures of Andrew Jackson. The crisis of 1857 followed a period of great prosperity marked by the discovery of gold in California in 1848, by great expansion of commerce, by the building of railroads, and by a great increase in foreign trade. The crisis of 1873, probably the severest in our history, is attributable to great speculation, especially to railroad-building on an unexampled scale following the war. The blow, when it fell, was intensified by the contraction of currency leading to the return to a specie basis and lower prices. The crisis of 1884, a comparatively slight one, occasioned (rather than caused) by the discussion of the money question, was followed by some years of noticeable depression. The years 1889 to 1892 witnessed a prosperity that culminated in a crisis in September, 1893, (likewise generally explained as due to the unsettled state of our monetary system) followed by a period of depression lasting until 1897.

The period from 1897 to 1903 has been marked by great prosperity and by rising prices. The over-hasty prophecies of collapse in the last two years have thus far been falsified,[3] but there is now a general feeling of distrust in investing circles. Already there has been a reduction of dividends in leading industries, and here and there a fall in the value of stocks. High prices have greatly checked building. The great credit advances made on "industrials," the stocks of manufacturing corporations, are one of the main sources of danger. Caution, however, has been learned by experience; the banking interests are more closely coördinated and give better mutual support than in the past, and a considerable decline in stocks has already occurred without as yet affecting general prices of commodities. Various novel features in the situation make prophecy difficult, but a period of liquidation and lower prices appears to be at hand.

General features of crises

4. *Irregular in time, and unlike in their immediate occasions, crises show some general features.* The chief of these are told in the brief story of the course of prices. Crises are less severe in countries with less developed money and credit systems. They are harder in the United States and England than in Germany, harder in Germany than in France, harder in western Europe than in eastern Europe, harder in Christendom than in heathendom. They are less severe in rural districts, where prosperity depends more on crop conditions, and business has in it less of financial speculation. Their effects are least felt in the staple industries, for when hard times come, people economize on the less essential things. The glove-factory, the silk-factory, the golf-club-factory are more likely to close than the flouring-mill. They

[3] These statements are retained as they were made in March, 1903. In the following September occurred a very remarkable panic in stocks which had the minimum of effect on general business. While stock prices have somewhat recovered since that time, general business conditions, on the whole, tended for a while toward the worse until the spring of 1904.

are felt less by classes with fixed incomes than by those with variable ones. They affect wages and salaries less than profits. The rate of wages is affected only in a moderate degree, but laborers suffer in the loss of employment. The money-lender who has eliminated chance as far as possible and has taken a low rate of interest loses little; the risk-taker who draws his income from dividends on stock probably loses much.

§ III. Various Explanations of Crises

Glut theories of crises

1. *Over-production and under-consumption theories are those most widely held.* In the first annual report of the United States Commissioner of Labor (1886) is given a long list of theories, more or less wild, that have been advanced in explanation of crises. It is simply a catalogue, not a logical grouping. Most of the views can be classed as under-consumption or over-production theories, which are but two aspects of the same idea. One view is that too many things are produced, another that too few are consumed. The over-production theorist, seeing that warehouses are filled with goods that cannot be disposed of for what they cost, that factories are shut down and men are out of employment for lack of demand, declares that productive power has grown too great. The under-consumption theorist, seeing the same facts, says that the trouble is lack of purchasing power. He admits that there are people who would like to buy these things, but he asserts that such people lack money because production grows faster than wages, wages being fixed, as he believes, by the minimum of subsistence—a theory akin to the iron law of wages. In both over-production and under-consumption theories the inequality of demand and supply is looked upon as a general one. There is supposed to be not merely an unequal and mistaken distribution of production, but a general excess of productive power.

Defects of glut theories

The wide vogue held by these views would justify a fuller discussion and disproof of them here, did space permit. It must suffice to indicate merely that they have the same taint of illogicalness as the "fallacy of waste," the "fallacy of saving" and, still closer likeness, the "fallacy of luxury." They overlook the fact that an income, either of money or of other goods, coming even to the wealthiest, will be used in some way. It may be used either for immediate consumption or for further indirect use in durable form. Through miscalculation there may be, at a given moment, too many consumption goods of a particular kind, but the durable applications can find no limit until the inconceivable day when the material world is no longer capable of improvement. At the time of a crisis, there is unquestionably a bad apportionment of productive agents, and a still worse adjustment of their valuations, but these in no wise negative the basic economic fact of the scarcity of wealth.

Money theories of crises

2. *Another group of theories explains the crises as being due to money, either too much or too little.* The unregulated issue of bank-notes has been assigned as the cause of crises, especially under the circumstances accompanying such crises as those of 1837 and 1857 in America, when bank-note issues chanced to be the agency most marked in the undue and unsound expansion of credit. The issue of government paper money, leading to inflation and speculation, is assigned as a cause leading up to such a crisis as that of 1873, following our Civil War. The reverse view is taken by the advocates of a cheap and plentiful money. They say that these crises were caused, not by the expansion, but by the reduction of bank-notes; for example, not by the inflation of prices through the issue of greenbacks in 1862 to 1865, but by the contraction of the currency from 1866 to 1873.

Their inadequacy

There is only a fragment of truth in these various views. It is always lack of money at the moment of the crisis that causes any particular failure, and in that sense it is always lack of money that causes a crisis. But the question is, whether in any reasonable sense it can be said that it was lack of a circulating medium before the crisis that brought it on. There is no support for this view, except in the rare case when the money standard is undergoing a rapid change, as in the United States from 1866 to 1873, and the statement then needs much modification and explanation. The money theories of crises are nearer to the truth than are the over-production type, for the crisis is always connected with money and prices. But it cannot be said that the absolute amount of money in circulation in the period preceding crises gives occasion to them. In a few instances a rapid change in the amount has had an important effect, but this fact does not explain crises in general.

Lack of confidence is said to be a cause of crises. This is a truism, but the lack of confidence is not without reason and cause. Over-confidence in the period of expanding prices is succeeded by extreme depression when many false hopes are shattered.

Capitalization theory of crises

3. *Crises must be explained essentially as the forcible and sudden movement of readjustment in the mistaken capitalization of productive agents.* Capitalization runs through all industry. The value of everything that lasts for more than a moment is built in part upon rents that are not actual, but expectative, whose amount, therefore, is a matter of guesswork, or "speculation." Many unknown factors enter into the estimate of future rents. The universal tendency to rhythm in motion (material or psychic) manifests itself in an overestimate or underestimate of rent and of every other factor in value. This is emphasized by a psychological factor called the "hypnotism of the crowd," Most men follow a leader in investment as in other things. The spirit of speculation grows till it becomes almost a frenzy, and people rush toward this or that investment, throwing capitalization in some industries far out of equilibrium with that in others.

The use of credit enhances the rhythm of price. A large part of business is done practically on margins. If the value of a thing fully paid for falls in the hands of the owner, he alone loses; but if the value of a thing only partly paid for falls so much that the owner is forced to default in his payment, the loss may be transmitted along the line of credit to every one in the series of transactions. A credit system, highly developed, is a house of cards at a time of financial stress. There is an element of credit in all modern business. Enterprisers enter into strenuous rivalry to secure the profits of a rise, ever hoping to get out whole before the crisis comes.

Psychological nature and objective conditions of crises

The fundamental cause of crises thus is seen to be psychological; it is the rhythmic miscalculation of rents and of capital value, occurring to some degree throughout industry, but particularly in certain lines. But this subjective cause in men is given full opportunity for action only when certain favoring objective conditions are present. Most noteworthy of these besides the credit system is a dynamic condition of industry. The past century has opened up new fields for investment on an unexampled scale. Investment has advanced both intensively and extensively in a series of great waves. New machinery and processes have given undreamed of opportunities for enterprise in the older countries, and the physical frontier of investment has moved outward with the march of millions of immigrants to people the fertile wilderness. Such factors disturb the equilibrium of prices both in time and space, give a powerful impulse toward higher values in the older lands, and stimulate the hopes of all investors. When the balance between the capitalizations of various industries and between the rents of the various periods proves to be false, the inevitable readjustment causes suffering and loss to many, but particularly in the inflated industries. But, because of the mutual relations of men in business, few even of those who have kept freest from speculation can quite escape the evils.

Widespread effects on incomes

4. *Crises must be discussed in connection with other subjects than profits.* In the textbooks the subject of the crisis is variously classified. It may well be discussed with money, credit, and banking. It has its bearings on wages, justice in distribution, the theory of interest, and the consumption of wealth. But the reasons for taking it up in connection with the subject of profits are strongest. In no other connection is the presence of the element of speculation and of chance profit and loss in business so forcibly seen.

Their probable mitigation

The income of every class of society is to some extent affected by these more or less periodic fluctuations. They are in part the price paid for progress under the constantly shifting conditions of our dynamic industry. In part they are the proof of industrial maladjustment. The force of the shocks will no doubt be much reduced by better banking and business methods, and by a sound currency system.

More important still, the development of moderation, conservatism, and a less speculative spirit among the leaders of business will do much toward softening the asperity of these scourges of industry.

PART III
THE SOCIAL ASPECTS OF VALUE

DIVISION A—RELATION OF PRIVATE INCOME TO SOCIAL WELFARE

Chapter XXXVIII
Private Property and Inheritance

§ I. Impersonal and Personal Shares of Income

Functional vs. personal distribution

1. *Under the title "the social aspects of value" are to be considered the influences exerted upon incomes by various social acts, ideals, and institutions.* The incomes from the wages of free labor and those from the rent of wealth, as studied in the abstract theory of value, are alike in their impersonal aspect, their relation to utility. But while wage flows from a personal source—is an income appearing to reward the personal effort of the laborer, the income of the wealth-owner is due to the uses of goods. In the abstract theory of value we do not seek to get behind this impersonal phase of rent. The income arising from goods goes to the de facto owner of the goods. We do not ask how the goods first came into his possession, whether through labor or as a gift, whether stolen or inherited. Indeed, the economic theory of competitive rent may be said not to recognize the personal fact of ownership; it is concerned with the impersonal fact of usufruct. The theory of economic rent, of time-value and capital, and of wages, as measured by efficiency, is impersonal, is a study of functional distribution. In the problem of monopoly the personal factor is more prominent, but the economic study of rent cannot well stop there.

Social institutions and personal incomes

An answer, at least in broad outline, must now be given to the question why some men are permitted to hold wealth as their "own," that is, as "property," while other men are propertyless. Why do the owners exact payment for the use of goods, and why are they allowed by their fellows to do so? Back of these facts is a great system of social institutions that helps to determine what men will do. Market value is a social fact; price is determined by the bidding of men under the existing social and political conditions. These broader social aspects of value remain for consideration. The influence of lawmaking, of collective action, and of social institutions on value must be noted. Incidentally, this has been done in speaking of patents, political monopolies, and related questions; but mainly the subject has been viewed from the individual standpoint; now it must be looked at more fully from the social side.

Harmony of the studies of impersonal and of personal distribution

2. *The study of personal distribution should include a further explanation of the various elements that unite to form the individual's income.* "Distribution" in economics is the reasoned explanation of the way in which the total product of a society is divided among its members. It is a logical question and not an ethical one. The economist first asks, What is the effect of utility on value? and, next, What is the relation of these goods to the personal incomes of the members of society? It is not his peculiar part to say whether this is the best distribution in an ethical sense, yet in pursuing the question of distribution one comes to the border of certain moral questions.

The impersonal and the personal views of distribution are not, however, contradictory; they are different aspects of the same question. It cannot be said that the analysis of economic rent is a purely abstract piece of work. In fact, the impersonal view of distribution is essential to an understanding of the personal view of it. The one gives general principles, the other the special cases. In the practical economic issues of the day, the most urgent need is a better popular understanding of the abstracter theory of value. It is a guiding thread through otherwise bewildering mazes.

Composition of personal incomes

The actual incomes of individuals are made up of different elements. The wage-earner and the salaried man are rarely quite without material wealth. The enterpriser gets some income also in the form of contract interest, or as rent from machinery. Actual personal incomes are therefore a sum of various functional or impersonal incomes. The earnings of every agent may be thought of as always going either to some individual or to some group. By social convention the receiver of incomes that are not personal gifts is supposed to have produced them. This involves the great assumption that the owner of a piece of land has produced or contributed in some way to society an amount equal to the rent. This may be true in many cases, but in many cases this view cannot be accepted without close scrutiny.

Law in relation to wealth

3. *Property and wealth are respectively the personal and the impersonal, the legal and the economic, aspects of productive agents.* Law holds an important place in the discussion of actual economic questions. This fact was not overlooked by John Stuart Mill, and it has been far more clearly recognized in the last few years, especially by the German economists. Political law in the broadest sense, as embodied in the state, is, in the first place, a set of rules to guide the conduct and regulate the relations of men in society—a legal code; it is, in the next place, a governmental machine to determine disputes between men—a judicial system; and it is, finally,

physical power to bring contestants into court and to secure and protect their rights—a police force. Whether acting through legislature, courts, or police, in all its dealings with wealth the law is predominantly personal. The question the law asks and answers regarding wealth is not *What*, but *Who?* Who is the owner, who should control, receive, enjoy the income? Economic wealth consists of scarce things, of valuable agents, and because they are scarce, men quarrel over them. Because of the impersonal economic fact that a field and a machine produce scarce goods, arises the legal question as to which man is entitled to enjoy them.

Property and wealth

In the case of material things, property value and capital value must be exactly equal. Property rights cover the ownership of a material thing. Material property consists of things viewed with reference to ownership; capital consists of the same things viewed with reference to their economic services. There are other property rights besides those in material things, various immaterial rights controlling the action of the individual and thus giving a sort of ownership of the individual's actions. Such are patents which forbid other men making a particular kind of machine; copyrights which forbid other men printing certain writings; legal contracts that limit the action of men in various ways, and thus appear to abridge their liberty.

§ II. The Origin of Private Property

Property and income

1. *Property is ownership, the legal control over the sources of economic income.* The Latin word property means ownership, and hence that which pertains to the individual, that which is a man's own. The control of property is greater or less. The law makes between property rights and equity rights certain subtle distinctions which have their reason in the history, if not in the logic, of the law, but which are not essential to economic discussion. What we are interested in are the equitable claims of men to wealth rather than the technical property rights. With that thought let us consider the value of the control of wealth. If a farm worth ten thousand dollars is mortgaged for five thousand dollars, its economic worth is ten thousand dollars after as before the mortgage, but the equitable claim is divided into two shares of five thousand dollars each. The value of the property right cannot, in a reasonable view, be greater than the value of the economic wealth it covers. There is much confusion in the law of taxation on this point. The law treats the farm as property and the debt upon it, whether secured by a mortgage or not, as another body of property. Needless to say, this leads to absurd conclusions in reasoning, and to gross injustice.

Forms and modes of ownership

There are different forms of ownership: first, private, as that of individuals, families, partnerships, or corporations; second, public or state, as the ownership of the state house, the highway, the Adirondack forest-reserve or the Erie Canal. These are equally effective as against the claims of outsiders, but the rights of those inside the circle of ownership differ. For example, the rights of one shareholder against another, or the rights of one member of a family as against another, are not the same as the rights against outsiders. Private property is the characteristic feature of our present industrial society, but it exists side by side with state property and with many intermediate grades between private and common property. Private property, while attacked on some sides, is usually accepted without question; but in this age of inquiry its origin should be examined, its limits and the reasons for them should be noted, and its purpose, faults, and effects should be set clearly before the judgment.

Various theories of property: Occupation

2. *The older theories of the origin of private property are those of occupation, conquest, labor, natural rights, and law.* The theory of occupation is that property is based upon the priority of claim of one who finds wealth without an owner and appropriates it. This, to be sure, is a statement of what happens in the settlement of new countries, but it is not an explanation of the property rights that are arising every moment, nor does it give a logical reason for the continuance of ancient property rights.

Conquest

The same can be said of the conquest theory, the theory that property is based on force. It applies to the invasion of the Roman provinces by the barbarian tribes who divided the country and enslaved the population. But it rarely applies to present-day happenings and at its best it cannot, to modern minds, "justify" present property rights.

Labor

The labor theory, meeting some queries where others fail, is that ownership is based on production, on the right of a man to that to which his brain and his muscle have imparted value. It is evident that this test leaves without explanation or justification a great number of things that do exist and have existed as property.

Natural rights

The natural-rights theory is that property is necessary for the realization of the dignity of human nature. This, if true, would be not so much an explanation as a condemnation of private property as it has existed in most cases, as millions of men are in every land all but lacking in property, and inequality of possession is everywhere marked. This theory expresses, however, one of the worthy ideals of modern democracy. Although, in common with the various other "natural rights"

PRIVATE PROPERTY AND INHERITANCE

theories, it must to-day be deemed too absolute and too individualistic, it contains a far-reaching truth, of which due account must be taken in our social philosophy.

Law

The legal theory is that property exists because the law says it shall. This expresses a truth, but is no more than a truism. The law determines the limits of property, but what determines the limits of the law? What practical or social justification is there for passing and continuing such law? The legal theory does not explain anything finally. Each of these theories has its defects, but each points to some fact important and significant, at certain times and places, in the explanation of this widespread institution.

Property in early societies

3. *The institution of private property has evolved under diverse conditions; the question of its origin is not the same as that of its present justification.* In early societies individual property rights were not very clearly marked. Every tribe asserted against other tribes, and tried to uphold, by war, its claims upon its customary hunting-grounds; but the claims of the individual hunter and fisher within the tribe did not often come into conflict. Private property at the outset was in personal possessions, ornaments, weapons, utensils, which were very meager in that primitive society where it was the custom "to go calling with a club instead of a card-case." Only later came individual property in land. A few years ago it was generally believed that the organization of the old German tribes was politically an almost perfect democracy, and economically a communism wherein all had equal claims on the land. To-day this opinion is very seriously questioned. It seems probable that the so-called communism was really an oligarchy of the favored, and that the masses lived in subjection, cut off from all but a meager share in the public property.

Origin vs. present justification of property

However that may have been, strong forces within historic times have put an end to the common ownership and tillage of land as it existed among the serfs of Europe. The common tillage of land was shown by experience to be wasteful. Not only did competition tend to bring the economic agents into more efficient hands, but the movement was furthered by many acts of injustice and violence on the part of those in power. Inquiries into the origin and development of this social institution are interesting and helpful in forming an estimate of its present significance, but the problems of the past are not those of to-day. Whether or not the ancient beginning of property in Europe was in violence and evil has but a remote bearing on the question as to the present working of it. Social conditions and needs have not changed more than have the forms and limits of property itself. Each generation has its own problems to solve, and each must test existing institutions by their present results, ignoring for the most part the evils of the past.

Social expediency the ground of private property

Shifting limits of the law of property

4. *Private property may now be justified mainly on the grounds of social expediency.* This is a broad explanation under which can be brought the many varying conditions; but it has the fault of a broad explanation, that it needs to be further explained. Conceding that private property works hardship to the individual in many cases, it must be justified on the ground that, on the whole, it furthers the progress of society. Private property is looked upon by some as merely reflecting or expressing the economic inequalities of men; the man poor in ability is the man poor in property. It is looked upon by others as exaggerating, indeed at times reversing, the economic abilities of men. In general, it must be judged by this test: Does it further the welfare of society better than would any alternative plan for the control of economic wealth? The question is not whether it is faultless, for no human institution is so. Nor must it be assumed that property is a fixed and uniform mode of control; there are many kinds of property. Different parts of wealth may be treated in different ways: there may be private property in wagons, and public property in roads; private property in houses, and public property in forests; private property in automobiles, and, in some countries, public property in railway-carriages. But any rule of property, like any other workable human law, must be applicable to all individuals that meet the conditions. Hence any human institution must be judged by its average working, not by exceptional cases.

The very acceptance of the theory of social expediency implies the need of a readjustment of the institution of private property; for private property, as it is found to-day, is complicated by many historical accidents. Survivals of ancient injustice and relics of feudal institutions that rest on no vital reason remain in our new country as well as in the older ones. The limits of property in many respects are determined, not according to the logic of expediency, but by the social inertia which often governs succeeding generations.

§ III. Limitations of the Right of Private Property

Public interests limiting property rights

1. *Unmodified private control of property is unknown: the public makes many reservations in its own interest.* Few realize the manifold ways in which property rights are limited. There is, first, a whole set of limitations to prevent nuisances. An owner in many situations is not free to build a slaughter-house or to start a glue-factory on his land. Property is governed by general public utility, and anything that threatens to become a nuisance or a danger is excluded. When, under the right of eminent domain, the state or the railroad takes the old homestead from its owner who would live and die there, the payment of money damages to him does not make this the less a limitation of his property rights. Rights of way on property exist either through contract or by prescription permitting its public use.

Most important of all limitations is the right of taxation, by which society takes more or less of private incomes for purposes of which the individual owners may in no way approve.

Private claims limiting property rights

2. *The law enforces a multitude of private claims against private owners.* A variety of rights called easements or servitudes may attach to private property, modifying its exclusive use. Leases for any period are a virtual limitation of the control and division of the ownership. Both the holder of the lease and the owner of the property have certain rights before the law. The lender of money secured by mortgage has a legally recognized and enforceable interest in the mortgaged wealth. Property is left in trust for the benefit of persons or of institutions or of the public, and is administered by trustees who are strictly bound to the execution of the terms of their instructions. Contracts of many sorts are entered into by owners, limiting their control in manifold ways, and the law enforces these contracts. These all form a complex of equitable claims, which together equal in value one undivided property right, which in turn equals the value of the wealth. These claims mutually limit each other (whether they be called equitable claims, or liens, or property rights), and wealth is not multiplied by multiplying the claims, as the lawmakers unfortunately sometimes assume to be the case.

Limitation of bequest

3. *The right of bequest, or of gift at death, is limited in various ways in different countries.* The term bequest implies a will, usually a written will in which the person, foreseeing death, has expressed his wishes as to the disposition of his property. It is said sometimes that bequest is a "logical" result of private property, but the law does not treat it as such. In countries where hereditary aristocracies exist, primogeniture is in some cases required by law, in others so strongly favored by public opinion that it is practically always followed. Custom limits bequests in England to members of the family, and wills giving outside the family are rare, and are almost always broken in the courts. John Stuart Mill contrasts this with the frequent practice by rich men in America of giving for public purposes. In France the right of bequest outside the family is legally limited; only the share of one child can be willed away by the father, and the rest must be equally divided among the children. Settlements and *fidei commissa* are limited in many countries, because of the recognized social evils resulting from the tying up of estates for generations. Throughout the history of England, Parliament has given attention to the question of mortmain, which chiefly concerned the drifting of great estates into the hands of the church or of corporations, as a result of bequests by the pious. Only recently in England, and to a less extent in this country, has been seriously discussed the policy of permitting unlimited endowments to charitable institutions, and new legislation has diverted from their original purposes some of the old endowments. These varied and often strict limitations of the right of private property are all determined by some thought, wise or foolish, of social expediency.

Limitation of right of inheritance

4. *The law of inheritance varies greatly with time and place.* Inheritance, in contrast with bequest, usually means succession to the property of one who has died intestate, that is, has made no will. The old idea of family unity survives in great measure in modern laws of inheritance. The nearest living relatives, no matter how distant they may be, inherit property when there is no will. When a miser dies in solitude and neglect, the world must be searched over to find a remote cousin to take the hoarded wealth. Inheritance is limited largely at present by the power of taxation. The view is growing that the claims of the society in which wealth has been acquired are stronger than those of relatives distant alike in space, in blood, and in affectionate interest. This view is reflected in many recent inheritance-tax laws which take from the shares of distant relatives a goodly portion for public purposes.

The question is raised in many minds, If private property is not an absolute right, what shall be its limits? What changes should be made in it? The essential thought in the various attacks on the institution of private property is that, because it occasions inequality in incomes, it is not socially expedient. The conviction is growing that, in some general way, incomes should correspond to, and reflect, social service. It is well to consider more closely what the terms social expediency and social service imply.

Chapter XXXIX
Income and Social Service

§ I. Income from Property

The justice of property questioned

1. *Property rights must meet the test of social expediency.* If private property is defended on the ground of social expediency, it must show good social results. It is not a sacred thing; it is open to examination, and must be judged by its fruits. Of all the forms of income, that from property has been most strongly attacked. The thought is that enjoyment of wealth should not be found apart from labor, and that it should bear some proportion to services performed. The enjoyment of an ample income by one who does no more than to draw checks or to sign coupons seems to many minds to be unjust; and it is often questioned whether there is any social service performed by the receivers of the rent from land. Property seems in many cases to be distributed without rule or reason. It does not correspond with beauty, strength, wit, wisdom, temperance, gentleness, or charity. Since the beginning of the Christian era, reformers have assailed and preached against the prevailing inequality of wealth. The idea that incomes, if not equal, should correspond to social service has always been present in some vague way in the minds of men.

Social effect of the right to give

2. *The right to transmit property by inheritance or by gift may be judged with reference to its effect on the giver, on the receiver, and on society at large.* It is well to take these three points of view. The right to dispose of property either during life or at death has undoubtedly in many ways a good effect on the character of men. It stimulates the father to provide for his children, the husband to provide for his wife. There is a joy in giving, a joy in the power to bestow one's wealth on those one loves. The right to give stimulates industry, frugality, ingenuity, and yields productive results. Much of the existing wealth probably never would have been created if men did not have this right of gift. But there is a limit to the working of this motive, and other motives often are much more effective. Many men after gaining a competence continue to work for love of wealth and power in their own

lifetime, as the miser continues to toil for love of gold. When men without families die wealthy, when men that have not the slightest interest in their nearest relatives labor and amass wealth till their dying day, it is evident that the right to bequeath property has little to do with their efforts. Love of accumulation and love of power in these cases supply the motive. A more limited liberty to dispose of property at death might still suffice, therefore, to call out the greater part of the efforts now made to accumulate property.

Effect of the right to receive

That the effects on the receiver of the property are good is somewhat more doubtful. It is true that children raised in great comfort or luxury would be more than ordinarily unhappy if plunged into poverty or even into humble circumstances on the death of their parents. There is much social justification for permitting families to maintain an accustomed standard of comfort. Few would deny that a moderate provision by parents to provide education and opportunity for their children is commendable and desirable. But the evil effects of waiting for dead men's shoes are proverbial. Many a boy's greatest curse has been his father's fortune. Men of native ability wait idly for fortune to come, and opportunities for self-help slip by unheeded. The world often exclaims over the failure of the sons of noted men to achieve great things, for, despite confusing evidence, men still have faith in heredity. A too easy fortune saps ambition and relaxes energy; and thus rich men's sons, if not most carefully and wisely trained, are made pitiable paupers in spirit, while the self-made fathers think their boys have chances they themselves did not enjoy. The greater social loss is not the dissipated fortunes, but the ruined characters.

Broader social effects of inheritance

The effects of inheritance on the community are good in so far as it secures efficient management of wealth. If the son or relative has been in business with the deceased, there is a reason that he should inherit the property, and his succession to it makes the least disturbance to existing business conditions. But every profligate son is an argument against inheritance; every incompetent heir is an argument in the hands of the enemies of the existing order of society. It is to society's interest that no able-bodied member shall stand idle. Every child should have presented to him the motive to devote his powers to the social welfare in economic or other directions. Moreover, many feel that the great fortunes now accumulating through successive generations in the hands of a few families are endangering our free society, even if these fortunes should continue to be well administered. There is a widespread feeling that the heredity of great wealth is, like the heredity of political power, out of harmony with the democratic spirit—though this may easily become a misleading comparison. Still, democracy wishes to see men as individuals put to the test, not profiting forever by the deeds of their forebears. This feeling is shared by those who cannot be charged with radical prejudices. A few years ago the Illinois Bar Association passed a somewhat startling resolution favoring moderate limits to inherited fortunes. Every year sees bills of this purport introduced in the

INCOME AND SOCIAL SERVICE

legislatures and in Congress. Andrew Carnegie says it would be a good thing if every boy had to start in poverty and make his own way. Cecil Rhodes recorded in his will his contempt for the idle, expectant heir.

The test of wise inheritance laws

3. *Social expediency will limit the right of intestate inheritance to persons in essential economic and social relations.* Public opinion is not yet crystallized in favor of this formal proposition, but tends strongly toward it. The foregoing considerations show that the right of gift in the lifetime of the giver should be the freest. The right of bequest, that is, of gift by will, should be liberal. The man who has acquired wealth may well be trusted to decide who bear to him a close social or personal relation, and to say whose lives have in a measure furnished the motives of his activity. But the right of intestate inheritance by distant relatives is one that stands on weak social foundations to-day. It appears to be an unreasonable survival from more patriarchal conditions. The true test is whether the wish to provide for these heirs has furnished the motive for the producing and preserving of the wealth. The claims of those nearest in blood and closest in personal relations are strongest. Family affection and friendship form the strongest of social ties, and it is socially expedient to cultivate them. Motives for abstinence and industry must be strengthened. But the same test shows that the zealous regard of the American law for the rights of grandnephews in Australia, or even of brothers long absent in distant quarters of this country, is irrational, and is unjust to the community where the fortune lies.

Social services of favored classes

4. *Many fortunes built on favoring legislation are defended as due to social service.* In the Middle Ages kings often granted great estates to nobles as rewards for past merit and as a payment for expected public actions. The great landlords were the magistrates, military leaders, and supporters of social order, and thus, in the judgment both of the king and of the commonalty, the nobles earned their incomes by their social service. While this practice has disappeared under constitutional government, large grants are still made to royal families. Many Englishmen who are democratic at heart uphold such grants as the price of social stability. Regard for royalty is so deep-rooted in the minds of the people of any long-established monarchy that there is always danger in change. England must pay many millions annually as the price of loyal and conservative sentiment. So long as this is true, a family of royal figureheads and idlers performs a social service.

Possible social service of protected industries

Protective tariffs sought by wealthy manufacturers are granted, not ostensibly to help them, but to help the country. The argument is that the benefits are diffused. Aid to enterprises in private hands, such as ship subsidies or as the grants to the Pacific railroads, are defended on the ground that, as a whole, society benefits by thus increasing the income of one class. The promise of social service is most urged by those who get the immediate benefit. Their eyes are keenest. The manufacturer sees clearly the benefits that will come to his factory from a protective tariff, but before he can get it he must convince many others that they too will gain. The majority of the American electorate is not voting a special favor at the polls, but is recognizing what it believes to be in its own interest. Most students of social questions doubt the wisdom of most of these grants to the wealthy on grounds of social service. The burden of proof is on their advocates, but few to-day are so rash as to say that such a claim of social service is never sound.

Private property in land questioned

5. *Property in natural agents is the most strongly attacked.* In the case of great natural deposits, such as those of coal or iron, the social service that is performed by the mine-owner is hard to see. Great incomes are drawn in the form of royalty or rent by those who never lift a pick or direct a stroke of work. Agricultural land in the hands of absentee landlords yields an income not very clearly due to social service, and this phase of property has been especially assailed during the past century. The modern form of this discussion is concerning "the unearned increment," the rise in the value of lands as a result of social growth. It is proposed to appropriate by "the single tax" the entire rental value of the land for the use of the public.

The defense of property in land is first positive: taking not the extreme but the usual case, private property secures the discovery and development of natural resources and their thorough use and good management (not necessarily by personal labor with the hands). If this is true, it is well for the individual and for the community to have this wealth in private hands. But in other cases there is merely a negative argument for property in land: no other better method of employing it has been devised and found practicable The experience with state ownership of mines, forests, and estates has not definitely answered in every case the question whether the social results of state ownership are more favorable than those of private ownership. In some cases they clearly are not, in others they may be; and as the balance of opinion inclines in the direction of public ownership, other reforms will doubtless be undertaken.

Inequality of fortunes

6. *The present inequality of wealth, not private property as such, is often attacked.* It is estimated that in the United Kingdom two per cent. of the families own seventy-five per cent. of all the wealth, while ninety-three per cent. own less than eight per cent. In the United States it is estimated that one per cent. of all the families own more than the remaining ninety-nine per cent.; and at the other part of the scale eighty-seven per cent. of all the families own less than twelve per cent. of all the wealth. The trend has been toward concentration of fortunes and a larger proportion of the growing income from property is in a few hands. Many feel that the law of property is defective when this is possible, although at the same time the average income of the wage-earner is increasing. Yet, it is not the institution as a whole that is attacked, but its details. The custom of equal division of property

among children in the United States has not been as effective in keeping fortunes small as was expected. The wealthy American families have averaged small, and in some of the most prominent the rule of equal division has not been followed. Opportunities for the investment of small savings at low interest are not lacking, but the great fortunes overtower the little ones, securing the great profits and great political and economic power. The farms and the villages are refuges for the small industry and for the small fortunes, and this fact has a great influence on our national character. The whole social atmosphere in the cities, with their extremes of wealth, differs from that in the country, and this contrast promises to become greater as the years go on.

Private property vs. socialism

7. *The ideal of property rights is that they shall furnish the highest motives for efficient social service.* Private property furnishes such a motive in a broad way, but its most ardent defenders will recognize that it does so imperfectly. It is an institution that has been tried and that does the work, while other methods suggested to do away with it are found to be dreams. The ideal of socialism is the abolition of private property, the centralizing under the control of the state of all wealth, except the simple personal belongings, clothing and other consumption goods. But history and human nature unite to testify that extreme socialism is an unworkable plan, excepting under special conditions, as in barbarous times and under a political despotism. The modern ideal for the control of wealth is the best attainable harmony of liberty and efficiency. If private property as it is, falls short of that ideal, at any rate it works either on a small or on a large scale, and socialism does not work at all. Property rights as they exist are not a product of pure reason. They are the result of social evolution, of historical accidents, of class legislation, and of selfish interest in many cases. Changing social conditions and ideas are bringing many changes in law, and further change must be expected to come.

§ II. Income from Personal Services

Some anti-social speculative gains

1. *Incomes from legitimate enterprise and speculation correspond roughly to social service.* It has been recognized above that there are many grades of chance, of speculation, and of enterprise. The extreme cases are bald crimes and are punished as such. Over some men that never directly break the law there always hangs a suspicion of guilt. It is the purpose of the law to make dishonesty unprofitable, but how imperfectly it does so! There are many cases of chance gains where the lucky man without social service legally enjoys his fortune. The law must be framed in broad terms, and cannot provide for every case. It may broadly forbid lotteries whose evils clearly exceed their benefits. But what would be the effect of taking away reward for the discovery of a gold-mine, even though sometimes it is awkward stumbling, not industry, that reveals the veins of metal? Society has

studied that question in the past; even now changes are being made in the laws; and in their turn the citizens and legislators of the next generation must decide the question. It is always under consideration.

Reward and enterprise

Are the rewards of the successful enterpriser greater than he deserves? How shall it be judged what he deserves? The answer is in the form of a question, Could society have the service without the reward? Society may be thought of as hiring the services of the efficient business man at the lowest price. Does it wish the services of Cornelius Vanderbilt in organizing a great system of railroads, of Andrew Carnegie, of Pierpont Morgan? What can it get them for? It must appeal not only to their love of money but to their love of power. Large services and large results can be bought only with large rewards. The shrewd enterpriser is not to be paid with abstract social gratitude. He is not to be tricked, as is a Chinese god, with tissue-paper gold.

Unmeasured gains of vast wealth

But in many ways fortunes appear to grow without social services, and sometimes with social harm. Russell Sage, the noted capitalist (who should know something of Wall Street), in speaking of the greatest of American corporations, said: "They dominate wherever they choose to go. They can make and unmake any property, no matter how vast. They can almost compel any man to sell out anything, at any price." Henry Clews, the well-known New York banker, said of a certain group of financiers: "Their resources are so vast that they need only to concentrate on any given property in order to do with it what they please.... There is an utter absence of chance that is terrible to contemplate. This combination controls Wall Street almost absolutely. With such power and facilities it is easily conceivable that these men must make enormous sums on either side of the market."

Anti-social use of rare ability

2. *The high pay of rare ability and skilled labor reflects in general a high social service.* The large income of some men reflects service to a narrow class, not to society as a whole. Lawyers as a class aid in maintaining right, but a corporation lawyer may get enormous fees for defeating just public claims; a skilful criminal lawyer may grow rich aiding the guilty to escape justice. Other service ministers to the whims, follies, and vices of the men who pay the bill. Such a service is "social" in a mean sense, corresponding to the low standards of desire in that social group. But what of the high rewards of skilled service ministering to worthy ends? Such favorites of fortune as Jenny Lind and Patti have received five thousand dollars for a single concert. Is this because they are the lucky possessors of a rare gift, or because they perform a social service deserving such reward? Certainly many of their auditors get what they want and believe they are getting the worth of their money.

INCOME AND SOCIAL SERVICE

General social result of rewarding talent

In general the legal right of everyone to get the highest pay he can in a free and open market is essential to the calling forth of ability. In a particular instance it is possible that the service would continue if one half or more of the income were confiscated by the public; but such a personal discrimination would introduce an arbitrary and demoralizing uncertainty into the problem. Who can tell how far the exceptional money rewards have inspired to the highest cultivation of great genius and of many minor talents? In a broad but very true sense, therefore, it appears that high personal achievement, large economic reward, and large social service are connected.

Social service of manual workers

3. *The low income of unskilled labor seems to fall short of its social service.* This does not refer to the feeble-minded or utterly inefficient, but rather to honest, industrious, "day-laborers," and to the low-paid manual workers in field, on railroad, and in factory. Their service is essential to the existence of society as it is, to all the higher arts, to the sciences, and to the amenities of life; their tasks are the roughest, most painful, most dangerous; yet their pecuniary rewards are the lowest. There is such a unity in society that each more fortunate man is dependent on the services of the humbler laborers who make up a large part of society. According to the breadth of social sympathy their claims seem more or less urgent.

The problem of increasing their reward

There is a vaguely recognized and growing conviction that these hewers of wood and drawers of water should enjoy a larger income. But how are they to get it? How is society to grant it to them? They get what they can under the competitive conditions, they get what their service is worth in the market. Are the conditions of the competition fair? If not, what will be the effect of a change? If they get more, others will get less; and with what result? However great the wish for better things, the attempt to change conditions fundamentally in a forcible and artificial way is both dangerous and foolish. Improvement must come through the coöperation of many indirect agencies gradually changing the nature and direction of the deeper economic forces.

Imperfect social and individual estimates of service

4. *The services of each are being measured and paid for by each and all.* In two ways society is putting its valuation on the economic services of other members of society: first, by law, or formal social convention; secondly, by individual estimates. By formal law is determined what institutions shall be continued. If the class of property owners is considered worthy of this reward, the institution of property will be continued; if not, it will be altered or destroyed. These decisions are made imperfectly, but as well as men of limited intelligence and honesty can make them. If men were more capable in both these ways they would enact better laws. Again, individuals are putting their estimates on others in bidding for services to minister

to wisdom and virtue or to ignorance and vice. If there is to be a much juster estimate of social service, there must be wiser men in society.

The ideal of social service

Does the world owe each man a living? No; on the contrary, each man owes the world his services in exchange for his living. The pauperism of spirit that consists in taking something for nothing is found in every rank of society that enjoys the blessings of progress without giving its best services in return. The ideal of a better adjustment of reward and service grows in the minds of men. Social evolution, shaped by this changing ideal and by accumulating experience, will bring into closer relation the social services and the economic rewards of men.

Chapter XL
Waste and Luxury

§ I.   Waste of Wealth

Loss of wealth in an isolated or an exchanging economy

1. *The accidental destruction of wealth is a loss to the owner, rarely with benefit, on the whole, to others.* In the consumption of wealth the loss of its utility is accompanied by the gratifying of wants; in the destruction of wealth utility is lost without the gratifying of wants. In a simple society, without exchange, the result of such a loss is evident. If food is destroyed, men suffer from hunger or gratify appetite less perfectly; if clothing is destroyed, they are cold; if houses are destroyed, they have no shelter. Likewise, if the self-sufficing family on a farm loses wealth by fire or storm or blight, its economic environment is made less fitted to gratify wants. In the conditions of our society, where goods are exchanged, the result appears to be different. The need to replace the lost goods makes a demand for special kinds of labor or goods. There may be, therefore, an immediate benefit to some, which obscures the corresponding loss to others. If a part of the income of the loser must be diverted from other uses to replace the wealth destroyed, those from whom he would have bought suffer an unexpected falling off of their sales, and he has himself gained nothing. The net result is a loss of wealth and gratification to the community as a whole.

There is a real exception where the accidental destruction removes some social difficulty. The great fire in London and the great fire in Chicago resulted in wonderful improvement. When an old city is built almost entirely of wood, each owner may think it to his interest to keep the old buildings. A great fire sweeps them all down and compels the rebuilding of the city on a new and higher standard. But the usual social result of accidental destruction is a loss. It is a use of wealth without a fulfilling of the purpose of production, the gratifying of wants.

Intentional destruction of wealth by the owner

2. *The intentional destruction of wealth by the owner, to make trade good, benefits neither himself nor others.* The case in mind is one where there is full choice between

keeping or losing the good, not such a case as the throwing overboard of a part of the cargo when the ship is in danger of sinking, in the hope thereby of saving the rest, or as the blowing up of buildings to prevent the spread of a fire. In such cases the destruction is inevitable without man's action; he merely tries to minimize it. The case in mind is the deliberate destruction of wealth that might be kept for use. One labor leader, for example, boasted that when he drank pop he always broke the bottle "to make trade good" by helping the glass industry. The refuting of this fallacy is one of the time-honored tasks in political economy. There is, it is true, an increase in the demand for glass and glass-blowers' labor, but without an increase in gratification; but at the same time there is a decrease in the demand for other goods which would afford additional gratification. The proverb, old in Shakespeare's time, runs, "Nothing can come of nothing." What is spent for one purpose cannot be for another; "you cannot eat your cake and have it too." A given income can be spent in one of many ways, but not in all ways or even in two ways at once. It is a question of this *or* that. At the same moment that the demand for pop-bottles is increased, the demand for other things is decreased, possibly that for pop-corn or pop-guns or Populist papers—who can tell? Such a form of benevolence is a mistaken, uneconomic attempt to provide labor for one man by taking it from another.

If the advocate of wealth-destruction would be consistent, he should break, not merely the pop-bottle, but the water-pitcher and the table as well; he should make a bonfire at least once daily of his clothing, his house, and its furnishings; he should advise blowing up the steamboat and ripping up the railroad when they have carried a single load of passengers. Thus, when all men were naked and starving, and civilization had sunk to savagery, trade would have been made as "good" as, by the policy of destruction, he could ever hope to make it.

Intentional destruction of others' wealth

3. *The intentional destruction of wealth owned by other persons is falsely thought to benefit trade in general.* The cases referred to are not acts done with criminal motives, but those done with a view to the public interest. If one sets fire to the property of another, seeking revenge or plunder, he is guilty of the crime of arson. But what shall be said of volunteer firemen that let an old house burn down to provide labor for carpenters and "to make business good"? The duty of firemen is to put out fires, no matter what the building is; but they choose sometimes to be ministers to the social interest as they interpret it. The more spent for carpenters' work out of any income, the less can be spent for other objects. It is true, however, that if in a small town the money to rebuild is borrowed from a distant loan or insurance company, there is an increase in employment in that town for one season; and that is as far as most men try to carry their economic analysis. Let the student carry it further.

The seen and the unseen

Servants sometimes excuse the breaking of dishes and furniture on the ground that it makes work, and that the employer can afford it. But income is thus diverted from other expenditure, either for production or for consumption. In the light of the theory of wages, it would appear that carelessness reduces the servant's own efficiency, and in the long run the loss comes, in part at least, off the wages of that particular servant. Bastiat's discussion of the broken window-pane is often and deservedly quoted. What is seen is a certain immediate benefit that the glass-maker and glazier get; what is not seen is that the power to expend an equal amount for other things is thereby lost by the owner of the house.

The wasteful use of wealth

4. *The destruction of unnecessarily large value to secure a given gratification is not economically sound.* The careless use of wealth to secure an inadequate result is likewise justified as "making trade good." The blunder that compels the rebuilding of a wall in a rich man's garden is an occasion for congratulation to those who see in it a happy provision of work for the unemployed. It is easy to forget that the proper use of goods is the final step in production. According as goods are well or poorly used, the production—that is, the real income or gratification they afford—is large or small. Differences in skill in the use of wealth are great. A French cook, we are often told, can make a palatable soup from what goes from the average American kitchen into the swill-pail. Waste in the use of goods is more likely to be found in new countries where wealth comes more easily and necessity does not enforce frugality.

The praise of waste implies the error noted in the preceding propositions. Deliberately securing less than the maximum result from wealth is merely a minor degree of the intentional destruction of wealth. The mistaken view is essentially that of the opponents of labor-saving machinery. It may be true, if the interests of a small class of workers or of tradesmen for the moment are looked at; it is false, if the interests of society as a whole be considered. Far more of wisdom lies in the proverb, "A penny saved is two earned." The economic use of wealth as surely adds to wealth (and, ultimately, to the income of society) as any other mode of production.

Waste in public outlay

Some government expenditures, as for river and harbor improvements, are sometimes favored, not because their immediate purposes are good, but because they "make work" and "distribute money" throughout the country. This money comes from taxation, and no matter what the system of taxation, the burden falls on some one, reducing the incomes at the disposal of the people to expend for objects of their own choice. If the work is not worth doing for itself, the collection of money in small amounts from many taxpayers and its expenditure as a large sum in one locality results in a net loss to society as a whole. Where the result is worth something, but not enough by itself to justify the expenditure, the fallacy of the destruction of wealth is present in a smaller degree. Examples are seen in the extreme use of pensions and in some public subsidies.

The fallacy of waste

5. *The supposed benefits of destruction and waste are due to a narrow and incomplete view of the question.* Let us restate the ideas that have been touched upon. In many cases it is possible that one person may benefit by another's mishap or folly in the use of wealth. The complex interrelations of men in society make this inevitable. But, to appreciate the final effects of such action upon society, one needs but to go back to the essential thought of wealth and its purposes. As the average efficiency and bounty of the world fall, so fall the income and welfare of men. As it rises, the social and economic levels rise also. Every kind of economic wealth has potentially two kinds of uses: to gratify wants—thus fulfilling its destiny—or to be converted into higher and more efficient agents—consumption or production. That the possibilities of the latter are boundless is overlooked in the fallacies here criticized. An efficient world would be the result of "economy" and saving; a wasted and used-up world, the result of the fallacy of the destruction and waste of wealth.

§ II. Luxury

Luxury defined

1. *Luxury, while variously defined, involves always the thought of great consumption of wealth for unessential pleasures.* It is not possible to define luxury absolutely; it is a relative term. Those opposed to it condemn it in their definition of it, as, for example: "an excessive consumption of wealth," or "devoting a relatively large amount of wealth to the satisfaction of a relatively superfluous want." Those who take a more moderate and favorable view say: "It is the enjoyment of forms of wealth not obtainable by the mass of men." The difficulty in the definition as well as in the problem of luxury is that it involves a mixture of economic and of ethical questions.

Extravagance "to give employment"

2. *Luxury is erroneously justified by some as giving employment to labor.* Typical instances are extravagant dress and elaborate balls where fine and costly flowers, decorations, music, coaches, require the expenditure of a large amount of money. It is said of the Empress Eugenie, wife of Napoleon III, that, in order to help the glove industry of France, she wore no pair of gloves more than once; in order to help other French industries, she purchased many silks and laces. It is a very comfortable doctrine to some people that the oftener they change their dress, the greater benefactors to society they are. A few years ago the "Bradley-Martin ball" was given in New York city. It was possibly little more elaborate and expensive than many another ball, but it chanced to be a dull time for news and the papers all over the land gave columns to its discussion. In the many interviews with ministers and business men, the thought appeared over and over that the ball had at least the merit of giving employment to labor.

The fallacy of luxury

The fallacy of this is essentially the same as that in the argument for waste and destruction. From the fact that these particular tailors, musicians, and florists would have less employment if this ball were not given, it is falsely concluded that, but for this ball, this particular income, or capital, would not be used at all. The average of employment in those special industries which minister to luxury is the result of and is determined by the average level of demand. There are more caterers and florists in Ithaca than in Hayt's Corners. A more than ordinarily gay season gives unusual profits to these enterprises, and it is true that an abrupt and extreme falling off in demand would cause them large losses, and leave many workers lacking employment for that one season. But, if this limited demand became usual, capital and labor would shift to the other industries to which expenditure had shifted. Other modes of expenditure than twenty-five thousand-dollar balls are possible, as, for example, twenty-five thousand-dollar public libraries. Mr. Carnegie takes his dissipation in that form. That gives employment also; not less does investment in new houses, in new railroads, and in new factories. More employment of a particular kind of labor is caused in one case than in another, but not more employment of labor as a whole and on the average.

Results of a sudden change in standards of living

3. *If all extreme luxury ceased, men of means would improve durable agents more or would give more or would take more leisure while producing less.* The question of luxury is most difficult when put thus: What would happen if everybody began suddenly to live on the simplest food and to confine himself to the bare necessities of life? A sudden change of this sort is almost unthinkable, but if it took place, all the factories and agents used for non-essentials would lose their value at once. A great industrial crisis would follow, as industry would have to adjust itself abruptly to an unprecedented standard of desires. What would happen if that standard continued would vary as human nature varies. There might follow increase of population, or a heightening of the efficiency of such agents as were of use, or, more probable than all else, a progressive lightening of labor, a use of the surplus of energy in study, rest, and recreation. It is, of course, illogical to suppose that with limited desires for the objective goods of the world there would continue undiminished efforts to produce goods and to save for future superfluities. In actual life changes of standard occur gradually. Economizing in material things by simpler living makes possible not only the increased efficiency of productive agents but the increased enjoyment of immaterial goods.

Luxury as an incentive to progress

4. *The defenders of luxury claim that it is the great incentive to progress.* It is undoubtedly true that a dead level of conditions is unfavorable to the progress of society. There must be in society some motive for emulation and ambition after the bare necessities of life are provided. There is therefore much strength in the defense of luxury. Necessities, strictly understood, are things absolutely essential to life and health. No hard line can be drawn between necessities and comforts,

between comforts and luxuries. The level rises; it is a trite and true saying that the luxuries of one age become the necessities of the next. The rise of the bathtub in the nineteenth century is an epitome of the progress of civilization in that period. The free baths in our cities surpass the hopes of the wealthy of a century ago. Even the meaner motives of envy may have their social function. The lower social grades, emulous of the higher standard held before them, labor with greater energy. The successful and capable, not content with necessities, continue to give their efforts to production. The destruction of the motive of luxury before the development of a substitute in a higher social conscience, would be paralyzing to industry. Luxury in a moderate measure may be defended by the same arguments as those for private property. True as this view may be in many cases, in others it seems directly opposed to the facts. Let us look at the economico-moral questions involved from the side of the individual who is indulging in luxury, and from that of the society in which he lives.

Happiness and the simple life

5. *As a question of consumption luxury involves for the individual both an economic and a moral problem.* The economic question is, Does luxury enhance the man's real income? Does a greater expenditure on himself give him a larger sum of gratification in life than a moderate expenditure would give? Ostentation has its penalties. Undue striving after effect defeats its own purpose. This is the cold fact of experience, not a speculative proposition. To get back to the fundamental principle: gratification results from a harmonious relation between man's nature and the world. Life loaded with too much luggage staggers under the burden. The tired faculties of the Sybarite cease at length to respond to natural pleasures. When the senses are robbed of their fineness, youth grows blasé, mature manhood is ennuied, life is empty. The praise of "the simple life" has lately been heard in a quarter whence such counsel does not usually come. In gay Paris, a wise pastor has made one of the most beautiful and rational pleas for plain and sincere living that society has heard since the time of the stoic philosophers. The word is needed. With the growth of incomes grows the strain to reach the self-imposed standards of frivolity. Insanity and suicide are on the increase. The stress of modern life makes men yearn for the simpler joys. Happiness dwells not outside of men; they must seek it within.

Luxury vs. social welfare

An economic failure, luxury is likewise in most cases a moral failure. Morality has to do with others; the social aspect of luxury is its effect on other people. The mere spending of a large income in selfish indulgence absorbs all the energies and interests of some men and women. Not only happiness in the narrow sense, but self-realization, is to such lives impossible. Those absorbed in display can give no due measure of thought to social obligations. A society made up of self-absorbed and self-centered individuals is a selfish society, foredoomed to decay.

WASTE AND LUXURY

Luxury generally condemned

6. *The larger moral problem involved in luxury is connected with distribution or the justice of the income, rather than with consumption or the spending of the income.* The individual effects of luxury broaden thus into the larger social effects. Most of the enemies of luxury condemn all expenditure of wealth above a very moderate sum, declaring that it is "unjust" for one man to have much while others are in poverty. This communistic doctrine pervades the teaching of many moral teachers, pagan and Christian. In many ways a public opinion can be developed to disapprove and condemn ostentation. Frivolous display becomes bad taste. Flaunting riches meet the public frown. The spending of income for dress and display has never been successfully forbidden by law. The Middle Ages are full of futile sumptuary laws which sprang from the envy of the nobles for the wealthy merchants. The growth of good taste may do what formal law found impossible.

Increasing social uses of wealth

The use of wealth in these days is taking more social directions. It turns from dress toward education, art, music, and travel; then ceases to be applied merely to self and family, and benefits the community. Nowhere and never before has this movement gone so far as in America. Andrew Carnegie, with his gifts of millions annually to public libraries; Peter Cooper, founder of the People's Institute; Ezra Cornell, the patron and prophet of the modern type of higher education—are citizens of a kind better known in this country than in any other.

Justice of the large income

Legal repression of luxury inadvisable

The immorality of luxury rests in most minds on the conviction that it is unjust that any one should have so large an income to use. The question of luxury leads back to the question of distribution: Has the man honestly gained his wealth? If so, he may spend it with good judgment or poor, with good taste or bad, but, so long as he does not injure others in the spending of it, there is much vagueness and confusion in the talk of "justice" or "injustice." Each must in large measure be his own judge of the wisdom of expenditure. Luxury is not always a question of wealth. Every person of moderate income has relatively superfluous and expensive tastes. One spends more for music than many a millionaire does; another more for books. How many college students' budgets could pass the censorship of Hetty Green, reputed to be the richest woman in America? If expenditures were regulated by the public, few persons would be within the law. But whatever the goods that are bought, if income is unjustly acquired, if its distribution is by rules that do not give the best possible approach to social service, there may well be talk of injustice. There is need of better standards of taste and judgment in expenditure, but not of sumptuary laws. If there is any legal change, it should be rather in the law of property.

Chapter XLI
Reaction of Consumption on Production

§ I. Reaction upon Material Productive Agents

Essential mark of the consumption of goods

1. *Economic consumption is the enjoyment of the utilities which wealth is capable of affording.* All wealth looks toward consumption. To take away the prospect of the enjoyment of goods is to take away all their value. Consumption involves generally the using up of a thing. Food is consumed quickly, clothing more slowly, and houses wear out after many years. The using up is, in some cases, due to the forces of nature, and is not hastened by enjoyment. A house goes to ruin more rapidly if uninhabited than with a careful tenant; clothing is destroyed more quickly by moths than by wear. The use of many goods that give esthetic pleasures, as art, painting, sculpture, and the enjoyment of fine scenery or of beautiful building sites, does not destroy the things that afford the pleasure. The idea that all value originates in labor has led to false views on this question. The essential mark of consumption is the using of the income as it arises, not necessarily the using up of the material agents that afford it, though this frequently occurs as well.

Consumers' choice as influencing value

2. *The kind of consumption affects the value of material agents.* Each buyer helps to determine the use of productive agents. The control of purchasing power means the potential control of industry to that degree. It was necessary in discussing the enterpriser to recognize that the buyer eventually dictates the direction of industry; the enterpriser seeks to produce that for which there is most demand. A change of taste affects the value of natural agents. An increase in the demand for meat affects the value of wheat and potatoes, and also the land used for producing them. A change in the national diet may be equivalent to the discovery or to the destruction of half a continent. If one chooses to drink wine instead of buying statuary, he increases the value of vineyards and decreases that of marble quarries. If one drinks beer, he bids for barley; if he eats candy, he may be offering a bounty for beets. Therefore, choosing vines or violets, pictures or pretzels, each with his

nickel helps to determine what shall be produced.

Inventions influencing value

The distribution of wealth thus affects the value of agents. The wealthy spend relatively more for luxuries, the poor for food and other essentials. Where wealth and incomes are very nearly equally distributed, the demand of different families will be for much the same kinds of goods. If there were no rich men, the demand for vineyards producing fine wines would be less. The very best qualities of goods take on the highest prices when there is a small, but very wealthy, class of purchasers.

Inventions often shift demand, and value follows. The invention of the bicycle with pneumatic tires, coincident with the adoption of electric traction for street cars, reduced the price of horses between 1890 and 1895. This doubtless was a factor in agricultural land values at that time. This change was sudden, extreme, and temporary, and there has since been a gradual adjustment and a return to the former values.

Consumers' choice as affecting productive forces

3. *The production of the next period may be radically affected by the use now made of agents.* Some consumption takes the form of using up and reducing the stock of wealth. The demand for lumber causes the disappearance of the forests, whereas the demand for oranges stimulates the planting of orange trees. The reckless exploitation of natural resources leaves society poorer. Great herds of buffalo were slaughtered to get the hides, which were of comparatively slight value. Rich land has been exhausted to get a few harvests.

War is a use of wealth for ends believed at the time to be necessary and believed to forward social welfare better in the long run than would dishonorable submission; but it causes misery and leaves industry prostrate. The forms taken by saving are affected by the choice of expenditure. In war the savings of individuals are given to the government and used for destructive purposes. The lender parts with his wealth and society uses it up. While the lender has a claim on the industry and on the remaining property of the community, society as a whole is the poorer. If the savings had taken the form of public buildings, libraries, railroads, and factories, the wealth and income of society as a whole would have been enhanced.

Consumers' choice as affecting wages

4. *The kind of consumption affects the wages of the various classes of labor.* That an increase in the supply of a given grade of labor reduces its wages and encourages its use, and vice versa, is a truth that became familiar in the study of wages. An influence also is exerted from the side of goods upon the price of labor. A shift of demand from one kind of goods to another depresses the wage of the one kind of labor and raises that of the other. A low grade of labor that performs only simple tasks, and those but badly, is injured if demand shifts to better products. Back of the sweat-shop shirt is the problem of the inefficient worker. Progress takes

place by the effort of labor to increase its efficiency and to move into higher paid callings, and at the same time by the desire of the purchaser to buy as good a quality as he can.

The consumer's responsibility

Every buyer then determines in some degree the direction of industry. The market is a democracy where every penny gives a right of vote. It is the thought of the society called "The Consumers' League" that through purchases, pressure may be brought to bear upon the employer to provide better conditions of work. The members of The Consumers' League refuse to buy goods not made under sanitary conditions. Undoubtedly there is here a great economic force which an enlightened public opinion, even without a formal association, can make in large measure effective. Every individual may organize a consumer's league, leaguing himself with the powers of righteousness. Will he read a yellow journal or a pink or a white one? A nickel or two will buy either. He has a dollar; will he go to the theater or buy ten dishes of ice-cream? He decides to buy a book, and more type and paper are made, and more printers are employed; he subscribes to foreign missions and Christian workers penetrate farther into Africa. Every purchase has far-reaching consequences. You may spend your monthly allowance as an agent of iniquity or of truth. You cannot escape a choice even by burying the money, for that is either a demand for gold or a gift to the issuer of paper currency.

§ II. Reaction upon the Efficiency of the Workers

Instinctive choice as related to welfare

1. *All consumption works some temporary change in the consumer, making him a more or less efficient producer.* Most consumption goods are used to gratify a wish of the moment. Many actions are governed by impulse rather than by reason; but in general this impulse is in harmony with the interests of efficiency. In primitive society instinct and appetite must generally have been safe guides. Food not merely appeased hunger and gratified the palate, but it gave strength. Sensations of cold, hunger, and thirst were developed by nature to stimulate men to do the things that helped them to survive. In primitive societies there are few chances to seek pleasures that are not favorable to efficiency. In the struggle for existence the more efficient tribes survive, and those that develop many abnormal tastes must perish. But the conditions of modern life are more complex, and temptations beset men on every side. Tastes are pampered and appetite is gratified at the expense of later welfare.

Choice of foods

2. *The physical efficiency of the worker is conditioned on wise consumption.* Chemists and physiologists are telling now in accurate terms how the nutritive values of

REACTION OF CONSUMPTION ON PRODUCTION 289

foods differ. Food values are not measured by the pleasure afforded the palate. The wide variety and greater choice now possible, even to the modest purse, make the chance of error much greater than in simpler conditions. This subject, already touched upon in the sections on the efficiency of labor, deserves further notice. From youth to age, the foolish choice of goods yields its harvest of ultimate misery. When babies are fed on crackers dipped in coffee, or, as among the Italian immigrants, on stale bread dipped in sour wine, there is a poor foundation laid for a vigorous manhood. Rich and poor cook too much for taste and too little for nutrition or digestion. Much cooking is still done in ways fit only for our grandfathers who had cast-iron stomachs and worked in the open air. Culinary methods have not been adapted as yet to a sedentary life.

Of drinks

Drinking tempts some men not only by taste, but by the appeal to sociability; to other coarser natures the joys of Bacchus offer the one hope of exhilaration. The pleasure from alcoholic liquor may at the moment outweigh the cost in money, but a diseased appetite forbids any reckoning of the vast psychic cost that follows. The coin paid for the drink is the beginning of the expense; misery, disgrace, degeneracy, and bestialty too often are the unreckoned items.

Of clothing

Clothing is primarily for ornament, secondly for physical comfort. That was the historical order, and it is the logical order in most minds to-day. How badly the two needs are harmonized! No wonder that the savage suffers in adopting civilized dress. Travelers describe the African potentate, attired in a high hat and a bracelet, striving to outshine his rival resplendent in full-dress coat and a palm-leaf fan. Civilization is making headway there; but the student of primitive peoples finds one of the important causes of their decay to be their bad judgment in adopting civilized dress, unsuited to their customs and climate. A mistake is made likewise by workers in physical tasks in imitating the dress of the wealthy and professional classes. The dress of the higher classes often is chosen because of its unsuitableness for an active worker. It serves thus to mark its wearer as one engaged in delicate tasks or as a person of leisure. Possibly, therefore, because of their strong social ambitions, the manual workers in America more than elsewhere adopt a costume that is not sensible or sanitary.

Reactions of enjoyment upon the intelligence

3. *The intelligence of the worker is affected by the form of his enjoyments.* This does not refer to the use made of spare time for regular study in night schools, correspondence schools, vacation work, but to the use of time when seeking recreation. The choice of recreation reacts upon the nature of the man. Will he read a book or play billiards? In proper proportions both may be good, in excess both are evil. Liking realism, does he read Howells or the blood-curdling serial entitled "Piping the Mystery"? Does he devote his spare hours to the "Scientific American"

or to the "Police Gazette"? At the moment there may be as much pleasure in one as in the other (and one might add, in Hibernian phrase, "Yes, and more too."). Does he enjoy music, the theater, or the cheaper attractions of Coney Island and the Bowery? Is his recreation permeated with a certain intellectual ambition? There may be just as much momentary joy in one choice as in another, and life is shaped by the direction of one's enjoyments. Much depends on the natural bent; some natures incline to the healthy as the plant grows toward the sun. With most characters much depends on the influences of neighborhood life; thus the boy's clubs and college settlements of the cities, the schools and playgrounds of the villages, are tending to surround child life with healthier conditions, that will mould it into better social habits.

Reaction upon the character

4. *The form of the worker's expenditures affects his industrial virtues.* This is not a moral lecture; it is a look at the economic side of the subject. There are some moral qualities, however, that are closely connected with efficiency, while others are not. Some individuals are corrupt in private personal relations, but "square" in business dealings. But usually there is some connection between the two, and under modern conditions this is becoming closer. Fitness for daily tasks is affected by the daily thoughts of the worker. Sordid and foul thoughts, like an internal malady, sap the economic efficiency of the worker; clean, bright thoughts act as a tonic. Drink, gambling, fast living, unfit men for positions of trust, while many pastimes leave the moral nature cleaner and stronger. Few can live a double life—honorable, conscientious, and exact in one part of the day, and corrupt in another. Dr. Jekylls and Mr. Hydes are not often found in real life. The habitual train of thought in leisure hours possesses and controls the man throughout his work. It is said that "A man is what his work makes him," but it is equally true that a man's work tends to become what he is. A man fit for a higher kind of work rises to it in the usual order of things; but no matter how humble the task, it partakes of the worth and wholesomeness of its doer.

§ III. Effects on the Abiding Welfare of the Consumer

Production vs. welfare

1. *Man and his welfare are the end and aim of the economic process.* The starting point of industry is wants; the goal is welfare. Momentary gratification is only a way-station, not the journey's end. Too often, in economic reasoning, things are looked at from the employer's point of view. The older writers, such as Ricardo and Mill, were inclined to take what John B. Clark has called the "feed and work" view,—the view that the workman is merely an agent of production, a means to an end; that his food, the same as coal for an engine, is to be thought of rather as employer's cost than as consumer's gratification. But, in the broader view, the welfare of men as men is the subject most worthy of economic study. The

workman's food is to gratify his hunger, primarily; not merely to make him a better working machine. This reverses the order of the older reasoning. The use made of the income is itself a kind of production—its last stage. Is the process, on the whole, worth while? This can only be judged by finding whether, on the whole, the welfare of man has been furthered.

The marginal application of income

2. *An income yields the maximum gratification when it is apportioned among goods so that their marginal utilities, as nearly as possible, are equal.* Even a small income is income capable of many applications. The choice lies among many thousands of articles. Utility varies not only according to the kinds of good, but according to the varying quantities of each. Every moment, therefore, the conditions of a choice are changing. The best use of income forbids the purchase of an additional unit of any good unless it affords the highest gratification obtainable, at the moment, at an equal price. Various circumstances prevent the exact application of this rule. Expenditure is a matter of habit, in large measure, rather than a matter of judgment. The knowledge needed for a rational choice very often is lacking. Appetites change, making unwise the old purchases, yet men go on buying the same things in the same proportions simply because a readjustment that would give greater gratification requires thought. Finally, the best economic adjustment must conform to the abiding physical and moral welfare of the user, not to a temporary impulse; and such a choice is far more difficult than that of the temporary good.

Progress and the refinement of desires

3. *Progress takes place where new wealth gratifies marginal wants as intense as those of the preceding period.* If the utility of every kind of goods decreased uniformly as wealth increased, desire would steadily decline in intensity. But old wants vary and new wants develop with prosperity. Desire grows by what it feeds on. Ambition passes on to other and higher peaks. The direction of the individual man's life thus is determined by the expenditure of his increasing income. Wealth makes possible a new adjustment of life, a new character, both in the individual and in the society.

Wealth a means to living

The thought that needs emphasis in this connection is that, while production and consumption are separable in thought and distinguishable in practice, they are not opposed in their ultimate purpose. The highest fruits of production are in the lessons of sacrifice and discipline, and in its opportunities for experience and self-expression. The best result of the consumption of wealth is not the gratification of appetite, but the strengthening of the spiritual forces within men. The world is to rise to a higher social stage not by banishing labor and by multiplying sensual enjoyments of the commoner sort. Wealth, even in an economic view, is not the end of life, but merely the means to its realization.

Variety and harmony in the choice of goods

4. *Enjoyment is increased by a proper variety and harmony of goods.* As the old kinds of goods increase in amount and fall in value, there must be a substitution of new goods. An element added to the dress or to the diet heightens greatly the total gratification. The result is a unit. Think of a dinner without butter, or a cranberry-pie without sugar, or a dress-suit without a linen collar. Certain combinations are essential to the requirements of developed taste and present a problem of complementary goods. Combinations of complementary goods enhance the enjoyment; inharmonious combinations decrease it. That certain things "go together" is a fact that rests often in the nature of things. Complementary colors please the eye; well-seasoned dishes please the palate.

Again, the harmony of goods is affected by the special nature of the occupation. A farmer with his out-of-door life can use tobacco with far less danger than the sedentary worker. A piano player cannot be a base-ball player: the one requires soft and supple hands, the other hard and callous ones. The young man must give up the piano or the game, or play both badly. The harmony may rest on a still more complex social adjustment. The loss to the man whose life is in the main on a higher plane is greater if he descends occasionally to a lower. A ditch-digger, looking at the question short-sightedly, may deem "a good drunk" a very desirable form of enjoyment. But a brain-worker, whose joy as well as efficiency depends on the clearness of his intellectual processes, must see that in his case the perils and the costs are much greater.

Unity of choice in happiness and in character

Wise consumption depends not alone on physical pleasures, but on the spiritual unity of the uses made of goods. Happiness and character are akin in the qualities of simplicity and unity. Happiness, so far as it depends on wealth, is a harmony of gratifications. Character is a harmony of actions, a group of complementary deeds. There can be no harmony, without a central, simple, guiding principle. The wise and moral use of goods and the economic use of them are therefore for the individual essentially the same. Life is a unity. The results of the choice of goods are reflected in the health, intelligence, happiness, morality, and progress of society. It is vain for the economist to ignore the ultimate relations between economic choice and morality; it is folly for the moralist to ignore the economic bases of right and wrong in human conduct.

Chapter XLII
Distribution of the Social Income

§ I. The Nature of Personal Distribution

Definition of personal distribution reviewed

1. *Personal distribution, in economics, is the reasoned explanation of the ways in which income is divided among the members of the community.* Before noting more exactly the ways in which distribution can and does take place, it may be well to review briefly some definitions that have been given in other connections. Distribution is bound up in practice with production, but it can be thought of as a more or less distinct problem. Functional distribution is the attribution of value to agents or classes of producers, to land, machinery, and labor considered impersonally as groups of productive agents. Personal distribution is the actual apportioning of income to living persons. This theme now to be dealt with is the more important practically, for the abstract discussion of rent and interest is of use only as it helps to an understanding of this vital human problem. It is well to recall also the distinction between wealth income, money income, and psychic income. The first is the objective aspect, the last is the subjective aspect, of income; the second, money income, may be an expression, in money form, of either of the others, but commonly of the former. The money expression of psychic income can be only approximately attained.

Personal affection and distribution

2. *The individual's income is determined by a number of forces, only part of which are primarily economic.* Many persons derive income directly neither from property nor from labor. They neither toil nor clip coupons, but they flourish in the favor of others—parent, husband, wife, friends, patrons. So long as the good-will continues these persons may be as well off as if they drew a salary or owned a bank. If a person in control of goods shares them with another, it is a matter that economists must recognize, but cannot well reduce to rules of value. It is not the task of economists to explain why the impulses of generosity arise, but only how they affect distribution. The economic problem of distribution really ends where owner

or worker secures his income. Giving a part of it to some one else is essentially a form of consumption, and only secondarily a mode of distribution; it is the way chosen to spend the wealth income.

Complex source of psychic incomes

The psychic income of individuals, therefore, is often made up of many elements. Some parts are due to services performed by the person himself. When one combs his own hair he is adding to his income. Benjamin Franklin said it was better to teach a boy to shave himself than to give him a thousand dollars. Other goods are the uses and fruits of legally controlled wealth: chance finds, as gifts of value or lost and abandoned goods; goods assigned to one by authority; wealth inherited; illegal gains by robbery; goods secured on credit; gifts either of things or of services. The uses of this university are a gift forming a part, first, of the student's income, and, finally, of the social income. Such gifts can be traced back to large-hearted, public-spirited men like Ezra Cornell, but they must be looked upon as coming from some one. This list, incomplete as it is, suggests that the real income of most individuals has manifold sources. Let us undertake to examine and analyze the various methods in actual use in the distribution of income to the persons making up society.

§ II. Methods of Personal Distribution

Compulsory distribution; violence

1. *Distribution is sometimes compulsory, by force or fraud.* This crude and primitive mode of distribution, the negation of personal liberty, never has been quite eliminated. In every country an unhappily large number of men from time to time break over into crime, from violence and highway robbery down to sneak-thieving, pocket-picking, and bunco games. Not more than ten per cent. of this criminal element is at any one time in prison. This method of personal distribution, not hinted at in most theories of distribution, determines a large part of the income of tens of thousands of men in this country and concerns the distribution of millions of dollars. These enemies of society appropriate whatever they can, and the law stops them if it is able.

Chattel slavery

Slavery is distribution by legalized force, but the force is not legalized by the consent of the victims. The evolution of the harsher slavery may be traced through various forms of milder serfdom. There is found an element of this in the freest existing societies; men unwilling are forced to do things. A patent example is the convict on a chain-gang, a slave to society as a penalty for his violation of its commands. But some radical reformers to-day claim that present society is wholly based on legalized force, and that the working-man is essentially a slave. Their ideal

DISTRIBUTION OF THE SOCIAL INCOME

cannot be realized without dissolving social bonds and destroying civilization; yet the presence, even in our society, of this forced, unwilling submission on the part of some of its members cannot be ignored.

War indemnities

A similar example of forcible taking is seen in case of war. Savage tribes plunder and take captive their weaker neighbors. Conquering modern nations usually exact tribute from defeated enemies. Germany got a billion dollars from France, Japan a quarter of a billion from China. The terms of peace at the close of our great Civil War were the most liberal ever granted by conqueror to vanquished; and yet the federal pensions granted to Northern soldiers are a form of tribute, being paid by taxes falling alike upon the North and the South. In all these cases the distribution by force is unwillingly suffered. In none of them is it reducible to economic rules or capable of a strict economic explanation.

Charitable distribution within the family

2. *Distribution may be charitable, that is, determined by considerations of benevolence and affection.* Charitable is here used in its original sense, as synonymous with love or affection. First to be mentioned is the love of parents, the root and type of all the forms of charity. The lack of economic equivalence in the relation of parent and child is complete in early years. The helpless infant gives nothing economic to the parent, the parent gives all to the child. Gradually, however, the balance is regained; as the years go on, not only does the child repay in affection but in many cases he repays in material ways. In the factory districts and on the farm the child in early years begins to reëstablish the balance, becomes a worker, and contributes as much as the cost of his support, and finally more. A student of modern English town life has traced the curve of poverty traversed by the average child of the poor, as the family moves, now below, again above, the level of minimum income required for physical efficiency. In the middle or propertied classes the children do not for many years take the burden from the parents, and it is doubtful whether in most cases the economic balance is ever reëstablished. It is not to the parents, but to the succeeding generation, that the debt is vicariously paid.

And in larger circles

Friendship widens the range of generosity and multiplies the mass of gifts. Broad sentiments of humanity lead to gifts outside the range of personal affection and personal interest, to the beggar on the street, to institutions devoted to charity. In New York state about twenty million dollars a year is given to charity, and in the country at large many times as much. In the year 1901 over one hundred million dollars was given to education in the United States by private donors; and that high mark will no doubt soon be passed. Gifts in cases of great disasters, as the Irish and Indian famines, the Chicago fire, the Galveston flood, the eruption of Mount Pelée, bespeak a widening generosity. Religion impels to the building of churches, to the support of priests, missions, and manifold religious undertakings.

Charity in this connection is the expression of a sentiment that varies from the broadest and most general humanitarian sentiment to the most intense and ardent personal affection.

Authoritative distribution in the despotic state

3. *Distribution may be by an authority willingly acknowledged.* The two preceding forms of distribution, force and love, shade off into this form. In them the ones from whom goods are taken or to whom they are given have no power to change the conditions; here is to be considered the case where the person bows willingly to the superior power and takes what that power accords him. There are few despotisms in which the government is not based on the wishes and average capacities of the governed. If the citizens as a body really desired and were deserving of better government, in most cases they could get it. Much is heard, for example, of despotism in Russia, and of the abject condition of the people; but travelers testify that while many in the educated student classes are filled with the greatest discontent, and the intelligent subject peoples, such as the Finns, detest their rulers, such sentiments are far from general throughout the empire. The power of the Czar could not exist for a single moment if the mass of the people did not look to him as the great father whom they venerate and love. If this is true, the despotism in Russia, though abhorrent to our ideals of freedom, is fitted to the aspirations of the mass of the people. So far as government determines income, the authority distributing income there, as elsewhere, is one willingly acknowledged.

In communities and families

In patriarchal tribes, in communal societies, in monastic and other religious orders distribution is by an accepted authority. Each person works at what he is commanded to do, and some one in authority (the patriarch, head of the community, the father of the monastic order) portions out the work and the reward. In the family this rule largely prevails, and even after the children have come to years of discretion they not infrequently accept, from habit or affection, the will of the parents, and give up their entire wages to receive back a portion. The method of charitable distribution while the child is young gradually changes to authoritative distribution after the child becomes a worker. The untrained and indocile youth, however, is made the subject of compulsory distribution.

In much governmental action

The collection and distribution of taxes is by public authority. No attempt is made to give back an exact equivalent to the tax-payer. The money is taken and spent by authority for the public good. This method is exemplified in the work of certain commissions appointed by law to fix rates or settle disputes, as boards of conciliation and arbitration and railway commissions. The courts sometimes find themselves obliged to enter this field, although they do so most unwillingly. They try to confine their efforts to interpreting the contracts men have voluntarily entered into, and they avoid, so far as possible, the making of contracts or the fixing of rates.

In various contests

In many cases, little thought of as economic distribution, the authoritative method is followed. Literary and oratorical contests are passed upon by a set of judges whose opinion of merit determines the award. It is a poor method, often resulting in injustice (as every defeated candidate will admit); but it is the only way practicable for deciding such contests. Yet there are literary and oratorical contests decided very differently. If a man advertises himself as an orator and charges fifty cents admission to his lecture, everyone who goes to hear the man votes that he is an orator; everyone having money but staying away votes that he is not of such value. The one is judgment by the authoritative, the other by the competitive, method. The essence of the method of distributing by authority is that one individual (or group of individuals) judges of the deserts or duties of others, decides what others must get or must pay, not what he himself is willing to pay. Authoritative distribution is necessary in many cases, but it is fraught with dangers. It is the essence of socialism that it would make this plan universal.

4. *Distribution of psychic income may be in part by the collective use of social wealth.* By collective use in the full sense is meant the continuing enjoyment at the same time by all caring to partake and without limit as to amount.

Distribution by collective enjoyment

Now it is evident that, because of difficulties that arise, not all things are capable of this kind of enjoyment. Free water for private use from public waterworks is wasted; free meals and clothing to school-children are open to still greater abuses. Men cannot thus collectively enjoy rare wines or good confectionery; they cannot partake without limit of a limited supply. But libraries and schools may practically be managed in this way. They require both certain qualifications and certain sacrifices on the part of the user. Collective enjoyment is most completely possible where the use of a permanent form of wealth, such as a park, can be made free to the public. All individuals may enjoy equal privileges, though general rules may limit the kind of use; for example: no one may be permitted to pull flowers or to walk on the grass, but all who make use of the park enjoy equal privileges. Henry van Dyke in one of his essays puts into the mouth of his boy the question, "Father, who owns the mountains?" and the answer is, He who can enjoy them. Every man without covetousness, as he stands on this hilltop, owns the mountains, the lake, and this beautiful valley.

In some ways the amount of public enjoyment is decreasing, as by the growing density of population, by the loss of open spaces and commons for playgrounds, by the destruction or fencing in of natural scenery; but in other ways it is growing and must grow rapidly. The spirit of civic improvement spreads. The streets are better paved than formerly; there are more public buildings, art galleries, and noble monuments. Every cross-road in the land will some day have its fountain and its statue. The coöperation of the whole community gives to collective use many of the advantages of large production, and the maximum of enjoyment.

Distribution by custom and status

5. *Distribution may be by status or set rules and customs.* Distribution by status fixes the shares of men independently of their effort and without their control. It is guided neither by their personal merit nor by the economic value of their services, but by the merits and acts of men not living. This method has prevailed and still prevails to a great extent, though in our society this is hardly realized. Feudal society was built on status. Men were born to certain privileges and positions; they inherited property which could neither be bought nor sold; they followed trades which could rarely be entered by any outside of favored families. Caste in India and in other Oriental countries regulates by status a large part of the life. In western countries to-day inheritance of property is the main legal form of status and it shades off into other forms of distribution. While in some cases inheritance may be looked upon as a gift to the heir, in other cases, elsewhere noted, it is partly earned by the heir who has helped to produce it. By public opinion and by prejudices, status is still maintained even where the law has formally abolished it, as is seen in modern race problems.

Competitive distribution the dominant form

6. *Distribution is usually competitive in accordance with the value of the product.* This is the dominant form of distribution in modern society. It is the essentially economic form, as contrasted with the legal and personal forms just described, because it is impersonal and reducible to a rule of value. Distribution under competition is made not with reference to abstract ethical principles or to personal affection, but to the value of the product so far as it is honestly controlled. Monopoly, it may be noted, never has ceased to rest under the ban of Anglo-Saxon law, hence to exemplify compulsory, as opposed to competitive, distribution. A striking feature of the competitive method is its decentralization. Each helps to value the economic services of each. If one pays more for the services of the singer than for those of the cook, it is not because he would rather listen to the singing than to eat, but because by apportioning his income he can get the singing and the eating too. In the existing circumstances, the singer's services seem to him worth paying for, and he backs his opinion with his money. So each is measuring the services of all others, and all are valuing each. It is the democracy of valuation, while the method of authority is an oligarchy or monarchy.

Various ideals of distribution

7. *The best distribution in practice must be sought in union and harmony of these various methods.* Various social reforms propose simply the extreme application of one kind to the exclusion of the others. There are two opposing views of competition: one, that it is the ideal to be sought; the other, that it is inherently bad, and therefore should be abolished. Extreme individualists, believing that everything would be settled for the best by free competition, wish to make it

universal. They ignore the many cases where it does not, should not, and cannot exist.

Socialists, ill content with the share secured by the less skilled laborer, say that the competitive plan is unsound at the core. They say that distribution should be not in proportion to value, but in proportion either to needs or to deserts (they are not agreed which), judged by a vague ethical standard. But this involves the principle of authority in its extremest form. It intrusts to some men the function of passing upon the economic merits or desires of all others. Yet that alone is not a conclusive argument against all use of authoritative distribution. In many practical cases the intrusting of power and authority to men to judge of the value of others cannot be avoided. Whatever is indispensable, whatever is the best possible, is, humanly speaking, just. Assessors, judges, jurors, must be employed. Interstate commerce commissioners determine whether rates are reasonable, boards of arbitration settle disputes, the strike commission adjudicates difficulties in the coal regions. Doubtless these methods will be increasingly used.

Need of a wise blending of methods

There is no other kind of distribution than those enumerated. The strongest contrast is between the competitive and the authoritative principles; the others are minor and modifying. None of them alone is sufficient; each has its merits and each has its defects; they must supplement each other. Actually they are employed in modern society side by side; each seems essential and best in some special application. But it does not follow that exactly the proper use is now made of each. No two generations have followed the same rule, and the proportions in which use has been made of them has constantly shifted. It must be recognized that the principle of diminishing utility applies to each method of distribution as it does to the productive processes. Each may be best under certain conditions and circumstances, but, extended in application, each reveals its weaknesses. In any productive process the best method depends upon the proper proportion and combination of elements. Progress toward the best possible distribution is to be sought in the wise adjustment of the various methods to human nature and to human needs.

Chapter XLIII
Survey of the Theory of Value

§ I. Review of the Plan Followed

The cycle and order of economic study

1. *The beginning and end of economic study is man.* Before leaving the more theoretical and abstracter part of the theory of value, it may be well, at the cost of some repetition, to restate and review the relations of the various parts of the argument. Intent on details of the theory of value the student is in danger of losing its broader perspective.

The proposition with which this section opens was accepted as our axiomatic starting-point. It was not so in the older political economy; men too often were looked upon rather as a means to an end, namely, the creation of wealth. This proposition refers to all classes, not to a small group of men. The aim of economic study is democratic, being the welfare of all men. Economics does not purpose, however, to explain man's action with reference to all things. It asks and attempts to answer the question: "Why does man attach value to certain things and actions; why does he measure them in certain ratios as expressed in terms of each other; and why do these ratios change with changing conditions?" This purpose has determined the order of our study. Beginning with an analysis of the nature of wants, and of the mental process of valuing consumption goods, the circle of inquiry widened to the problem of valuing things whose relation to wants is more remote and indirect (though not less important).

The problem of future uses, the major part of the theory of value, leads back to the question of the use man makes of things—a field claimed by the moralist, but one that cannot be neglected by the economist. Economics is not the whole science of social relations. It is a restricted part of the field. But it comes into relation with great practical questions that touch all sides of life. Thus economics broadens and unites with the general stream of sociology. In the pursuit of our study one comes back to the starting-point and cause of value—human wants and the use made of wealth to gratify them. The circle is completed. We have surveyed, rapidly and imperfectly it is true, the whole range of economic inquiry.

SURVEY OF THE THEORY OF VALUE

The unit in value problems

2. *The central point in economic study is the simplest problem of exchange value.* The first look at the economic world reveals so many things that have relation to wants, and relations so complex, that the mind is confused. The object of science is to simplify; it seeks unity in the midst of chaos. Relations exist between wants and things that certainly never can gratify them directly. Where is the simplest aspect of the problem to be found? Evidently in the exchange of consumption goods, for these are in closest touch with wants. Out of the complex of direct and indirect goods, those few which are at the moment gratifying wants must be somewhat abstractly, but logically, set apart and studied. In the simplest problem, the exchange of the most typical consumption goods, is the key to the larger problem of value. If one could follow it step by step into its complexer relations, he might hope to understand everything in economics.

Former or conventional conceptions of rent and interest

3. *The problems of rent and of time-value are successive steps in the explanation of the exchange value of indirect agents.* The term rent has been so variously defined that no caution to the student as to its use can be deemed superfluous. Until recently economists sought to confine the term to the income from natural resources (or land). Rent, in their conception, was the income from one group of goods, physically distinguishable from another group of goods, called capital, which were supposed to yield interest. That is, rent and interest was each supposed to bear much the same relation to a particular set of durable agents; the difference between them was primarily in the agent that yielded them (though there were other complicating thoughts) rather than in the aspect of value they represented.

Rent and time-value as here used

Rent as defined in this volume has the much broader meaning of the usufruct of any material agent as contrasted with the use-bearer. Usufruct is a conception most intimately related to that of consumption goods, but is logically one step further removed from want. Time-value, as here considered, is a broader conception than that of contract interest, for it has to do with the all-pervading element of time in its influence on value. Some rents are logically, and in practical business as well, not measured over periods of time, but at the moment of their accrual. The measurement of time differences is mainly required in setting a valuation upon a more or less permanent use-bearer. This process, which is capitalization, has only recently been recognized to be the discounting of all the future uses to their present worth. While in its essence this is merely a problem in exchange value, it is the highest, subtlest, and most difficult of such problems. Its understanding presupposes rent, just as rent presupposes the analysis of wants and marginal utility. It is the outer zone of the value problem, carrying the thought of value years away (all but an eternity away) from present enjoyment.

Different stages in value

While both rent and time value are widened so that each applies in some manner to all durable agents, it is a grave error to conclude hastily that the intention is to make synonymous the old terms rent and interest. Rent and time-discount remain essentially different stages in the value problem. Actual concrete net *economic incomes* as they arise *are always rents*. Interest never accrues in a concrete form except under the interest contract for a money loan (a contract income, not an economic income), and this evidently is a species of contract rent. Time-value is a phase of value connected logically with investment, or the calculation of future earning power; rents are both actual and expectative, or future, but as realized incomes they always express present earning power. Together, rent and capitalization embrace the whole problem of valuing durable material agents.

Wages and profits related

4. *Wages and profits are of the same genus, the value of human services of different grades*. The attempt has been made in the foregoing treatment to show the unity between the problems of wages and profits, and to point out the difference between the conditions that surround them. Through the common characteristic, social utility, the employer's service can be compared with the most ordinary or the most artistic labor. Profits and wages, therefore, are simply different aspects of the same question. A common power, or principle, is found in all objects of value, a power to gratify human wants. In the variety of human services and in material goods must be sought this unity.

The different kinds of services range from direct to most indirect goods. The commonest labor may serve welfare at the moment or may be embodied in a form to be used years later. In that light, wages seems a more complex problem than either rent or capitalization. But the moment the service embodies itself in a material good with future uses the general theory of capitalization applies to it.

§ II. Relation of Value Theories to Social Reforms

"Orthodox" political economy

1. *The earlier theories of political economy implied a dismal view of the future of the masses*. The theory of value one holds is sure to affect his view of economic progress and of social reform. The theories from the middle of the eighteenth to the middle of the nineteenth centuries, however varied they were in other respects, nearly all gave a gloomy view of the condition of the laboring-men. The physiocratic school in France, the so-called "orthodox" economists in England (that is, the writers from about 1800 to 1850 that were in sympathy with the landholding or commercial classes), and the socialistic or laboring-class theorists, all inclined to this view. It was while this view prevailed that Carlyle characterized political economy by the term still sometimes heard — "the dismal science." The thinkers of that time started

SURVEY OF THE THEORY OF VALUE

their study of value at wages, and assumed that population would always increase so fast as to force labor to a bare subsistence. The other shares (or the other classes of society) were supposed then to absorb all the surplus income. Economics to-day is not especially lugubrious, and its more cheerful note is due as well to its changed theory of value as to the evidence of advancing welfare among the masses.

The gloomy socialistic theory

2. *The socialistic theory of value, akin to the other, holds that capitalists absorb all the benefits of progress.* The socialists (of the radical school) claim that their theory is merely the logical conclusion to be drawn from the old "orthodox" theory, stated in its extremest form. Usually, however, the orthodox theorists softened and modified greatly the statement of their harsher views. The socialists have not been willing to recognize any ameliorating conditions. They say: economic theory shows that under a competitive condition of society the laboring-man must be forever ground down in helpless misery; therefore the only hope of the laboring masses is to do away with competitive society and to substitute for it central, governmental control of all industry. They did not and do not attempt to distinguish carefully the part of production, due to brains and effort, from the part due to ownership of capital. The socialist theory is a plan for political agitation rather than a scientific theory of value. It was originated or elaborated by men such as Karl Marx, Frederick Engels, and Ferdinand Lasalle, as labor leaders and political agitators, who found a ready weapon in the bungling economic analysis of the time. The claim of a scientific basis for socialism has continued to be proudly made by their followers, but it has a tottering support in their defective theory of value.

George's single-tax theory

3. *The single-tax theory of value is that ground-rent automatically absorbs all benefits of progress.* This is the most notable example of a plan of social reform growing out of an abstract theory of value. While the socialists first had their plan of social reform (or revolution), in whose support Marx's fanciful theory of value was invented, Henry George appears first to have got hold of a theory of value that suggested his plan of social reform. Studying the political economy of Ricardo and Mill, he accepted their ideas regarding the hopeless outlook of the laboring classes, and their conception of the theory of ground-rent with its false implication that land-owners get all the surplus in society. George thus came to believe that, with private ownership in land, competition steadily robbed all but landlords, even the non-landholding capitalist, of any share in the benefits of progress. This theory of value is thought to explain all the poverty in the world. It calls, in the single-taxer's opinion, for a radical measure of reform, namely, the taking of all rent of land for public purposes as a common instead of an individual income. If the theory of value on which it is based were sound, the doctrine would have irresistible reasons in its favor; if it is false, most of the argument falls to the ground, though there may still be substantial reasons of a different nature for the exceptional treatment of ground-rents for purposes of taxation.

Recent hopeful theories of wages; Walker's

4. *Recent theories of value assign to labor a more hopeful position.* A most optimistic theory of wages is "the residual claimant theory," presented by Francis A. Walker. His view was that the various shares of production, such as land-rent, the income from machinery, etc., and the enterpriser's profits, were fixed by forces independent of wages, and any increase in the product must therefore fall to the laborer as the residual claimant. This conclusion has the one merit of explaining somehow the rise in wages in the past century, but the fallacy of its method is too evident to call for exposure. Not to enter into the details of the method, it is enough to note that it involves the circular reasoning that land-rent is a surplus over cost of production, and is fixed regardless of wages, whereas the cost of production itself is made up of money wages.

Clark's wage theory

Another American economist, John B. Clark, is led by his theory of profits to a most hopeful conclusion as to the future of wages. Profits he considers to be essentially the reward for improvements in productive processes, which gradually accrue to the general benefit. As profits thus disappear, the average wage-earner is correspondingly uplifted, a conclusion quite as hopeful as that of Walker. In discussing profits above, dissent from the narrow conception of their source has been expressed.

Some facts lend support to every one of these theories of social progress, but other facts refuse to be harmonized. The temptation to get a simple, dogmatic explanation of value should be resisted. When the interrelation of the factors is recognized there is little likelihood of concluding that some one of them will absorb all the benefits of progress. One is not driven to the extreme either of optimism or of pessimism. While the theory of value is not in itself a theory of society, it greatly influences social conclusions. Clear economic analysis is a condition to sound thinking on practical questions.

§ III. Interrelation of Economic Agents

Organic nature of the productive process

1. *The industrial process is a unity and the different agents bear an organic relation to each other.* The problem of value is not one of physical division; it is one of logical analysis, and this is not possible in isolation or without the competition of men. Production as now carried on is a social process; the determination of market price is a social process. The different agents are complementary goods, each necessary to the best use of the various other agents. The value of seed is not to be found apart from the use of the ground; or the value of the leather apart from the shoemaker or the thread he uses. When these things are brought together in society their value is found by the comparison and measurement of marginal utilities. Economic

forces, like other classes of forces, act and react upon each other. Two bodies attract each other in space; two chemicals uniting are both transformed into a substance differing from either. The economic result of materials and men coöperating is something differing from either factor, yet dependent on both.

The conventional divisions of economics

2. *The divisions of the older political economy are aspects of the general problem of value.* The divisions conventional in the text-books on political economy, namely, "production, exchange, distribution, and consumption," have not been observed in the plan of this work. It has not seemed possible to accept the view that each of these phases of the vital economic process could be discussed completely apart from the others. *Consumption* must be studied at the beginning, as the basis of exchange value, and again at the end, when the circle of thought has returned to the use man makes of wealth; and it pervades the whole subject of value, for back of every price is the potential utility of the good. *Exchange* is coextensive with the whole process of associated industry; for wherever there is a price, there is exchange. Subjective value outside a market forms a small, though not negligible, part of the problem for the student of to-day. *Production* is implied in every exchange, as exchange is in all social production. They are, indeed, but different phases of the larger phenomenon, the economic process. Nor is *distribution*, considered in its impersonal or economic form, any other than the logical valuing of the shares of the factors in economic production. Impersonal distribution is coextensive with economic production. Whatever a good, logically considered, contributes to value in production, that is its share of the product. Personal distribution, it is true, brings in other great influences which have been partly considered, but which will be treated more fully in the division to follow, on the influence of the state in the distribution of income.

The broadest principle of value

3. *The law of diminishing returns is the broadest principle of value.* The one character common to all goods is that their importance varies with their quantity in any given connection. This is true of direct goods whose power to gratify wants falls as the supply grows; it is true of indirect goods, whose technical importance diminishes as the quantity increases, and which when taken at any given cost can be applied, after a point, only with diminishing advantage. The gradual extension of the marginal principle from land used in agriculture to every conceivable economic agent is the most important development of the last century of economic theory.

Generality of the law of value

It being true that things are measured by the utility of the unit used last, logically considered, the least change in the combination alters the value of all the factors. Practical economic problems, therefore, are dynamic, not static. The view that the shares of the different factors are fixed by quite separate laws has not been accepted here. The law of rent is the same as the law of wages in its essential point and principle. It is a general law of value applied to a particular kind of want-gratifier. The law of substitution likewise is a general law, for within limits some substitution of factors is always possible along the margin. That being true, every movement of price creates its own resistance; substitutes will be found for materials, demand will decline, and a new equilibrium of price will be attained.

Mutual employment of the factors

An ever changing problem

4. *The factors and agents of production mutually furnish the field of employment for each other.* Each factor is dependent for its technical efficiency on the presence of the other factors. If labor is plentiful and machines are scarce, machines bear a high rent. In accordance with the law of diminishing returns, the last unit of labor in that case contributes little to the product, and labor gets low wages, while more is attributed to the machine. Each machine thus may be considered to offer a field for the employment of labor. If population increases and land remains fixed, the need for food raises the rental value of land. But if population increases slowly, and capital and science progress, the field for the employment of labor is enlarged; and if new lands are opened up or new resources are discovered beneath the surface of the land, the field for labor is still more enlarged and a greater share is attributed to labor. This changing character of the problem must be recognized; no share is foreordained in size.

The pursuit of the analysis of value along the lines of marginal utility thus leads to conclusions far less mechanical, and, to the superficial student, less simple than were the doctrines prevailing in the older economics. But the conclusions are, let us hope, more exact and more applicable to the real world, enabling the student to arrive at juster views of the present interests and of the future welfare of society.

DIVISION B—RELATION OF THE STATE TO INDUSTRY

Chapter XLIV
Free Competition and State Action

§ I. Competition and Custom

Definition of economic freedom

1. *Economic freedom exists when men's goods or their own services may be exchanged as they choose, without hindrance.* Competition is but another expression for economic freedom. Where men are *free* to exchange their goods and to get the best price they can, and actually do so, they are said to compete. The action of men in the mass follows pretty regular lines, corresponding to certain abiding motives. If one man dictated all industry, a very fragmentary science of economics would be possible; but the mass of men act according to some rule and are free so to act. When men are free to bring their goods to a market and get the best price possible, a single market price results.

When cost of production was believed to be the regulator of value, it was said that the law of value laid down was true "within the limit of free competition." Market price varied ceaselessly from cost of production, and whenever it did "the law of value" as then formulated was admittedly invalid or inapplicable. The law of monopoly price was supposed to be in marked contrast to the law of competitive prices. The law of prices, as followed in our study, stated in terms of marginal utility, is equally valid in competitive and in monopolistic conditions if there is merely one-sided, or buyers', competition. Two-sided competition is not the sole, though it is the usual condition, which the economist takes account of in reasoning on the problem of price. Anything that keeps men from exchanging what they have for the best price, interferes with competition. Some of these hindrances have been noted, others are now to be.

Economic freedom vs. equality of efficiency

2. *Economic freedom does not mean equality of power or of efficiency.* It was said in discussing monopoly that it was not to be understood to be merely either scarcity or superiority. To speak of the class of laborers of ability above that of the average day laborer as having a monopoly is certainly a confusion of monopoly with the

FREE COMPETITION AND STATE ACTION

scarcity of efficiency. The term competition is not easy to define in practice; for it is not easy to see just what part of a man's inability to exchange is due to his own lack of efficiency, and what to things outside of himself which prevent him from exchanging his labor. But the thought is clear that free competition—economic freedom—is limited whenever men are hindered by any power outside themselves from using their economic power as they prefer. The limitations of competition, thus understood, are essentially social limitations, imposed by other men either unconsciously by custom, convention, tradition, or consciously by force or by laws. When, among Polynesian tribes, the custom of taboo prevailed, by which certain things were reserved to the rulers and were forbidden to the common man, there was a limitation on his economic freedom. Contrast such limits with those set by the penury of nature. The savage may like best to hunt, but if there is no game, he must fish; he may like best to make arrowheads, but in need of food he must dig roots. Economic action is limited by lack of knowledge and skill; the resources of nature lie unused under the feet of savages who are suffering from their lack. These are limitations not of economic freedom but of economic efficiency.

Limitation by custom in early society

3. *In early society custom limits economic freedom in many ways.* The savage is not a man without law; he is bound in many ways to prescribed lines of conduct. Primitive custom usually takes on a religious sanction, and every member of the tribe is compelled to do as his fathers have done and as his neighbors are doing. He is not free to choose. Custom in some ways is favorable to the welfare of society, for it limits the power of masters and rulers, preserves the rights of individuals to common property, and is in the interest of the weak as well as of the strong. In an age of force if it were not for custom, he who had might on his side could take all. So in early society even economic relations were complex and yet almost fixed—changing only slowly from generation to generation. Every such social custom that limits the choice of men limits economic freedom.

Limitation by custom in the Middle Ages

4. *Custom ruled a large share of the industrial life of the Middle Ages.* Political and economic interests were not clearly divided in the Middle Ages. Land was the all-important kind of wealth. Military and other public services were performed by the vassal, who thus at the same time paid his taxes and the rent of the land. The landlord was at once the ruler, the receiver of rents, and the collector of taxes. The rent, however, was not a competitive price, but consisted of the dues and services the forefathers had been accustomed to pay. This limited slavery, like all other slavery, was wasteful, as it did not give to the individual the strongest motive to increase the quantity and to improve the quality of his service. Trade became limited in almost every direction. Crafts and gilds arrogated to themselves the right of employment in their industries. No matter what talent the son of a peasant might show, he usually found it impossible and always found it difficult to follow the occupation of his choice. Privilege pervaded all the life of that time. In such conditions economic friction is great. Men are kept in trades below their ability,

while others gain command of monopolistic and unearned returns.

Yet through all the Middle Ages ran the forces of competition. The inefficiency of customary services was a constant invitation to competitors. Men were striving to break over the barriers of custom and prejudice. The strife for freedom was the vital economic force even of the Middle Ages. The industrial history of that time is largely the story of the struggle of the forces of competition against the bounds of custom.

§ II. Economic Harmony through Competition

Effect of modern forces on custom

1. *The industrial events following the discovery of America strengthened the forces making for economic freedom.* Discoveries in the Western hemisphere opened up a wide field for the adventure and enterprise of Europe. Commerce is the strongest enemy of custom, and new opportunities gave a rude shock to the conservatism both of the manor and of the village. With the rapid growth of industry and manufactures, old methods broke down. In an open market custom declines; it flourishes best in sheltered places. Further, the movement of thought in the Reformation and the spirit of the time, expressing the principle of personal liberty, allowing the individual to follow his own opinions and take the consequences, were favorable to competition. Despite these facts the restraints of the national governments on trade continued great, in some respects increasing during the seventeenth and eighteenth centuries, in France, Holland, and England. The regulation before attempted by towns and villages was employed on a larger scale by national governments with their commercial systems. The colonies in America were used for the economic ends of the "mother countries" and for the selfish interests of the home merchants in Europe. The American Revolution was one of the bitter fruits of the English policy of trade restriction.

Adam Smith's influence

The philosophy of natural law

2. *Adam Smith's work advocating greater economic freedom had a profound influence upon public thought.* "The Wealth of Nations," the first great work on political economy, was published in the year 1776. That was the "psychological moment," as public thought was so prepared for it that it had its maximum possible influence. The year of the American Declaration of Independence gave the most striking object lesson on the evils of a selfish colonial policy that interfered on a grand scale with economic freedom. The old customs had become ill fitted to life, ill adapted to the rapid industrial changes that were going on. What was needed in many directions, both in politics and in industry, was negative action by the government, the repeal of the old laws, the overthrow of old abuses. The French Revolution, following a few years later, emphasized this thought in the political

field. The philosophers of the time believed in a "natural law" in industry and politics. The reformers of the time wished to throw off the trammels of the past and to give men opportunity to exert themselves "naturally." In America the old abuses never had taken deep root, as the conditions of a new continent were not favorable to monopoly and privilege. Although the movement for the repeal of medieval laws has continued in Europe from 1776 till the present time, yet to-day custom is stronger in Europe than in America. Serfdom was not abolished until the nineteenth century in Austria and southeastern Europe, and not until a few years ago in Russia. Many economic and cultural forces furthered this movement, but the most powerful intellectual force in its favor was the work of Adam Smith. So strong an impression did Smith's book make, that in the minds of men "free trade" became almost identical in thought with political economy, whereas that was but the temporary economic problem of the eighteenth century.

The doctrine of the economic harmonies

3. *The doctrine of the "economic harmonies" is the extremest form of belief in the virtues of competition.* Every truth in political philosophy finds some exaggerated expression. The main task of the student is to determine what shade of gray things are, rather than whether they are white or black. The belief in the benefits of competition and the virtues of economic freedom found expression in the doctrine of "the economic harmonies." This is the faith that if men are left entirely free to do as their interest dictates, the highest and best efficiency for all will follow; it is the belief that the economic interests of all men are in harmony. The most striking evidence in support of this thought is the stimulating effect of self-interest freely working in the field of competition. Each strives to do what will bring him the largest return, and the price others pay measures their estimate of the service. Each seeking his own interest is led to make himself more useful to others. Thus are men stimulated to sacrifice, to invention, to preparation; thus is zeal animated and are efforts sustained.

Good social effects of self-interest

Through self-interest the working force is distributed over the field of industry wherever it is most needed. The remarkable adjustment of industry to the needs of each neighborhood is brought about by individual motives, not by centralized authority. It is not mere chance that produces this harmony. Wherever consumers settle, stores are started and factories are built. Wherever work is to be done, men come in about the right number to do it. Skill is adjusted to needs by the delicate measurement of the market rate of wages. Competition gives a definite rule of price—certainly the only definite impersonal rule; some say the only just rule. The competitive price must be appealed to even in arbitration. It is the standard to which things tend constantly to adjust themselves in an open market.

Conflicting interests in the business world

4. *Experience shows that the economic interests of men are only partly, not wholly,*

in harmony. That there is a great measure of truth in the statements just made, all must admit; but their application is limited. They are partial truths, never to be ignored, but quite false if taken, without modification, as practical rules of conduct. There are three species of competition in every market: that between sellers, that between buyers, and that between sellers on the one hand and buyers on the other. It is to the interest of the buyers that the sellers shall be numerous, eager, and freely competing. It is to the interest of the seller that supply shall be small, that sellers shall be united, and that buyers shall compete sharply. If at any point free competition is hindered, even the disciple of economic harmony must expect a discordant result. But in reality competition is rarely quite complete on both sides, and when it is not, the weak suffer. Men do not start with fair and equal opportunities. All that they may be entitled to under competition may be so little that social sympathy seeks to better the result; hence poor relief, public and private. Society as a whole has an interest in the outcome of the individual's economic struggle. It cannot see men starving or driven into crime. But the argument need not be confined to such crude and extreme cases, for wherever economic interests are not in harmony and it is possible to further the social welfare, will not society be justified in acting?

§ III. Social Limiting of Competition

Imperfections of economic freedom

1. *Undoubted evils result from some forms of competition under the conditions actually existing.* Complete freedom must remain a somewhat abstract ideal, and actual conditions must be recognized. Entire freedom of choice means freedom to make mistakes, a privilege whose enjoyment society cannot always permit. The child should be raised to good citizenship, and entire freedom of choice makes that impossible or improbable. The freedom of choice of the insane, the feeble-minded, and the criminal, cannot be recognized. Even where competition is the ideal of sound adult humanity, it is not to be too suddenly or extremely applied. The inequality of faculties, the prevailing dishonesty, the mass of inherited abuses, cannot be either ignored or at once ended. The immigrant from Europe, plunged into the trying conditions of city life, suffers in health and in morals, and often becomes a burden upon society. One of many competitors may drive competition to an evil extreme. The "problem of the twentieth man" is presented when nineteen men desire to limit competition in ways not socially harmful, as by closing shops on Sunday or in the evening, and the one man refuses. The appeal to economic harmony often is the cry of "peace, peace, where there is no peace." The highest social result may be attained now by limiting, again by directing, in other cases possibly by fostering, competition.

Forces opposing competition

2. *The main rivals of competition are custom, religion, morality, combination, and*

state action. The first three of these were the strongest forces in the past and they are still operating; but combination and state action are more characteristic of the present. The influence of custom, of morality, and of religion on value, has been touched upon at several points in our study; that of combination has been recently and more fully discussed. But state action, one of the most important of all the limitations, has been reserved for the concluding portion of our work.

The state's part in directing competition

3. *It is a function of the state to determine in part the ways in which men shall exert their powers.* This is not the sole function of the state, nor is its influence toward this end exclusive. The state puts limits to the physical rivalry of men. In the distant past no doubt physical rivalry between men was an agent of progress. The strong drove out the weak; physical contest developed more vigorous limbs, keener senses, and higher sagacity. To-day it is one of the principal functions of the state to suppress the physical contest between men. The citizen is surrounded with a network of rules and regulations of which he is hardly conscious. Most men easily avoid coming into contact with the police and feel no irksomeness in the control of the civil courts. The state regulates economic interests in many other ways; it controls the building of streets; it inspects the material and construction of houses; it forbids acts injurious to the public welfare; it regulates the issue of money; it determines the manner in which credit may be extended, the forms of taxation, and the direction which trade may legally take. The state has a part in shaping great industries of a public or semi-public nature, such as waterworks, railroads, and the postal system.

Aim and failings of state action

The state is as wise as the men who constitute it. Men make mistakes, therefore men collectively will make them. The state regulates and limits—now wisely, now foolishly; but its aim is to preserve the benefits of competition without its evils, to lift the competition to a higher plane, and, by determining the direction in which men shall put forth their efforts, to give a higher and truer economic freedom.

Chapter XLV
Use, Coinage, and Value of Money

§ I.   The Precious Metals as Money

Money defined and reviewed

1. *Money we have defined as a material means of payment and medium of exchange, generally accepted and passing from hand to hand.* The origin and function of money were set forth in the study of capital. The subject must now be approached from a different side and with the two-fold purpose of seeing whether there is anything peculiar in the relation of money to the general problem of value, and what is the influence of the action of the state on the value of money. The definition of money implies several ideas. First, the words "generally accepted means of payment" imply that money, as something bearing the stamp of social approval, has a peculiar social character, is not an ordinary good. Second, the definition implies that money itself must be a thing having value, otherwise it could not serve as a medium of exchange. Exchange means the taking and giving of things of value. Money is, therefore, not merely an order for goods, as a card or paper requesting payment; it is itself a thing of value, though this value may be due solely to its possessing the money function. This point is one of the most difficult in the subject. Third, the definition implies that money is a material thing. The telegram when transferring an order for the payment of money, the spoken word, the promise to pay, etc., are not money. Fourth, it implies that money passes from hand to hand, is a thing that can be handled, and is or can be bodily transported.

Difficulty in applying the definition

The application of the definition is not always easy, for money shades off into other things that serve the same purpose and are related in nature. Even special students differ as to the border-line of the concept, but as to the general nature of money there is essential agreement. In many problems it appears to be at the same time like and unlike other things of value, and just wherein lies the difference often is difficult to determine. The use of money is of such social importance, and it touches so many practical interests, that it raises many questions of a political

USE, COINAGE, AND VALUE OF MONEY

and ethical nature. There are perhaps more popular errors on this than on any other one subject in economics. Yet the general principles of money are as fully understood and as firmly established as any parts of economics.

Standard, or primary, money
Gold-using countries

2. *The precious metals, gold and silver, are the standard, or primary, moneys in the world to-day.* Primary, typical, standard money is the unit in which the value of the money of a country is expressed, no matter what its form is; the standard is a certain weight and fineness of a particular metal. Coins of this standard are called full, or real, money by some writers who deny the title of money to everything else. It has been shown before that there has been an evolution in the use of money. The more efficient forms, gold and silver, have competed with copper, iron, tin, cattle, salt, tobacco. In this contest silver had proved itself a few centuries ago to be the fittest medium of exchange, but in the last century gold has, among the leading nations, been displacing silver rapidly. In a higher degree than any other material, gold has the qualities of a good standard money in rich and industrially developed communities. The gold-using countries to-day are those of the western world. England for perhaps two centuries practically has had gold as its standard money; the United States since 1834 (except for the period of paper money from 1862 to 1879); France since about the year 1855, at which time she shifted from silver under the working of the bimetallic law; and Germany, then more backward industrially, since 1873. Australia and Japan have reached that result only within the last few years, and Italy, Russia, India, Mexico—even China and other Oriental countries—are striving to attain it.

Subordinate kinds of money

In all these countries other kinds of money are used side by side with gold and silver. The actual money consists of a wide and confusing variety: silver, nickel, copper, paper in various forms and issued by various authorities. But among all the kinds, either gold or silver is found standing preëminent and in a peculiar position. The difficulties of the money problem must be attacked at the point of standard money where it is nearest to ordinary value problems and is less complicated than when the various money substitutes are included. Most of the fallacies regarding money have arisen not about standard money, but about paper and light-weight silver.

Coinage defined

3. *Coinage is the act of shaping and marking a piece of metal to be used as money so as to indicate its weight and fineness.* The precious metals can and do circulate as money without coinage. Any other mark equally plain and equally recognizable serves for many purposes just as well as the government stamp on the standard metal. The use of metals in antiquity was without coinage, by weight and test of fineness. In backward countries to-day most payments are made by weight. International

payments are made by means of gold ingots that bear the mark of some well-known banking-house, and for that purpose gold bullion is money without the coiner's stamp. But for most uses government coinage has marked advantages. It is far more convenient for the average citizen to handle coins uniform in size and design than the diverse coins that would be put out by private enterprisers.

Technical features of coinage

An established rate of fineness insuring uniform quality is a great convenience. In the United States all gold and silver coins are nine tenths fine; in Great Britain, eleven twelfths. The established weight of the gold dollar in the United States is twenty-three and twenty-two hundredths grains of fine gold or twenty-five and eight tenths grains of standard gold. The limit of tolerance is the variation either above or below the standard weight or fineness that a coin is allowed to have when it leaves the mint. The par of exchange between standard coins of different countries is the expression of the ratio of fine gold in them. Thus the par of exchange between the American dollar and the English sovereign (the "pound") is four and eighty-six and two third hundredths, that is, four and eighty-six and two third hundredths dollars contain the same amount of gold as an English gold sovereign. The embossed design, milled or lettered edges, and other similar devices are merely to make the coins easily recognizable and difficult to counterfeit.

Seigniorage defined

4. *Seigniorage is the right the ruler or state has to charge for coinage, or it is the charge made for coinage.* Coinage as a function of great importance politically as well as economically was early exercised by governments or rulers. The prince, king, or emperor stamped his own device or portrait upon the coin; hence the term seigniorage from seignior (meaning lord or ruler). The right to issue money came to be one of the most essential prerogatives of sovereignty. Coinage is rarely without charge, and often has been a source of revenue to the ruler. In the Middle Ages this right was frequently exercised by princes for their selfish advantage to the injury and unsettling of trade.

Free or gratuitous coinage

When no charge is made for coinage, the coinage is said to be gratuitous. Coinage is said to be free if the subject or citizen can take bullion to the mint whenever he pleases, paying the usual seigniorage. Coinage is limited if the government or ruler determines when coinage is to take place. Thus, coinage may be both free and gratuitous, when citizens are allowed to bring bullion whenever they please and have it converted into coins without charge or deduction. But coinage is free without being gratuitous when any citizen may bring metal to the mint, whenever he chooses, to be coined subject to the seigniorage charge.

Money value under free coinage

5. *Where coinage is free and gratuitous the coin is worth the same as the bullion that*

is in it. This evidently and necessarily must be near the truth if the citizens exercise their right. They will not long keep metal uncoined in their possession when it is worth more in the form of money, nor will they long keep money from the melting-pot when it is worth more as bullion. Yet there may be a slight disparity between the bullion and the money values before the metal is converted into coin or the coin melted down into metal. A motive for action must exist before either change will be made; but a thing cannot have considerably different values in two different uses at the same moment.

Adjustment of supply to value

There is here no special problem of value. The value of gold as bullion and money is fixed by marginal demand. The several uses of gold are constantly competing for it: its uses for rings, pens, ornaments, championship cups, photography, dentistry, delicate instruments, and as a circulating medium. If the metal becomes worth more in one use, its amount there is increased and correspondingly diminished in the others. The supply likewise is influenced by changes in price. Gold-mining is one among various industries to which men may apply their labor and capital. Some mines are superior, others average, others marginal which it barely pays to work. There is, therefore, a rise and fall of the margin of production with change in price and change in cost of production. If at a given moment, when it barely pays to work a mine, gold becomes worth less, that mine will go out of use. As gold rises, some mines that did not pay before, come into use. A similar variation has been noted in the case of marginal land, marginal factories, marginal forges, and marginal agents of every kind.

"What is a dollar?"

The question was once asked in Parliament, "What is a pound?" and a good question to ask in beginning the study of money is, "What is a dollar?" The answer, so far as it refers to the standard money, is: a dollar is a convenient name applied to twenty-three and twenty-two hundredths grains of fine gold or twenty-five and eight tenths grains of standard fineness. The exchange value of gold varies in different places and conditions, but the name remains the same. A dollar exchanges for more wheat in Dakota than in New York or for more iron in Pittsburg than in Oregon, yet it is sometimes asserted that the value is always the same because the name is always the same. The fallacy of this may be seen in the equivalent expression that twenty-three and twenty-two hundredths grains of gold have the same value always and under all circumstances.

The problem of the bullion value of money metal, under gratuitous coinage, presents no special difficulties. The ordinary theory of value applies to it. The difficulties of the money question begin at the point where the money value is seen to diverge from, and depend on, something else than the value of the bullion. Yet in the principles just discussed are found a firm foundation for any further study of the question.

§ II. The Quantity Theory of Money

The money use

1. *The fundamental use that money serves is to apportion incomes of goods so as to make them yield the maximum gratification.* Money first increases utility by increasing the ease with which exchange takes place. Like any tool or agent, it is valued for what it does or helps to do. But further, it enhances the sum of enjoyments by the division of goods into proper quantities, making them available at the best time. It follows from the principle of diminishing utility that the particular time at which goods are available for wants has an essential bearing on their value. A hundred loaves of bread in the hands of a single individual would mold long before they could be consumed. Money enables men in society to acquire these hundred loaves in a series so that they can be used when most needed. Money is the most successful device man has ever discovered for distributing the supplies of a journey along its course, and the goods of daily need over a period of time. The use of money as a storehouse of value is merely an extreme case of keeping things for the future when they will have a greater gratifying power.

Concept of the money demand

Variation in the average

The fact that money is essentially a valuable good kept on hand as the best possible provision against emergencies points to the essential nature of the money demand. Money is sought, in order to form a cash reserve, up to a point where the loss from keeping it balances the probable gain. The money use is subject to the law of diminishing utility; beyond a certain point its added convenience is purchased at too great cost. Every man may be thought of as having an average, or usual, money demand, which is that proportion of his income that gives him more utility retained in money form than if at once expended. A man with an income and expenditure of fifty dollars a month paid monthly has use ordinarily for no more than fifty dollars as his cash reserve. While under ordinary circumstances this is his maximum demand, various circumstances may diminish it. If his expenses are distributed in two equal parts (the one on pay-day, the other thirty days later) his average money demand is twenty-five dollars, not fifty dollars. If most of his purchasing is done at the beginning of the month, his average money demand may be perhaps ten dollars. Many a workman purchases on credit, spends his fifty dollars within an hour after he receives it, and goes without money for the rest of the month. The average demand of a community for money required as a reserve is affected by the methods of doing business. With a given method of use a reduction in the supply of money results in loss of time and waste of effort; an increase in the supply results in a lowering of its value relative to other things. In either case the equilibrium of the marginal utilities of income must be restored. The thought of an average, rational, money demand relative to money income is the fundamental requisite for clear thinking on the question of money, but to grasp this thought there is needed a certain power of scientific imagination lacking in some minds.

USE, COINAGE, AND VALUE OF MONEY

The quantity theory of money

2. *The quantity theory of money is that, other things being equal, the value of money falls as its quantity increases, and vice versa.* This is an abstract statement of a concrete and difficult problem. The phrase "other things being equal" betokens the statement of a tendency where there are several unknown factors. In recent discussion the quantity theory of money has been questioned by some critics; yet it is held by most economists to be merely the general law of value as applied to money. There are three sets of facts to be brought into relationship with each other in the quantity theory: (1) amount of business or exchanges to be effected; (2) the methods by which this is done; (3) the amount of money available to do it. According to the quantity theory we must expect that when conditions (1) and (2) remain fixed, the value of money will vary inversely as its quantity. This conclusion follows from the conception of the money demand as the value of circulating medium that bears an average proportion to the value of goods exchanged.

Example of its application

Let us consider various conditions. When a number of men, by reason of increasing gold supplies, get larger stocks of money than they have had, the former proportion between their money incomes and their money is altered. In reducing their stock of money by buying goods they bid up the prices of goods until the total value of goods exchanged again bears the same ratio as before to the total value of money. Taking an extreme case: if twice as many dollars get into circulation in a community, either some few men must have several times as many dollars as before, while others have the same; or every man will have his due proportion, just twice as much as before. The latter, "other things being equal," must be the logical result after equilibrium has been restored. Is any other result thinkable? Now if prices of goods remained the same as before, there would be twice as great a value of money available to effect exchanges. There is no reason why each should tie up twice as large a proportion of his income in a supply of the medium of exchange. If, however, there is a concerted movement to spend the surplus money, there results a general bidding down of the exchange value of money, a general bidding up of prices of goods. At what point will this movement stop? The rational conclusion must be that "other things being equal" equilibrium will be reëstablished only when the ratio between the value of money and the price of goods becomes the same as before. The money being doubled, prices must be double, and likewise for any other change in quantity.

Objections made to the quantity theory

3. *The quantity theory is misunderstood, and is criticized on the ground that the facts oppose it.* If but one kind of metal were used as money, and this were coined of uniform weight and fineness, the problem would be comparatively simple. But in fact gold and silver, full-weight and light-weight coins, circulate side by side. More mysterious still, the money in circulation is partly coin and partly paper. How can the quantity theory hold in these conditions? Several objections to the quantity theory are presented. It is said, first, that prices do not vary exactly

with the per capita circulation of different countries at a given moment. The per capita circulation in Mexico may be five dollars and in the United States twenty-five dollars, while prices are much less than five times as great here as in Mexico. Secondly, it is said that prices do not vary directly with changes in the amount of money in a given country. There is now perhaps five times as much money per capita in the United States as fifty years ago and yet prices are not five times as high. Thirdly, it is said that credit methods change, and therefore that money does not fix prices. Fourthly, it is said that even if true of primary money the theory fails to apply to actual conditions with many forms of money in circulation side by side. Fifthly, it is said that there are too many unknown quantities to permit the rule to be used.

The objections examined

4. *A reasonable interpretation of the quantity theory makes it a statement of the effect of a change in a single factor.* The objections to the quantity theory assume that it is a statement of what occurs under all conditions, instead of what it is, an index to the working of one condition at a time. The foregoing objections need but to be further analyzed to show that in each of them it is not merely the quantity of money, but a number of other factors that differ in each of the propositions. We may note briefly in turn the defects in the arguments of the preceding paragraph.

Not a per capita rule

First, the quantity theory does not remotely imply that prices in different countries differ at a given moment according to the per capita money. In the case of the United States and Mexico not only the amount of exchange per capita but the method of exchange, and the rapidity of the circulation of money differ quite as much, doubtless, as does the per capita circulation. The quantity theory would lead any fairly careful student to a conclusion the exact opposite of that which its critics have twisted from it.

Recognizes the growth of trade

Second, the quantity theory does not imply that during a period of years when a country is changing in a multitude of ways, as in population, methods of industry, modes of exchange and transportation, and in wealth and income, the prices will vary directly either as the absolute or per capita amount of money does. In the light of the quantity theory the inquirer must be led to just the opposite of the ridiculous conclusion imputed to it.

Recognizes use of credit

Third, the theory does not overlook the effect of an increased use of credit, for it fully implies that any such a change, by economizing the use of money, would enable the same amount of money to support a higher scale of prices.

USE, COINAGE, AND VALUE OF MONEY 321

Not confined to primary money

Fourth, the theory does not overlook the variety of forms, and is not true merely of primary money. However great this variety, the money demand of individuals and of communities still represents a pretty definite ratio of the value of exchanges effected. If the primary money alone were doubled in quantity, while the various forms of substitute money (smaller coins, bank-notes, government notes, etc.) remained unchanged, the quantity of money as a whole would not be doubled, and according to the theory, prices would not be expected to double. Indeed, in such a case, the method of exchange would be very greatly altered, and the case is fully covered by the statement of the theory.

Is a practical rule

Fifth, despite the number of changing factors affecting the methods of exchange, the method of business, etc., the quantity theory is a rule usable at any moment. These various factors change slowly, and the quantity theory answers the question, What change occurs in prices as a result of an increase or decrease of the money in a given community at a given moment? Like the law of gravitation, the law of projectiles, and the statement of the chemical reaction to be expected when adding some substance to a given compound, the theory must be interpreted with practical limitations. When the quantity theory is thus stated and understood, its negation is unthinkable, as is evidenced by the involuntary use made of it constantly by every one of its few critics in explaining the simplest monetary phenomena.

Practical application of the quantity theory

Recent price changes

5. *The quantity theory makes intelligible the great and rapid changes in price that have followed sudden changes in the money supply.* Inductive demonstration of broadly stated economic principles is difficult, but in no other economic problem is laboratory experiment so nearly possible as in that of money. Many inflations and contractions of the circulating medium have occurred, now in a single country, again in the entire world, and the local or general results have served to exemplify richly the working of the quantity principle. With the scanty yield of silver- and gold-mines in the Middle Ages, prices were low. After the discovery of America, especially in the sixteenth century, quantities of silver flowed into Europe. The great rise of prices that occurred was explained by the keenest thinkers of that day along the essential lines of the quantity theory, though there were many monetary fallacies current at the time. The experience in England during the Napoleonic wars, when the money of England was inflated and prices rose above those of the Continent, led to the modern formulation of the theory by Ricardo and others. The discovery of gold in California and Australia, in 1848-50, increased the gold supply marvelously, and gold prices rose throughout the world. Between 1870 and 1890 the production of gold fell off greatly while its use as money increased and prices fell. A great increase of gold production has occurred in the period since 1890. In

part the rising prices from 1897 to 1902 are explicable as the periodic upswing of confidence and credit, but in part doubtless they are due to the stimulus of increasing gold supplies. These are but a few of many instances in monetary history which, taken together, make an argument of probability in favor of the quantity theory so strong as to constitute practically its inductive proof.

Chapter XLVI
Token Coinage and Government Paper Money

§ I. Light-weight Coins

Seigniorage and the value of coins

Saturation point for coinage

1. *When the number of coins issued is limited properly, a seigniorage charge does not reduce their money value; they are worth more as money than as bullion.* The coinage thus far considered has been that of full-weight coins without seigniorage. The question now is, What is the effect of a seigniorage charge on the value of the coin as compared with the bullion that is in it? This is one of the most difficult phases of monetary theory. Two values must be thought of: one the value of the coin as money, the other the value of the bullion in it. When coinage is free and gratuitous, these two values are the same. How can they ever be different? The answer to the question is found in the theory of monopoly value. If the supply of coin is limited by the sole agency of issue, the value can be kept above the cost of production (*i.e.*, in this case the bullion value), the seigniorage being the profit of the government. The limit within which the coinage must be kept is the number of coins that would circulate freely if they were made full weight without a seigniorage charge. This is the "saturation point" of the money demand of the country; it is a certain number of pieces of full-weight metal. If more than that amount gets into circulation it becomes worth less as money than as bullion, and it is melted or exported.

Example of seigniorage value in coins

If this full supply of money at a given moment is 100,000 pieces or dollars, a seigniorage charge of ten per cent. could be made if the number of pieces were not increased above 100,000. The government alone having the right of coinage, the need of money would give the circulating medium a monopoly value. The value of the money would rise until the coin would buy one ninth more bullion than was in it, but if there were any further rise the citizens would begin to take coins to the mint. After the ten per cent. charge was taken out they would receive a coin which, though containing one tenth less bullion, would be worth very nearly the same as the metal taken to the mint. No considerable depreciation could take place unless the volume of business fell off so that less money was needed than at the old standard. In that case there would be no outlet for the excess of coins until they fell to their bullion value, *i.e.*, till they lost the entire value of the seigniorage, the monopoly element in them. Melting or exporting them before that point was reached would cause the loss of whatever element of seigniorage value they contained.

Example of excess and depreciation of coins

Assuming that the volume of business, or sum of exchanges, remains unchanged, let us consider what will result if the government begins to issue "on its own account." The number of coins might be increased until at the bullion price the total money value were equal to the original 100,000 full-weight coins, at which point exportation would take place. There being nine tenths as much precious metal as before, it would require ten ninths as many pieces, or 111,111 pieces, to have as great a value as the 100,000 had before. At this point there is no further profit to the government in issuing coins of that weight. To make a further profit it must again reduce the amount of pure metal in the coin.

Medieval examples of depreciation

This is essentially what occurred often throughout the Middle Ages. A ruler debased the quality or reduced the weight of money, but for a time the new coin, having the same money use, circulated as freely as the old coin. If, as so often happened, the ruler yielded to the temptation to issue more in order to get the profit, the older, heavier coins at once began to go abroad or into the melting-pot. Then occurred a fall in value, mystifying alike to the prince and the people. The reason is now perfectly plain: the number of pieces issued had not been kept within the proper limits, and the coins went down to their bullion value.

Difficulties with full-weight subsidiary coins

2. *Subsidiary coins of lighter weight than the standard, if properly limited, will remain in circulation at par.* Money to serve all of its purposes must be of different denominations. The amount required of each denomination is determined by the volume of exchanges for which each is most convenient. Each kind of money, as the penny, nickel, dime, has its own peculiar demand and its saturation point. For the smaller denominations the standard metal is not suitable. A gold dollar cannot well be cut into twenty or a hundred pieces. Thus copper, nickel, silver remain in restricted use. When these are issued at their bullion value, difficulties arise; not only are they too heavy, but as they vary in bullion value, some of them become worth more as bullion than as coin, and suddenly disappear from circulation.

Adoption of light-weight minor coins
Theory of light-weight coins

This happened often throughout the Middle Ages and until the nineteenth century. Gold and silver generally were coined at a ratio of weight corresponding exactly to their market ratio at a given moment, and every time the market conditions varied, one kind of the money went out of circulation, and the country was left either without the larger gold coins, or without subsidiary coin, or "small change." At length the plan was hit upon of issuing a limited number of subsidiary coins of less than full bullion value, that is, as "token coins." By this plan there is given to the minor coins a value greater than that of the bullion in them. The small profit made by the government on every penny, nickel, or dime issued, is a seigniorage charge. These minor coins, in somewhat confusing variety, circulate side by side with full-weight money, their value depending on the monopoly principle. The result of a large issue of any one denomination would be a lowering of its value. In practice their issue is determined by the needs of business and by the requests of citizens for small coins in exchange for standard money. One needing "change" gets it at the bank; when the bank finds its supply falling short it gets more from the government mints. As business increased in 1898, the demand for nickels, dimes, and quarters became unprecedented, and the mints worked night and day to supply them.

Gresham's law

3. *Gresham's law of the circulation of coins of different bullion value is: bad money drives out good money.* This so-called "law" was stated in these circumstances: England had two kinds of metal money, silver and gold, which were coined at a fixed ratio in weight; and as the market value of the bullion changed, the new full-weight coins of the metal rising in value went out of circulation. The coining of the cheaper metal caused the melting or exporting of the one becoming dearer, and for those purposes the coins containing the most bullion were picked. Likewise full-weight coins disappear whenever money of less bullion value (either because containing more alloy, or because made of a cheaper metal or of paper) is poured into the circulation in large quantities.

Proper interpretation of Gresham's law

Gresham's law needs some explanation, for it is frequently misunderstood. "Bad" money means money that has not the bullion value equal to its money value, money that is either debased in quality or light in weight. But not every piece of bad money will drive out every piece of good money. If that were so, a single bad penny would drive out of circulation all the gold. The law applies only under certain conditions. The "good" will leave the country only if the total amount of money in circulation is in excess of what would be needed if all were of full weight or best quality. Paradoxically speaking, if there is not too much of the bad money, it is just as good as the good money. The good money may not leave the country. It may be hoarded, or be picked out by banks and savings-institutions to retain as their reserve, or it may be melted for use in the arts. Gresham's "law" is thus a practical precept: keep the amount of token or light-weight coin limited to the field of its peculiar use, or it will cause the other forms, the fuller weight money, to leave for a better market. That better market may be the melting-pot or it may be a foreign country.

§ II. Paper Money Experiments

Nature of paper money

The legal-tender quality

1. *Government paper money may be defined as money for which a seigniorage of one hundred per cent. is charged.* The order in the study of the money question is from seigniorage to paper money, because paper money embodies the principle of seigniorage in its extremest form. The issue of paper money grew out of the practice of debasing metal. The gain of seigniorage from paper money is greater and is just as easily secured. Government paper money is sometimes called "political money," in contrast with money whose value rests on the value of its material. In this sense, however, all coins containing an element of seigniorage, or monopoly value, are to that degree "political" money. The typical paper money is irredeemable, that is, it cannot be turned into bullion money on demand. It was simply put into circulation with the legal-tender quality. The "legal-tender" quality is the declaration of the government that the paper money must be accepted by citizens as a legal discharge for debts due them. The object of this is to compel people to use it as money whether they will or not. The purpose of the government in thus employing its power over the circulating medium is usually to profit, that is, to secure the value of the seigniorage for public purposes. Paper money differs from bank-notes in that it does not depend for its redemption on the credit of the issuer. It differs from bonds in that its value is not based on the interest it yields, but solely on its money uses. The issue of paper money may save the government the payment of interest on an equal amount of bonds. The promise to receive paper money in payment for taxes or for public lands, may help to maintain the value of the notes by reducing their quantity, but nothing short of prompt exchange for standard coins makes them truly redeemable.

Examples of paper money in the eighteenth century

2. *The most notable examples of paper money in the eighteenth century were the American colonial currencies, the continental notes, and the French assignats.* In all the American colonies before the Revolution notes or bills of credit were issued which were in most cases legal tender. Without exception they were issued in large amounts and without exception they depreciated. Parliament forbade the issues, but to no effect. The continental notes were issued by the Continental Congress in the first year of the war (1775), and for the next five years. The object at first was to anticipate taxes, and it was expected that the states would redeem and destroy the notes, but this was not done. The notes passed at par for a time, but depreciated rapidly as their number increased. The country had less than $10,000,000 of coin before the war, and when, in 1780, over $200,000,000 of notes were in circulation

TOKEN COINAGE & GOVERNMENT PAPER MONEY

they were completely discredited; hence the phrase "not worth a continental." Specie quickly came back into use. A few years later the leaders of the French Revolution, failing to learn the lesson of the American experience, issued, on the security of land, notes called assignats in such enormous quantities that they became worth no more than the paper on which they were printed. In a figurative sense they may be said to have fallen to their "bullion" value.

More recent examples of paper money

3. *Notable examples of paper money in the nineteenth century were the English bank-notes in the years 1797-1820, and the American greenbacks, 1862-79.* There have been many other examples. During the Franco-Prussian War, France, through the medium of its great state bank, issued notes which only slightly depreciated. At the present time many countries—Russia, Austria, Portugal, Italy, all the South American republics—have depreciated paper currencies. But the English bank restriction of 1797-1820 is notable because it gave rise to the controversy which did most to develop the modern theory of the subject. The Bank of England was forbidden to redeem its notes in coin because the government wished to borrow all the coin the bank had. The result was the issue of a large amount of bank money not subject to the ordinary rule of redemption on demand. It was virtually government paper money. The notes depreciated and drove gold out of circulation, and not until 1820 was there a return to specie payments.

The greenbacks

The United States under the constitution did not try paper money till 1862 when paper notes (called greenbacks, because of the color of ink with which the reverse side was printed) were issued as a war measure to the amount of about $450,000,000. Other interest-bearing notes were issued with legal-tender quality and circulated as money to some extent. Greenbacks depreciated in terms of gold, and gold rose in price until, in June, 1864, it sold at two hundred and eighty a hundred. Fourteen years elapsed after the war before these notes rose to par, in terms of gold.

Evil effects of political money

4. *Paper-money issues usually have had injurious effects on general industry.* The purpose of the issue of paper money is generally to relieve the financial necessities of the government. It is a costly expedient, resorted to only in desperate extremities. A result usually unintended is the derangement of business and of the existing distribution of incomes. The rapid and unpredictable changes in prices give opportunity for speculative profits, but most legitimate business is injured. This incidental effect on debts and industry becomes the main motive of some citizens in advocating the issue. It is peculiarly liable to be the subject of political intrigue and of popular misunderstanding.

§ III. Theories of Political Money

Commodity-money theory

1. *The commodity-money theorists declare that government is powerless to influence value, or to impart value to paper by law.* There are two extreme views regarding the nature of paper money, and a third which endeavors to find the truth between these two. First is that of the commodity-money theorists, or the cost-of-production theorists, who will not admit that there is any other basis for the value of money than the cost of the material that is in it. Money made of paper, on a printing press, has a cost almost negligibly small, and, therefore, they say it can have no value. The fact that it does circulate, and is treated as if it had value, is explained by the commodity theorists as follows: While the paper note is a mere promise to pay, with no value in itself, it is accepted because of the hope of its redemption, just as is any private note. Depreciation in this view is due to loss of confidence; the rise toward par measures the hope of repayment. Such a view overlooks the feature in which paper money differs from ordinary credit paper. The value of one's promise to pay depends on his reputation and his resources; the resources constitute the basis of value. Bonds have value because they yield interest and are payable at a definite time in standard money. But paper money, lacking this basis for its value, has another basis in its money use, in its power to buy goods. The money demand in connection with the monopoly power of government over the money supply, furnishes a satisfactory logical explanation of the value of paper money.

Fiat-money theory

2. *The fiat-money advocates assert that government has unlimited power to maintain the value of paper money by conferring upon it the legal-tender quality.* The meaning of fiat is "let there be," and the fiat-money advocates believe that the government has but to say, "let it be money," to invest paper with value. The typical fiat advocates in the United States were the "Greenbackers," those voters who wished to retain the paper money issued in the Civil War, and to increase its amount greatly. They saw in paper money an unlimited source of income to the government. They proposed the payment of the national debt, the support of the government without taxes, and the loan of unlimited money without interest to citizens. All might live in luxury if the extreme fiat-money theorists could realize their dream. There are still some survivors of this faith in the power of the government fiat. The depreciation that has taken place in every case where government notes have been issued, they declare to be due to a too mild enforcement of the law of legal tender. To them the fact that paper money may circulate for a time at par appears a reason why it always should. They do not admit that there is a saturation point in the use of money, and that its use is still further limited by the fear of larger issues. They do not see that the ultimate basis of the value of paper money is economic,—is in its money use, not in the fiat of the government.

Theoretical possibility of a good paper money

3. *A sound theory of paper money makes it a special case of monopoly value.* It has

TOKEN COINAGE & GOVERNMENT PAPER MONEY 329

been seen that the power of almost every monopoly over price is relative, not absolute. As the power of a great private corporation over the price of its product is limited, so is that of the government over the value of political money. The money use is the source of value to the paper notes. Business conditions remaining unchanged, the limit of possible issue without depreciation is the number of units in circulation before the paper money was issued, the saturation point of full-weight and full-value coins. Because governments generally have not stopped at that point, paper money has depreciated. Popular error and selfish interests force legislation beyond the reasonable limit. In a few cases only have there been public integrity and courage enough to retrace the steps before great harm resulted. It is principally this lack of control that prevents paper money from being a good circulating medium.

Influence of law on value

It is sometimes said that government cannot affect value in any way, but it can do so in many ways. Certainly one of the most remarkable is by the use of its monopoly power over the medium of exchange, whereby it can, under certain conditions, cause a piece of paper to have the value of a piece of gold. Thereby at the same time it affects the interests of nearly every member of society, raising or lowering the value of many kinds of property, and of many incomes.

Chapter XLVII
The Standard of Deferred Payments

§ I. Function of the Standard

Definition of the standard

1. *The standard of deferred payments is the thing of value in which, by the law or by contract, the amount of a debt is expressed.* A credit transaction is a lengthened exchange; one party fulfils his part of the contract, the other party promises to give an equivalent at a later date. The equivalent may be in any kind of goods; for example, in barter one may part with a horse on the promise of a cow to be received later; or a small horse on the promise of a large one; or a flock of sheep on the promise of its return at the end of the year with a part of the increase of the flock. A simple standard in which to express the debt is the thing borrowed, as horse, sheep, wheat, house, etc. This involves the use of the renting contract. Again, the thing to which the value of debts is referred may be a thing quite different from the goods borrowed, and with the growth of the money economy and the use of the interest contract, money comes more and more to be used as the standard. The parties express the debt in terms of the standard unit established by law.

Increasing use of the interest contract

2. *The importance of the standard of deferred payments increases with the use of money and with the amount of outstanding debts.* Until the use of money develops, the use of credit is difficult and limited; it becomes easy when the value of all things is expressed in terms of a common circulating medium. If all business were done for cash there would be no great interests affected when a change in the value of money occurred. Every dollar would change in value in the hands of the holder, but there the effect would cease. But the volume of outstanding debts expressed in terms of money now exceeds many fold the total value of the circulating medium. The value of all these debts changes in the same proportion as does that of the standard unit of money; when this is cheapened either by law or as a result of increasing supplies, a creditor to whom a thousand dollars are due loses the same as if he had a thousand metal dollars locked up in a strong chest.

THE STANDARD OF DEFERRED PAYMENTS 331

Great effects of money changes

Outstanding contract debts may be roughly divided into three classes: short-time loans, running less than a year; medium-time, running from one to five years; long-time, running over five years. Fluctuations are rarely rapid and great enough to affect appreciably the debtors and creditors in the case of short-time loans. The results are greater in the case of long-time loans, such as national, state, and city debts, bonds of corporations, mortgages given by farmers on their land or by owners of city real estate. A multitude of interests are affected by a change in the value of money. When, as in the years 1873-96, money gains in purchasing power (prices fall) receivers of fixed incomes are gainers. When, as in the years 1896-1903, the value of money falls, the revenues from educational and charitable endowments, the salaries of public officials, and all fixed incomes, lose purchasing power. In a capitalistic age, therefore, almost every individual is affected in some way by a change in the value of money. In most cases the change escapes recognition; people do not trace out the relation that an industrial change bears to their own interests. In a few notable cases, however, the change has been revolutionary as in the period following the discovery of America, when the feudal dues had come to be expressed in terms of money instead of labor services. In modern times, the mass of debts being greater than ever before, such changes as those following the discovery of gold in California or the decrease in gold production between 1873 and 1890 have the gravest economic results.

Merits of gold and of silver as standards

3. *The best standards of deferred payments available—the precious metals, gold and silver—are still imperfect.* The good that is most convenient as a standard of deferred payments is the one used as money. Gold to-day is constantly expressing the value of all other things. Borrowers prefer to make loans in the form of the general medium of exchange. From the usage of speaking of all things in terms of money, the false idea arises that the value of other things changes, but that the value of gold is always the same. Money is no such a fixed objective standard as a foot-rule or a pound weight. The value of gold rests on the estimates made by men, and is constantly changing according to conditions. A fixed objective standard of value is not possible of attainment. The value of the precious metals is stable as compared with most things. The current new supply is comparatively regular. For generations at a time there may be no radical changes in the output of gold and silver. For centuries there was no change in the methods of extraction. Recent inventions, however, have considerably altered these conditions. The nature of the use of gold and silver, likewise, is such as to make the demand for them, under ordinary conditions, most stable. The precious metals are but slowly worn out; only a portion of the annual output is used in the arts; there is, therefore, a large reservoir into which flows steadily a small stream; the existing stock is twenty or thirty times the annual output. Yet the value of the standard metals is never quite stable, and sometimes several influences combine, as in the last century, to affect their value greatly and suddenly.

Various standards suggested

Enjoyment

Sacrifice

Labor

Tabular standard

4. *Various ideals for a standard of deferred payments have been suggested—as return of equal enjoyment, of equal sacrifice, social expediency; and various standards—as labor, commodities, and the tabular standard.* The ideal standard of deferred payments is one that will insure justice between borrower and lender. Different views have been taken as to what constitutes justice in this matter. The suggestion is attractive that the sum when returned should represent the same amount of enjoyment as it did when it was borrowed. Such a standard is impossible of realization in any general way, for men's circumstances are constantly changing. To insure even to the average man the same amount of enjoyment is only roughly possible. The same goods do not afford the same enjoyment when conditions have changed. Another suggestion is that the goods returned should represent the same sacrifice as those loaned. Here again the difficulty is in the lack of an objective standard. Whose sacrifice? That of the lender, who may be rich, or that of the borrower, who may be poor? Some have supposed the conditions of equal sacrifice were met by the labor standard, according to which the sum returned should purchase the same number of days of labor as when borrowed. But what kind of labor is to be taken, that of the lender or that of the borrower, or that of some one else? Labor is of many different qualities, which can be exactly compared only through their objective value in terms of some one good. The ideal of equal enjoyment has been supposed to be realized by the tabular standard, which consists of a number of leading commodities in fixed proportions. The money returned is to be enough to purchase the same goods at the expiration as at the making of the loan, and thus may be a larger or smaller sum than was borrowed. While this does not, as is sometimes claimed, insure equality of enjoyment, it averages the fluctuations of many goods, and thus prevents great extremes. This standard has been favored by notable monetary authorities, but the difficulties of its practical application are prohibitive.

It must be recognized that any possible concrete standard of deferred payments will sometimes work hardship to individuals. The best average results for justice and social welfare will be secured by measuring debts in goods that change least often, least rapidly, and in the least unpredictable manner. Gold thus far has proved itself worthy to serve as the standard.

§ II. International Bimetallism

Examples of price fluctuations

1. *The fall of prices in 1873 and the following years meant a great change in the*

THE STANDARD OF DEFERRED PAYMENTS

standard of deferred payments. The monetary changes following the discovery of America were due to the inflow to Europe of great quantities of silver taken by force from the native American rulers, and from the rich mines. Silver, at that time throughout Europe the main standard of deferred payments, was thus greatly lowered in value. This change lightened all outstanding obligations, lowered the money rents of the peasants, and the customary dues of labor wherever they had come to be expressed in money form. By the third quarter of the nineteenth century gold had become in Europe and America the main standard, though silver still served as such in some countries. The output of gold in 1849-57 caused the greatest money inflation that has occurred since the sixteenth century, favoring in a similar manner the debtor classes. The substitution of gold for silver by some countries at that time, by making a great additional market for gold, helped in some degree to check the fall in its value.

The recent great fall of prices

The decline in the output of gold was a change of the opposite character, causing a fall of prices and increasing the burden of debts. From 1873 to 1896 there was almost constant decline of the prosperity of the agricultural classes, due in part to this money influence, but in part to influences which cannot be dwelt upon here, as they had nothing to do with the money question. There was complaint, agitation, and demand for relief on the part of many interests in France, Germany, England, and the United States.

Bimetallism defined

2. *Bimetallism, the use of two metals as standard moneys, was the remedy proposed.* Bimetallism is legally complete when both metals are admitted to the mints for free coinage at an established ratio of weight; it is halting or limping when one of the metals is not freely coined. Bimetallism may be legally authorized, but not actually working. As soon as the legal ratio varies appreciably from the market value, only one of the metals will in fact be brought to the mint. National bimetallism is confined to a single country, as that in the United States before the Civil War, or in France before 1867. International bimetallism is an agreement among several nations to use two metals on the same terms, the only case in history being that of the Latin Union, which included France, Italy, Switzerland, and other countries. The discussion of international bimetallism in recent years has been on the proposal to make a much larger league of states than the Latin Union, embracing all the leading countries.

Object of international bimetallism

3. *The main object of international bimetallism is to prevent the fluctuations of the standard of deferred payments.* Commercial dealings between gold-using and silver-using countries are of great magnitude, and the use of different standards leads to many difficulties. Fluctuations in the ratio of the two metals occasion much uncertainty and loss to individual traders. The rise in the value of gold meant an

increase in the burden of the public debts of silver-using countries which collect their revenues in silver, but which must pay their debts, principal and interest, in gold.

Its theory

The theory of bimetallism is that the government can act on the value of the two metals through the principle of substitution. The metal tending to become dearer will not be coined, the other will be coined in greater quantities. The degree of influence that can thus be exerted on the value of the two metals depends on the size of the reservoir of the metal that is rising in price. When it all leaves circulation, the law on the statute book permitting it to be coined becomes a mere sounding phrase. In such a case there is bimetallism *de jure*, but monometallism *de facto*. The greater the league of states, the greater is the likelihood that the scheme will work. The economic theory of bimetallism was recognized by a majority of economists to be abstractly sound, but the political difficulties in the way of international agreements are great, and have proved to be insurmountable.

§ III. The Free-silver Movement in America

Conditions leading to the demand for free-silver

1. *International bimetallism, despite many efforts, failed of adoption.* This brief proposition sums up the history of the movement, from 1878 to 1892, to form a league of states and an agreement for international bimetallism. International conferences were held, and taken part in by the leading financiers of the world. France at first favored the policy, and the United States was always foremost in advocating it, while England in the main was opposed. Some of the advocates of bimetallism argued that the fall of prices was due not alone to economic forces, but also to a money conspiracy which had influenced legislation to introduce and continue the gold standard. This, of course, was strenuously denied. It is true that the commercial classes found gold the form of money most suitable to large business, and no doubt class interests entered into the question in some measure. The difficulties of the debtor class in America were peculiarly great, owing to the inflated paper currency, from 1862 to 1879, which had made our conditions quite abnormal. In the period of speculation following the Civil War an enormous mass of debts had been accumulated. The hopes of thousands of tillers of the soil suffering from a fall in prices, and of the great debtor class, clamoring for relief, were centered upon the success of this movement. Banking and other large business interests in general opposed it.

Purpose of the free-silver movement

2. *The plan of the free-silver advocates was to legalize national bimetallism in the United States at a ratio between gold and silver very different from the market ratio.*

THE STANDARD OF DEFERRED PAYMENTS 335

Gold had become, long before 1860, the real standard of our money system, and after 1873 it was the only metal admitted to free coinage. Silver, little by little, was losing purchasing power in terms of gold, until from being worth, in 1873, one sixteenth as much, ounce for ounce, it became, in 1896, worth but one thirtieth as much as gold. It must be recognized that the power of silver to purchase general commodities fell much less than the change in its ratio to gold would indicate, gold having risen in terms of most other goods as well as of silver. Nevertheless, the proposal to open the mints to free silver at sixteen to one in the year 1896 meant a sudden and marked cheapening of money. The prime purpose was to lighten the burden of debts by making the standard of deferred payments cheaper. It was at first a debtors' movement, but to succeed it had to enlist the support of other large classes of voters. And thus, by force of political necessity, but doubtless in large part naïvely, it developed into the more sweeping theory that wages, welfare, and prosperity called for a larger supply of money independently of the effect on debts.

The free-silver theory

In its extreme form the free-silver plan was a fiat scheme, for some of its supporters believed that by the mere passage of the law the two metals could be made to bear to each other any ratio desired. But its most intelligent and high-minded advocates (who were moved to its support by a sincere sympathy and concern for the distressed agriculturalists) recognized fully that the force of the law was limited by economic conditions. The extreme opponents of the plan, ignoring the evident fact that the adoption of a metal as a standard money is one of the most essential of the market conditions, denied that government action could in any way affect the value. Most of the arguments presented on either side in the political campaigns showed little evidence of a sound theory of money. The victory of the gold standard in 1896 and 1900, it would seem, was due more to the well-founded fear that a sudden change of the money standard would cause a panic, than to a thorough understanding of the question.

Increase of gold production

3. *The increase of the gold output has for the present checked the fall of prices.* Before 1890, for a number of years, the average output of gold was shrinking till it reached a scant hundred million per year. At the same time, nations which recently had gone over to the gold standard were striving to secure large stocks for their banks and general circulation, and those great reservoirs, as a result, became better filled than they ever were before. After the opening of new gold-yielding territory in South Africa and in the Klondike, the annual output of gold became greater than it had ever been, being at the opening of the South African War in 1898 nearly three times that of ten years earlier. The present methods of extracting gold resemble those of fifty years ago as civilized industry resembles that of savages. Intricate machinery has taken the place of crude tools, chemical processes have been introduced, and the principal product results from the regular and certain working of deep mines rather than from chance surface discoveries. Great masses of debris can now be reworked profitably. In many parts of the world are enormous deposits of low-

grade ores, before useless, that can be worked economically by present methods. For a generation at least the world's supply of gold is likely to continue larger than ever before in history, and prices in terms of gold probably will rise.

Rising prices the temporary solution

Though no change seems likely or possible at the present time, the free-silver advocate has been justified by events against those gold advocates who said that the amount of money has nothing to do with prices. Prices have gone up as gold has increased. The free-silver advocates have gotten what they wanted through a change for which neither party can claim the credit. Yet the present situation is unsatisfactory and undeveloped. A standard better than a single metal, more stable than a single commodity, is desirable if it can be found. The money question must arise again and in a new form before many years. The difficulty has not been finally settled; it is but postponed.

Chapter XLVIII
Banking and Credit

§ I. Functions of a Bank

The essential banking function

1. *A bank is a business whose income is derived chiefly from lending its promises to pay.* Banks have passed through many changes in the past three centuries. Originating on the street corner for exchange of money, they have evolved into great institutions of many forms, and performing many functions. The definition seems paradoxical, but it expresses what in modern thought is the essential feature of a bank: the lending of its credit. A reserve of money is needed by the man of business. But for the banks each man would have to keep his reserve in his own till. Except the small sum needed for current uses, a bank can keep this reserve more economically than individuals can. It has the advantages of large production similar to those of a large factory. The process of lending credit is called deposit and discount. It grew out of the deposit of actual money for safe keeping and the loaning to borrowers by the method of discounting their notes. The term now has a somewhat different meaning, for a merchant may obtain a deposit to-day without putting any money in the bank. He gets the bank to discount his notes or collateral security, and to enter the sum to his credit as a deposit. He becomes a depositor by borrowing, not by lending to the bank. The sum is under the borrower's control; he can check it out when he wishes; but he usually keeps a certain balance to his credit. The bank's gain is larger than ordinary interest, because it gets a discount on the large sums left in its possession. The bank increases its funds also by attracting deposits from those who do not care to borrow.

Other functions usually performed

2. *Functions not essential to banking are ordinary money-lending, money-changing, exchange to distant points, safe deposit, and issue of bank-notes.* Banks often lend in the ordinary way, allowing borrowers to draw the money out at once, but this is not the business they prefer. Many individuals and corporations, such as endowed charities, colleges, insurance companies, lend great sums of their own

money without thereby partaking in any degree of the peculiar character of banking. Money-changing (the exchange of coins of different countries) is done by banks, but likewise by many other agencies not sharing the essential banking character. Foreign and domestic exchange is the issue and cashing of "drafts" for money payments between distant places. Most banks are well fitted to perform this function, but some banks do not undertake it, and it is performed also by some business houses that are not banks. Safe deposit is the keeping of things to be returned in identical form, as silverware, notes, and papers. By banks in small towns this is sometimes done freely, sometimes for a slight charge; but in large cities safe-deposit vaults are generally quite unconnected with banks. Even bank-note issue is not essential to banking; most banks in the United States issue no notes, others issue very few. All these functions may be united under one management, but the essential banking function is deposit and discount.

Sources of the income of banks

3. *The income of banks is derived from discounts, interest on their own capital, charges for exchange and collection, rents on investments, and profit from the loan of their bank-notes.* The income of banks is drawn from different sources, according to the size of the community and the nature of the banks. While in the villages and smaller cities they perform a number of functions, in the larger cities they usually specialize in a far greater degree. Like every other enterprise, a bank must start in business with some paid-up capital as a guarantee of credit. Further security is afforded by the limited liability of shareholders for losses, in proportion to their capital stock. The same amount of money could be loaned with less trouble and more cheaply without starting a bank, but used as a banking capital a part of it can be loaned while still serving to attract money deposits. Charges to smaller customers for exchange are a source of income to some banks, but in many cases this service is freely performed for regular customers and becomes a considerable expense. Banks make few investments in real estate or other physical property; it is, in fact, their duty to keep out of ordinary enterprises, but they are forced sometimes to take for unpaid debts things that have been held as security. Profits on bank-notes have at times been the main, possibly the sole, motive for starting banks; but that is not the case to-day when the right of issue is so strictly limited.

Productive services of banks

4. *Banks are productive economic agents performing important industrial services.* False ideas have long been entertained about the magic power of banks to produce wealth from nothing. To many, banks are a mystery much like paper money. Their opponents sometimes have pictured them as vampires fattening on the blood of industry. That they have shown abuses at times is undeniable, but, like other economic agents, they are to be judged by their net efficiency. The bank is a tool performing services similar to those of money. For some purposes money is an awkward and costly agent in comparison with banks. For remitting payments from New York to San Francisco or Hong Kong, money is a medieval device. Money can more safely be entrusted to a bank than to a strong chest in one's

own house. The man who refused to make use of banks in this day would isolate himself economically, and would soon find himself out of any but the smallest business. He could no more get along without the banks than without the post, the telegraph, or the telephone.

The bank as a labor-saving device

The gathering of loanable funds by the banks, making them available at once, reduces hoarding, makes money move more rapidly, and creates a central market between borrowers and lenders for the sale of credit. While not creating more physical wealth directly, it adds to the efficiency of wealth; it oils the bearings of the industrial machine. To abolish banks would be to destroy labor-saving machinery. Banks perform incidentally a further service in developing better business methods in the community. In supplying credit to active business, banks are constantly passing judgment on the collateral security presented to them and on the solidity of the enterprises that are seeking support. They enforce promptness and exactitude in business dealings.

Because in their public nature banks are very analogous to money, they have always been looked upon as properly subject to more supervision than most private business, and government has always exercised a considerable measure of control over them, sometimes for good, sometimes for evil.

§ II. Typical Bank Money

Nature of typical bank money

1. *Typical bank money consists of notes issued by banks on the credit of their general assets, without special regulation by law.* As no two leading countries have quite the same system of bank-notes, the subject is a difficult one. It is well to begin, therefore, with a clear conception of typical bank money, unregulated by government. Such a form of note is one with which few now living in the United States have had any experience, as the present national bank-notes differ in essential ways from the typical form. Typical bank-notes are notes issued by banks as a means of loaning their credit. The borrower, instead of receiving a credit balance at the bank subject to check, gets notes which he hands on to other men. These notes are returned for redemption to the issuing bank as soon as any one wishes specie in their stead. The limit of the issue of such notes is the need of the community for that form of money, and if they are promptly redeemed in gold on demand, they never can exceed that amount. A holder of a note (in the absence of special regulations) has the same claim on the bank that a depositor has. As it is to the interest of the bank to keep in circulation as many notes as possible, there is a temptation to abuse the power of note-issue, to which many banks yielded in the period of so-called "wild-cat banking" before the Civil War.

Bank-notes viewed as commercial paper

2. *Bank-notes are viewed by some as a form of commercial credit.* Typical bank-notes are not legal tender, and every one has the legal right to take or refuse them as he pleases. It is therefore said by some that bank-note issue is of no special concern to the state, that it can safely be left to individual self-interest. It is said that if one has little faith in a note, he may refuse to accept it. But in reality every one is compelled to take the money that is current. The average citizen cannot know the credit of distant banks, and thus has not the same power of judging wisely in taking bank-notes that he has in making deposits in the bank of his own neighborhood. Between bank-notes and ordinary promissory notes, there are other differences of a nature pretty generally recognized. Bank-notes pass without endorsement and thus depend on the credit of the bank alone, not like checks, on the credit of the person from whom received. They yield no interest to the holder. They are intended to be used as money and are so used. Thus they come near to paper money in their nature, and the banks are near to exercising the right of coinage.

Bank-notes viewed as a form of political money

3. *By others, bank-notes are considered to be almost identical with government paper money.* Some opponents of bank-note issue declare that it is a usurpation of the prerogatives of government, and that no power but the sovereign state should issue money. While many in America to-day hold this view, the comparison probably is false and strained. Typical bank-notes, unlike inconvertible paper money, depend for their value on the credit of the bank, not on their legal-tender quality and on political power. They must be redeemed on penalty of insolvency; government notes need not be, and yet will circulate at par if properly limited.

While these differences mark off government paper money pretty sharply from typical bank-notes, it must be noted that in many cases actual bank-note issues have been far from this typical form. In the days of "wild-cat" banking, bank-notes were issued in excess and fell below par, yet the man in a Western community who dared to ask the bank to redeem the notes in specie was not only frowned on by the bank, but condemned by the public, which felt that business was endangered by such a demand. Redemption on demand would have required a reduction of the amount of money in circulation and would have caused a fall in prices. Inflation of the bank currency went on with results almost identical with those following an excessive issue of government paper money. Not formal law but public opinion made such bank-notes essentially political money.

Policy of public regulation of bank-notes

4. *The public nature of bank money has led to many forms of public regulation of their issues.* Bank-notes thus stand midway in their economic nature between political money and private notes, sharing something of the character of each. An extreme analogy in either direction is misleading. It is of great social importance that the circulating medium should be reliable. The least possible amount of the citizen's energy and thought should be required to decide whether the money is good or

bad. Nevertheless, those opposed to state interference in industry declare that if the citizen is not left to look out for himself, the growth of stupidity will be encouraged; and they say that it is no more essential for the state to guarantee the quality of bank-notes than the quality of woolen cloth or of sugar. Few, however, take so extreme a view, and it is generally held that it is a function of the state to insure in a greater or less degree the quality of the money in circulation. The actual bank-notes of the leading countries are thus of many varieties. The Canadian notes are the most nearly typical bank-notes issued to-day; those of Germany come next, while those of the United States have little of the typical character.

§ III. Banks of the United States To-day

Forms of banks in the United States

1. *The three forms of banks in the United States are private, state, and national.* Any one with a little capital may become a private banker. There are "curbstone brokers" in almost every town, and some of the great financial houses are private banks. But the law will not allow this to go very far. Some states will not allow a man to put up a sign announcing himself as a banker unless he complies with certain banking laws. In some states even private banks are subjected to the same inspection as the state banks and are required to make the same reports to the state officials. State banks are those organized under special state banking laws. They are usually subject to inspection by state-bank commissioners, must make regular reports, and are required to comply with certain rules as to their reserves, rates, and investments. In any case they do not issue bank-notes, because the national laws now tax the notes of state banks so heavily that they are unprofitable. National banks, the largest and most important portion of our banking system, were authorized by law in 1863, during the Civil War. They are subject to stricter regulation and inspection than are other banks, and that regulation is perhaps an advantage to them, as it strengthens public confidence in their stability. Yet this regulation does not insure the depositors against loss, as some national banks fail every year. They may be organized with twenty-five thousand dollars capital in towns of less than three thousand population, with fifty thousand dollars in towns of less than six thousand, with one hundred thousand dollars in cities of less than fifty thousand, and with two hundred thousand dollars in larger cities.

Nature of our national bank-notes

2. *Our national bank-notes have no essential mark of typical bank money.* The one marked peculiarity of the national banks of the United States as compared with those of other countries, is their mode of note-issue. They perform all the other functions of banks, essential and unessential, and perform them well, but the issue of bank-notes is optional with them, and some of them do not issue any bank-notes. The legal condition to their issue is that bonds of the United States shall be purchased in the open market and deposited with the treasurer of the United

States. Until 1900, notes might be issued only to ninety per cent. of the value of the bonds deposited; but now they may be issued up to the par value of the bonds. The notes, being secured by the value of the bonds, rest on the credit of the government, not on the credit of the bank. These notes are not promptly sent back for redemption to the banks issuing them, as is done with typical bank-notes. They may circulate thousands of miles away from the bank that issued them, and for years after that bank has gone out of business. They are not an "elastic currency" increasing or diminishing with the needs of business. The changes in their amount depend upon the chance of the banks to make more or less in this way than by any other use of their capital, and this in turn depends largely on the price of bonds and on the rate of interest they bear. From 1864 to 1870, fortunes were made from this source, but in recent years there has been little opportunity of gain from note-issues. Our present bank-note issues are not on a logical basis, and satisfy no one entirely. They are of importance neither to the bank, to which they afford little or no profit, nor to the public, for which they do a service equally well done by silver certificates, greenbacks, or coins.

Suggested reforms of the bank-note system

Along with the discussion of the currency has gone, since 1896, a vigorous discussion of the banking system. The two problems are so closely related that a change in the one suggests readjustment of the other. One extreme plan is to abolish bank-notes entirely and to replace them with additional issues of greenbacks; the other extreme plan is to authorize the issue of almost typical bank-notes. A modification of the Canadian banking system, which has great merits, is held up for imitation. Bills have been repeatedly before Congress authorizing the maintenance of a general guarantee fund with which the notes of failed banks could be redeemed, and at the same time authorizing branch banks such as those in Canada. Public sentiment has never strongly favored this plan, however, and there is more likelihood of the passage of a bill providing for emergency notes in time of financial stress, after the plan followed in Germany.

Bank regulation a protective measure

That the control of banking is an important duty of government is the conclusion of the practical world. The various banking systems of the leading countries embody different plans for the one purpose of the adequate control of banking in the public interest. Government control of bank-notes is felt to be of the same nature as factory inspection, that is, to be a protective measure. When public interests are at stake and private interests conflict with them, government acts to forbid one citizen from doing harm, and to protect other citizens from injury.

Chapter XLIX
Taxation in its Relation to Value

§ I. Purposes of Taxation

Taxation defined

1. *Provision for the expense of organized government is the fundamental purpose of taxation.* Taxation may be defined as the taking by the government of private property for public uses. This implies a certain degree of compulsion. When the national government accepts ten million dollars in trust for the Carnegie Institution, it is not taxation, though wealth is given for public uses. The effects of taxation pervade all industrial affairs, but they will be discussed here only in relation to the value of goods and to the distribution of incomes. By taxation the government interferes with the individual's free choice and with the impersonal economic forces. It expends income in different ways from those which would be chosen by the individual.

Taxation for public defense

The primary purpose of taxation is public defense. War often has driven men into closer social relations. Public defense requires sacrifice on the part of the family and of the individual. In family or patriarchal communities all share a common income and combine in the common defense, but self-preservation compels such small communities to form a larger, stronger state for the common defense. Personal service in the field gives place to money taxes permitting a more regular, continuing, and perfect organization of military forces.

To preserve domestic order

Next comes the need of civil government to insure domestic tranquillity. As political unity grows, the citizens need less often protection against foreign foes, and they need more often, relatively, defense against the aggressions of some of their own countrymen. The preservation of domestic order requires police, courts of justice, and other agencies. The ideal of the anarchist to do without government is nowhere realized. Everywhere there must be government to preserve peace and to protect property. Unfortunately, this need grows with the growing density of population. Crime increases when men swarm in great cities. To maintain and operate the social machinery requires ever-increasing resources. The courts which settle disputes between men, and which interpret their contracts, are agencies of peace, displacing physical contests. Many other public expenses tend to enlarge, as those for legislative bodies, public buildings, statistical inquiries, the printing of public documents. Government on these accounts has become in modern times an increasingly costly institution.

Developing public wants; social and industrial welfare

2. *The promotion of the social and industrial welfare of society has come to be an important purpose of taxation.* Some functions of government, less essential than the primary ones just mentioned, seem naturally to grow out of them. In a democratic society, popular education is one of the necessary conditions of good government, as it appears that domestic order is not possible in a democratic state without intelligent citizens. Step by step the functions of government are widened. Some industrial functions are performed by the government in connection with the primary needs. Light-houses are necessary to guide the navy, but they also serve to guide the merchant marine and to aid industry. The post was established as an agent of political and military government to connect the ruler with the outposts (a fact the name post indicates), but the postal service has grown in every country to be a great industrial and social agency. The consular service, beginning in the political need of keeping official representatives in foreign lands, has grown to be a great economic agency. Consuls are commercial travelers, advancing the trade-interests of their countries in all quarters of the globe. These social and industrial functions have been increasing of late. As the national and local governments engage more in industry, they usually make larger demands in the shape of taxation.

The sphere of the state expands

It is along the border-line between the primary and the secondary purposes of taxation that the contest goes on regarding the proper functions of government. If they are to stop short of the extreme of socialism, where shall the line be drawn? The movement has been of late toward greater government activity; more of the wants of men are thus supplied through the agency of the state. That year by year a greater sum is taken by taxation and spent for the citizen is a fact that may be recognized without debate here. The toll-road becomes a public road, the toll-bridge becomes free, more is supplied by taxation for schools, for advanced research, and for technical training. In our country great wealth was given by the Morrill Act to scientific and technical schools. The state universities, against much opposition, have become in many states of the Union the dominant educational force. Moreover, taxation often is used as a means not merely of raising revenue, but of discouraging one kind of industry and encouraging another. One industry wanes or dies under increasing burdens, another waxes strong by fostering exemptions and bounties. A large share of this "protective legislation" is done under the guise of taxation.

Government as a consumption good and as a means of production

3. *Shifting of the limits of state action and corresponding changes in the weight of taxation are constantly affecting value and incomes.* Society as a whole is made up of many groups of industry. Government is the largest of these, collecting and expending more than any individual or corporation. Government is in one aspect a consumption good. In return for its collective cost men collectively get the enjoyment of social organization, markedly in contrast with the uncertain ties and hazards of primitive communities. But government becomes also a mode of social investment, an indirect agent, a productive enterprise. Wealth applied through it secures a greater product than is possible by individual action. Government can maintain light-houses more economically than individuals could otherwise secure them.

Apportioning of the cost

But when the government undertakes these various tasks, the expense falls unequally on individuals and affects differently their incomes. When free schools take the place of private schools, the law compels every one to contribute to education. To many individuals it is a matter of indifference whether they pay tuition or taxes, but the wealthy bachelor sometimes grumbles when forced to help in educating the day-laborer's family of twelve. The average result may be right, but individuals diverge from the average and thus have constantly a motive to attempt to change the limits of governmental action. Happily the subject is not always viewed with selfish eyes. The ethical and patriotic thought is not, "How will this affect my interests?" but, "How will it affect the general interests?" But as the question of value is always involved, men are usually found favoring or opposing a measure of taxation according as it affects their own income. Thus taxation is inevitably an economic question.

§ II. Forms of Taxation

The various forms of taxes

On incomes

On property

On expenditure

On business

1. *Taxes usually are a portion taken from the income arising from labor or from wealth.* In rare cases more than the net income of wealth may be taken, but the aim of taxation in general is to take only a portion of the income for public uses. As

economic income has many sources, it may be intercepted at many different points, and taxation may take various forms. First, private income may be appropriated by a tax on income. This is the simplest in thought, but the administrative difficulties of the income-tax are great in practice. It is not easy to determine the money value of the various sources of enjoyment that come into a man's possession in the course of a year, including, as the ideal requires, the immaterial gratifications along with the material. A second form is a tax on property in proportion to value. Since the value of material wealth is the capitalization of the rentals at the prevailing rate of interest, the property tax, so far as it applies to material wealth, should take an approximately equal proportion of incomes. If it were accurately assessed, it would be in some respects better than a tax on actual rents, for it reaches the prospective, or speculative, rental. A third form of tax is one on consumption, or expenditure. This is but another mode of attacking income, for in the long run income is spent, not always by the individual who earned it, but by some one, and thus it is reached by a tax on expenditure. The principal consumption taxes in the United States are the tariff duties and the internal revenues of the national government. In time of war, internal revenues are extended in the United States to a multitude of articles, but usually they are limited (with minor exceptions) to liquor and tobacco. A fourth form of tax is one on selected agencies of industry; such are business taxes, licenses, taxes on investment in business, corporation taxes, etc. These burdens are diffused and rest eventually on some income, not always exactly ascertainable. Actual tax systems combine these forms in great variety, subtracting many minute fractions from each citizen's income in ways unsuspected by him.

Changes of taxation and in capitalization

2. *The immediate effect of a change in the form of taxation is a change in the market value of goods.* If the new tax reduces the net rent of any productive agent, it reduces likewise its value, which is but the capitalization of its net rental. If taxes are taken off of factories and put upon farm rents, factories rise and farm-land falls in value. The immediate change in value is much greater than the annual tax, for if five dollars is to be taken permanently from the annual rental of the farm, nearly one hundred dollars is taken at once from its selling value.

Taxes are reckoned by enterprisers as a part of the cost of production whenever the conditions of competition and of substitution make it possible to do so. In such a case the products rise in price and most of the tax falls upon the consumers. In the Civil War an increase in the tax on whisky increased its selling price, and distillers who owned stocks on which a smaller tax had already been paid reaped profits of millions of dollars. When recently the tax on tea was increased in England, all dealers who had accumulated a stock before the law went into effect were gainers. Every change in taxation inevitably affects, either favorably or unfavorably, many interests. The chance to anticipate a change in tax laws or to get, from those in power, information of a proposed change, makes speculation possible and political corruption profitable.

Shifting and incidence of taxation

3. *After every change in taxation, competition among bargainers goes on and a new equilibrium of prices results.* The citizen who pays a tax into the public treasury is not always the one whose income is reduced in the long run. In most cases the final and regular burden of the tax is distributed over a number of incomes. The passing on of the burden is called the shifting of the tax; the location of the final burden is called the incidence of the tax. The lawmaker cannot tell exactly where the weight will fall. The principles of value give some guidance in the inquiry, but the workings of the principle are difficult to follow. Certain it is that the new tax, both in its collection and in its expenditure, becomes a new influence in industry. Some occupations are made more attractive, others less so. Some places are made more, others less, desirable to live in. As property thus fluctuates in value, as investments become more or less remunerative, the market price of corporation stocks rises and falls. The rate of adjustment varies greatly under different conditions. The inflow and the outflow of labor and capital are more or less rapid in the various industries.

Many personal incomes affected

The fact that a change in taxation is a disturbing element in price is not to be thought insignificant merely because "all comes out right in the end." Every change in taxation is an element of uncertainty in business and increases the fortunes of some men at the expense of others. Hence no considerable change should be made without good reasons in its favor. The older taxes have the virtue of stability, but in many cases they have grown out of harmony with the industrial conditions. While, therefore, from time to time there is a real need of a reform in the tax system, it should not be undertaken without recognizing the many and complex interests involved.

§ III. Principles and Practice

Various standards of justice suggested

1. *Taxation should be adjusted with reference to the general social interest.* Many standards have been suggested to measure the distribution of the burden of taxation, such as benefit, equality, and ability. Each of these terms is capable of various interpretations which have changed from time to time. The benefit derived by any citizen from most of the public services evidently cannot be measured with exactness. The standard of equality cannot be applied in any literal sense to strong and weak, to rich and poor. It is possible, however, to interpret equality with reference not to objective goods, but to the psychic sacrifice occasioned by taxation. Ability thus is of many kinds and may be differently understood. Some think ability to bear taxation is "in exact proportion to the money income"; others believe that it increases at a greater rate than money income, and favor, therefore,

progressive taxation, that is, higher rates on the larger incomes.

Social welfare as the aim

The conflicting interests of the classes in each period are to some degree softened by the social conscience, and taxes are adjusted according to a vaguely held ideal of the social welfare. Social expediency, more or less broadly interpreted, determines who shall be taxed and what will give the best social results. The exemptions from taxation in feudal times were great, and viewed from our standpoint were inequitable, for it was the upper classes who escaped while the peasants bore all the burdens. The landlords and nobility who were assumed to be performing important social functions, often had outgrown their usefulness. Exemptions are granted liberally in most states to-day for some purposes and to some classes of citizens; to educational, religious, and charitable institutions; to the homes of priests and ministers; to homesteads purchased with pension money, etc. California alone of all the states in the Union continued until 1903 to tax churches and private schools. The social interest requires that taxes be both elastic and productive, so that the needs of the government shall be amply provided for. The harmonizing of these needs in the laws of taxation requires a high degree of wisdom, of foresight, and of integrity, in the legislator and in the citizen. No hard-and-fast rule for the apportioning of taxes can be laid down. The decision must be made in each generation by social opinion, guided by the social conscience.

Principles of administration

2. *The administration of taxation should be economical, certain, and uniform.* Whatever taxes are adopted, whether on property or income, whether at a proportional or a progressive rate, their justice and expediency depend largely on their administration. Principle and practice in this as in most affairs may go far apart. Some laws are more easily and economically executed than others. The time of collection should be as convenient as possible for the citizen, and the mode of payment should be the most simple. As to the time, method of payment, and amount, the utmost certainty is desirable. Taxation that is variable, shifting, dependent on personal whim and favoritism, is despotism. Above all, the administration of the law should be uniform and impartial,—yet this is a principle most frequently departed from in practice. The assessment of taxes has to be intrusted to men with fallible judgment, imperfect knowledge, and selfish interests. The assessor is as near a despot as any agent of popular government to-day. Not infrequently it is to men incapable of earning two dollars a day in any private business that the power is given of passing judgment on the value of millions of dollars' worth of property. Under the circumstances, evils are to be expected and they occur. The small property-owner often is crushed under the unequal assessment while the large owner comes lightly off. Political friends are favored, political foes are made to suffer. Woman nearly everywhere pays more than her fair share of taxes, a fact that the advocates of woman suffrage do not fail to urge as an argument for their cause, although women's disadvantage in this matter is little greater than that of any man without special political influence.

TAXATION IN ITS RELATION TO VALUE

Importance of taxation as a public question

3. *The relation of taxation to private incomes makes it one of the largest public questions of the day.* The discussion of taxation has accompanied the growth of free government in England and America from the time of Magna Charta. The control of the public purse frequently was the occasion of conflict between the monarch and the people. Taxation was a leading issue in the American Revolution. While, therefore, it cannot be said that the subject has been of no great importance in the past, it is true that in our own national history since the adoption of the Constitution, taxation has not been much discussed, except in the one aspect of the tariff. Constitutional and political questions, states rights, and the question of slavery, long absorbed the interest of citizens and legislators. But with the aroused interest of the public in economic problems, taxation is attracting, and is certain to attract in the next few years, increasing attention in local, commonwealth, and national politics.

Chapter L
The General Theory of International Trade

§ I. International Trade as a Case of Exchange

The motive of individual gain in foreign trade

1. *International trade is exchange between individual men, and has the same object as other exchange of goods.* The term international trade should not be misunderstood as meaning that nations rather than individuals engage in it. International trade differs from domestic trade only in the fact that the parties are citizens of different sovereign states. Exchanges between men in the same village, between those in neighboring villages, and between those in different countries, are prompted by essentially the same economic motive — the wish to increase the want-gratifying power of goods. In every such case both parties gain or think they are gaining. In international trade there is the same chance for mistake as in domestic trade, but no more. In a single transaction in either domestic or foreign trade one party may be cheated, but the continuance of trade relations is dependent on continued benefits. The once generally accepted maxim that the gain of one in trade is the loss of another, is rarely applied now except to international trade. The starting point for the consideration of this subject is in this proposition: Foreign trade is carried on by individuals, for individual gain, with the same motives and for the same benefits as are found in other trade.

Natural differences affecting foreign trade

Political boundaries and trade

2. *As commerce has grown, the territorial division of labor has correspondingly increased.* Although economic motives have had influence in political affairs and have helped to determine political groupings and the limits of modern nations, there is to-day no very close correspondence between political and economic boundary lines. Both industrial and political conditions have changed so rapidly that the lines often have tended to diverge rather than to agree. It is common for two portions of a nation to exchange far less than do two portions of entirely different nations. The great territorial divisions of industry are determined first

and mainly by differences of climate, soil, and natural resources. Thus trade arises easily between north and south, between warm and frigid climes, between new countries and old, between regions sparsely and regions densely populated. Foreign trade with distant lands is as old as history. In medieval times the luxuries of the temperate zone were mostly articles produced in the tropics. Political divisions usually have not been large enough to embrace widely varied soils and climates, the Roman Empire being an exception in marked contrast with the comparatively small political units of the Middle Ages. Before modern methods of transportation, a large free federal state like our republic was impossible. As in recent centuries the large political units have been formed, the question has arisen, Shall the political boundary be likewise the economic boundary marking the limits of trade? The firm constitutional Union of the American states arose out of difficulties with regard to trade. The German Zollverein, the forerunner of the modern German Empire, had a similar origin. The Australian Federation consummated within the last few years has grown out of the need of adjusting tariffs and tariff boundaries. These larger political units containing such varied resources can in larger measure, but never completely, become independent of the rest of the world if they will.

Differences in culture and industry

Territorial division of trade is determined secondly by differences in the accumulation of wealth, in the development of capital, of invention, and of organization, in the degree of intelligence of the workers, and in the grade of civilization. It is mainly trade due to this second group of causes, and carried on between old and new countries of about the same latitude, that is the subject of discussion in economic treatises on international trade.

Comparative costs as between individual workers

3. *The doctrine of comparative costs is that relative, not absolute, advantages of production determine for a country the benefits of international trade.* The free-trade question in any country is whether it is for its interests as a whole to permit trade between its citizens and the citizens of other countries. The question appears especially difficult where both countries have natural resources of about the same character (as iron and coal in the case of England and America), and where, therefore, both can produce the things that are exchanged. If American labor can produce as much iron in a day as English labor,—or more,—is it not foolish and wasteful, it is asked, not to produce that wealth? Now, exactly the same case is presented in simple neighborhood exchanges. The merchant may be able to keep his books better than does the bookkeeper whom he employs. The proprietor may be able to sweep out the store better than the cheap boy does it. The carpenter may be able to raise better vegetables than can the gardener from whom he purchases, and yet the merchant and the carpenter do not quit their better-paying work and turn to clerking or to raising vegetables.

As between communities differing in advantages

It often happens that both countries can technically produce both the articles that are internationally exchanged. It may frequently happen that one of the two countries has an advantage in amount of sacrifice and effort, as to both articles; but if the advantage is greater in one article than in the other, the foreigners, like the low-paid clerk, will be willing to exchange at a ratio that will make it profitable to specialize in the product wherein the greater superiority lies. Therefore not the advantage as to a single product, enjoyed by one country over the other is most important in determining whether to produce at home or to exchange, but the comparative advantages enjoyed in the production of the two articles in question.

Examples of comparative costs

It must be remembered that comparative cost as here used refers to cost in effort, not to money cost,—a point on which there is often confusion. The money cost of a certain product is often greater in a new country because wages are high, and wages are high just because psychic cost is low, that is, because labor can produce so much. At the time of the great gold discoveries in 1849-50, the price of goods in California was much higher than in the East, and much higher in Australia than in Europe. A day's labor doubtless would produce as much food in Australia and in California as in New England and in Norway, but it produced far more gold. Hence butter and cheese were shipped by long routes from Norway to Australia and from New England around Cape Horn to California, to be exchanged for gold. One of the standing arguments against foreign trade is based on the idea that a country cannot profitably import goods unless it is at an absolute disadvantage in their production. It is declared that as our country can produce these goods "as well" as foreign countries (meaning with as few days' labor), there is a loss on every unit imported.

Selection of the most paying industries

4. *The equation of international exchange is that adjustment of prices which results in the equalizing of the imports and exports of the country.* The superiority of a new country over an old one is not equally great in every line of industry. It is almost certainly most marked in those enterprises where natural resources are employed. To compete with the older country in less favored industries, capital and labor in the new are forced to take a lower rate than they can earn in the more favored. Without any government supervision, therefore, but simply through the choice of enterprisers seeking the best investment of capital, industries are developed in which the country is either most markedly superior or least inferior to its neighbors.

If the productive energies of men interchanged between industries and between countries with perfect readiness, a perfect equilibrium of advantage would everywhere result. In every country, in every occupation, labor and capital of given quality and amount would receive the same reward. But the interchange of labor and capital between countries is never without friction. Adam Smith said that "a man is of all sorts of luggage the most difficult to be transported." The higher wages in a new country are sufficient to attract constantly from the older lands a portion of their labor supply; the higher rate of interest in the new countries attracts constant additions of capital; yet, despite these forces working toward equalization, the inequality may remain and through the working of other influences even increase in the course of years.

Persistence of the differences

The laborers, enterprisers, and investors in the one country are thus in a position of more or less enduring advantage relative to those of the other countries. The advantage is sometimes said to be a "monopoly" which they, or the country as a whole, enjoy; but in the absence of any contractual limiting of competition, this is a misuse of the term monopoly. This variation in the degree of scarcity of agents in different territories is not peculiar to nations as a whole. Differences of the same nature exist between the Northern and the Southern states of the American Union, have continued for decades between Eastern and Western states, and are found even between neighboring counties. The differences between two countries, however, are likely to be more marked, the circulation of factors being so active within a country that it is allowable to speak broadly of prevailing national rates of wages and of interest.

The ratio of international demand defined

Every exchange of goods between the countries is made at a ratio that reflects, or expresses, this abiding difference in comparative costs. The imports into the favored country represent regularly the results of more units of labor of a given grade than do the corresponding exports. The ratio which expresses the disparity of advantage of productive factors is called "the equation of international demand." This does not mean that the money value of the imports exceeds that of the exports, or vice versa. On the contrary, the equation itself embodies a maxim of international trade that "in the long run," or "on the average," imports and exports must be equal in value (*i.e.,* equation of demand). This brings us to the theory of foreign exchanges, which is essential to an understanding of this feature of international trade.

§ II. Theory of Foreign Exchanges of Money

Purpose of foreign exchange

The rate of foreign exchange

1. *Foreign exchange of money is the purchase and sale of the right to receive a given kind and weight of metal at a specified time and place.* Par of exchange is the number of units of the standard coin of one country that contain the same amount of fine gold (or silver) as the standard coin of the other country. Usually the English pound is

taken as the basis in the tables which express the ratio of the gold in the standard coins of different countries. The *gold shipping point* is par of exchange plus or minus the cost of moving the actual metal; it varies with means of transportation and communication. The par of exchange between England and America being $4.866 and the cost of expressing and insuring a gold pound between New York and London being approximately .03, the shipping point for the export of gold from New York is $4.896. At the upper and lower limits, there is a motive for shipping gold as a commodity. If each transaction were independent of all others, the cost of exchange would be the weight of metal called for, plus grains enough more to pay for loss of interest, cost of freight, risk, and trouble. In such a case it would cost $4.896 to remit one pound; while a debt of one pound payable in London would at the same time be worth $4.836 to the creditor in New York. When, in New York, a number of men having bills to pay in London meet a number of owners of bills receivable in London, a market for London drafts is created and a rate of exchange results somewhere between the shipping points. In this is the explanation of the variation of the rate, and of the facts that the cost of outward exchange sometimes is less than the par of exchange and that the value of foreign drafts sometimes is above par.

Variation about par of exchange

The balancing of foreign exchanges is of essentially the same nature as the domestic cancelation of indebtedness. It is going on constantly between two merchants in the same town, between two banks in the same town who represent groups of merchants, between men in neighboring towns, between distant states like New York and California, and between the trading nations of the world. The price of exchange to the individual is reduced by the specializing of the business in the hands of a few dealers, permitting cancelation of indebtedness or offsetting of exchange, and greatly reducing the amount of bullion to be transported. Exchange varies above and below par as conditions change. When the movement of money is into the country, drafts on London are bought and sold for less than par, for every pound draft thus remitted to London reduces the need of shipping gold to this country, while every London draft collected in New York at such a time increases the need to ship gold.

The cash balance of international trade

2. *International shipment of money is always just the amount needed to balance the accounts due.* The proposition that in the long run the value of imports must equal the value of exports, while the fundamental truth in the theory of international trade, must be understood in a broad sense. Into the balance between the traders of two nations enter many items: the cash values of the imports and exports of each; freights, insurance premiums, and commissions; the expense of Americans traveling in foreign lands, and the cost of the foreign service of this government (such as the salaries of consuls and of diplomatic representatives) which count as the importation to America of an equivalent amount of food, clothing, and sundry services; subsidies and war indemnities to foreign nations representing, as they

GENERAL THEORY OF INTERNATIONAL TRADE 355

do, an expenditure, which at the moment may be paid in coin, but which, as is to be more fully explained, must be offset ultimately in some way by exports.

Various credit items entering into the balance

Many credit transactions affect the balance one way or another until settled. The loans made by European capital to the American government or to individuals and corporations in America, as well as the European capital expended in purchasing American enterprises, require the remitting of gold to New York, and thus offset many imports of goods to New York otherwise calling for the remitting of gold to London. In the direction opposite to this, act the interest payments and the eventual repayment of the principal loan, for these require either money or goods to be exported from America to the value of the obligations. Loans that run for years thus offset annually (in their accruing interest) a portion of the exports of the debtor country. An excess of exports may therefore at any given moment indicate either that the country is in debt or that it is getting out of debt. An excess of exports is generally looked upon as an evidence of national prosperity; but it is absolutely inconclusive on the point. Finally, after all the items of imports and credit paper purchased abroad are set opposite the items of exports and promissory papers sold abroad, the balance is paid in gold bullion and is shipped one way or the other. Evidently the amount of gold shipped is but a small fraction of the total volume of transactions.

Industrial indebtedness is represented in various forms: bills of lading for goods shipped, drafts made by the creditor on his debtor for goods shipped or property sold, checks or letters of credit of travelers, bonds and notes public and private. These are the objects dealt in by the bankers who are the agents to carry on the work of exchange.

Relations of the international flow of goods to the flow of money

3. *The territorial distribution of money is both a determined and a determining factor in international trade.* It appears to be determined in that the balance of all accounts for or against the country must be settled eventually in money. After any such a settlement one country has less, the other more money than before. The change in the amount of money at once reacts on prices and becomes a determining factor in international trade. The flow of money out of a country causes money to tighten, interest rates on short loans in the large cities to stiffen, and prices slightly to fall. When prices fall, imports decline, as the country is not so good a place to sell in; when prices rise, imports increase, as it is a better place to sell in. As the opposite effect is produced on exports, there occurs immediately a change in the quantity of money which continues until the national credits and debits balance and for a brief time remain in equilibrium. If the trade of a country with its neighbors continued long to give a balance of imports of goods and of debit items (exclusive of money) it would ultimately be drained of all its coin, and would default payment or cease to import. If the trade constantly gave a balance of exports and credit items, money would continue to flow in, until prices rose to unexampled heights. In fact no such extreme is even remotely approached, for a slight movement of money in either

direction at once influences prices and sets in motion counteracting forces. Decade after decade the circulating medium of leading countries changes only slightly in amount, and the fluctuations during periods of so-called "favorable balance of trade" and of "unfavorable balance of trade" represent only the smallest fraction of the value of goods passing through the ports of the country.

§ III. Real Benefits of Foreign Trade

Fallacious explanations of the gains from foreign trade

1. *The direct advantages of foreign trade consist in the increased efficiency it imparts to productive forces.* In explanation of the advantages of foreign trade it is said to be a vent for surplus production and to give a wider market to what would otherwise go to waste. This involves the same fallacy as the "lump of labor," the destruction of machinery, and the praise of luxury. If backward nations now give a vent for products which would otherwise rot in the warehouses, at length a time will come when the world will have an enormous surplus unless neighboring planets can be successively annexed. Again it is said that the great purpose of foreign trade is to keep exports in excess of imports so that money may constantly increase in amount. The ideal of such theorists is an impossible condition where the country would constantly sell and never buy. In the commercial view the sole object of foreign trade is to afford a profit to the merchants, regardless of the welfare of the mass of the citizens.

The real advantages of foreign trade

The main advantage of foreign trade is the same as that of any other exchange. It is hardly necessary to review the explanation here: the increased efficiency of labor when it is applied in the way for which each country is best fitted; the liberation of productive forces for the best uses; the development of special branches of industry with increasing returns; the larger scale production with resulting greater use of machinery and with increased chance of invention; the destruction of local monopolies.

The moral and intellectual gains of foreign commerce were formerly much emphasized. Commerce is an agent of progress; it stimulates the arts and sciences; it creates bonds of common interest; it gives an understanding of foreign peoples and an appreciation of their merits; it raises a commercial and moral barrier to war; and it furthers the ideal of a world federation, the brotherhood of man.

Conflict between general and special interests

Prevalence of protective tariffs

2. *Free foreign trade thus has in its favor the presumption of advantage to the citizens; but various interests may be adversely affected.* The general attitude of economic

GENERAL THEORY OF INTERNATIONAL TRADE 357

students for a century and a half has been favorable to a large measure of freedom in foreign trade. But the actual practice of nations is opposed to the principles laid down by the philosophers and accepted by nearly all serious students of the question. Germany adopted very restrictive measures under Bismarck in 1879 and by a recent law has discouraged trade still further. France, Italy, and other smaller nations of Europe have strong protective tariffs. The United States has followed a restrictive policy for the last century almost unvaryingly. The explanation of this contradiction is not entirely simple. Free trade is not the most desirable thing for every one. Great interests are affected by foreign trade and certain of these interests are able to dominate legislation. The general proposition of free trade between nations, as advocated by most economists since Adam Smith, is rejected by a majority of the people, by the politicians, and by the legislators.

Chapter LI
The Protective Tariff

§ I. The Nature and Claims of Protection

Nature of a tariff for revenue

1. *A protective tariff is a schedule of import duties so arranged as to give appreciably more favorable conditions to some domestic industries than they would enjoy with free trade.* Tariff duties were first laid to get revenues for the government. The first effect of the tariff is the same as that of any tax that enters as a new factor into enterpriser's cost—the domestic price of the taxed article tends to rise. Other results then follow. If the article cannot be produced within the country (as oranges, spices, and coffee, in England, Norway, and Sweden), its consumption is reduced. The lessening of demand may affect somewhat the price in the producing country and may compel the foreign producers to sell each unit for less than before. As such a tariff does not increase home production, it is for revenue, not for protection.

Effects upon home industry

But if the article can be produced in the importing country at the new price, "home industries" will start. If the whole demand at home is thus supplied, imports stop and therewith stop all revenues to the government from that source. This is a prohibitive or completely protective tariff. Most tariffs combine the characters both of revenue and protective measures. Where the freight charges are low along the coast and on the main lines of transportation, some imports take place; while farther inland, where freight charges are high, some home production of the same goods takes place. A tariff that reduces imports but does not cut them off entirely is either a revenue tariff with incidental protection or a protective tariff with incidental revenue. The difference is partly one of legislative intention, partly one of degree only.

The beginning of the tariff under the Constitution

2. *The tariff question has been the most discussed of economic questions in American*

politics. The tariff bill passed by the first session of Congress in 1789 was primarily a revenue measure with rates averaging only about five per cent.; but incidentally it was protective (as most tariffs are), being laid on imports of iron and cloth, the production of which had been undertaken to some extent before, but which thus were further encouraged. Between 1808 and 1812, the United States and England were in constant disagreement, and our government repeatedly laid an embargo on British commerce, closing our ports to British ships, and British ports to our ships. The war from 1812 to 1815 almost annihilated American trade on the ocean. Added to this discouragement of foreign trade was the high tariff imposed, in the vain effort to get revenue from greatly decreased imports. Altogether these causes almost completely stopped importation and forced the American people to rely on their own efforts for such goods. Some industries having been "stimulated" in a high degree, their destruction was threatened by the repeal of the high war tariffs. Many investments and interests were at stake, and the tariff became a most important question.

The tariff controversy before 1865

The first period of real discussion of the protective policy was between 1816 and 1846. The result of the first twelve years was an increase of the tariff rates which, in 1828, reached a high point. By the compromise of 1832, the rates were reduced by steps till 1841. Again from 1842 to 1846 was a brief period of higher duties, followed by a policy which, relatively speaking, was one for revenue, from 1846 to 1860. Again in the Civil War, 1861-65, the rates were steadily increased without much discussion, the tariff not being the leading question at a time when the prosecution of the war was absorbing nearly all attention.

Recent discussion of the tariff

The latest period of discussion was from 1874 to 1892. In the Tilden and Hayes campaign of 1876 the tariff was made the leading issue and the advocates of a lower tariff were very nearly successful. In 1880, protection again triumphed in the election of Garfield. In the election of Cleveland in 1884, the issue of tariff reform had some part, but no effective legislation on the subject was enacted in the next four years. In 1888, Cleveland was defeated in a campaign fought mainly on the tariff issue, and Harrison was elected as a pronounced protectionist. In 1892, Cleveland was reëlected on the issue of tariff reform. From that time, however, there has been a lull in the discussion of the tariff question. The campaign of 1892 was the last presidential election in which the tariff was the dominant issue. Since 1896, the money question and imperialism have quite crowded the tariff issue off the stage.

The "balance of trade" argument

3. *A leading argument in favor of a protective tariff is that by encouraging an excess of exports it maintains a favorable balance of trade.* This notion of the favorable balance of trade appears in several forms. One of these, already discussed in connection with

foreign exchanges, is that the exports of a country in the form of merchandise must exceed the imports if the country is to prosper. The ideal cherished is to keep more merchandise constantly flowing out of the country than comes in. An interesting commentary on this delusion is the fact that this is the usual situation in poor debtor countries having constant interest payments to meet; while the opposite of the ideal is the situation in rich creditor countries. England for many years in the period of her greatest prosperity has had a constant excess of imports, these being goods to the value of the interest payments due to Englishmen from investments abroad.

"To keep money at home"

4. *Another argument is that the protective tariff keeps money at home which, if trade is free, will be sent abroad to buy foreign goods, thus impoverishing the country.* This is the "favorable balance of trade" argument, with the emphasis on money rather than on goods. A superficial glance at the trade relations of an old and rich country with a new province seems to give evidence for such a belief. The older country is lending capital (which it sends to the debtor country in the form of goods) and it has at the same time a larger supply of money. These two facts—the lack of money and the poverty of the newer country—are looked upon by the protectionist as due to the importation of goods. The real cause of the imports to the newer country and of its scanty money-supply, it need hardly be said, is its comparative poverty. Europe and the United States, in their trade with China and South America, do not get gold in exchange, but merchandise of various sorts. It is true that in the trade of England and New York with great gold-producing districts, such as California, South Africa, and Alaska, gold is received in return for merchandise, for to these districts gold is merchandise and its export does not drain them of their supply. The richer states in the Union do not drain the poorer states of money. A few years ago the states of Kansas, Nebraska, Iowa, and their neighbors were filled with resentment against the money-lenders of the Eastern states. There was a widespread belief that hard times were due to an insufficient currency. Attempted action took the form of the greenback and free-silver movements, which were defeated by the opposition of the East, but there can be little doubt that if the Federal Constitution had not forbidden it, the discontented states would have established a protective tariff "to keep their money at home." Few advocates of protective tariffs are ready to admit that the money-supply of the country is dependent on the general wealth of the country, and on the methods of doing business, rather than on a protective tariff.

The "two profits" argument

5. *It is said that the tariff keeps "two profits" at home, foreign trade gives but one.* The word "profits" is here used in the popular sense of gain from a single transaction. This argument becomes somewhat confused, for certainly in the admission that there are "two profits" in a trade, the notion that "one man's gain is another's loss" is rejected. Both parties are said to profit and both profits are thought to be secured at home when two citizens are forced to trade with each other. There is an error in

elementary arithmetic here, both as to the number and as to the aggregate amount of profits. The purpose of a protective tariff is to compel *two* of the citizens of a country to trade with each other instead of trading with *two* citizens of a foreign state; the number of profits is therefore not increased by substituting domestic for foreign trade. What, then, as to the size and aggregate amount of the profits? The margin of advantage is not the same on all exchanges; the exchange is made if there is a margin to both parties, no matter how small it is; but the generous "profit" on one transaction where the conditions of the two parties are very different may be greater than the total of petty margins on a dozen exchanges between two traders of evenly matched powers. Can it safely be assumed that every trade with a foreigner is less advantageous than one with a fellow-citizen? Diamond cuts diamond, but two shrewd Yankees left to themselves surely should not be worsted in bargains with the universe. If they could exchange to better advantage with each other they probably would discover it as soon as the interested manufacturers and political orators who can prove so eloquently that they know the other man's business better than he knows it himself. Forcing the home trade is doubtless to the advantage of one citizen, but it is not likely to be to the advantage of both citizens.

The claim that protection raises wages

6. *The most effective popular argument for protection is that it raises, or maintains, the general scale of wages in the country.* This argument is two-fold: first, when wages are low in a country it is claimed that a tariff is needed to raise them; and, secondly, when wages are high it is argued that a tariff alone can preserve them. In Germany the fear is of the higher paid and more efficient labor of England. In America, where wages at all times have been higher than in England, it was first argued that because of the greater cost of production, due to high wages, the tariff was needed to start certain industries; but after the tariff had long been established and the old argument had been forgotten, it was said that the tariff was the cause of the high wages and must be maintained to protect against the (so-called) "pauper" labor of the older countries. That wages generally are higher in new countries and where a tariff prevails is always claimed to be one of the chief fruits of a protective policy. The cause of the high wages in America appears to be the productive efficiency of industry under existing conditions. Labor is surrounded here with advantages in the forms of rich natural resources and of mechanical appliances such as never before were combined. Because of the scarcity of workers in particular protected industries, wages may be higher in them than in some other industries; but such workers form a small fraction of the population. The claim that the general scale of wages in all occupations is raised by the tariff protecting this fraction, is no less invalid than the sweeping claims in favor of trade-unions.

§ II. The Reasonable Measure of Justification of Protection

Political arguments for protection

1. *For military and political reasons an otherwise uneconomic tariff may be justified.* It usually is admitted by the believers in free trade that in the interest of diplomacy, to secure proper concessions, tariffs may sometimes be levied. Even in England, where protective arguments long have had little acceptance, Mr. Chamberlain, with his eye on a tariff union and imperial federation of England and her colonies, has been advocating this policy. In such a case there is no pretense that the justification of the tariff is its immediate economic advantages; it is an expenditure for ultimate gain. By the same argument a protective tariff is upheld as a means of defense — to encourage the building of ships, arsenals, and factories for munitions. It is always questionable whether an outright expenditure would not be better, whether the government cannot build its own arsenals, ship-yards, etc., more cheaply than it can foster private enterprise by means of a tariff.

The infant-industry argument

Applied to America

2. *Protection may be defended as encouraging infant industries and thus diversifying the industries of the country.* Most free-trade writers concede a limited validity to this argument. If the natural resources of a land are adapted to an industry, it may be called into being early by a fostering protective tariff. This is merely anticipating and hastening the natural order of progress. In the American colonies the manufactures of iron, cloth, hats, ships, and furniture sprang up not only without "protection," but despite numerous harassing trade restrictions made in the interest of the English merchants; and they continued in some cases despite their absolute prohibition by Parliament. Can it be doubted that many of these industries would have developed and flourished in America under no other fostering influences than those of rich resources and of economy in freights? The growth of industries in the Middle West in the last twenty-five years has been phenomenal. The discovery of natural gas and the presence of abundant coal, ore, and timber have enabled them to develop without protection against the Eastern states. Industries capable of eventual self-support must in most cases naturally appear in due time. Economic forces will bring them out. It is a trite but valid remark that protective tariffs are often like hothouse culture, anticipating the season by a few weeks and at great cost. The question is whether the mere possession of the hothouse is a luxury worth the price, if meantime the products can be gotten more cheaply by exchange. English manufactures flourished because they were well established, had excellent coal supplies, great stores of iron ore, and low-paid labor which did not have the opportunity of better alternatives, as did the American workman. If America had imported *more* (it would not have been *all*) of her iron and coal, the English mines would have been exhausted earlier, and America's advantage surely would have asserted itself in time. Her iron manufactures undoubtedly were hastened — they cannot truly be said to have been created — by the protective tariff.

Social effects of the tariff

Industries are forced into an earlier diversification by tariffs. The peculiar advantages of a new country attract labor and enterprise into a few lines. Is it an evil? Contrast Iowa, Dakota, and Minnesota, or Kansas, if you please, with New York and Pennsylvania. Is it so certain that a dense population congested in cities and crowded in factories and mines is a more ideal social aggregation than is a community of prosperous farmers? The smoky industrialism fostered by protection often puts a premium on a low grade of immigrant and keeps him an alien to the American spirit. It would be surprising if Americanism on the Western plains were not as good as in the Eastern cities. But the infant-industry argument appeals strongly to the enterprise and the speculative spirit of Americans, who like to do all things rapidly and on a large scale. Every village aspires to be a great industrial center. Americans are impatient of the suggestion that things "will come in time"; they like things to come at once.

The "home-market" argument as to freights

3. *The tariff develops a home market for the products of agriculture.* It has been especially hard to reconcile the farmers in America to the tariff. While in England the protection that existed before 1846 was almost entirely for the benefit of the landholding interests, the tariff in America has been peculiarly favorable to manufactures. The "home-market" argument is the protectionist appeal that has proved most effective with the American farmers. This argument, which takes on several aspects, is akin to the "two-profits" argument when it declares that the shipping of food to Europe and the importing of manufactures involve a great cost for freight which could be saved by manufacturing "at home." Of course the farmer is supposed to pay this cost, although there is nothing in the argument to show that it is not all paid by the European, either the manufacturer or the food consumer. Home trade "saves the freights" for the farmer only in case he can buy goods under a tariff with less of his own labor and products than under free trade. The payment of freight charges is true economy when the goods can be bought at a distance on more favorable terms than near home. The freight-argument proves too much, for it condemns every exchange, within the country, of goods produced a stone's throw away from the consumer.

As to security of trade

Again, the home-market argument dwells on the greater steadiness of domestic trade. War or political changes, it is said, may change the demand for products. This is true, but no other changes have affected American agriculture so radically as the peaceful development of domestic transportation and the opening of the West.

As to the value of farm-lands

The home-market argument is strongest when addressed, not to all farmers, but to one class of farmers, those whose lands are situated nearer the manufacturing cities. The higher value taken on by land as it is converted from the extensive cultivation of corn and wheat to dairying, fruit, and market-gardening, is pointed to as a benefit of protection. The decaying agriculture and deserted farms throughout the great industrial states during the past twenty-five years are pathetic evidence that this benefit has failed to come to the average farmer just where it should be most expected. There is, however, a partial validity in the argument as applied to a comparatively small number of farmers, who gain as landholders, not as tillers of the soil.

Exports and exhaustion of the soil

4. *The tariff may keep some of the natural resources of a new country from becoming quickly exhausted.* The export of food takes out of the soil and out of the country fertile qualities never to be returned. The shipment of several hundred million dollars of food products year after year represents a tremendous drain from the soil of the United States. The assumption, however, that the use of the food in this country would preserve the fertility of our own fields has been in the main mistaken. The fertile material in the food shipped for human consumption five miles away from the field is almost absolutely lost. Engineering skill has as yet succeeded in saving hardly a fraction of the fertile organic matter that flows into the sewers, that is dumped into river and ocean, and that is buried in heaps at the borders of our cities. On the other hand, the increased use of iron, coal, and timber, as a result of encouraging manufactures, has very effectually aided in exhausting the natural resources of the country.

Protection as a monopoly measure

5. *A new country has a limited potential monopoly in certain kinds of products; a tariff may make it effective.* The opening up of a new country with rich natural resources may be a great gain to the average consumer in the older countries, although it causes a loss to a special class of landowners. Whether the citizens of the older or of the newer country shall reap the greater benefit in the trade depends on the reciprocal demand for the two classes of goods, as was seen in discussing the equation of international demand. A wide margin of advantage may go to one party and a narrow margin to the citizen of the more favored land. To put it concretely: if America, having great natural resources for agriculture, continues to exchange food for manufactures up to the narrowest margin of advantage, England reaps most of the benefits of the trade. An American tariff on manufactures from England will, under such conditions, check the demand for English products and compel some Americans to leave farming. This reduction of the American supply of wheat or corn and of the American demand for English manufactures compels a new ratio of exchange. It is conceivable that exchanging fewer goods at a larger margin of advantage, will give a larger total of gain to the favored nation. Thus, by the shifting of the ratio of exchange, foreigners may be compelled to pay a part of the tariff to enjoy the favored market. This is but a special case of the monopoly principle; the government by law artificially limits the supply of goods offered by its citizens.

Limited monopoly advantages of America

This argument is somewhat subtle, but probably is the soundest one in the theory of protection. The supposed conditions seldom occur, but they may exist, and probably have existed in America. When the great system of internal transportation was developed in the United States before that of the other new countries, this country had such peculiar advantages for the production of food that the quantity was enormously increased and the prices fell. At such a time the tariff may work toward retarding the unfavorable turn in the ratio of exchange and toward reëstablishing early a more favorable ratio. But the limited application of the principle must be recognized. The potential competition of undeveloped countries on all sides, seeking to develop their resources, to raise their own food, and to profit by the higher prices in the world-market caused by the tariff, threaten the peculiar advantages of the favored land. A great nation with its manifold interests is not eminently fitted to practice the gentle art of monopoly.

§ III. Values as Affected by Protection

Influence on the value of capital

1. *An increase of the tariff is favorable to many capitalists and to many owners of natural resources.* A denial of large general advantages in protection is not the denial of all its influence on value. On the contrary, it cannot be too strongly emphasized that manifold interests are affected by the tariff. Owners of natural mineral resources are among the first to benefit. When the price of iron is low, many iron- and coal-mines may yield no rent and have small prospective values. A tariff forcing home production opens the marginal resources and gives them a large capital value. Factory sites and surrounding lands leap from the level of rural prices to that of city real estate. The owners of farms situated near the new industries have a home market and get scarcity prices, as they alone can supply the needed fresh vegetables and dairy products. Wealth less favorably situated, however, is in many cases depressed in value because its products exchange for smaller amounts of other products.

The special gains and the general burden

2. *A tariff is immediately favorable to some enterprises and to special classes of workmen.* Enterprisers already acquainted with and engaged in a business always may hope to gain by the higher prices immediately following a rise in the tariff rates on their particular products. Though they are granted no enduring monopoly by the protection, they for the time enjoy the advantage of being on the ground and reap the first fruits of the favoring conditions. The enterpriser usually profits when the price of his product suddenly rises. Usually skilled workmen are affected slowly by competition when there is any considerable increase of their special industry. The burden of higher prices is very soon distributed to a number of less favored

citizens. A part of it may be borne by the retail merchant, a part by his customers. The weight falling on each is usually small, often unsuspected, always hard to measure. The increased benefit is concentrated in a few industries and accrues to a comparatively few producers. Here is a recipe for riches: get everybody to give you a penny; they'll not miss it, and it will mean a great deal to you. Something like this happens in the case of many protected industries; every consumer of the article pays a penny more, a few wage-earners gain, and a few enterprisers wax wealthy.

Sudden tariff reduction injurious

3. *A sudden reduction of the tariff causes local crises and may bring on a general crisis.* The repeal of the tariff works in a direction the reverse of its enactment. The benefits of the lower prices are diffused; the immediate injury is concentrated and acute. Factories are closed, capital is depreciated, labor is thrown out of employment. The organic nature of local industry causes the evil to be felt by many classes. Merchants, professional men, servants, and skilled laborers that are tributary to the depressed industry, suffer. The effects are transmitted to commercial and financial centers and credit is shaken. The readjustment of industry is slow and much capital is lost in the process.

The two policies in political discussion

It is rarely appreciated how great is the tactical advantage enjoyed in political contests by the advocates of a high tariff. They can so easily impress the popular judgment with the evident fruits of their own policy, and with the immediate dangers of the policy of their opponents. The low-tariff advocates in America undoubtedly have made the mistake of underestimating or of quite overlooking these immediate effects. They have been too abstractly doctrinaire, and have argued too absolutely for the merits of free trade. They have opposed one extreme system by another, with no thought of the inexpediency and injustice of sweeping changes. There is a strong feeling among business men that any tariff, be it high or low, is better than a shifting policy. Despite the great preponderance of domestic production over foreign trade, it is perhaps too much to say that the tariff is unimportant in our present conditions. It can, however, be said that the tariff agitation has taught that radical changes, especially sudden and large reductions, are fraught with evils, and that business can adjust itself in large measure to any settled conditions. The future of the tariff discussion in America is hard to prophesy. The infant-industry argument now is of little force. With the widening of our international relations are growing interests favorable to reciprocity or to other freer trade relations.

Chapter LII
Other Protective Social and Labor Legislation

§ I. Social Legislation

City growth and new social problems

1. *Under modern conditions many laws restricting free competition are required to secure the health and convenience of the citizens.* The rapid growth of city populations has brought new social and economic problems. The friction in social relations is greater when men are crowded together. In 1790, three per cent. only of our population lived in cities of over eight thousand; to-day the percentage is thirty-three. Then the city dwellers numbered one hundred and thirty-one thousand; now they number twenty-five millions. Then there were but six cities of eight thousand or over; now there are five hundred and forty-five. Then the largest city (Philadelphia) numbered fifty thousand persons; to-day the largest city (New York) numbers three millions. Many laws are survivals suited only to the older rural conditions. In London, these problems were first forced into prominence, and a law passed after the great fire of 1665 to regulate the rebuilding of houses, streets, sidewalks, and sewers, foreshadowed alike the American law of special assessments and the modern tenement-house legislation. A mass of laws wise and foolish has resulted from the attempt to meet the new conditions. The laws of nuisance and of sanitation have been rapidly changing.

Need of social regulation

Why not leave such subjects to individuals? It is for the interest of every one that his back yard should not be a place of noisome smells and disagreeable sights. But men are at times strangely obstinate, selfish, and neglectful, and through one man's fault a whole community may suffer. The refusal of one man to put a sewer in front of his house would block the improvement of a whole street. The obstinacy of one may bring an epidemic upon an entire city. There must be a plan, and by law the will of the majority must be imposed upon the unsocial few. Where voluntary coöperation fails, compulsory coöperation often is necessary. Thus health laws, tax laws, and improvement laws regulate many of the acts of citizens, limit the use of property, and compel men to a course against their own wishes and judgments. The justification for these limitations on the right of private property, on free choice of the individual, on "free competition," must be found in the social result secured.

Tenement-house laws in cities

Interests affected

2. *Tenement-house legislation is an important recent expression of this social protective policy.* As city population grows denser, land increases in value, and the evils of bad housing threaten the welfare of the great majority of city dwellers. Light, sun, air are shut out, and cleanliness, decency, and home life are made impossible. Two policies are open to the public. It may be left to private enterprise to solve the problem. If the tenant agrees to rent a disease-breeding house, he is the first to suffer. The interests of investors, it is said, will supply as good a house as each tenant can pay for. The other policy now adopted is to set a minimum standard of sanitation and comfort, to which all builders and owners must attain. Property owners are no longer left free to determine plans, height of building, proportion of lot built on, lighting, materials, and workmanship. Complying with the legal requirements, they are left quite free to collect whatever rent they can get. Such legislation is partly in the interest of the body of landowners as against the selfish desires of some individuals. One bad building may bring down the rent of all on the street. Partly, however, the regulation is in the interest of the tenants and of society as a whole, and against that of the landlord. The rents from slum property are threatened; hence the strong opposition always manifested against tenement-house legislation by some landlords, architects, and contractors, who fight it bitterly as an interference with their interests and as a confiscation of their property. It is not quite certain how marked will be the effect of this policy in making the rents too high for the poorer tenants and driving them into the country. But this result, predicted by the enemies of the policy, is not so undesirable, and the enlightened sentiment of the public to-day favors all efforts to destroy the breeding-places of disease, misery, and crime.

Public inspection of goods used in the homes

3. *Laws forbid adulteration of products for domestic use and provide for public inspection.* English laws of the Middle Ages forbade false measures and the sale of defective goods, and provided for the inspection of markets in the cities. Recent legislation in many lands has developed much further the policy of insuring the purity or the safety of articles consumed in the home. The oleomargarin law passed by Congress was, however, designed as protective legislation in the interest of the farmer. Usually, the self-interest of the purchaser is the best safeguard for the quality of goods; but personal inspection by each buyer frequently is difficult and time-consuming, requiring special and unusual knowledge of the products, and special costly testing apparatus. The state undertakes, therefore, to set a minimum standard of quality, and to apply it by the economical method of social coöperation. This policy extends only to staple products and to a comparatively

few articles. It would be impossible as well as unwise to apply it to art products, except to protect the morality of the community. This inspection sometimes raises the price, but the evils are small compared with the convenience and the benefits resulting to the citizen. He is assured that the article he buys is of standard quality, and if he wishes a cheaper quality there is no law to prevent his adulterating it for his own use.

State support of education

4. *Other kinds of social amelioration undertaken by the state, through free, compulsory education, charity, and temperance legislation, are likewise interferences with competition and freedom of contract.* Many of these are so customary that they are not thought of in this light. Schools are productive enterprises, education is industry, and the supply of this service is always in large measure undertaken by private enterprise and could be left entirely to it. But free elementary education is the established policy, and is no longer debatable in America and France. In England the policy is still debated, much as is that of public ownership of trolley lines in America. One by one the states are passing compulsory education laws, and thus interfering still further with the freedom of the individual. The affection of parents can in most cases be trusted to provide for the education of children, but when family affection fails, the child and the state are the victims of the resulting ignorance, crime, and pauperism. State support of higher education is more in dispute. It is a universally accepted view that social welfare requires a more generous support for higher education than could be secured if it were sold at a competitive price; but while in eastern America its provision is left mainly to private gifts, in the West and South it is undertaken largely by the state. The justification of this policy must be found, not in the benefit to the particular students, but in the benefit diffused throughout the commonwealth by the encouragement of science, arts, and letters.

Public charity
Temperance legislation

The system of public relief for the defective classes of blind, deaf, insane, feeble-minded, and paupers, are examples of the social protective policy. The public interest undoubtedly is served by having these suffering classes systematically relieved, but the extent and nature of the provision are questions ever in debate. Still more debated is temperance legislation, both as to licensing and as to prohibiting the liquor traffic. Nowhere is the manufacture and sale of intoxicating liquor treated quite like the traffic in most other goods, because it is recognized that the public interest is affected in a different way. While it is beyond question that society should protect itself against the drunkard, it is more doubtful whether it owes to the man, for his sake, protection against his own blunders. Not even the gods can save the stupid. Temperance legislation is strongest in its social aspect. The opponent of it usually champions the individualist view; its partisans uphold, in varying degrees, the social view.

Other laws to protect public morals

Similar questions arise regarding lotteries, gambling, betting, horse-racing, etc. When a man backs a worthless horse against the field, money probably is transferred from the stupider to the shrewder party. The philosopher may say that the sooner a fool and his money are parted the better; but the broken gambler remains a burden and a threat to honest society. Gambling, lotteries, and speculation cause embezzlement, crime, unhappy homes, and wrecked lives. Here are to be found with difficulty the true boundaries between ethics and expediency. A busybody despotism may protect the fool, but it thereby helps to perpetuate and multiply his folly; yet if the fool is left alone, he too often is a plague to the wise and the virtuous.

Usury laws as social legislation

5. *Usury laws are found almost universally in civilized lands.* By usury was formerly meant any payment for the loan of goods or money; now it means only excessive payments. In former times moralists and lawmakers were opposed to all usury or interest. Most loans were made in times of distress. The sources of loanable capital and the chances of profitable investment were fewer in the past than to-day. For the last four centuries there has been on the question of usury a gradual change of opinion, beginning in the commercial centers and most rapid in the countries with more developed industry. A moderate rate of interest is now everywhere permitted; but in all but a few communities the rate that can be collected is limited by law, and penalties more or less severe are imposed on the usurious lender. It has been noted in another connection that usury laws are practically evaded in a number of ways within the letter of the law. Many writers maintain that usury laws do more harm than good even to the borrower, whom they are designed to protect. In a developed credit economy, where a regular money-market exists, they are superfluous, to say the least, as most loans are made below the legal rate. Such laws, however, have a partial justification. In a small money-market they to some extent protect the weak borrower at the moment of distress from the rapacity of the would-be usurer. Their utility is disappearing, but in simpler industrial conditions usury laws are fruits of the social conscience, a recognition of the duty to protect the weaker citizen in the period of his direst need.

§ II. Labor Legislation

Growth of child-labor legislation

1. *Factory laws now limit in many ways the employment of women and children, and the hours of work.* Factory legislation began in England, early in the nineteenth century, to check some of the worst evils then showing themselves in the factories. It has since increased in England and has been copied rapidly by other countries. Some of the agricultural states of the Union have as yet no factory laws, but the

states industrially more advanced have many. They are made, first, to apply to children. The evil of forcing children into factories is easily recognized. The child, subject to the commands of his parents or guardians, is not a free agent. At times a lazy father is tempted to support himself in idleness on the wages of his young children. Often poverty leads the parents to rob their children of health, of schooling, and of the joys of childhood. Child-labor depresses the wages of adults and the evil grows. Children laboring long hours in close and grimy factories, and growing into blighted and ignorant manhood, are a threat to society. In agricultural conditions, such as have prevailed generally in America, there is far less need of limiting the hours of work and the age at which children may begin to work. The barefoot boy trudging over clover-fields to carry water to the harvesters may be the happier, healthier, and better for his work.

Women's work and shorter hours

The work of women in factories tends to depress the wages of men, is inevitably harmful to family life, and, when the work is arduous and continuous, the evils are visited upon succeeding generations. In the early days of the factory system in England, the hours of work were lengthened in order to make the machinery earn as much as possible. The first laws regulating hours applied especially to women and children, limiting their work to ten or twelve hours daily. Later, this regulation was made to apply to men, and now is found in most civilized lands. In recent years the agitation has been for an eight-hour day, and doubtless it will some day be adopted in the majority of trades.

The workmen's remedies for injuries

2. *Many laws provide for the health and safety of workers in factories and mines.* Both workman and employer are in many ways interested in providing against danger from fire, bad ventilation and lighting, bad sanitation, unprotected and dangerous machinery, and bad moral conditions in the factories and other places of work. What can the workman do to protect himself? (1) He may refuse to work whenever the conditions are bad. But this requires that he inspect the factory and judge of the sanitary conditions in each case, and that he then resist the temptation to accept employment of which he may be sorely in need. (2) He may ask higher wages to compensate for the added risk. But this is not practically possible with his insufficient knowledge of conditions, and it supposes an equal caution in many other workers. It is well that individual men are not excessively cautious, or the state would lack brave citizens and defenders. It is better that the forethought be in part exercised by the community collectively. (3) The person injured in health or limb may sue for damages. But this, with his means and knowledge, is often impossible, and is a costly process, yielding a pitiful recompense for a blighted life.

Factory laws to reduce accidents

The employer is interested in attracting better workmen at lower wages, and in avoiding damages by making the conditions of work favorable. The law seeks the same end by more economical ways when it sets a minimum standard. Experience shows that certain safety appliances should always be present to prevent the evils; for a state to leave their provision to self-interest, is to trifle with the welfare of its citizens. Factory legislation usually is opposed by employers because of the expense it causes; but if the regulations apply to all factories, the expense becomes a part of the cost of production and is shifted, like the other expenses of production, to the general body of consumers, of which the employers form only a small part.

Legal regulation of wage-payment

3. *Laws regulate the form, time, and methods of payment in manufactures and mining.* Companies sometimes keep stores and pay the workers in mines and factories in goods, instead of money. Such a store in the hands of a philanthropic employer might easily be made, without expense to himself, a great boon to his workmen, giving them more than the benefits of consumers' coöperation. But the usual result is told by the fact that such stores are known as "truck stores," "pluck-me stores." They are most often found where some one large corporation dominates in the community, as in mines, where the workers are in a very dependent condition. If the higher prices demanded practically lower real wages, it would seem that the worker had an immediate remedy in his power to demand higher money-wages. Recognizing that this is for the most part an illusion—for it is just in such places that the conditions for free competition are least present—the law in many states prohibits these stores. It regulates also the measuring of work, fixing the size of screens and of cars used in coal-mining. The law is especially favorable to the hand-laborer in regard to the collection of his wages, requiring regular monthly or fortnightly or sometimes weekly payments. Mechanics' liens give to workmen in the building trades the first claim on the products of their labor.

Limitation of freedom of contract

4. *In some cases the law forbids "contracting out," and the courts fix the terms of the contract.* In general, the law does not interfere with the right of the citizen to make any formal contract he chooses. It confines itself to providing rules and agencies for interpreting and enforcing the contracts when made. Employers often compel workmen to sign a release from damages in case of accident. This practice was forbidden even by common law, and many recent statutes have specifically provided that employers cannot "contract out" of the right to claim damages. The courts are particularly watchful of the interests of children, who are usually deemed incapable of entering into contracts binding them to their injury. Sailors, likewise, have long been protected and guarded by the law, because, journeying far from home, they are peculiarly in the power of their employers. The English courts may even change the contract if the sailors have been coerced by their masters. The rights of married women to mortgage their property is limited in some states in recognition of the undue influence that may be exercised by their husbands. The attempts in the last twenty years to settle the Irish land-question have resulted in a steady increase of the interference of law and courts with the freedom of contract between tenant and landlord. Though in many ways freedom

of contract is thus limited, competition is not entirely destroyed; it is turned in other and usually better directions.

General nature of this social legislation
Economic or moral objects primary

5. *This group of social laws resembles protective tariffs in preventing free competition, but differs from them in varying ways and degrees.* Writers class all such laws as protective legislation, in that they depart from the rule of free trade taken in its broadest sense. It does not follow, however, that all these laws stand or fall together,—that if the protective tariff is wrong, all are wrong. The justification of every such measure is limited and relative, and therefore of varying strength. All protective measures are alike in that the free choice of the citizen is forbidden by law. The argument for the tariff is economic and political. The tariff does not seek to prevent a moral evil; foreign trade is morally as good as other trade. In a large majority of social laws the moral purpose is fundamental. It is the demand of humanity that competition be placed on a higher plane. Tariff legislation is primarily in the interest of a special well-to-do class, with which other citizens are compelled unwillingly to trade. Most social legislation is to protect the weak from being forced into contracts injurious to their welfare and happiness. In any case, social legislation is not to be justified by any but the most general abstract principle,—the attainment of the best social result. The best test of social protective laws is their contribution to a higher independence and to a freer competition on a higher, more worthy, and more humane plane.

Chapter LIII
Public Ownership of Industry

§ I. Examples of Public Ownership

The kinds of political units

1. *Local political units generally acquire only industries whose products must be used in the place where produced.* The word industry is used here in a broad sense, including agents of psychic income not usually so classed, such as public parks. The grouping of publicly owned industries according to the size and importance of the political units cannot be exact, because some classes of industries are owned by several kinds of political units. Yet, especially with application to American conditions, an approximate classification may be made on this principle. Federal states consist of three main groups of political units: national, provincial, and local. Provincial units are the largest subdivisions, as the American "states," or commonwealths, the German states, and the provinces in other countries. The term local political unit is more complex and may mean county, township, village, city, and school or sanitary district; but most of what is to be said of local ownership refers to cities or to incorporated villages.

Municipal ownership of parks, libraries, &c.

Of bridges, markets, waterworks, &c.

Nearly all public parks and recreation grounds are owned by cities. As population has become more dense, private yards of any extent become impossible, in cities, for all but the wealthy. Public ownership of parks insures recreation grounds to the common man in the most economical way. Of late the movement for large and small public parks and playgrounds has gone on rapidly in American cities. Related to parks are public baths, public libraries, art collections, museums, zoölogical gardens, etc. Some have declared that such a policy stops little short of a paralyzing socialism for the masses. Reason and experience fail to reveal any such danger so long as the things supplied gratify the higher tastes—as art, music, literature, innocent social recreation. Not until the necessities of life, as bread, clothing, and houses, are supplied, is encouragement given to the increase of improvident families and to the breaking down of independent character. The means of local communication—streets, roads, bridges—were once owned largely by private citizens. Here and there still are found toll roads and toll bridges built under charters granted a century ago, but tolls on public thoroughfares are for the most part abolished. A public market, where the producer from the farm and the city consumer can meet, is an old institution that is now being established anew in many cities. The providing of apparatus for extinguishing fires is always a public duty; the conveyance of waste water is increasingly a public function; and the supply of pure water, while often a private enterprise in villages, and sometimes in large cities, is increasingly undertaken by public agencies. Public ownership of gas and electric lighting is less common, as the utility supplied is not so essential and the industry is somewhat less subject to monopoly; but the difference is one of degree only. Street-railroads are often under public ownership in Europe; but there has thus far been no case of the kind in the United States, and only one in Canada.

American failures in state industry

2. *The American state owns and conducts industries mainly whose products have a wider territorial use.* The American commonwealth has retired from some fields where once it was engaged in industry. Students of American history know that between the years 1830 and 1840 some states engaged largely, even wildly, in the building of canals and undertook to construct railroads, to start banks, and to engage in other enterprises. The undertaking of these industries was determined often by political and by selfish local interests, and their operation often was wasteful. A few enterprises succeeded, the most notable of these being the Erie Canal in New York. The unsuccessful ones remained worthless property in the hands of the state or were sold to private companies, as in the case of the Pennsylvania railroad. This reckless state enterprise was a bitter lesson in public ownership, and even after seventy-five years is not without effect on public opinion. For a long time no proposal for public ownership could have a fair hearing in America. But railroads and canals are publicly owned, and more or less successfully operated, in many foreign countries, as in Prussia and other German states, in Switzerland, and in the new states of Australia.

State ownership of various kinds

There has been recently a rise of interest in forestry in America. This is especially likely to be a state enterprise wherever the forest tracts are entirely within the limits of the state, as is the case of the Adirondacks in New York. Most of the forests in Germany are either communal or state-owned. The schools, a great industry for turning out a product of public utility, are largely conducted by the American state and by local units rather than by the nation or by private enterprise. The state encourages researches in the arts and sciences, and gives technical training. A variety of minor enterprises have been undertaken by states to supply salt, phosphate, banking facilities, even some manufactures. In the prisons and public institutions, states, such as New York, that have adopted the system of labor on public account engage in agriculture and manufacturing on a large scale, the products, amounting to millions of dollars annually, being used almost entirely by public agencies.

National ownership of various kinds

3. *The nation owns and controls many industries of the widest use and most general interest.* Some industries grow out of the political needs of government. Established as a means of communication with military outposts, the post became a convenient means of communication for merchants and other citizens and grew into a great economic institution. In most countries the telegraph is publicly owned and has been annexed to the post, to which it is very closely related in purpose. The national improvements connected with rivers and harbors were first political—that is, they were for the use of the governmental navy; they became, secondly, commercial—for the free use of all citizens engaged in trade; and they continue to unite these two characters. Forestry is most largely undertaken in this country by the national government, doubtless because the large forest areas in the West extend over state boundaries, and because large tracts of public lands were still unsold at the time public attention was attracted to the subject. Since 1890, the policy of reserving great areas for forests, and picturesque districts for national parks, has developed greatly. In some countries mines are thought to be peculiarly fitted for national ownership and control. In Germany, the state owns some coal, salt, and other mines. Coinage and banking are everywhere looked upon as a function of sovereignty, and yet it is no more necessary for a nation to own its own mint in order to control the monetary system than for it to print the bank-notes in order to regulate their issue. The American government has its own printing office and therewith its share of troubles with organized labor. The fish commission, and the various branches of the department, coöperate with private industry in many ways. In Germany, compulsory insurance is provided for the workingman. This hasty survey suggests that the industries undertaken by government are both varied in nature and large in extent, although small in proportion to the mass of private industry.

§ II. Economic Aspects of Public Ownership

The primary need of public ownership

1. *Public ownership is primarily to control the essential agencies of government.* A large part of public ownership and activity in industry develops from political functions. As society evolves, what was unessential to political life becomes essential. Civilized government requires the use of a number of material agents. Buildings for legislative and executive officers, custom-houses, post-offices, lighthouses, can be rented of private citizens, as post-offices usually are in small places; but it is obviously economical and convenient in large cities for the government to own the public buildings. Government can reduce to a minimum

PUBLIC OWNERSHIP OF INDUSTRY 377

its employment of labor by "farming out" the taxes, as all countries once did to some extent, and as France continued to do up to the French Revolution. It is now the settled policy for government to own or control its essential agencies, but this does not involve in every case the employment of day-labor direct to clean the streets, to collect garbage, etc. The more simple political functions shade off into the economic. To coinage usually are added the issue of legal-tender notes and certain banking functions; the post carries packages, transmits money, and in some cases performs the function of a savings-bank for small amounts. The only open question is as to the proper limit to this development.

Conflict of public and private interests

2. *Public industry expands to supply as free goods many essentials of good citizenship, and to insure cheaper and more bountiful supplies of others.* It is the ideal of Herbert Spencer and of a small surviving group of *laissez faire* philosophers that government should confine itself exclusively to the most essential political functions, leaving the economic functions absolutely alone. It should keep the peace, prevent men from beating and robbing each other, and preserve the personal liberty of the citizen. They assume that all of the economic needs will be provided by competition, in the best way humanly possible, in quantities and at the rate needed. In many cases, however, the general interest fails to harmonize with that of the individual. The forest has an immediate utility to the consumers of lumber, and it has also a diffused utility in its influence on industry, on climate, and on torrents and floods. Yet, as the private owner cannot control enough of the forest to affect the climate, and could not sell climate even if he could affect it, he will cut down the tree whenever he can gain by doing so. In this situation either government control or government ownership of forests is essential.

Social economy of some public industry

In some cases the difficulty of private ownership is in the excessive cost of collecting for the service. The cost of maintaining tollhouses at short intervals on a turnpike sometimes exceeds the amount collected. Collection in other cases, as for the service of lighthouses to passing ships, is impossible. Public industry secures, through the economy of large production, a cheaper and more efficient service, the benefits and costs being diffused throughout the community. The benefits of the work of experiment-stations for agriculture are felt immediately by the farmers, but are diffused to all citizens. A manufacturer able to keep his methods secret, or to retain his advantages for a time, can afford to undertake experiments in his factory, but the farmer seldom can. The public ownership of parks for the use of all gives a maximum of economy in the production of the most essential utilities—fresh air, sunshine, natural beauty, and playgrounds in the midst of crowded populations. Municipal ownership of waterworks is an extension of the same idea. Not only because large amounts of water are used by the public, but because cheap, pure, abundant water is an essential condition to good citizenship, speculation should in every possible way be eliminated from this industry.

378 THE PRINCIPLES OF ECONOMICS

Monopolistic nature of localized industries

3. *Public ownership tends constantly to include the industries of a monopolistic nature, locally supplying general necessities.* This is no abstract principle; it is merely a statement of what is seen to be happening. Some industries are of such a nature that they drift inevitably into monopolistic control. Waterworks, gas, electric lighting, street-railways, telephone systems, are among these. However fierce may be the competition for a time, sooner or later either one company drives out the other or buys it up, or both come to an agreement by which the public is made to pay higher prices.

Localized production favors monopoly

A feature favoring the growth of monopoly when such industries are left to private enterprise, is the need to produce and supply the utility at a given locality. While two street-railways can compete on neighboring streets, it is physically impossible for two or more to compete on the same street. Two systems of water-mains or gas-mains can be put down, as sometimes is done, but this is not only a great economic waste, but the tearing up of the streets is an intolerable public nuisance. This difficulty is less marked in the case of telephones and electric lighting, and some persons still cling to faith in competition to regulate the rates in those industries; but faith in competition between water-companies and between gas-companies has been given up by nearly all students of the subject.

Gains from large production favor monopoly

4. *A second feature favoring monopoly in such industries is the marked advantage of large production in them.* These industries are usually spoken of as "industries of increasing returns." This advantage is enjoyed in some degree by every enterprise, but it is gradually neutralized and limited (as has been noted elsewhere). The need to extend an expensive physical plant to every point where customers are to be served, and the very much smaller cost per unit of delivering large amounts of water, gas, electricity, transportation, etc., on the same street, offered a greater inducement for one competitor to crowd out or buy out the other at a more than liberal price. Even then, larger net dividends and correspondingly larger capitalization are secured than were before possible to both companies combined.

Uniformity of products favors monopoly

5. *A third feature favoring monopoly is uniformity in the quality of the product furnished.* It is a general truth that competition is most persistent where there is the greatest range of choice open to the customer, and consequently the most individual treatment required in the enterpriser. An artist, even a storekeeper, attracts about him a body of patrons who like his product (for the merchant's manner and method of dealing are a part of the quality of his goods), and who cannot be tempted away by slight differences in price. Rival companies in the stage of competition are seen to claim superiority for their particular goods and to improve their service in every way possible. A new telephone company, entering

where a monopoly has held the field, works at once a wonderful betterment in rates, courtesy, and service. But as the product of all competitors attains the highest technical standard possible at the time, the rivalry is reduced to one of price, and it is usually a "fight to the finish."

Franchises favor monopoly

6. *A fourth feature favoring monopoly in these enterprises is the necessity of making permanent and exceptional use of the public streets and alleys.* If this right were granted by a general law to every citizen, this feature would be sufficiently implied in the foregoing discussion. As it would be intolerable to allow private interests to use public property in whatever way they wished, the legislative body makes special grants in such cases in view of the circumstances. Not only is the legislature (or council, or county board of commissioners, etc.) induced by the economic difficulties to withhold a charter to a second company, but it is exposed to the greatest corrupting influences by the one already established. The knowledge of the opposition to be encountered in getting a franchise must keep competitors out, even though monopoly prices are maintained.

In view of these several features, which are so closely related that they form a common character, more or less fully shared by various industries, and especially in view of the necessity for the formal granting to them of peculiar privileges in the form of a public franchise, the public, in order to protect the general interest, is forced to undertake an exceptional control of these industries.

Modes of controlling public utilities

7. *Several courses are open to the public, acting in its political capacity, to retain these monopoly advantages for the general welfare.* First, it may do nothing, trusting vainly to competition to regulate the rate, or consciously leaving the result to be worked out by the monopoly principle; this is what in most cases has been done in the past in America. Second, in granting the franchise it may attempt to fix near cost the charge for the service or product, so that the franchise will be worth little or nothing. Third, it may leave the rate to be fixed by the monopoly principle, but charge for the franchise so much that the value of the monopoly is appropriated into the public treasury. Fourth, it may have public officials carry on the business, either selling the product at cost or making monopoly profits that go into the public treasury. Various combinations of these plans are followed in practice, the most common plan being the fixing of maximum rates which, with improved methods, generally become ineffective. It is difficult to fix a uniform rate that is equitable, because conditions change, and, further, because a uniform rate must be applied to all parts of the town, although the cost of service varies greatly. It is difficult to sell the franchise for near what it is worth, because of the uncertainty, of the political blackmail, and of the limited number of competent bidders. There remains only the policy of public ownership to secure the profits of monopoly to the public, either directly or in a diffused manner.

Economic basis of public ownership

Cost under public or private ownership

8. *Public ownership is economically justified when it secures a utility of widespread consumption, otherwise impossible, or insures the public a better quality or a lower price.* The question of public ownership is not exclusively an economic question. There are incidental problems, such as its effects on enterprise and on political integrity, with which it is not possible here to deal. In the main, however, public ownership is simply a business proposition which must be justified by its economic results. In the case of a general social benefit not to be secured without public ownership, as popular education or the climatic effect of forests, the only question to answer is whether the utility is worth the cost. In the case of industries already in private hands, as waterworks, gas and electric lighting, there is needed, to make a wise decision possible, a knowledge of the effect a change to public ownership will have on value. If public officials can furnish some goods cheaper than they are furnished by private enterprise, it is because of the wide margin of monopoly profit, not because there is any magic in public ownership. The same general items of cost must be met. The first cost of the plant and the annual interest payments are much the same. Experience shows that, because of political influence, wages are likely to be higher under public ownership, but salaries of officials are higher under private ownership. On the whole, public industry in these respects probably has no advantage. Some items of cost may be less under public management. Public collection of dues along with taxes is an advantage not enjoyed by private companies. Several public officials sometimes share the same office and thus reduce expenses. In small towns the public electric lighting and waterworks have been operated more economically under one roof. Public industry does not have to meet the cost of lobbying and blackmail which are often forced upon private companies. But the greatest source of saving in public ownership is the value of monopoly privileges that, under private management, go into private pockets.

Character of public officials

Limits and effects of public ownership

The temptation to political corruption may be more insistent when a large force of men is constantly employed, and when large supplies are constantly purchased, by public officials, but the temptation is not so strong or so centralized as it is in the granting of franchises to wealthy corporations. Public industry is weakened by the absence of certain motives to excellence that are present in private business. The income of public officials not being dependent on the economy of management, the spur and motives of competitive industry are lacking. No social discovery has made individual honesty and civic virtue useless to good government.

The decision in any specific case is one dependent on local conditions, and the exact limits of public ownership are not fixed. Industry is changing so rapidly that new experience is needed each year. The main outlines of public ownership, however, are now in large part determined. Some industries do well, others ill, under public management, and between these lie many debatable cases.

Waterworks and probably electric lighting, because of the comparative simplicity of their operation, are more suitable for public ownership than are gas-works. No absolute line divides the one group from the other. But whatever the changes, the student of the theory of value must never overlook the fact that the increase of public ownership is altering in manifold ways the prices of goods, and is reacting also on the production, distribution, and consumption of incomes.

Chapter LIV
Railroads and Industry

§ I. Transportation as a Form of Production

Productivity of transportation

1. *Transportation of goods and men is one of the most important modes of production.* When utility was thought of as inherent in things rather than as resulting from a relation between things and wants, it was usual to consider only those industries as truly productive that brought something physical into existence, as do agriculture and the extractive industries. Even after it was recognized that a change of form also imparted value, it was still denied that a changing of place could be truly productive industry. But when production is seen to be the bringing of things into right relations with wants, transportation may be deemed to be the primary and typical mode of increasing income. Movement is necessary to the existence of animals. The animal, in the order of evolution a higher form of life than the more fixed plants, goes to seek food, and has open to it a wider range of possibilities in life. With slight exceptions, it is true that the only way in which animals can bring about better place-relations between their wants and goods is by moving themselves. To this power man has added that of moving goods and thus adds enormously to income. Agents being valued in accordance with their net productiveness, the nearness to market and the ease of transporting the product are large factors in price. The location of a field enters into its value as truly as do the chemical qualities of the soil. A rocky field near a market may be richer, in an industrial sense, than the richest soil far remote, which can be used by men only at the cost of their alienation from society. Means of transportation set a limit to social and political groupings, to the size of the market, and to the possibility of exchange. Indeed, all exchange value is conditioned upon the possibility of transportation.

Original local advantages

2. *Natural differences in the grades of fertility and of accessibility determine first the most valued locations.* Primitive man, dependent on the bounties of nature, had to

take things as he found them. Few places unite the best grades of the essential things: water, food, fertile soil, a favorable climate, protection against enemies. Between tribe and tribe went on ceaseless war for the few favored spots of the earth. Where transportation is possible, trade can supply one or more of the missing elements. International trade began early, wherever it could, to strengthen economically the weak localities. Advantages in transportation are sometimes better than fertile soil and rich resources. The early centers of civilization were on the banks of rivers and the shores of seas. Around the Mediterranean were the ancient empires. Trading-towns grew up at ports and at the favored points of trade: Tyre, Sidon, Carthage, Florence, Genoa, Venice, Antwerp, London, New York. The early settlements in America were grouped along the coast. Without the cheap communication afforded by water, the colonies would have been cut off from the benefits of continuing contact with the older civilization. It would have been a great price to pay, even for a rich continent.

Influence of waterways on local advantages

3. *The opening up of new water-routes of travel has profoundly altered the prosperity of nations.* Sometimes the relation of cause and effect is the reverse of that just noted. The conquest of Asia Minor by the Turks closed the lines of travel with the East, destroyed the trade of the Italian cities, and stimulated exploration for new routes. The War of 1812 in America stopped the coast trade and forced on the wagon-roads between the New England and the Southern states a great traffic, which declined quickly at the close of the war. Again, the growth of population and industry shifts the center of trade, as it did from the south to the north of Europe, and as it is doing from England to America. The discovery of new routes, however, has wrought the most rapid and sweeping changes. These three causes united, about the time of the discovery of America, to overthrow the prosperity of the older cities of Europe, while the opening of the resources in America, the abundance of silver and gold, trade with the colonists and the Indians, showered wealth and trade into the lap of Spain, Holland, Belgium, England, and the northern cities of Germany. Such changes continue under our eyes. The Erie Canal has an influence on values in every township from New York to Buffalo, and along the lake shores to the head of Lake Superior. The Suez Canal marked an epoch in ocean travel. The American Isthmian Canal will affect the value of many investments, from the Gulf of Mexico to the Pacific Coast. A marked change in transportation thus shifts the level of values in a locality. Fortunes are made and lost. One community rises and another sinks. Increments and decrements of value on a great scale are unearned, and all classes of goods are affected, though in varying degrees.

§ II. The Railroad as a Carrier

Technical vs. economic efficiency of transportation

1. *Different modes of transport are more or less economical relatively to the other*

industrial conditions. Not only new routes but new agents of travel change the scale of values. In early societies, undeveloped industrially, first men, then domestic animals, were used as beasts of burden. The first vehicles are technically simple in design and construction; on land are used drags, sleds, carts; on waterways are used rafts, canoes, barges, and boats. Primitive means of transportation had to be inexpensive, for poverty and the uncertainty of early society forbade the tying up of large resources in them. Technical efficiency of means of transportation may be contrasted with economic efficiency. Technical goodness is absolute, and is measured in speed and weight of cargo; economic efficiency is relative, and varies with the money cost and money value of the services. A turnpike is more efficient than a mud road, yet in some districts it is bad economy to build it. A railroad is more efficient than a cart, yet in some places even pack-horses are more economical. To be economical, the expenditure needed to supply the efficient agent must be warranted by the volume and value of traffic.

Economic advantages of natural waterways

2. *The most economical means of transportation before the railroad were the waterways, natural and artificial.* Some natural waterways still afford the most economical means of transportation between favorably situated ports. Coal is shipped most cheaply in sailing vessels from Wales around Cape Horn to ports along the western coasts of America. A part of California's regular fuel-supply is obtained in this way. Coal has been shipped from Pennsylvania to Europe, and in the anthracite coal-strike in 1902, some was shipped from England to America. Invention has reduced the cost of construction and operation of vessels and has increased their safety and speed, thus multiplying the efficiency of the natural waterways. The large cities in America are situated on waterways, usually where there is a break in transportation requiring reshipment, as, for example, at New York, San Francisco, Buffalo, New Orleans, Cincinnati, Chicago, Minneapolis, and St. Paul. Likewise many of the small cities and villages, serving as local trading centers, owe their existence to similar though less powerful influences.

Merits and defects of canals

Canals are begun as connecting links in a system of natural waterways to extend the advantages of cheap transportation. The Erie Canal not only serves the three hundred miles of territory along its banks, but it opened to commerce all the lands tributary to the Great Lakes. The great advantage of canals is cheapness of operation due to the simplicity of the machinery needed and to the great loads that can be moved with small power. A cent a ton-mile is a paying rate on a canal. For heavy, slow-moving freight, the railroads can hardly rival the canals at their best. As canals, however, can be built only along a level country and where the water supply is at a high level, their construction is limited to a small portion of the country. The law of extensive diminishing returns applies strongly to the construction of canals. The first canals are easily constructed and economically operated, but it is only with greater cost and difficulty that the system can be successively extended. In temperate climates their use is limited by ice to a part of the year, and the summer's drought sometimes limits it still further. At its best, therefore, the small land-locked canal is fitted only to be a supplementary agent in the system of transportation wherever industry demands high speed and great regularity. Far different is the case of the oceanic canal in a tropical climate.

Superior advantages of railroads

3. *The railroad is rapidly surpassing in importance every other agency of transportation.* Even in respect to cheapness, the unique virtue of waterways in favored localities, the railroad has been making rapid gains. Improvements in roadbed, rails, cars, engines, and other equipment are reducing greatly the cost of conducting traffic on the main lines of roads. The adaptability of the railroad excels that of any other agent of transportation; it can go over mountains or tunnel through them. In certainty its superiority is marked; floods and snows may delay it for a day, but there is no seasonal stoppage of traffic. In speed, the railroad so far excels that the canal can survive only by dividing the traffic, taking the lower grades of freight, and leaving to the railroad the passenger traffic and fast freight.

Results of the rapid growth of railroads

Because of these qualities, the extension of the railroads in the last fifty years has been so rapid that it has not given time for a gradual adaptation of industry. It has worked in many places revolutionary changes. The building of railroads in the Mississippi valley in the seventies lowered the value of Eastern farms, ruined many English farmers, and depressed the peasantry in all western Europe. With the prices that resulted when the fertile lands of the Western prairies were opened to the world's markets, the stony and worked-out lands of the older districts could not compete. Great regions are still to be opened in this manner in Russia, Siberia, Africa, and South America. While one can only speculate upon the effects this development will have, the changes promise to be less sudden and tremendous than those of the last twenty years. Many minor changes, of no less moment in limited districts, result from the building of railroads. Local trading-centers decrease in importance. Villages and towns, hoping to be enriched by the railroads, see trade going to the cities. Commerce becomes centralized. Enormous increase of value at a few points is offset by losses in other localities.

§ III. Discrimination in Rates on Railroads

Monopoly power of railroads

1. *The railroad has more monopoly power in fixing rates at points along its lines than is the case with other agents of transportation.* The ownership of the wagons, ships, and canal-boats of a country is usually divided. Every point along the line of the turnpike or the canal and at ocean ports enjoys competition between carriers, the great shipping combinations not having been successfully formed as yet. In

the early days of the railroads it was believed that a company or the government would own the rails and charge toll to the different carriers, who would own cars and conduct the traffic as was done on the canals. Experience soon showed the utter impracticability of this scheme and the need of unified management. The railroad, therefore, has a monopoly at all points on its line not touched by other carriers. This, like all other monopoly, is limited by the need to secure some business and to meet competition at terminal points. The railroads in private hands early began to "charge what the traffic would bear" at every station, thus practising various forms of discrimination disastrous in their effects on the citizens.

Discrimination as to goods

2. *Discrimination as to goods is charging more for transporting one kind of goods than for another without a corresponding difference in the cost.* When reasonably understood, this proposition does not apply to a higher charge for goods of greater bulk, as more per pound for feathers than for iron, the "dead weight" of car being much greater in one case than in the other. It does not apply where there is a difference in risk, as in carrying bricks and powder, or coal and crockery; nor where there is a difference in trouble, as in shipping live stock and wheat. Any difference that can reasonably be explained as due to a difference in cost is not discrimination; on the other hand a difference in cost without a difference in rate is discrimination. Discrimination as to goods may be by value, as low rates for heavy, cheap goods and high rates for lighter, valuable ones. Coal always goes at a low rate as compared with dry goods, and sometimes more is charged for coal to be used for gas than for coal to be used for heating purposes. Discrimination as to goods is the most usual and, if reasonably employed, one of the most justifiable of the various kinds of rate discriminations.

Local discrimination

3. *Discrimination between places (local discrimination) is charging different rates to two localities for substantially the same service.* This occurs when local rates are high and through rates are low; when rates at local points are high and at competing points are low; when less is charged for shipments consigned to foreign ports than for domestic shipments; when more is charged for goods going east than for goods going west. The causes of local discrimination are: first, water-competition, found at great trade centers such as New York and San Francisco; second, differences in terminal facilities, making some places better shipping-points than others; third, competition by other railroads, which is concentrated at certain points, only four thousand (one tenth) of the stations of the United States being junctions; fourth, the influence of powerful individuals or large corporations and the personal favoritism shown by railroad officials.

Its effects

The effect of discrimination is to develop some districts and depress others; to stimulate cities and blight villages; to destroy established industries; to foster monopolies at favored points; and to sacrifice the future revenues of the road by forcing industry to move to the competing points to get the low rates. The power of railroad officials arbitrarily to cause rates to rise or fall is happily limited in practice by the need of earning as large and as regular an income as possible, but even as exercised it has been at times as great as that possessed by many political rulers.

Personal discrimination

4. *Discrimination between shippers (personal discrimination) is charging one person more than another for substantially the same service.* This most odious of railroad vices, rarely practised openly, is done by false billing of weight, by wrong descriptions or false classification to reduce the charge below published rate-sheets, by carrying some goods free, by issuing passes to one and not to all patrons under the same conditions, or by donations or rebates after the regular rate has been paid. In some cases a subordinate agent shares his commission with the shipper, and the transaction does not appear on the books of the company. In other cases favored shippers are given secret information that the rate is to be changed, so that they are enabled to regulate their shipments to secure the lower rate.

Causes of personal discrimination

One group of reasons for personal discrimination is connected with the interests of the road. It is to build up new business; it is to make competition with rival roads more effective by favoring certain agents, as is very commonly done in the Western grain business; it is to exclude competition, as by refusing to make a rate from a connecting line or to receive materials for a new railroad which is to be a competitor; and it is to satisfy large shippers whose power, skill, and persistence make the concession necessary. Another group of reasons has to do with the interests of company officials. It is to enable them to grant special favors to friends; or it is to build up a business in which they are interested; or it is to earn a bribe that has been given them.

Evils of personal discrimination

That the evils of personal discrimination are great, need hardly be said. It introduces uncertainty, fear, and danger into all business; it causes business men to waste, socially viewed, an enormous fund of energy to get good rates and to guard against surprises; it grants unearned fortunes and destroys those honestly made; it gives enormous power and presents strong temptations to railroad officials to injure the interests of the stockholders on the one hand and of the public on the other.

Apart from government, the railroad represents the greatest single economic factor in personal distribution. It has introduced a new form of problem into economic society. It has created a monopoly comparable to the prerogatives of feudal lords. No other industrial agency in private hands so affects all the producing forces of society and exercises such a potent influence on values.

Chapter LV
The Public Nature of Railroads

§ I.   Public Privileges of Railroad Corporations

Public nature of railroad franchises

1. *Railroads enjoy peculiar public privileges through their charters, franchises, and the right of eminent domain.* Railroads in our country are owned by private corporations and are managed by private citizens, not, as in some countries, by public officials. They have been built under the motive of private enterprise, in the interest of the investor, not as a charity or as a public benefaction. Railroad-building appears thus at first glance to be a case of free competition where public interests are served in the following of private interests. But, looked at more closely, it may be seen to be in many ways different from the ordinary competitive business. Competition would make the building of railroads a matter of bargain with proprietors along the line, and an obdurate farmer could compel a long detour or could block the whole undertaking. But the public says: a public enterprise is of more importance than the interests of a single farmer. By charter or by franchise the railroad is granted the power of eminent domain, whereby the property of private citizens may be taken from them at an appraised valuation. The manufacturer, enjoying no such privilege, can only by ordinary purchase obtain a site urgently needed for his business. Why may the railway exercise the sovereign power of government and invade other private property rights? Because the railway is peculiarly "affected with a public interest." The primary object is not to favor the railroads, but to benefit the community. These charters and franchises are granted sparingly in most European countries. In this country they have been granted recklessly, often in general laws, by states keen in their rivalry for railroad extension. When thus great public privileges had been granted without reserve to private corporations, it was realized, too late in many cases, that a mistake had been made and that an impossible situation had been created.

State and National aid to American railroads

2. *In America and in many other countries, large grants of lands and money have been*

made to railroads on the ground of their peculiar public nature. Railroads were granted not only peculiar powers and privileges, but also material aid. The railroad enterprise was uncertain, the possibilities of its growth could not be foreseen, and private capital would not invest without great inducements. In European countries where capitalists were less enterprising or venturesome than in America, railroad extension was very slow except where the state in some manner extended its aid to the enterprise. The American states abandoned the principle of non-interference most recklessly, and vied with each other in giving lands, money, and privileges, in loaning bonds, in subscribing for stock, and in releasing from taxation. These protective measures fostering a special enterprise were expected by increasing wealth to diffuse a greater welfare throughout the community. Many of the states were forced to the point of bankruptcy by their reckless generosity, and some of them repudiated the debts thus incurred. The national government then took up the same policy and granted lands to the states to be used for this purpose. The first example of this was the grant to the Illinois Central road, in 1850, of a great strip of land through the state from north to south. Grants were made in fourteen states, covering tens of millions of acres of land. Then the national government, between 1863 and 1869, aided the building of the Pacific railroads by granting outright twenty square miles of land for every mile of track and by loaning the credit of the government to the extent of fifty million dollars—a debt settled by compromise only after thirty years.

Railroad grants by localities

Counties, townships, cities, and villages along the line of projected roads then entered into keen competition to secure them. Bonds, bonuses, tax-exemptions, and many special privileges were granted. To obtain this new Aladdin's lamp, this great wealth-bringer, localities mortgaged their prosperity for years to come. The promoters bargained skilfully for these grants, playing off town against town, cultivating the speculative spirit, punishing the obdurate. Not the civil engineer, but the financial engineer platted the devious lines of many a railroad on the level prairies of America. The effects of these grants were in many cases disastrous, and since 1870 they have been forbidden in a number of states by legislation and by state constitutions. But before this era of generosity ended, probably the railroads had received more public aid than has ever been given to any other form of industry in private hands.

Investors' view of railroads' obligations

3. *The railroads are now generally held to have peculiar public duties corresponding to their privileges.* Do all these grants in the past make the railroads other than mere private enterprises? One answer, that of those financially interested in the railroads, is No. They say that the bargain was a fair one, and is now closed. The public gave because it expected benefit; the corporation fulfilled its agreement by building the road. The terms of the charter, as granted, determine the rights of the public; but no new terms can now be read into it, even though the public now sees the question in a new light. Similar grants, though not so large, have been made to

other industries. Bounties have been given to sugar-factories; tariffs have favored iron-forges and woolen-mills; factories have been given, by competing cities, land and exemption from taxation; yet no attempt is made on that account to control these businesses in a peculiar way and to treat them as public enterprises. So, it is said, the railroad is still merely a private business.

Social view of railroads' obligations

But the social answer is stronger than this. As to the precedent of tariff- and bounty-favored enterprises, most careful students would admit a close analogy in the two cases, but would maintain that the tariff policy also has been carried to an unjustifiable extreme, and that it could not be used to vindicate a still greater assault on public rights. But, further, privileges of railroads are greater in amount and more important in character than those granted to any ordinary private enterprise. The legislatures recognize constantly the peculiar public functions of the railroads. In other private enterprises, investors take all the risk; legislatures and courts recognize the duty of guarding, where possible, the investment of capital in railroads. Laws have been passed in several states to protect the railroads against ticket-scalping. Whenever the question comes before them, the courts maintain the right of the railroads to earn a fair dividend. Private enterprise has been invited to undertake a public work, yet public interests are paramount.

Need of harmonizing public and private interests

If an extremely abstract view is taken there is danger of losing sight of the real problem, which is that of harmonizing these two interests in thought and in public policy. Yet the extreme advocates of the private control of railroads have resented indignantly any public interference with railroad rates and with railroad management as an infringement of individual liberty. At the time of the passage of the Interstate Commerce Act this position was inconsistently taken by those in whose interests free competition had been violently set aside at the very outset of railroad construction, and for whom government interference had made possible great fortunes. The railroads cannot change from a public to a private character just as it suits their convenience. They cannot be allowed to play Dr. Jekyll and Mr. Hyde; smooth and affable in the character of public agents when public advantages are to be gained, and then as private enterprises ugly and scowling, flouting the public interests, charging all the traffic will bear, and resisting all reasonable regulation and conditions. Though railroads are private enterprises as regards the character of the investment, they are public enterprises as to their privileges, functions, and obligations.

§ II. Political and Economic Power of Railroad Managers

Railroad rates like taxes

1. *In various ways railroad managers exercise great political influence and power.* Some writers maintain that the power to make rates on railroads is a power of taxation. They point out that if rates are not subject to fixed rules imposed by the state, the private managers of railroads wield the power of the law-maker. By changing the rates on foreign exports or imports, the railroads frequently have made or nullified a protective tariff and have defeated the intention of the legislature. High rates on state-owned roads have openly been used in lieu of protective duties. These facts go to show that a change of railroad rates between two places within the country is similar in effect to the imposing or repeal of tariff duties between them.

Political influence of railroads

The wealth and industrial importance of the railroads give them widespread political power in other ways. It is commonly charged in some states that the legislature and the courts are "owned" by the railroads. The railroads, in part because they are the victims at times of attempts at blackmail by dishonest public officials, are compelled in self-defense to maintain a lobby. The railroad lobby, defensive and offensive, is in many states the all-powerful "third house." Railroads even have their agents in the primaries, they enter political conventions, they dictate nominations from the lowest office up to that of governor, and they elect judges and legislators. The extent to which this is done differs according as the railroads have large or small interests within the state. How is this great political problem to be met except by an appreciation of its importance and by a growth of public integrity?

The complex obligations of railroad directors

2. *The economic power of the higher railroad officials enables them to exercise certain functions of an important public nature.* When the railroad was a young industry, its essentially public nature was not recognized. It was at first thought to be simply an iron-track turnpike to which the old English law of common carriers would apply. As this and similar notions proved illusory, the railroad manager became invested with complex and often conflicting duties to the stockholders and to the public. He wore his conscience-burden lightly, and frequently made little attempt to meet the one and no attempt whatever to meet the other obligation. The new field offered for speculation gave opportunities for great private fortunes. There were no precedents, no ripened public opinion, no established code of ethics, to govern. It was a betrayal of the interests of the stockholders when directors formed "construction companies" and granted contracts to themselves at outrageously high prices. It was an injury not only to shippers, but also to the stockholders, when special rates were granted to friends and to industries in which the directors were interested.

392 THE PRINCIPLES OF ECONOMICS

Unclear convictions as to the railroads' public nature

It is believed that a better code of business morality has developed, and that the officers' relation of trusteeship toward the shareholders is now more often recognized. But practical ethics need to be developed much farther than this. A railroad manager is engaged by the stockholders, is responsible to them, and looks to them for his promotion. Hence their interests are uppermost whenever the welfare of the public is not in harmony with the earning of liberal dividends. The manager feels bound to defend the principle of "charging what the traffic will bear" in the case of each individual, locality, and kind of goods. If this ruins some men and enriches others, if it destroys the prosperity of cities to increase the earnings of the road, at all events he feels he has done his full duty. Railroad directors do not yet recognize, and possibly never will, that their office is more than a private trusteeship, that it is a public trust.

Progress of railroad consolidation

3. *The progress of consolidation among railroads is putting into fewer hands greater financial and economic power.* The early railroads, many of which were built in sections of a few miles in length, have been slowly welded into continuous trunk lines with many branches. The New York Central between Albany and Buffalo was a consolidation, by Commodore Vanderbilt, of sixteen short lines. The Pennsylvania system was formed link by link from scores of small roads. The growth of consolidation recently has been more rapid than ever before. Sixty per cent. of the mileage of the United States is under the control of five interests; seventy-five per cent. is controlled by a group of men that can sit about one table. The country is being divided territorially into great railroad domains, within each of which one financial interest is dominant. Great financial alliances and "community of interests" still further unify the policy of the leading roads.

Economic results of consolidation

Toward this result strong economic forces are working. Consolidation has many technical advantages: it saves time, reduces the unit cost of administration and of handling goods, gives better use of the rolling stock and of the terminal facilities of the railroads, and insures continuous train service. It has the advantages of other large production and the possible economies of the trusts. Most important, however, from the point of view of the railroads, is the prevention of competition and the making possible of higher rates and larger dividends. The statement that competition is not an effective regulator of railroads often is misunderstood to mean that it in no way acts on rates. It is true that competition between roads does not prevent discrimination and excessive charges between stations on one line only; but competition usually has acted powerfully at well-recognized "competing points." The larger the area controlled by one management, the fewer are the competing points; the larger, therefore, is the power over the rate and the more completely the monopoly principle applies. It is a grim jest to say that consolidation does not change the railroad situation as regards the question of rates.

§ III. Commissions to Control Railroads

Railroad evils and the old legal remedies

1. *Most of the states have undertaken, through commissions, to regulate the railroads in the public interest.* When it became evident that public and private interests in the railroads were so divergent, it still was not easy to determine how the public was to be safeguarded. At first, some general conditions such as maximum rates were inserted in the laws and charters; but these were not adaptable to changing conditions and, for lack of administrative agents, could not be enforced. The early efforts at state ownership were, as was noted above, futile and disastrous, the remedy of state ownership, as then applied, being worse than the disease. The old law of common carriers gave to individual shippers an uncertain redress in the courts for unreasonable rates; but the remedy was costly because the aggrieved shipper had to employ counsel, to gather evidence, and to risk the penalty of failure; it was slow, for while delay was death to the shipper's business, cases hung for months or years in the courts; it was ineffectual, for even when the case was won, the shipper was not repaid for all his losses, and the same discrimination could be immediately repeated against him and other shippers.

Object and working of the state commissions

Attempting to remedy these evils, thirty-one of the states have appointed commissions and, as the most important states are included, this mode of regulation applies probably to four fifths of all traffic beginning and ending in a single state. These commissions differ in power, but in general they attempt to prevent excessive discrimination in rates and to check all railroad practices injurious to the public welfare. The commission principle, strongly opposed at first by the railroads, has been upheld by the courts and is now an established public policy. The state commissions, however, have fallen far short of a solution of the problem. Though they have done much to make the accounts of the railroads intelligible, something to make the rates reasonable and subject to rule, and much to educate public sentiment, on the whole their results have been disappointing. It has been difficult to get commissioners at once strong, able, and honest; the public does not yet know its own mind well enough to support the commissions properly; and—more fatal weakness still—the courts early decided that state commissions could regulate only the traffic originating and ending within the state, and this left untouched the much greater volume and more important class of interstate traffic.

Passage of the Interstate Commerce Act

2. *The Interstate Commerce Commission is an agency by which it was hoped to secure a uniform national public control of railroads.* Public hostility to private railroad management was greatest in the regions where the most rapid building of roads occurred from 1866 to 1873. One center of grievances was in "the granger states" of Illinois, Wisconsin, Kansas, Nebraska, Iowa, and Minnesota; another center was in the oil regions of Ohio and Pennsylvania. The Eastern states were not without their

troubles, for the report of the Hepburn Committee of the New York legislature in 1879 shows that discrimination between shippers prevailed to an almost incredible degree in every portion of New York state. When the courts, in 1886, decided that the greater portion of the railroad rates could not be treated by state commissions, national control was loudly demanded. Scores of bills were presented to Congress between 1870 and 1886, and, despite the bitter opposition of the railroads, the Interstate Commerce Act was passed in 1887.

Its provisions

The act laid down some general rules: that rates should be just and reasonable; that railroads should not pool, or agree to divide, their earnings to avoid competition; that they should, unless expressly excused, fix rates in accordance with the long- and short-haul principle (to charge no more for a shorter distance than for a longer one on the same line and in the same direction, the shorter being included within the longer). The act provided for a commission of five men, to be appointed by the President, which might require uniform accounts from the railroads, and which should enforce the provisions of the act.

Results of the act

3. *The object of the Interstate Commerce Act has been but imperfectly attained.* This brief proposition sums up the story of years of efforts and defeated hopes. The powers of the commission have proved inadequate to attain the main purposes of the act—the prevention of discrimination and the securing of steady and equitable rates to all shippers. By the decisions of the federal courts, the commission's power has been reduced far below the intentions of the Congress that passed the law. The railroads have in many cases refused to obey the orders of the commission and have succeeded in maintaining their refusal. Admirable results have been secured in the way of uniform accounting, uniformity of rates has been somewhat furthered at times, and the public has been in many cases enlightened. But the greatest evils remain. Railroads still give secret rates in great numbers; many competent witnesses before the Industrial Commission in 1900 and 1901 testified that discrimination had never been worse. From time to time the recognition of the injury to dividends wrought by discriminating rates prompts some railroad to offer its coöperation to the commission, and this inspires new hopes of an effective administration of the act. The pressure of competition, however, soon forces the penitent road back into its old ways. On one thing the railroads and the commission are agreed: that pooling should be permitted, though the commission wishes to have this under strict supervision. To this point the public has not yet advanced.

The railroad problem unsolved

Despite the general acceptance now of the principle that the railroads should be controlled in the public interest, despite the barren legal triumph of the commission principle, it is evident that the railroad is not yet under social control.

THE PUBLIC NATURE OF RAILROADS   395

The future must determine whether the solution is to be found in effective public regulation or in public ownership.

Chapter LVI
Public Policy as to Control of Industry

§ I. State Regulation of Corporate Industry

The social problems of corporations

1. *The great increase of late in the number of industries under corporate control has brought new problems of social regulation.* Inventions, machinery, better transportation, better communication, widening markets, have united to favor large-scale production, and this in turn to multiply corporations. Corporate organization makes possible greater massing of capital, greater stability of policy, and (because not dependent on a single life) greater permanence than does individual ownership. With these advantages the corporation brings also new social problems. The relations in corporate business are more complex than those in individual enterprise. The ordinary stockholder cannot have personal knowledge of the business or exercise personal supervision over his investment. The corporate official controls chiefly not his own wealth, but the wealth of others. When men deal personally with each other their sympathies are more appealed to. But, as noted in the case of the railroad, the corporate official at best seeks to satisfy his employers, often to the detriment both of the employes and of the public. Corporations are "soulless" because they permit less of the close personal relation that makes for morality. At various points in these later chapters on the relation of the state to industry, mention has been made of the measures society has taken to regulate corporate industry. The purpose now is to survey the field more systematically and to see the extent of this regulation, the difficulties arising, and the principles involved.

Examples of public control of corporate industry

2. *Numerous laws and commissions recently have been established to provide public regulation of industry.* The Interstate Commerce Commission is the most prominent of the agencies for regulating corporate industry, as the railroad problem is the most prominent of the corporation questions. But before the advent of the railroad, banks had been recognized as having an exceptional public character. Not only

stockholders, investors, depositors, and note-holders, but a large part of the public suffers losses by the failure of banks. As investigation by the various interested persons is quite impossible, the state through its agents inspects the books of the bank in a manner not thought of in the case of ordinary private business. The bank commission is the eye of the public, safeguarding the public welfare. State inspection of insurance companies, a later kind of corporate enterprise, grew out of a similar need. Insurance to provide for sickness, old age, or death is socially desirable and is possible in an equitable way only by the association of a large number of policy-holders. But inspection of the business by each policy-holder being impossible, regulation and control through some public agency is needed. The tax commissions now found in a majority of the states have been created principally to deal with corporations. In California, a debris commission regulates the relations between the farmers and the miners using hydraulic processes. A number of states have mining commissions, harbor commissions, labor commissions, boards of arbitration, and other similar bodies. The increase of these public agencies to regulate corporate industry has lately been condemned by some as a useless multiplication of state machinery. Doubtless some commissions have, through improper influences, been needlessly created; others having important duties have been intrusted to incompetent political appointees. But most of these commissions are needed, though at first their work may be ineffective.

Helplessness of the small investor

3. *There is a strong and increasing demand for publicity in the business of the ordinary corporation, as a protection to investors.* The law has looked upon corporations, with few exceptions, as private businesses, having the right to keep every detail of their management secret from their rivals. The inner management, therefore, has been closely hidden from most of the stockholders, who, in the economic analysis, are in the main the enterprisers. More and more the business and capital of the country has thus come into the control of the few. The ordinary investor in corporate stock "buys a pig in a poke" and trusts to the integrity of officers working behind closed doors, responsible to no one, too often speculating in the stock of their own companies. The unearned gains thus secured have tainted with dishonesty many a large fortune. No small part of the evil is the closing of the avenues of safe investment to the small capitalists, giving to a favored few a measure of monopoly in investments yielding large returns. Only recently has it been recognized that no large corporation can now be a private business in the old sense. The evolution of industry has left investors and shareholders without protection in advance of a wrong, and usually without legal redress when a wrong has been committed.

Steps toward publicity to protect investors

The demand for some remedy for a condition whose seriousness has been steadily increasing has not come so much from radical quarters as from business and financial circles. In England, some of the worst abuses have been corrected by legislation. In 1900, a bill was drafted at the suggestion of Theodore Roosevelt, then Governor of New York, which aimed eventually to make the corporation a quasi-public institution, open to inspection. The organizers of a company voluntarily accepting the act were to be personally responsible for the statements in its prospectus; its issue of stock was to be limited to actual investment and to be publicly made; its office and records were to be open to inspection. Though public opinion was not ready for this bill, and it failed of passage, the bureau of corporations of the new department of commerce of the federal government, established in 1903 under President Roosevelt, may be looked upon as a fruit of this initial attempt.

Broad social grounds for publicity

4. *Greater publicity of corporation business is essential in the interest of the public.* With the interests of the investor are usually united more general public interests; but in many cases the two groups of interests conflict. Some persons favor control of corporations only to the degree needed to protect investors, but others place the policy on broader social grounds. The ability of a manufacturing corporation, at times, by threats of removal, to coerce unfair terms from the community, from its employees, and from those who supply it with materials, has led to the proposal that factories shall be forbidden to change their location without the consent of the state.

Publicity to insure just prices

Especially does it seem desirable, if it is possible, to preserve the benefits of competition, by forbidding rates and agreements in restraint of trade. The old English idea, inherited in our law, is that the highest price that can be got in an open market, under ordinary conditions, is in general a just price. The control of any line of industry by a few corporations makes secret agreement much more easy, and thus replaces a general market-price by a discriminating rate, the highest that each individual will bear. A trust's price might still be a reasonable one if the seller met competition in every market; but it is not reasonable when opposition is crushed by local and by individual discriminations. The methods by which this result is obtained shrink from the public gaze. They include secret agreements with railroad agents, a system of espionage on the business of competitors, secret special rates to the competitor's customers, to say nothing more of corrupt political influence. Publicity in corporation accounts is the first condition to a public and uniform price. The need thus to develop potential competition is especially strong where a monopoly in a natural product exists. A more general recognition of the public nature of corporations will lead to further legislation and to the appointment of corporation commissions, as has been done already in some states.

§ II. Difficulties of Public Control of Industry

Growing need of social coöperation

1. *The progress of industry is compelling greater social contact and more use of the*

PUBLIC POLICY AS TO CONTROL OF INDUSTRY 399

agencies of government. The numerous exemplifications of this general statement that have been met in the course of this study have a common cause. In simple conditions of industry, where most of the productive energies were given to securing the necessities of life, the struggle of men was with nature. Social relations then were simple and crude, such as those of chattel slavery. Now, most men get their livelihood from their bargains with other men. The relations of men with nature now are fewer, and less close; the relations of men with men are more numerous and complex. Efficient coöperation is a factor in production. Right social relations are more essential to industry than a fertile soil.

The practical limits of legislative reform

The social institutions of any community are its answer, expressed in human consciousness and in formal laws, to this difficult problem of living together. Laws and ways for regulating industry may be good or bad. The good laws are those in harmony with human nature, giving the best motives for work and the greatest happiness both in the effort and in its reward. The merit of laws, therefore, is relative to human nature; those good for one kind of citizens may be bad for another. Men cannot be legislated into honesty without limit. The best that is possible is to enact laws that encourage the best in men as they are. A dishonest community neither has, nor is capable of choosing, men honest enough to supervise the others. Society cannot, by any amount of tugging and pulling on legislative boot-straps, lift itself above its own moral plane. But though the change in formal law cannot far precede, it may lag behind and retard, social progress. Law tardily adjusted to social needs tempts and corrupts men. A time has never been when a higher wisdom could not have corrected some ancient grievance, have leveled some unmerited inequality, and, by making laws as good as men were capable of administering at the moment, have freed their energies for further advances. It is only a spirit of moderate expectation that will not be cast down by the results of legal "reforms." Hence it cannot be hoped that abuses will not appear in the attempts to regulate private industry. Fallible men make mistakes and commit injustice, sometimes greater than that which they are seeking to prevent.

Local selfishness in industrial legislation

2. *Legislative interference with industry presents temptations to community selfishness to misuse social legislation.* Community greed is not more lovely than individual greed. Many a citizen holds up a high standard for the public official and bewails the corruptions of politics when the legislator votes for his own interest instead of for his constituents' interests. Such a citizen rarely reflects that the responsibility for many legislative abuses comes back to the community and to the individual voter. Can the water rise higher than its source? Is it a high conception of a representative's duty that he should out-talk, outwit, and out-vote his fellow-representatives, to get "a graft" for the men who elect him? In many communities, the one public question of importance is tariff legislation in favor of the local industries. This selfish issue bribes the electorate, and blinds it and its legislator to every question of the general welfare. A great industrial commonwealth steeps its public life in

corruption when its voters sell their political birthright for a duty on iron. Many congressmen are so burdened with the task of securing some public expenditure in their district to help their constituents that they have little thought and less interest to give to larger public questions. If a local improvement will furnish labor and increase the value of surrounding property, though it is most uneconomic for the general community, the representative is expected to labor hard to secure it. Many citizens see little harm in "log-rolling" by the legislator,—that is, in his voting for a law without merit in order to get another law that his constituents want. The guilt of this worst form of bribery comes back to the community that forces its representatives to such a course, sinking public morality to a lower level.

Political corruption in industrial legislation

3. *The power of the legislature to affect private fortunes presents strong temptations to public representatives.* That the legislator is so often true to a high standard of public duty, goes to illustrate the familiar truth that the individual moral code is better than that of communities. That some individuals betray their trust is less surprising. The Credit-Mobilier scandal, in connection with legislation in aid of the Union Pacific Railroad, implicated many congressmen. A few years ago, in one of the greatest states, it was discovered that an innocent-looking bill, relating to the rights of property-owners on streams, practically involved the gift, to a ring of men, of a quarter of a billion dollars' worth of coal-lands, lying under the navigable streams, and belonging to the state. Such temptations for wealth-getting are too great for men selected solely for their ability to obtain offices and pensions for political supporters, and to secure class-legislation for reputable citizens. The power of the legislative bodies to grant franchises and to permit the use of public property to corporations, constantly gives opportunity for dishonesty and occasion for scandal in the larger cities. The histories of the granting of franchises in New York, Philadelphia, Pittsburg, St. Louis, and many other municipalities, are full of black pages. Public duties are too heavy for the public integrity. Industrial power has grown faster than the civic conscience, and somehow the balance must be made even.

Heavy duties of the courts

4. *The power of the courts and of executive officers in the interpreting and executing of laws governing business has become greater.* With closer contact of men there is greater friction in social relations, and litigation increases. Fortunes turn on the result of a civil suit. While juries often are corrupt, yet it is remarkable how well the courts have kept their integrity in the midst of great temptations. Professional pride and the noble traditions of the English judiciary strengthen the individual's character on the bench, not infrequently transforming a dishonest lawyer into a just judge; but popular elections, selfish interests, and the social forces of wealth and ambition make the task at times too heavy.

Integrity needed in public officials

The executive branch of government is necessarily intrusted with great power, increasing with the extent of social regulation. The Secretary of the Treasury has discretion as to the sale and purchase of bonds, and thus can affect the rate of discount and the selling price of securities. One man's decision, if known in advance, makes possible fortunes for private pockets. A recognition of the importance of these facts, which are typical of a great class of facts, must help to develop a higher sense of public duty. Patriotism has been thought of too narrowly. The enemies of early society were outside its borders, and the citizen who traitorously gave them aid was held in abhorrence. Now, independently, in many quarters is voiced the conviction that the greatest enemies of society are within its borders, and that political corruption is the modern form of treason. A higher conception of civic virtue is required to meet the added tasks of society. Public official control must be united with private industrial control in a way to present the fewest temptations to the betrayal of public trust. Now, as never before, must be felt the wisdom of Emerson's words: "The best political economy is the care and culture of men."

§ III. Trend of Policy as to Public Industrial Activity

Recent growth of state socialism

1. *There has been a large increase of state socialism in recent years.* The term state socialism, broadly understood, includes all the forms of public participation in industry that have been passed in review: ownership by towns, cities, state, or nation; laws regulating the freedom of contract; agencies to inspect conditions and to enforce the laws; commissions to supervise and control corporate industry. From every direction comes evidence of the increase of state socialism within the past twenty-five years. To those accustomed to think of the spirit of the Germanic races as that of individual liberty and enterprise, it seems remarkable that this increase has been greater among people of Teutonic origin (Germany, England, America, Australia) than among those of Latin race. The change seems to be a part of the movement of democracy, even the measures of Bismarck in Germany having been taken to ward off the demands of the radical party. The mere name of socialism no longer frightens the citizens of a free state, and when men of strong individualistic spirit even claim with pride that they are socialists, the meaning of that term is becoming very vague indeed.

Varieties of socialism

2. *State socialism must not be confused with collectivism, or radical socialism.* The word socialism is so variously defined that the earnest student sometimes despairs of getting a clear understanding of it. The thought of socialism ranges from the simplest form of state interference, such as the support of public schools and public fire-departments, up to complete public ownership of all industry. It is well

to describe as radical socialists those who would abolish private property, and would strike at the very root of the existing order of society. The modern form of radical socialism originated among German thinkers of the school of Karl Marx, but it has many supporters in other lands. The typical radical socialist claims to possess the only pure brand of social reform, disdains any interest in state socialism, and scoffs at state control as mere temporizing, as not even a single step toward radical socialism.

Aim of state socialism

The typical state socialist agrees that these measures do not logically force him toward the extremer view. He is at heart an individualist, believing that the motive forces of society are in human character, not in governmental machinery; but he seeks to prevent some kinds of competition, to put other kinds on a better basis; "to make the rules of the game fairer," but not to suppress it. According to this difference in ultimate plan, men and present measures can in general be classified. Yet one view sometimes shades into the other in the life-history of a single individual. Believers in moderate interference sometimes move toward the extreme, and the most radical thinkers, sometimes with no less honesty, become, with broadening experience, more and more moderate. It would be surprising if any one who is thinking and growing in social philosophy should succeed in so exactly adjusting to each other all his opinions, as to be absolutely consistent at a particular moment in his views on social policy.

Unripe social philosophy

3. *It is not safe to predict from present evidence a continued trend toward extreme social control.* Social prophecy is fascinating. Men like to answer out of their ignorance the question, Whither are we tending? A deeper study of social law should give this power, but it is not won by hasty generalization. Unripe social philosophers assume that because the theory of biological evolution is correct, the particular theory of social evolution which they choose to invent or accept is unimpeachable. Radical socialism is the exaggerated statement of a present social need. It is a bridging with hope, not with experience, of the chasm between reality and the dreams of the unsuccessful.

Progress of social control

True Aim of social control

It is true that many evidences point to an increase in social control for some time to come. The laws, the institutions, the prevailing morality of society, have not kept pace with industrial growth in this period of sweeping change. What is seen, however, is a small arc of the curve of progress. Much of the social regulation in the Middle Ages was similar to that which is now increasing. Legislation by gilds and privileges of private corporations hedged industry about. A reaction against this in the seventeenth and eighteenth centuries brought on national and state control, and state interference of another kind rapidly increased until the

PUBLIC POLICY AS TO CONTROL OF INDUSTRY

time of Adam Smith. Then a strong reaction came, and the next period of fifty years saw far less of interference. The years from 1825 to 1840 were those of the greatest state socialism ever seen in America, but the results were so unfortunate that a violent reaction followed. The recent great increase of state activity is not likely to be continued indefinitely. The path of progress is a spiral. There are forces already at work creating a resistance to any great extension of this movement. Competition of the healthier sort cannot be suppressed without paralyzing results. Inequality and the opportunity for ability to realize itself cannot be destroyed. The social regulations must be of a sort to liberate the best energies of men, not to enchain them. If the evils of state regulation increasingly appear to outweigh the benefits, a limit must be put to the movement. While social control may aid in lifting production and competition to a higher and more moral plane, the ability of society will refuse to be ruled by the standards of the weak and inefficient.

Chapter LVII
Future Trend of Values

§ I.   Past and Present of Economic Society

Definition of economics recalled

1. *The meaning and scope of economics can be better seen at the end than at the beginning of its study.* The proposition with which this inquiry opened may well be recalled in the closing chapter. The words of the formal definition of economics should at this point convey a fuller meaning. In the wide range of subjects passed in review has been sought the answer to one question: What determines and affects the values of good?

Influence of economics on practical life

Perhaps now also can be better appreciated what the influence of such a study might and should be on practical action. At times economic students have gained the ear of statesmen and rulers, and have exercised much influence upon practical politics. It is sometimes bemoaned that economists have to-day so small a direct part in the government of our republic. They certainly have a greater part to-day than they had twenty years ago, but if they had not, there would be small occasion for regret. The immediate influence of the specialist on those in authority is at most times less in a republic than it is in a monarchy, at those rare times when a ruler shows the students his favor. That influence in America is mostly indirect, but it is no less sure and lasting. The results of the earnest pursuit of economic inquiry in the universities and outside of them are already appearing, not in dramatic ways, but in the more subtle, surer form of an intelligent public opinion.

Examples of mistaken social prophecy

2. *Economic science has not reached a stage that permits of much prophecy.* Prediction is sometimes given as the test of science. This test, however, is one that only astronomy can meet in any remarkable degree. Chemistry can tell much of what will happen in the laboratory, but nothing of the date of future powder-mill

explosions. Geology answers the question "What?" with surmises, and "When?" with an estimate of a few million years more or less. Is it surprising that in human affairs still less prediction is possible? There are countless unmeasured factors in human action. Such generalizations as are possible must be based on actions that appear and reappear with practical constancy. Though a number of facts unite to suggest some conclusions as to the immediate future, the experience of the last century bids one beware of sweeping predictions. The close of the French Revolution was a period marked by much speculation regarding the future of society. The optimists, with faith in the perfectability of human nature and of society, believed that all social ills were due to bad government; if despotism were but overthrown, man's nature would develop, untrammeled, to perfection. The economists of that day were sceptical, because, looking deeper, they saw sources of misery in the scantiness of man's environment, and in the sloth, ignorance, and incapacity of human nature. The pessimists—the communists, and socialists of that day—seeing the same evils, had other explanations to offer. While the economists of that day believed the conditions of poverty and misery to be inevitable, the pessimists pronounced them unendurable, and advocated a radical social change as the only hope of saving the masses from starvation. In such a variety of mutually contradictory views there must have been much error, but likewise much truth if it could be disentangled.

Economic prophecies of the nineteenth century

3. *The unexpected changes in transportation and in industry altered the course of economic development in the last century.* Much of the economic theory of that day appears absurd in the light of history. The inventions of the period, from Adam Smith's writings to Ricardo's (1776 to 1820), were mostly for use in manufacturing. This suggested to the minds of that time the progressive cheapening of cloth, iron, pottery, and of all other products of machinery, but not the cheapening of food. Indeed, the situation in western Europe then suggested strongly the opinion that the products of the soil would steadily become more difficult to get. The railroad was not of practical importance until after 1830; the steamboat was not applied to ocean travel until 1837. The opening of a rich continent and its annexation, by these new agencies, to the available resources of the older countries were not dreamed of. It was not fully appreciated that a great change in social standards, controlling the growth of population, was in progress. This was the panorama of the progress of society as seen by both the conservative economists and the socialists of less than a century ago: continued invention, an increasing population, low wages, scanty food, growing wealth for the few, and growing poverty and misery for the masses.

Unexpected course of development in the nineteenth century

4. *The actual course of economic development in the nineteenth century falsified the predictions alike of optimists, economists, and pessimists.* Not foreseeing the great supplies of natural resources soon to be made available for the older countries, the men of that day naturally thought of the supply of land as limited and fixed. Supply

in the economic sense means the amount available at the given time in the market; but despite the great areas since brought into the world-markets, the false idea of a century ago still persists in the text-books, and shapes economic reasoning. It is vain to say that the circumstances have been unique and that the general principle is still valid. Much of the so-called orthodox economic analysis was essentially erroneous as applied to the conditions of the past century; it is erroneous to-day and will be so for years to come, if it ever fits the facts. New continents are about to be opened. The building of railroads the length of South America and to the center of Africa will make available new mineral wealth, rare woods, enormous forests, and some of the greatest food-producing areas on the globe. Population in Christendom has increased more rapidly than ever before in the history of the world, but it has not overtaken the progress in resources. The rate of increase of population is slackening. The result of this combination of events has been a general rise of the conditions making for popular welfare. Despite the problems and the abuses that every new change brings, the civilized world undoubtedly is more prosperous to-day than ever before. The greatest misery and discontent is in the more backward communities. This is past and present; what of the economic future? Is the present condition a normal one—is this prosperity likely to grow or to decline? Thus far, surely, the economic student may question the oracles; for though the distant future is veiled from man's view, the role of economic theory is to show causal relations, to convert mystery into reason, and thus to give a lamp to the feet of the present.

§ II. The Economic Future of Society

Exhaustion of certain natural resources

1. *Present industrial progress is largely due to material conditions, temporarily favorable.* Many of the materials now being destroyed in immense quantities have been slowly stored up through the ages and are not renewable.[4] Till modern times man knew little of the world beneath its crust. Living, he scratched the earth's surface, and dying, left his bones to fertilize the soil. But to-day, man exhausts the stores in the interior of the earth, burns the treasures of the carboniferous age, casts the fertilizing elements into the ocean, and leaves the world an empty shell. Forests are being so rapidly cut off that the price of fuel-wood and lumber in many parts of the United States has, within twenty years, been multiplied by three. The world's store of iron ore is not yet fully known, but much of it has been measured, and of the deposits known to be within the United States over one half are said to be owned by one corporation, and they are enough to continue its present output no more than sixty years. Many other natural products are in like manner gathered by civilized man from a stock created long ago. While the supply of vegetable food promises to be ample, the supply of meat will be maintained with difficulty as population becomes denser.

[4] Though at first glance this may seem contradictory to the statement in the foregoing paragraph regarding the nature of supply, it will not be found so on closer examination.

Possibilities of other resources

2. *Many other inexhaustible sources of essential materials have not yet been developed.* What has just been said is the darker side. The coal-mines can be emptied, but so long as the sun shines and the rains fall, Niagara will remain as a source of light, heat, and power. The tides flow on forever. In every thunder-storm enough force is dissipated to run thousands of factories. The heat in the center of the globe, though not inexhaustible, would suffice for man's needs for many centuries. The force in Mount Pelée, if chained and utilized, would run a million factories a million years. It is not too much to hope that engineering skill will some day reach and utilize these sources. Such a cheapening and diffusion of power would put a new face on many of the problems of industry. New sources of materials undoubtedly will be developed. It is reasonable to hope that before iron ore has become extremely scarce, a cheap and practicable method of extracting aluminium from clay will have been perfected. Secure of these permanent sources, civilization will stand on a firmer foundation.

Effect on values of shifting centers of power and materials

A great displacement of local values must accompany this shifting of the centers of power and materials. When the coal districts are heaps of slag and cinders, industry will be found near the water-power. Because of distance from raw materials, New England even now finds herself hard pushed in her rivalry with the Southern states in the manufacture of textiles. The industrial map of our country will be greatly altered a hundred years hence. The possession of rich natural resources to-day does not insure a community enduring prosperity.

Effect of accumulating wealth

3. *The mass and quality of wealth will increase rapidly if social and political conditions remain stable.* The main method of increasing wealth must be the putting of energies and resources into more abiding forms. In order that a motive for saving may be present, there must be stable conditions. Increasing subordination of present to future will be accompanied by a fall in the rate of interest. The growth of wealth means a higher quality of all artificial productive agents. A larger part of the energies of men will then be directed merely to supervising the developed machinery. Man will live in a better environment, in a better and richer world. Wages must rise as the quality of tools and machinery improves. Population most probably will not increase proportionately and the relation of the labor-supply to the resources with which it works should be more and more in favor of the laboring classes. The difficult problems of the concentrated control of industry and of the control of wealth must be solved in the interests of all.

Social progress vs. race progress

4. *Improvement of the race biologically, through selection of the ablest individuals, has been a great factor in human progress.* Social progress is not necessarily the steady biological betterment of the native ability of men. The education of the average

member of society is becoming yearly better; it is doubtful whether the innate capacity of a new-born babe in Europe and America to-day is greater than it was among our Germanic ancestors in Roman times. Indeed, the progress of the past two thousand years has been in social organization, in the enlargement and simplifying of the mass of knowledge which has to be reappropriated by each new individual, rather than in race-breeding and in quality.

Nature vs. culture

Few thoughtful persons now hold the view that the race can be rapidly improved biologically by the process of educating the individual. Education is cumulative in so far as it builds up a better environment into which other children will be born, but the betterment is not due to the inheritance by the child of the acquired knowledge and skill of the parent. If this question is open to dispute among biologists, it is only as regards a minute increment of improvement. Practically, selection is the only means of improving the innate capacity of any species in any large measure. Many forces were at work in the past to lift man above the brute, and especially to increase the average brain-power of the human race. The weak, the ignorant, the incapable in primitive societies were ruthlessly killed off. The strong, the sagacious, and the enterprising left the largest numbers of descendants.

Decrease of the successful elements

5. *Progress will be checked if the native quality of the race declines.* Under modern conditions, especially within the last quarter of a century, the successful elements of society are becoming less fertile. Large families were the rule among the capable pioneers of America; now they are rare except in the lower industrial ranks. Democracy and opportunity are favoring this process of increasing the mediocre and reducing the excellent strains of stock. Caste and status kept successful generations of capable men in humble social ranks from which only by chance some remarkable individual could rise. In a democracy, those of marked ability can more easily move into the better-paid callings and professions. This individual good fortune, however, reduces the probability of offspring. In the higher social ranks are more bachelors and old maids than in the lower ranks, and fewer children are born to each marriage. The president of our oldest university has shown that one fourth of the graduates of the last generation have remained single, and that the average number of children of the married graduate is two. That group of men, therefore, has left only three fourths enough descendants to maintain its numbers, and as the population has doubled within the same generation, that class represents only three eighths as large a proportion of the American stock as formerly.

The menace to progress

This sterilization of ability has cumulative results. If society were composed in equal parts of two distinct strains of stock, not intermarrying; if the total population kept intact from one generation to another (say each period of thirty years), but the superior strain contributed only three fourths of its own number, at the end of five generations it would have sunk from one half to a little more than one eighth of the population. A period brief in the life of nations would serve to leave it an almost negligible factor in social life. There can hardly be a doubt that at present our society is on the average increasing far more from the less provident, less enterprising, less intelligent classes. There has not yet been time for many of the cumulative effects of this process to appear. Progress is threatened unless social institutions can be so adjusted as to reverse the present process of multiplying the poorest, and of extinguishing the most capable families.

Sympathy and selfishness in relation to progress

6. *If progress is to continue, there must be left a wide field for the ambitions and for the competition of individuals.* The results of any given ability are dependent upon the energy with which it is used. The social machinery finds its motive force in the nature of men. In taking economic wants as the starting point of our study, it was not implied that men were entirely selfish. Sympathy widens; economic wants include family, friends, and, in a growing measure, humanity. The happiness of a truly socialized man consists in part in the happiness of his fellows. As social sympathy broadens, the sense of duty becomes a stronger economic force. Men change, but not rapidly, and not always for the better. It is unsafe to overestimate the generosity of men. Individual wants and interests must, so far as can now be seen, continue to be among the stronger forces that move society. Progress is made because to exceptional ability in general is now presented the hope of large rewards.

Status endangering progress

Envy endangering progress

These dynamic forces making for progress are at present, however, threatened from two sides. Enterprise is threatened from the side of privilege or status. The avoidance of certain kinds of work which, by social convention, come to be regarded as degrading, takes much ability out of business. The freedom of America to so great a degree from this disdain of honest labor has been a large factor in her progress, but it is endangered when men become timidly conservative of social position. Progress is threatened, secondly, by democracy, with its tendency to carry the notion of literal equality over into industry. When democracy becomes envious, it denies to exceptional ability an exceptional reward. The line of growth must be the resultant of the positive forces in these two principles. The energy of the social reformer must be directed along rational lines. If this can be done, the economic outlook is for a great development of wealth and popular welfare. Economics must be looked upon as the study of the forces in human nature as much as of the material resources of the world.

QUESTIONS AND CRITICAL NOTES

Questions and Critical Notes

THE QUESTIONS.—These questions are not intended to be used merely as tests of knowledge of the text. They leave untouched many of the most important questions in the reading, and they raise other inquiries hardly hinted at in it. The list began ten years ago with one or two questions on each topic, assigned in advance of lectures and recitations, with the object of arousing the student's thought, quickening his observation, and stimulating his interest in the subjects. The possibilities of helpful questions of this kind are hardly more than suggested by the examples given, and every teacher will find peculiar opportunities in his own neighborhood for other similar inquiries.

Other questions are more of the nature of those in *Problems in Political Economy*, by W. G. Sumner (published by Holt & Co., New York, 1884), which are intended to be reasoned out in the light of principles given in the class-room. Many teachers and students have found much help in that little book, which in turn acknowledges large obligations to earlier lists of questions. The changed point of view in economic theory has, however, made most of the older problems of this nature unusable except after reformulation. Fertile in suggestions of both of the kinds of questions mentioned are two books by H. J. Davenport, *Outlines of Economic Theory* and *Outlines of Elementary Economics* (The Macmillan Co., New York, 1896 and 1897), though some of the questions imply theoretical views differing from those of this book. Excellent lists of questions with references to reading have been prepared by W. G. L. Taylor, in his *Exercises in Economics* (The University Publishing Co., Lincoln, Neb., 1900). The list of problems of this kind can easily be extended to meet the special conditions of each community.

THE BIBLIOGRAPHICAL NOTES.--The few references and critical notes given are intended as a help to teachers and advanced students desirous of following some of the more recent contributions to controverted points in economic theory. No attempt has been made to furnish a list of books for the beginner or the regular reader. Among accessible books containing helpful lists of that kind may be mentioned:

The Reader's Guide in Economic, Social, and Political Science, by Bowker and Iles.

Outlines of Economics, by R. T. Ely (published by Macmillan, New York, 2d ed., 1900). Contains both questions and bibliographies.

Introduction to the Study of Economics, by C. J. Bullock (published by Silver, Burdett & Co., 2d ed., 1900). The references to the literature are given by pages or sections at the end of each chapter, and at the back is a list (about twenty pages) of the most useful texts, documents, and materials.

Financial History of the United States, by D. R. Dewey (published by Longmans, Green & Co., 1903). Contains excellent references on public finances, tariff, banking, and taxation of the United States.

Introduction to Economics, by H. R. Seager (published by Holt & Co., New York, 1903). Each of the first twenty-six chapters is followed by fresh and well-selected references varying from one line to nearly a page in length. A good general bibliographical note is given on pp. 61-2.

CHAPTER 1. THE NATURE AND PURPOSE OF POLITICAL ECONOMY

1. Has political economy anything to do with woman suffrage, the liquor problem, a republican *vs.* a monarchical form of government, the silver question?

2. Is political economy a study of things or of men?

3. Shall a piece of coal be studied in geology, botany, physics, chemistry, or economics?

4. Do you expect to acquire wealth more easily as a result of the study of political economy?

5. Of what practical use do you think political economy is?

6. Is political economy necessary to the understanding of the business world, or vice versa?

7. How wide a knowledge would a complete understanding of industrial society require?

8. Did the discovery of America make the study of political economy more important?

CHAPTER 2. THE ECONOMIC MOTIVES

1. If you found $10 to-day on the street, what would you do with it?

2. What would be the chief differences between your use of it now and at the age of five or the age of twelve?

3. Name Crusoe's wants in the order of their importance.

4. Is it well to be contented with your lot? Is it well to be discontented?

5. Why does a horse like hay and a man prefer meat?

6. Are the wants of a savage more easily satisfied than those of civilized men? Why?

7. How many motives led you to come to college?

8. If you ever worked for wages, or a salary, was that the only motive? What else?

9. James Bryce says that the incomes of American university professors are much less than those of men of corresponding ability in law and medicine. If true, why?

10. If you could, would you do nothing always? Why?

11. Which would you prefer, to clerk in a store at $1.50 a day, or to lay masonry at $2? Why?

12. Do men work better under threat or when their pride is appealed to?

13. Is pride as powerful a motive as greed, in economic action?

14. Do you know any persons that work from a sense of duty alone?

15. Are charity workers usually well paid? Why?

CHAPTER 3.   WEALTH AND WELFARE

1. What is it to be economical of money?

2. Why did Crusoe work at all?

3. When he began to work at one thing, why did he ever stop to work at another?

4. What is the difference in utility between the water in a solid mountain reservoir and the same water when it is flooding the valley?

5. Does it change the utility of a load of powder to touch a match to it?

6. Is water useful? Is dynamite?

7. Is the last bait worth more when the fish are biting well?

8. Are the following wealth: food, tobacco, medicine, whisky, good looks, good health, a wooden leg?

9. Is a book full of useful information, wealth? Is a head full of useful knowledge, wealth?

10. Is a ship at the bottom of the ocean, or gold in the mine, wealth?

11. Is well-being in proportion to wealth? Why?

12. Are services, music, a theatrical performance, a gambler's pack of cards, wealth?

NOTE.—The theory of marginal utility broadly outlined in chapters 3-5 has been worked out in detail by the group of writers called the Austrian economists. The mechanism, or the technique, of marginal utility and exchange as they conceive of it, is essentially what this text seeks to explain. Our application and development of the conception of marginal utility differs from theirs, however, in ways that will appear as the text advances.

For more detailed discussion of many points in chapter 3, see Smart, *Introduction to the Theory of Value*, pp. 9-17; Wieser, *Natural Value*, pp. 3-16; Böhm-Bawerk, *Positive Theory of Capital*, pp. 129-153.

CHAPTER 4. THE NATURE OF DEMAND

1. Give illustrations of the difference between desire and demand.

2. Do people actually expend their incomes so as to get the maximum utility judged by a standard they would admit to be morally sound?

3. What causes a demand for an additional supply of food? Of books?

4. If you never eat corn-bread, will the failure of the corn-crop affect your grocery bill?

5. Give examples you have seen of a higher price of one thing causing an increasing use of another.

6. Do you buy what you most desire?

7. Give examples of cases where supply is fixed, and demand varies.

8. Give examples of demand shifting from one product to another.

NOTE.—For a more detailed discussion see works cited: Smart, 18-33; Böhm-Bawerk, 159-169; Wieser, 16-36.

CHAPTER 5. EXCHANGE IN A MARKET

1. Are merchants producers of wealth, or are their profits merely subtracted from the wealth already produced?

2. Is the railroad productive? Why?

3. Give examples within your observation of improved productive processes increasing exchange; of the reverse.

4. Why is exchange profitable if it is fair?

5. Would doubling all commodities affect their exchange value?

QUESTIONS AND CRITICAL NOTES 415

6. Is part of a stock of goods ever worth more than the whole? Examples.

7. Do you ever take account of a difference of five cents in deciding whether to purchase?

8. Is barter more or less frequent now in America than formerly? In the world?

9. Is there any causal relationship between commerce and manufactures? If so, in what way?

10. In a time of high excitement gold was sold for more at one side of the room than at the other side; how account for this?

11. Give examples of, and reasons for, two prices in the same market.

12. What effect on prices should be expected from an invention that makes possible the carrying of fresh meat from South America to England?

13. Describe the method of selling any product you know about. What is the market in which it is sold?

> NOTE.—See works cited: Smart, pp. 40-63; Böhm-Bawerk, 193-222; Wieser, 39-53.

CHAPTER 6. PSYCHIC INCOME

1. Is it possible to compare the value of the portrait-painter's service with that of the gardener?

2. To call the teacher's work unproductive, and the ditch-digger's work productive was once usual, but is so no longer; give reasons for either view.

3. It is usual to call the use of a house for business purposes a productive use, but its use as a residence an unproductive one. What reasons are there for and against this?

4. Give a list of material agents that are yielding non-material uses.

5. Give examples of personal services that are most immediately expressed as gratifications.

> NOTE.—The phrase "psychic income," used here for the first time, expresses a conception long neglected, but essential to the advancement of psychological economics. The idea has been recognized in the writings of Edwin Cannan, Irving Fisher, W. M. Daniels, and perhaps of late by others. It was discussed by the author in the *Quarterly Journal of Economics*, Vol. XV, pp. 19-30, especially pp. 25-26, in an article called "Recent Discussion of the Capital Concept" (November, 1900).

Chapter 7. Wealth and its Indirect Uses

1. Give reasons for attributing exchange value to the waves of the ocean; to a waterfall, a water-wheel, a loom, a piece of cloth, a dress made of the cloth.

2. Show the connection between these things.

3. How can the use of a flock of sheep be of value to one who must return them all to the owner?

4. Why should the use of a machine that never can be a direct cause of gratification, have a value that men will pay for?

5. Give examples of wealth never becoming a direct cause of gratification, yet whose possession is greatly valued.

> Note.—The conception in this chapter was ably presented by Böhm-Bawerk in *Capital and Interest*, Bk. III, ch. v, pp. 219-227. He does not, however, make use of it in a theory of rent.

Chapter 8. The Renting Contract

1. What things beside land are rented?

2. What is the form of contract used in the renting of farms, business buildings, and residences, in the community where you live?

3. Does the rent of pianos, type-writers, or masquerade-suits depend on the value of the thing rented? Is the rental a moderate return on the investment?

4. What are the difficulties in determining tenants' improvements?

> Note.—Various writers have recognized that social, class distinctions had an influence on the conceptions of rent and capital in England in the eighteenth century; see Fetter, article on "The Next Decade of Economic Theory," in *American Economic Association*, 3d ser., Vol. III, pp. 236-246, especially 243-4; also A. S. Johnson, *Rent in Modern Economic Theory*, p. 19, and references there given. Heretofore, however, there has not been assigned to the form of the contract the significance here given it. A discussion of the points at issue will be found in *The Relations between Rent and Interest*, by F. A. Fetter and others (published by Macmillan, New York, 1904), pp. 8-10, on the renting contract.

Chapter 9. The Law of Diminishing Returns

1. Is it possible to do twice the amount of business in any store-room by doubling the stock and the force of clerks?

2. Is it possible to expand a university indefinitely by increasing the force of teachers and the equipment, without enlarging the buildings?

3. Why do men cultivate two acres instead of one? Where land is plentiful, why do not men cultivate two acres instead of one?

4. Are there any things, not free goods, that could be indefinitely increased without increasing difficulty?

5. English farmers raise thirty-five bushels of wheat per acre, Americans perhaps fifteen; why this difference?

6. Why did people go to Dakota and Iowa when there was still room in New England?

7. Why put up a twenty-story building? Why not build a fifty-story one?

> NOTE.—The broad reading here given to the law of diminishing returns is so recent that even the latest texts have recognized it only in a partial manner, defining "the law" in the old terms confined to land. For the old statement see J. S. Mill, *Principles of Political Economy* (1846), Bk. I, ch. XII. Writers even so advanced as Alfred Marshall follow Mill with no essential modification. For a good historical account of the doctrine see Edwin Cannan, *History of the Theories of Production and Distribution*, pp. 147-182 (1893; 2d ed., with additions, 1903), which advances no positive theory, but makes evident many inconsistencies in the older view. A keen analysis and important contribution to economic thought was made by J. R. Commons, *Distribution of Wealth*, pp. 116-159 (1895). John B. Clark, in various earlier articles, and in his *Distribution of Wealth* (1900), has done more than any one else to develop the conception of "a universal law of economic variation." In magazine articles by various writers, the same idea has been developed, but no thorough-going application of it has been made in the available text-books.

CHAPTER 10.   THE THEORY OF RENT

1. Is competition severe in the renting of land in your community?

2. Give examples you have seen of a rise of rent; the cause. Of a fall of rent; the cause.

3. Does the existence of the land of California have any effect on rents in New York city? On agricultural rents in New York state?

4. If all the land on an island were equally fertile and equally convenient of access, would any of it pay a rent?

5. If you owned the Golden Gate, or the harbor of New York, could you rent it?

6. How does the hire of a team of horses resemble the rent of land?

7. How do livery charges in a college town in commencement week illustrate the subject of rent?

8. Show how a change of circumstances may raise the rent of machinery.

> NOTE.—Although most texts still present the older, narrow conception of land rent, its defects have been revealed by many critics. J. B. Clark has been the chief champion of the broader conception; *American Economic Association*, 1st ser., Vol. III, No. 2, *Capital and Its Earnings* (1888); and *Distribution of Wealth*, ch. IX and ch. XIII. See our summary of the present situation, *American Economic Association*, 3d ser., Vol. II, p. 241 (1900). Alfred Marshall's effort to save the older conception by compromise on a "quasi-rent" doctrine has many supporters, but this doctrine is examined in detail and criticized adversely by the writer in an article entitled "The Passing of the Old Rent Concept," *Quarterly Journal of Economics*, Vol. XV, pp. 416-455 (1901). For both negative and positive reasons for a change in the concept, see *The Relations between Rent and Interest*, before cited (in note to ch. 8).

CHAPTER 11. REPAIR, DEPRECIATION, AND DESTRUCTION OF WEALTH

1. What is the difficulty in the definition: Rent is the payment for the original and indestructible powers of the soil?

2. If the value of improvements on land is all counted, is there anything over? Examples.

3. What is stumpage? Does it differ from rent?

4. What do you know about the methods of renting mines?

5. What methods are adopted to keep up the efficiency of factories?

> NOTE.—Compare and note the inconsistent use of the term "rent" by Ricardo, pp. 34-5 and 45-6, McCulloch's edition. See also article, "Depreciation," in *Palgrave's Dictionary*.

CHAPTER 12. INCREASE OF RENT-BEARERS AND OF RENTS

1. What are the most obvious ways of increasing the productiveness of land?

2. How does a new railroad affect the value of the land it passes through?

3. How would the rent of a rocky island be affected if it became a summer

QUESTIONS AND CRITICAL NOTES

resort?

4. Mention any cases you may have seen where a greater value was imparted to land by a newly discovered use.

5. A tunnel was made to drain a mine; the stock doubled in price. Was it really the stock, the old mine, or the new hole in the mountain-side that had increased in value?

6. Criticize the statement that, in an economic sense, land is a "fixed stock for all time."

> NOTE.—The changes which the rent concept is undergoing can be traced in the work of Alfred Marshall. See *Principles of Economics*, Bk. V, ch. IX on "Quasi-rent," and ch. X on "Situation Rent," and Bk. VI, ch. IX, Secs. 6-7, in which Marshall modifies the older conception of rent. This is discussed in "The Passing of the Old Rent Concept," cited above (in note to ch. 10).

CHAPTER 13.   MONEY AS A TOOL IN EXCHANGE

1. Why do you value money? Do you value it more than the things it buys?

2. What functions does money perform in society?

3. Could a country better do without money, horses, or roads?

4. If money is a tool, what does it make?

5. What is the difficulty in deciding whether to call the following money: gold ingots, gold coin, silver dollars, copper cents, greenbacks, bank-checks, chalk-marks to keep account?

6. Are men wealthy in proportion to the money they have? Are countries?

7. Would a nation be poorer if, like Sparta, it prohibited all money?

CHAPTER 14.   THE MONEY ECONOMY AND THE CONCEPT OF CAPITAL

1. Are national bonds or promissory notes, wealth?

2. Is it money or things that the borrower wants?

3. If you were starting a factory on credit, would you rent the machines or buy them with borrowed money? Why?

4. When a man says he has a certain capital invested in his business, does he mean to include the value of the land and buildings?

5. What is the meaning of the phrase, "a capitalistic age"?

NOTE.—We are indebted to the economic historians for a better understanding of the important influence money has had on economic organization. See Hildebrand's notable article in the first number of the *Jahrbücher*, and Ashley, *English Economic History*. J. B. Clark was the first among contemporary economists to emphasize the value concept of capital. The scholarly and judicial article by Irving Fisher on "Precedents for Defining Capital" in *Quarterly Journal of Economics*, May, 1904, makes possible better understanding and agreement on the subject. I am pleased to say that in this article, and in personal correspondence, Professor Fisher disavows the interpretation I had thought (see "Recent Discussion," etc.) that his words required. His conception of capital is thus, in essentials, the one here employed, differing from it not in thought, but merely in terminology. Professor Fisher's original studies of the capital concept, in the *Economic Journal* in 1896-7, are indispensable to an understanding of the development of this important phase of the new economic theory. The connection between the conclusions of economic history and the value concept of capital in economic theory has been made by the author in essays before cited under chapters 6 and 8: "Recent Discussion of the Capital Concept"; "The Next Decade of Economic Theory," and "The Relations between Rent and Interest."

CHAPTER 15. THE CAPITALIZATION OF ALL FORMS OF RENT

1. What relation is there between the rate of interest and the price of land bearing a given rental?

2. If a $100 share of railroad stock sells at par when interest on loans is at 5%, what will be its price when interest rises to 6%? When interest falls to 4%?

3. If a business is very successful and its dividends double, what will be the effect on the selling price of its stock?

NOTE.—The subject is almost foreign to the standard works on economics, which have continued to look upon capital as primary, and its income as derived. Numerous recent articles will be found, however, dealing with concrete problems where the logical and the practical views are seen to be the same; *e.g.*, W. Z. Ripley, *Quarterly Journal of Economics*, Vol. XV, p. 106 (1900), article on "The Capitalization of Public Service Corporations"; also article in *Engineering News*, Vol. XXVIII, p. 492 (November, 1892).

QUESTIONS AND CRITICAL NOTES

CHAPTER 16. INTEREST ON MONEY LOANS

1. Some money-lenders in cities get 10% a day from fruit-vendors for the advance of small sums of money, and the losses are very slight. Pawnbroking pays frequently 25 to 100% per year. In these cases what affects the rate of interest?

2. Through what agency does the Western farmer borrow Eastern capital?

3. How do Englishmen invest in American railroads?

4. In what ways can a lender collect a high rate of interest without appearing to do so?

5. What would be the effect upon the rate of interest in a new state if it passed a law preventing the collection of loans by outside lenders?

6. Why has interest been about 10% in the West, 7% in the Central States, 5% in New York, 4% in Germany?

7. What is the money market? Who are the buyers and sellers, and what do they buy and sell?

8. In a panic, interest rises on short loans and prices fall, while it is almost impossible to borrow money; does this show that the amount of money determines the interest rate?

9. When gold is leaving England, the bank raises the rate of discount (interest); does this show that the quantity of money determines the rate of interest?

CHAPTER 17. THE THEORY OF TIME-VALUE

1. Give examples of a high cost for the use of wealth without the borrowing of money.

2. Give some examples of the neglect of repairs through lack of resources, and show how it involved time-value.

3. What would be some of the first effects on production if interest on money loans fell to one half its present rate?

4. Which is the more important for the rate of interest, the amount of money in the banks or the amount of goods in the country?

5. How would the rate of interest be affected if the amount of money were doubled at once?

> NOTE.—In an interesting article on "Prestige Value," by L. M. Keasbey, in *Quarterly Journal of Economics*, May, 1903, has been developed one phase of the thought in Sec. II, proposition 2.
>
> The very active recent discussion of "the interest problem" has done much to clarify economic theory; but almost the entire recent literature of the subject (as seen from our point of view) is

based on a defective concept of capital. See in *Quarterly Journal of Economics*, Vol. XVII, pp. 163-180 (November, 1902), article entitled "The 'Roundabout Process' in the Interest Theory," the author's criticism of Böhm-Bawerk's *Positive Theory*. All the recent "marginal productivity" interest theories are at fault, we venture to say, in trying to derive income from capital instead of deriving the amount of capital from rent.

Chapter 18. Relatively Fixed and Relatively Increasable Forms of Capital

1. Why not raise seals in California and fruit in Alaska?

2. Has the rainfall any relation to the density of population?

3. Has the isothermal line any relation to the number of millionaires?

4. What physical reasons account for the greatness of ancient Egypt, of Venice, of Holland, of England, of the United States?

5. Is all land useful? Is all land wealth?

6 Is there a different term for land that is wealth and land that is not?

7. Are there different economic terms for hewn and unhewn blocks of stone? What makes the difference?

> Note.—A meritorious though fragmentary essay to rethink the old conception of natural resources and to express them in new terms, is *Natural Economy*, by A. H. Gibson, 1901, reviewed by the writer in *Journal of Political Economy*, March, 1902.

Chapter 19. Saving and Production as Affected by the Rate of Interest

1. The savings of the people of the United States are nearly a billion dollars a year. What and where are they?

2. What are the main social conditions necessary to saving?

3. What influence has commercial morality on saving?

4. Do savings-banks and insurance companies stimulate saving, or do they exist because of a disposition to save?

5. What influence has the formation of joint-stock companies on saving?

6. Will you save more or less if the rate of interest falls?

7. Distinguish between hoarding and saving.

8. A woman cut the wool from a sheep's back, spun and wove it by old hand-methods, and within twenty-four hours wore the dress made of it. Is more or less time needed in production with the best machinery and processes?

9. Ricardo said that on account of the cheapness of food in America there was less temptation to employ machines than in England, where food was high. What is the fact about this temptation in America?

> NOTE.—The older abstinence theory of interest is given by F. A. Walker, *Political Economy*, Secs. 87-93. A noteworthy advance was the able article, by T. N. Carver, in *Quarterly Journal of Economics*, Vol. VIII, p. 40 (1893), "The Place of Abstinence in the Theory of Interest." A number of writers have written (fallaciously, in our judgment) on the "fallacy of saving," arguing that the capital-market easily becomes glutted; the contrary view is well presented by Cassel, *The Nature and Necessity of Interest* (1903), pp. 96-157, in chapters on what he calls "The Demand for Waiting," and "The Supply of Waiting."

CHAPTER 20. LABOR AND CLASSES OF LABORERS

1. Is dancing labor? Is the dancing of a dancing-master labor? If he would rather dance than eat, is it labor?

2. Enumerate some kinds of labor necessary to produce bread.

3. "Washing of clothes is unproductive labor; therefore as little of it should be done as possible." Criticize the argument.

4. Would you say that differences in ability at manual trades are due to practice or to native talent? If to both, in what proportion?

5. Do sons usually follow the father's trade? Is it more or less common than formerly for them to do so?

6. Do you know from personal observation whether a Mexican, a German, or an American, is the best workman?

7. What important personal traits are needed to make a man an efficient market-gardener?

8. Which would be of the greatest economic advantage, to increase by 50% the intelligence, the physical strength, or the integrity of the workers of this country?

CHAPTER 21. THE SUPPLY OF LABOR

1. Has the principle of the survival of the fittest any influence on the population

of America?

2. What limits the number of wild rabbits? Of tame pigeons? Do the same influences act in the case of men?

3. What other influences affect population?

4. What relation is there between population and mountains, temperature and water-supply?

5. It has been said that the supply of labor is fixed by biologic laws. Is it therefore not subject to economic influences?

6. What application do you think the principle of diminishing returns has to the question of population?

7. What is meant by the standard of life?

> NOTE.—The subject of population generally is discussed under the name of "The Malthusian Doctrine" and much space is given to it in the texts. So much useless controversy has been occasioned by the ambiguities of Malthus's argument that it seemed best not to introduce this difficulty into the text. The subject is discussed with broadest view by A. T. Hadley, *Economics*, Secs. 47-60. The writer attempted to make a judicial study of Malthus and his work in *Versuch einer Bevölkerungslehre*, Jena, 1894, and sought to put the discussion on higher ground in an article in the *Yale Review*, August, 1898, "The Essay of Malthus, a Centennial Review."

CHAPTER 22. CONDITIONS FOR EFFICIENT LABOR

1. Is hunger the cause of food?

2. Is there any relation between a republican form of government and the growth of manufactures.

3. What are the necessary conditions to the building of a house: (*a*) natural forces; (*b*) changes in material things; (*c*) human activities; (*d*) social conditions?

4. Is the public school system an economic factor? Where among the four preceding heads would you classify it?

5. From an economic standpoint, can we say that robbery really reduces the wealth in existence?

6. When does an industrious man stop working on his own farm, and why?

7. With a given number of workers, what may be causes of differences in the labor-supply?

8. Would men work better if they ate more?

9. What moral agencies increase the efficiency of labor?

10. Is there a strong selfish motive for men to increase their efficiency in most industries? How effective is it?

11. What effect has republican government on the efficiency of labor?

12. Why is the variety of occupations greater or less than formerly? What is influencing the change?

13. What cases have you seen where great skill came from practice?

14. What gain is it for men to work together instead of singly?

15. With increasing division of labor is there greater or less opportunity for the payment of laborers according to the piece-wage plan?

16. Discuss the following statement: Under the piece-work system the foreman looks out for the quality and the operative for the quantity of the work; under the time-wage system the foreman looks out for the quantity and the laborer for the quality of the work.

17. What remedy has the foreman for an inefficient laborer working under the time-wage system?

18. Is time- or piece-work best adapted to the following kinds of laborers: coal-miners, coopers, farm-hands, printers, engravers, shoe-factory hands, railroad brakemen, telegraph operators?

Chapter 23. The Law of Wages

1. What is the effect of free common schools on the comparative wages of skilled and of unskilled laborers?

2. What would be the effect of technical and industrial schools on the wages of artisans?

3. If a man is not content with $2 a day, why does he not do work that is paid $5 a day?

4. What is the effect on wages of differences in the danger, pleasurableness, social distinction, expense of preparation, of occupation?

5. If women are paid less than men for the same work, why are men employed at all?

6. What is the difference between these definitions: wages is the share of labor; wages is the payment by one man to another for his services?

7. If the supply of labor of any class were to be decreased 10% would wages rise in like proportion?

8. Since under the piece-work system a man is paid only for what he does, is there any reason for discharging a workman employed under this plan whose efficiency falls below the average?

Chapter 24. The Relation of Labor to Value

1. May a singer of songs or a mixer of drinks be called a productive laborer?

2. Are fine products high in price because wages are high, or vice versa?

3. Is common, unskilled labor "scarce" (in any reasonable sense of the word) in China? in the United States?

4. Can a manufacturer pay the same to laborers if the product will be marketed next year, as he can if it is to be marketed to-morrow? If so, how is the value of the labor adjusted to its product?

> NOTE.—An able discussion of the effect of discounting in the sale of labor in the market is given by Böhm-Bawerk, *Positive Theory of Capital*, pp. 313-318 *et seq.*; see also Wieser, *Natural Value*, numerous passages. The changes in industrial organization are treated with historic insight by Hadley, *Economics*, Secs. 341-354. F. W. Taussig's *Wages and Capital* (1896) gives a sympathetic interpretation of the wage-fund doctrine; the work is especially valuable for its excellent review of the history of the subject and for the chapters analyzing the modern industrial process.

Chapter 25. The Wage System and its Results

1. Why has machinery changed the relations of workman to master?

2. In what ways does labor get paid for its share, and who pays it?

3. Will a day's work of a common laborer buy more to-day than it would a half century ago? Why?

4. Are the opportunities for workmen to rise to the rank of masters as great as formerly?

5. Are wages independent of the other kinds of income?

Chapter 26. Machinery and Labor

1. Do you think that the amount of work is reduced by new machinery? Point out ambiguities in the question.

2. What is the difference to the workman whether he becomes more efficient or works with a better machine?

3. Is the work of any kind fixed in quantity? What would cause it to change?

4. What kinds of laborers were thrown out of employment by the invention of the type-writer? What kinds of labor found employment as a result of its invention?

Was the net result a gain or a loss of employment?

5. Answer the same questions with regard to the invention of railroads, mowing-, binding-, and threshing-machines; or the new roller-process of flour milling.

6. Can you describe from your own experience any example of readjustment of labor due to introduction of new machinery?

Chapter 27. Trade-unions

1. Does it make any difference in the permanence of an increase of wages brought about by a strike, whether the employer is one of the more successful or one of the less successful in that business?

2. Is there any similarity between the methods of trade-unions and the etiquette of the medical and the legal professions?

3. If you were an officer of a trade-union, would you begin a strike when trade was good or when it was poor?

4. If you can do more work in two hours than in one, can you do more continuously in sixteen consecutive hours than in eight?

5. What determines the maximum study-time for the earnest student?

6. If as much is produced in a general eight-hour day, who benefits?

7. If production is reduced one fourth by shorter hours, is "work made" to that degree for the unemployed?

8. If all day-laborers should agree to work with one hand tied behind them, would their wages go up or down? Would it be good or bad for the whole class of laborers?

Chapter 28. Production and the Combination of the Factors

1. What is production? Does the economic idea of production conflict with the physical principle that matter cannot be created?

2. Is it production to buy fifty cents' worth of yarn and knit a pair of socks worth twenty-five cents if you enjoy doing it? If you do not enjoy it?

3. Give examples of factors of production.

4. What factors of production must be combined by a savage to produce a canoe?

5. Outline the combination of factors that has produced New York bread made

from Minnesota wheat.

6. What is the largest manufacturing establishment in your home town? Would a number of smaller establishments of the same sort and with the same aggregate capacity succeed as well? Why?

7. Have you observed the growth of any local industry from a small beginning to large proportions? If so, how do you account for it?

8. Would you prefer to begin your business career with a large company or with a small merchant? Why?

9. Through what historic stages has production passed?

10. Give examples of the industrial advantages of America as compared with Europe.

Chapter 29. Business Organization and the Enterpriser's Function

1. What is the relative importance of organization in sawing wood, building houses, running a small store, or a large factory?

2. Which wins the battle: the general, the soldiers, or the armament?

3. What determines whether a crop is poor or good: the ground, the weather, or the farmer?

4. Why do some businesses give increasing returns as they grow?

5. One has said: "The natural differences in powers and aptitudes are certainly not greater than are natural differences in stature." Is this sound in an economic sense?

6. Who runs the business in a large store owned by a large family? Who has the risk?

7. Who is the enterpriser in a stock company where there is a superintendent elected by a board of directors, themselves elected by shareholders with one vote per share?

8. Who is the employer in a coöperative cooper-shop whose superintendent is elected by the workmen?

9. Has "a good chance in life" much to do with success?

10. What are the chief elements of business success?

11. Is modern business competition a competition of men only?

QUESTIONS AND CRITICAL NOTES 429

CHAPTER 30. COST OF PRODUCTION

1. What is the cost of a good you have made entirely with your own labor?

2. What is the difference to the employer between rent, interest, and wages as items of cost?

3. Is there anything in common between "cost, the onerous exertion necessary to get goods," and cost as the money expenses of production?

4. Why does a merchant engage in one business rather than in another?

5. When prices fall, what determines which factories shall close, and which workmen shall be discharged?

6. Does the value of a product conform to the capital that has been put into it.

> NOTE.—For a fuller treatment of the more recent view of the subject, see Smart, pp. 64-83; Wieser, *Natural Value*, pp. 171-214; Böhm-Bawerk, *Positive Theory of Capital*, pp. 179-189, 223-234. The defects of such revisions as that attempted by Alfred Marshall are pointed out in *Quarterly Journal of Economics*, Vol. XV, pp. 432-452, article "The Passing of the Old Rent Concept."

CHAPTER 31. THE LAW OF PROFITS

1. Business being poor, one employer is making good profits; how different will be the wages he pays from those paid by the unsuccessful employer?

2. How many of the men you know at the head of large businesses started life poor?

3. Was the rise in fortune due most often to chance, inheritance of wealth, or exceptional ability and power of work?

4. How should the income of an inventor be classified, as wages or profits?

5. Are the profits of the employer deducted from wages? Are the high wages of skilled labor deducted from the wages of unskilled?

CHAPTER 32. PROFIT-SHARING, PRODUCERS' AND CONSUMERS' COÖPERATION

1. Describe any case of profit-sharing you may have seen in operation.

2. Is advertising of any social service or is its sole purpose to divert trade from one merchant to another?

3. In what ways are retail stores wasteful in their expenditures? Can this be avoided?

4. If you have seen a coöperative store in operation tell what was its success.

5. Are you willing to pay more for goods in order to have a choice of stores?

Chapter 33. Monopoly Profits

1. How is the blacksmith free to compete with the physician and how not? In what sense have we assumed that competition exists?

2. Is there competition between the owner of good land and the owner of poor land?

3. Has the owner of a poor gold-mine a monopoly? Has the owner of a rich mine a monopoly?

4. Does the ownership of land give a monopoly? The ownership of a horse?

5. In what sense is a street-railway a monopoly? What is the value of its franchise?

6. Why does the public consent to grant patents or public franchises?

7. If one company controlled all the petroleum in the world, what would it consider in fixing the selling price?

8. Why will railroads issue commutation tickets?

> NOTE.—Of the very large recent literature bearing on monopoly and trusts may be mentioned as especially useful: J. B. Clark, *Control of Trusts*; R. T. Ely, *Monopolies and Trusts*; J. W. Jenks, *The Trust Problem* (a summary by the expert for the Industrial Commission); J. E. le Rossignol, *Monopolies, Past and Present*; *Report of the Chicago Conference on Trusts, 1899*; *Report of the United States Industrial Commission*, 19 vols., 1900-2 (a mine of information).

Chapter 34. Growth of Trusts and Combinations

1. What advantages are there to manufacturers in combination? What to the public?

2. What relation has improved transportation and other means of communication to trusts?

3. Name as many economic monopolies as you can.

4. What large trusts have recently been formed?

5. Does the public consider the growth of trusts to be good or bad? What do students of the question think of it?

QUESTIONS AND CRITICAL NOTES 431

Chapter 35. Effect of Trusts on Prices

1. Can the large factory always outsell the small one? Why?

2. Why are trusts or selling agreements formed?

3. Describe any agreement of which you know, made between merchants or manufacturers for the purpose of regulating prices. Did prices go up or down as a result?

4. Would it be a good thing for society if a trust made great economies in production, crowded out its smaller competitors, and maintained prices just where they were before, dividing among its shareholders the amounts saved?

5. How would the effects on society be different if prices were reduced by better organization and the prevention of waste?

6. Is it good public policy to allow a trust to undersell its smaller competitor in one district while it keeps up its prices elsewhere?

Chapter 36. Gambling, Speculation, and Promoters' Profits

1. Do you think that store-keepers fix the price of the produce they buy of the farmers? If so, to what extent?

2. Can brokers fix the price of grain on the market? How, and to what extent?

3. What is speculation? Give examples you have seen.

4. Were they, on the whole, good for the community?

5. Give other examples showing the difference between a gambling-house and an insurance company?

6. Is the immorality of betting based on economic grounds?

7. Ought lotteries to be permitted by law?

8. Ought speculation in mines to be permitted by law?

9. Ought the profits of the farmer from a sudden rise in the value of wheat be confiscated to the public?

> Note.—The ablest study of the subject is by H. C. Emery, *Speculation on the Stock and Produce Exchanges of the United States*, in Columbia University Studies in History, Economics, and Public Law, Vol. VII, No. 2, 1896.

Chapter 37.   Crises and Industrial Depressions

1. What is a financial crisis? An industrial depression?

2. Define the expressions "over-production" and "under-consumption."

3. In a period of depression is there less money than usual in the country? In the banks?

4. If there were twice as much money in the world, would panics take place?

5. Before a financial crisis how are prices, high or low? After a panic?

6. What economic changes occurred in your own community in the panic of 1893-4, or in the years 1903-4?

7. Do people save more in good times or hard times?

Chapter 38.   Private Property and Inheritance

1. If the law permits certain classes to be fleeced without redress, is wealth thereby reduced?

2. What are vested rights? Do they ever stand in the way of progress? Examples.

3. Is it right that the lucky inventor of a popular toy should make $100 a day from it?

4. Is it right that an inventor should by patent laws be able to keep the profits of his business high?

5. Do you know of any father who created more wealth because he could bequeath it to his son?

6. Does the son work as hard when he inherits his father's wealth?

7. What is the effect of private property on saving?

8. If capital is needed in production why is the question of justice raised when its use is paid for?

Chapter 39.   Income and Social Service

1. What is it to earn a living? How many people do it?

2. When is a man poor?

3. Would it be a good thing if the boot-black got a dollar a shine?

4. Does luck have greater influence on business success in an old country or a new one?

5. Ditto in agriculture, mining, commerce, or manufactures?

QUESTIONS AND CRITICAL NOTES

6. A rare coin and a piece of land sold for the same price one year, and the next year both sold for double the amount. Was there an unearned increment in both cases, and of the same kind?

7. If rewards were equal, what would determine the choice of work?

> NOTE.—The most important contributions to the theory of consumption have been made by S. N. Patten in his numerous writings, among them: *The Consumption of Wealth* (1889); *Theory of Dynamic Economics* (1892); *The Theory of Prosperity* (1902). A number of the ideas are well restated in more simple terms by E. T. Devine in *Economics*, especially pp. 375-396, and 73-111 (applies to chapter 41).

CHAPTER 40. WASTE AND LUXURY

1. Can we determine what luxury is, or give the notion definiteness?

2. Do you feel a sense of injustice when you read of a millionaire's ball if you are not a millionaire?

3. Can you excuse the sense of injustice felt by the hungry man when he sees you wear patent-leather shoes and kid gloves?

4. Under private property, can men complain of the use made by others of their wealth on the ground merely that it was unwise?

5. Is luxury necessary to give employment to labor?

6. Is the spendthrift the best friend of labor?

7. Ought legislation attempt to prevent luxury, or can public opinion affect it?

8. Is smoking high-priced cigars economically justifiable, assuming that the smoker is wealthy and does not injure his health thereby?

9. Wines, balls, pensions are said to be good because they put money into circulation. Criticize.

10. What is the difference between the consumption of wealth and its destruction?

11. In what ways can a piece of iron be consumed, economically speaking?

12. Was the great Chicago fire, which led to the rebuilding of the city, a good thing economically?

CHAPTER 41. REACTION OF CONSUMPTION ON PRODUCTION

1. What are complementary goods? Give some illustrations.

2. Can people live on the future, consuming in advance of production? How is it with the nation in time of war?

3. Does economic theory throw any light on the ethics of miserliness?

4. It is said that the demand of the day-laborer for cheap white shirts has reduced the wages of the women who make them. Criticize.

5. What effect on wealth would a change of climate have, whereby the consumption of coal would be decreased?

6. If manna fell from heaven daily in a climate where clothing and shelter were unnecessary, what effect on wealth would result?

Chapter 42. Distribution of the Social Income

1. What different ideas does the expression "distribution of wealth" suggest to you?

2. What different methods of obtaining an income have you noted among the men you know?

3. How can a yard of cloth be said to be distributed to the labor and capital producing it?

4. If two men of equal skill go fishing together, how would they find a rule for dividing the catch?

5. If one is more skilful or stronger, or owns the boat and the tackle, how would it affect the division? Would any rule be attainable?

6. If socialism reduced the total product, would it still be desirable because of the better distribution?

7. What classes of thinkers are most inclined to take up socialism? (Classes considered socially, industrially, as to race, as to economic and historical training.)

Chapter 43. Survey of the Theory of Value

1. Mention any cases you can think of where merely changing the place of things added to their value; or changing their form; or where the mere lapse of time added to the value of the thing.

2. What effect on wages and interest does the bringing in of foreign capital have?

3. If, through greater efficiency of labor, wealth increases, which share benefits?

4. What would be the effect on wages, interest, and land rent of a sudden addition of rich land to the country?

QUESTIONS AND CRITICAL NOTES 435

5. What would be the effect on interest, land rent, and wages of a great increase of national saving?

6. What concern have the poor in the abundance of capital? The rich in the abundance of labor?

7. Walker says that the laborer gets what is left after the other shares are deducted according to their law; wages are the residual claimant. Are the other shares independent of wages?

8. Can wage-earners be shut out from all advantages in the land of the country?

9. Are high wages and high interest seen to go together? Give such examples as you think of.

10. Do improvements in agriculture increase or decrease the rent of land?

CHAPTER 44. FREE COMPETITION AND STATE ACTION

1. What is economic freedom? How different from political freedom?

2. Does the presence of a policeman increase or diminish competition among men?

3. Are most positive laws intended to hinder competition or make it freer?

4. In what ways does competition reduce the total product?

5. Is custom a better regulator of economic action than competition?

6. Criticize the doctrine of economic harmony, giving examples.

CHAPTER 45. USE, COINAGE, AND VALUE OF MONEY

1. If gold were to become as plentiful as iron, would it be worth more or less than iron?

2. Some say Providence has indicated gold and silver as the materials for money. How has this been done?

3. Why does nearly all the gold produced in California leave the state? What keeps any of it there?

4. Who makes coins? Would jewelers make better ones?

5. When gold comes out of the mine is the gain to the community greater or less than when the same value of grain is harvested?

6. Does gold cost the day-laborer as much in California as in New York?

7. What are the principal things besides money uses that cause a demand for gold and silver?

8. The mint price of an ounce of gold, .900 fine, is alike at San Francisco and Philadelphia, $18.604. Why is gold ever shipped from California to New York?

9. Give examples of things that increase the demand for money.

10. Note any habits of friends that result in their carrying more or less money than others of the same income.

11. What determines the amount of money needed by different persons, towns, states, and nations?

12. When goods are exchanged for money or money for goods, what is the gain?

13. On an isolated island would it make any difference as to the value of money if there were but one gold-mine or several competing ones, supposing that the output were the same?

CHAPTER 46. TOKEN COINAGE AND GOVERNMENT PAPER MONEY

1. Define legal-tender as applied to money. What is meant by fiat money?

2. Show the difference between convertible and inconvertible money.

3. The government of the island of Guernsey having no money, issued paper-notes to pay for the building of a market. They circulated and were gradually taken up as the market earned its cost, during ten years. When they were all redeemed and burned, the island had the market free of cost. Explain how this could be done. (This is from Sumner's *Problems in Political Economy*.)

CHAPTER 47. THE STANDARD OF DEFERRED PAYMENTS

1. If every piece of money should miraculously be doubled in a night, whose interests would be affected?

2. Is the fact of one man's gain and another man's loss by chance of any economic or political importance?

3. What gives rise to the belief sometimes held that money is an invariable standard of value?

4. Is there anything in the nature of mining that keeps the ratio of the supply of gold and silver nearly uniform?

5. Is the value of gold and silver due to the action of government?

6. Does the principle of the substitution of goods have any bearing on the value of metals under bimetallism?

QUESTIONS AND CRITICAL NOTES 437

7. Note carefully, and indicate the different meanings of bimetallism; of demonetization.

8. What is the extent of the influence one nation can have on the ratio of the two precious metals?

9. If money wages are higher and general prices are lower, how is the laborer affected? Is this due to the appreciation of money?

10. Can you get a kind of money that will make the things that are sold, dearer, and the things that are bought, cheaper?

11. What are the main reasons given for the ratio of 16 to 1?

CHAPTER 48. BANKING AND CREDIT

1. What does a bank do for a community?

2. What are the sources of income to a bank?

3. Can a bank that issues its own notes afford to lend cheaper than the ordinary capitalist?

4. What is discount and deposit?

5. Do all banks issue notes? Why?

6. What is the function of a clearing-house?

7. If there are twenty banks in a town and no clearing-house, how many collections would have to be made by all the banks daily assuming that each day depositors of each bank receive checks on the other nineteen banks?

8. Does a clearing-house enable the banks that belong to it to get along with a smaller cash reserve?

9. What element of security is furnished by clearing-houses during panics?

CHAPTER 49. TAXATION IN ITS RELATION TO VALUE

1. Does taxation ever infringe on the right of private property?

2. What is it a citizen gets in return for his taxes?

3. Is there any relation between the taxes paid and the benefits secured from government?

4. A recent newspaper item says: "This is the year real estate is assessed. Turn the cow loose in the front yard, tear down the fence, make things look generally dilapidated, for it will be money in your pocket." What does this indicate regarding taxation?

5. The parts of an estate divided into fifteen equal shares by expert real estate agents were soon after assessed variously from $900 to $2850 for purposes of taxation. What does this indicate? (From Sumner's *Problems*.)

6. In what ways may we understand the proposition that taxation should be proportioned to ability?

7. Can taxation be used to secure some of the profits of large corporations?

Chapter 50. The General Theory of International Trade

1. Is it bad policy to let the people of Palo Alto spend money in San Francisco for things that could be produced at home?

2. Pensions are defended as putting money in circulation. Is this like any tariff arguments you have heard?

3. Is it bad policy for California to buy New England manufactures?

4. If there were no legal bar to a tariff between the states, would a tariff probably be imposed? If so, would it be a wise measure?

5. A nation with n dollars in circulation has to pay a war indemnity of n dollars to another country having the same circulation, how much money will each then have, and what will be the effect on prices, foreign trade, rate of exchange? (From Davenport.)

6. If large shipments of wheat are made to England, will bills of exchange on London be higher or lower in New York?

7. What effect on exchange has the holding of American bonds abroad?

Chapter 51. The Protective Tariff

1. If all trade is exchange do not the members of a trust reduce their income when they raise the price of their products by artificial agreement?

2. Is there any likeness between trade-unions and tariffs? Between tariffs and factory legislation?

3. Can it be of advantage to trade freely with one nation if general free trade is bad?

4. Who gained when Hawaiian sugar (before annexation) was admitted free of duty, while other sugar was taxed?

5. If it would pay us to admit goods free, may we be justified in taxing them to force concessions from the other country?

QUESTIONS AND CRITICAL NOTES 439

6. What have you read this year about reciprocity?

CHAPTER 52. OTHER PROTECTIVE SOCIAL AND LABOR LEGISLATION

1. Is granting patents an interference with trade similar to tariffs?

2. What reasons are given in justification of laws closing barbershops on Sundays?

3. Can a person owning a lot on a residence street of a city erect a glue-factory on it?

4. What have you noted as to the benefits or hardships of restricting child labor in factories?

5. Are men less able to bargain for the loan of money than for other things?

6. Can law fix the rate of interest at any point desired? If so, then why not at zero; if not, then why fix any maximum rate of interest?

7. Are interest rates changing in America?

8. In what ways is the rate of interest affected by the rise or fall of the value of money?

CHAPTER 53. PUBLIC OWNERSHIP OF INDUSTRY

1. What are municipal franchises? Where are they?

2. What kinds of municipal industries have you seen in operation? How successful were they?

3. What are the main arguments for and against the city ownership and control of gas and waterworks?

4. What troubles arise from city politics?

5. Name the industries that are owned and controlled by towns and cities of which you have a personal knowledge.

6. Which of them are most satisfactory in your judgment? Which the least so?

7. What is the public sentiment in your home community as to the ownership of industries by the town or city?

8. What forms of state activity favor survival of unfit men and bad traits of character? What forms help the fittest to survive?

> NOTE.—For exhaustive and well-arranged references on all aspects of municipal control and municipal ownership see

R. C. Brooks, *Bibliography of Municipal Problems*, pp. 157-169, in *Municipal Affairs*, Vol. V, No. 1 (March, 1901).

Chapter 54. Railroads and Industry

1. Why is transportation a greater problem in the United States than in Europe?

2. Show in what way natural waterways have determined the location of leading cities in America.

3. Give examples of cities whose growth has been caused by railroads.

4. What interests favor and what oppose the building of an isthmian canal?

5. Mention in order of economic importance four things that would happen if all American railroads were suddenly to be destroyed.

6. What cases have you seen where the railways impose unjustly on the public?

7. Give instances you have seen or heard of where two shippers paid different rates for the same service.

8. Why should preachers get half-fare rates?

9. If your neighbor rides on a pass and you pay your fare, are you helping to pay for his ride?

10. Do you know any large cities that are more favorable shipping-points than neighboring towns? Give reasons.

Chapter 55. The Public Nature of Railroads

1. What legal rights do the builders of a railroad have that are not enjoyed by all citizens?

2. Can you see any clear distinction between the public nature of a railroad and of a horse and carriage?

3. What harm can there be in the acceptance of passes by judges, legislators, and other public officials?

4. Ought the law prohibit the sale of tickets by "scalpers"?

5. Who has the greater political power, the president of the Pennsylvania Railroad, or the governor of that state?

QUESTIONS AND CRITICAL NOTES

CHAPTER 56.   PUBLIC POLICY AS TO CONTROL OF INDUSTRY

1. What effect would it have if the state should make laborers work for unsuccessful employers at lower wages than for successful ones?

2. Or should reduce rents for the less capable merchants and manufacturers?

3. Is there any rule for determining the limits of state interference?

4. Why does the question of the control of the railways in the interest of the public present especial difficulties in America?

CHAPTER 57.   FUTURE TREND OF VALUES

1. Make a list of the things discussed in this course that tend toward improving the average condition of men.

2. Make a list of those that tend toward worse conditions for the mass of men.

3. State what kinds of material agents will probably increase in value relative to other kinds, giving reasons.

4. State what to your mind are three important economic problems whose answer is most uncertain, giving reasons.

5. If you had the power, what single public measure that you believe would be practicable and effective would you put on the statute books, in order to make a juster division of the social income? Give reasons.

> NOTE.—On the subject of this chapter, see Devine, *Economics*, ch. XVII (disposition of the social surplus); Jenks, *The Trust Problem*, pp. 190-211; Marshall, Bk. VI, chs. XI and XII.

Index

A

Ability *3, 22, 95, 131, 132, 133, 134, 144, 154, 156, 193, 195, 196, 197, 198, 199, 200, 211, 214, 218, 221, 223, 226, 227, 238, 247, 249, 251, 268, 272, 276, 277, 308, 309, 347, 398, 400, 403, 407, 408, 409, 413, 423, 429, 438*
Abstinence *121, 122, 123, 124, 160, 273, 423*
Accidental destruction *279*
Acquisition vs. social production *190*
Adam Smith *24, 78, 86, 134, 310, 311, 352, 357, 403, 405*
Advantages of large industry *235*
Agents of production *68, 129, 306*
Age of machinery *173, 180*
Agricultural classes *85, 333*
Agricultural stage *192*
A. H. Gibson *422*
Alfred Marshall *417, 418, 419, 429*
Alternative cost *201*
Alternative uses *204*
America *8, 37, 44, 45, 62, 64, 66, 69, 78, 86, 115, 116, 122, 123, 141, 143, 145, 147, 156, 166, 170, 171, 173, 177, 181, 186, 192, 193, 198, 199, 216, 218, 225, 230, 255, 258, 269, 285, 289, 310, 311, 321, 331, 333, 334, 340, 349, 351, 354, 355, 360, 361, 362, 363, 364, 365, 366, 369, 371, 375, 379, 383, 384, 385, 388, 389, 401, 403, 404, 406, 408, 409, 412, 415, 423, 424, 428, 439, 440, 441*
American Federation of Labor *180, 186*
American Revolution *4, 182, 310, 349*
American standard of living *141*
Andrew Carnegie *273, 276, 285*
Animals *1, 2, 6, 7, 10, 33, 37, 38, 77, 119, 137, 138, 161, 230, 382, 384*
Army rations *145*
A. S. Johnson *416*
Assignats *326, 327*
A. T. Hadley *424*
Austrian economists *414*

INDEX 443

Authoritative distribution *296, 297*

B

Balance of imports *355*
Balance of trade *356, 359*
Bank-notes *258, 321, 326, 327, 337, 338, 339, 340, 341, 342, 376*
Banks and credit *83*
Barter *23, 43, 75, 76, 82, 83, 84, 86, 107, 225, 330, 415*
Bequest *30, 269, 270, 273*
Bets *246, 247*
Bimetallism *333, 334, 436, 437*
Biology *134*
Boycott *184*
Broadest principle of value *305*

C

Canals *61, 68, 161, 375, 384, 386*
Capital Concept *86, 88, 415, 420*
Capitalistic *81, 86, 88, 186, 210, 225, 331, 419*
Capitalization *40, 54, 55, 74, 89, 92, 93, 94, 95, 97, 103, 106, 108, 109, 110, 111, 125, 251, 252, 258, 301, 302, 346, 378, 420*
Capitalizing of franchises *96*
Capital stock *86, 95, 338*
Capital sum *85, 87, 89, 90, 91, 92, 93, 95, 96, 106, 113*
Cash balance of international trade *354*
Cassel *423*
Cecil Rhodes *273*
Changes in industry *157, 169*
Changes in real wages *170*
Changing occupations *156*
Characteristics of value *189*
Charitable distribution *295, 296*
Cheating and gambling *246*
Child-labor legislation *370*
Choice of goods *19, 289, 292*
City ownership *439*
C. J. Bullock *412*
Class legislation *223, 275*
Closed shop *183*
Coal deposits *66*
Coal strike of 1902 *185*
Coal-supply *66*
Coinage *314, 315, 316, 323, 340, 376, 377, 435, 436*
Collective bargaining *182*
Collective enjoyment *297*

Collectivism *401*
Combination and Wages *185*
Combination of factors *427*
Combination of the Factors *191, 192*
Commercial monopoly *225*
Commercial paper *99, 340*
Commissions to Control Railroads *393*
Commodity-money theory *328*
Common denominator of values *79, 81*
Communism *139, 267*
Comparative costs *351, 352, 353*
Competition and Custom *308*
Competitive distribution *298*
Competitive price *42, 227, 240, 309, 311, 369*
Complementary agents *58, 59*
Compulsory distribution *294, 296*
Condition of continuing profits *214*
Conditions Favorable to Saving *122*
Conditions for Efficient *144, 424*
Conditions of Economic Wealth *37*
Consumers' choice *286, 287*
Consumers' Coöperation *215, 219, 372, 429*
Consumers' League *288*
Consumption Goods *13, 20, 31, 32, 36, 37, 39, 53, 55, 56, 57, 58, 59, 75, 90, 93, 98, 101, 106, 107, 118, 119, 121, 124, 129, 163, 189, 191, 204, 211, 239, 257, 275, 288, 300, 301*
Continental notes *326*
Contracting out *372*
Contract Interest *98, 103, 107, 109, 110, 264, 301*
Contract rent *42, 43, 45, 60, 81, 111, 302*
Contract wages *152, 154, 161, 166, 209, 212, 215*
Control of Trusts *238, 430*
Corporate incomes *97*
Cost of operation *125*
Cost of Production *41, 201, 202, 203, 227, 241, 304, 308, 317, 323, 346, 361, 372, 429*
Crises and Industrial Depressions *253, 432*

D

Death-rate *141, 142*
Decreasing death-rate *142*
Defense of property *274*
Deferred payments *331*
Definition of profit-sharing *215*
Degrees of durableness *36*
Demand curve *20*
Deposit and Discount *337, 338*

Destruction of Wealth *61, 279, 280, 281*
Development of natural resources *274*
Development of the Concept *52*
Differences in wages *156*
Differential Advantages *55, 57*
Diminishing Returns *46, 48, 50, 51, 52, 53, 59, 106, 109, 114, 136, 137, 138, 158, 159, 202, 384, 424*
Directive ability *193*
Discounting of commercial paper *99*
Discovery of mines *78*
Discussion of taxation *349*
Distinction between productive and unproductive labor *191*
Distribution of the Social Income *293, 434*
Division of Labor *148, 149, 150, 193, 196, 234, 350, 425*
Doctrine of Comparative Costs *351*
Doctrine of Population *136, 137, 138*
Durable agents *35, 36, 45, 94, 95, 101, 124, 283, 301, 302*
Durable goods *32, 36, 39, 40, 45, 46*

E

Economic and contract rent *42*
Economic Aspects of Public Ownership *376*
Economic diminishing returns *47, 48, 114*
Economic freedom *308, 309, 310, 311, 312, 313, 435*
Economic Harmony *312, 435*
Economic Harmony through Competition *310*
Economic issues *264*
Economic law *53, 152*
Economic monopoly *225*
Economic Motives *6, 8, 9, 350, 412*
Economic production *163, 189, 190, 305*
Economic rent *42, 43, 45, 60, 81, 210, 263, 264*
Economic wages *152, 153, 161, 210*
Economist's Standpoint *203*
Edwin Cannan *415, 417*
Efficiency of labor *144, 147, 148, 192, 289, 356, 424, 425, 434*
Enjoyable goods *15, 31, 33, 35, 36, 39, 40, 53, 55, 92, 110*
Enterpriser *166, 193, 197, 201, 202, 203, 204, 207, 209, 210, 211, 212, 214, 217, 218, 220, 226, 228, 245, 247, 249, 264, 276, 286, 304, 358, 365, 378, 428*
Equality of efficiency *308*
Equation of international exchange *352*
Evasion of legal rate *100*
Examples of Public Ownership *374*
Exchange in a Market *22, 414*
Expression of wealth *86, 88*
Extensive utilization *50*

Extreme socialism 275

F

Factory laws 370, 371
Factory legislation 370, 372, 438
Factory system 69, 178, 371
Fallacy of luxury 257, 283
Fallacy of waste 257, 282
Favorable balance of trade 356, 359, 360
Favored classes 273
Ferdinand Lasalle 303
Feudal estates 84
Fiat-money theory 328
Fixed charges 125, 209, 219
Fluctuation of profits 212
Food supply 52, 137
Foreign exchange of money 353
Foreign exchanges 354, 360
Forms of ownership 266
Forms of Taxation 313, 345
Franchises 72, 96, 224, 225, 379, 380, 388, 400, 430, 439
Francis A. Walker 304
Frederick Engels 303
Free and gratuitous 316, 323
Free coinage 316, 333, 335
Free Competition 152, 156, 168, 223, 238, 298, 308, 309, 312, 367, 368, 372, 373, 388, 390, 435
Free goods 13, 56, 57, 59, 60, 70, 113, 114, 146, 163, 177, 377, 417
Free or gratuitous coinage 316
Free-silver movement 334
Free-silver Movement in America 334
Free trade 311, 357, 358, 362, 363, 366, 373, 438
Functional distribution 263, 293
Function of the state 313, 341
Fundamental use 318
Funded income 31
Future income 106, 110, 124
Future rents 63, 92, 93, 94, 98, 103, 104, 108, 109, 110, 119, 258
F. W. Taussig 426

G

Gambling 245, 246, 247, 248, 250, 251, 252, 290, 370, 431
Gambling vs. Insurance 245
Genealogy of value 204
General rate 156

INDEX 447

General Theory of International Trade *350, 438*
General use of money *81, 90*
George Rapp *196*
Gold discoveries *352*
Gold shipping point *354*
Gold standard *78, 334, 335*
Gold supplies *319, 322*
Government Paper Money *258, 323, 326, 327, 340, 436*
Grades of labor *131, 147, 156, 168, 204*
Granger stores *220*
Gratuitous coinage *317*
Great corporations *178, 244, 252*
Greenbacks *258, 327, 342, 419*
Gresham's law *325*
Gross and net rent *42*
Gross income *30*
Growth of manufactures *424*
Growth of state socialism *401*
Growth of Trusts *229, 430*

H

Happiness and character *292*
Henry Clews *276*
Henry George *303*
Herbert Spencer *377*
Hildebrand *420*
Historical diminishing returns *51, 52, 114*
History of Contract Rent *42*
Household industry in America *230*
H. R. Seager *412*
Human population *138*

I

Illegitimate speculation *252*
Impersonal distribution *305*
Incidence of taxation *347*
Income and Social Service *271, 432*
Income as a Flow of Goods *29*
Income as a Series of Gratifications *32*
Income from Personal Services *275*
Income from Property *271, 274*
Income of consumption goods *30*
Increase of population *117, 139, 140, 159, 283, 406*
Increasing Role *95*
Indirect Goods *35, 37, 40, 43, 53, 54, 55, 57, 59, 60, 102, 108, 301, 302, 305*

Individual income *303*
Industrial changes *77, 78, 173, 174, 310*
Industrial legislation *399, 400*
Industrial stage *192, 230*
Inequality of talents *134*
Inequality of wealth *271, 274*
Integration of industry *236*
Intensive margin *48, 49, 59*
Intentional destruction *279, 280, 281*
Interest contract *44, 87, 88, 105, 210, 302, 330*
Interest on Money Loans *98, 103, 421*
Intermediary in industry *211*
International Bimetallism *332, 333, 334*
International demand *353, 364*
International trade *350, 351, 353, 354, 355, 383*
International Trade as a Case of Exchange *350*
Interstate Commerce Act *390, 393, 394*
Iron law of wages *159, 171, 257*
Irving Fisher *415, 420*
Isolated exchange *23, 24*

J

J. B. Clark *418, 420, 430*
J. E. le Rossignol *430*
John Stuart Mill *115, 218, 264, 269*
J. R. Commons *417*
Just price *398*
J. W. Jenks *241, 430*

K

Kinds of abstinence *121*
Kinds of Monopoly *224*
Knights of Labor *180*

L

Labor and Classes of Laborers *128, 423*
Labor Legislation *370*
Labor of different grades *164*
Labor services *30, 331*
Labor theory of value *163, 164*
Laissez faire *377*
Land changes hands *45*
Land continues to be rented *86*
Large capital *51, 229, 365*
Large Industry *178, 181, 193, 199, 229, 234, 235*

INDEX 449

Large Production *51, 149, 229, 230, 231, 233, 235, 239, 240, 244, 251, 298, 337, 377, 378, 392*
Latin Union *333*
Law in relation to wealth *264*
Law of Diminishing Returns *46, 51, 59, 305, 306, 416, 417*
Law of Diminishing Utility *16, 318*
Law of inheritance *270*
Law of Value *155, 157, 239, 244, 305, 306, 308, 319*
Law of Wages *151, 152, 157, 158, 168, 305, 425*
Legal-tender *326, 327, 328, 340, 377, 436*
Legitimate chance *246*
Legitimate risk-taking *246*
Legitimate speculation *252*
Light-weight Coins *319, 323, 324*
Limitation of right *270*
L. M. Keasbey *421*
Long leases *44*
Long-time loans *99, 100, 102, 111, 331*
Lump of labor *176, 356*

M

Machinery and Labor *173, 426*
Malthusian Doctrine *424*
Manipulation of dividends *97*
Manual workers *277, 289*
Marginal labor *155*
Marginal pair *25, 26, 108*
Marginal Utility *16, 17, 18, 19, 20, 23, 47, 48, 49, 55, 56, 57, 58, 59, 60, 75, 78, 80, 108, 119, 130, 155, 158, 204, 205, 239, 247, 248, 301, 306, 308, 414*
Margin of advantage *25, 26, 248, 361, 364*
Margin of cultivation *48*
Margin of profits *203*
Margin of utilization *48, 49, 56, 57, 59, 65, 70*
Market price *24, 27, 28, 77, 103, 107, 108, 154, 202, 203, 224, 227, 244, 304, 308, 347*
Market Value *25, 28, 42, 55, 90, 92, 95, 96, 97, 153, 154, 164, 168, 190, 238, 252, 263, 325, 333, 346*
Material agents *39, 59, 138, 144, 151, 152, 159, 162, 163, 191, 209, 223, 286, 302, 376, 415, 441*
Material resources *144, 409*
Material Wants *6, 9*
Medium of exchange *75, 76, 77, 79, 80, 81, 103, 314, 315, 319, 329, 331*
Mercantile business *219*
Methods of remuneration *155*
Middle Ages *27, 42, 43, 44, 83, 84, 85, 89, 90, 111, 142, 147, 167, 173, 248, 255, 273, 285, 309, 310, 316, 321, 324, 351, 368, 402*
Modes of Earning Wages *153*

450   THE PRINCIPLES OF ECONOMICS

Money as a Tool in Exchange 75, 419
Money-changing 337, 338
Money cost 201, 202, 203, 204, 352, 384
Money defined 314
Money Economy 82, 86, 88, 113, 254, 255, 330, 419
Money market 102, 103, 124, 198, 421
Money theories of crises 258
Money use 77, 79, 80, 81, 83, 318, 324, 328, 329
Money value 316, 317, 323, 324, 325, 346, 353, 384
Monopoly and supply 238
Monopoly of labor 183, 187
Monopoly Price 187, 226, 227, 228, 239, 240, 308
Monopoly Profits 222, 227, 240, 379, 430
Morality 97, 221, 246, 284, 292, 312, 313, 369, 392, 396, 400, 402, 422
Moral qualities 133, 195, 290
Mortgages 86, 89, 99, 331
Movement of money 354, 355

N

Nail trust 242
National bimetallism 333, 334
National ownership 376
Natural Economy 83, 422
Natural law 311
Natural resources 37, 44, 50, 62, 67, 68, 69, 86, 116, 117, 136, 139, 147, 158, 159, 170, 192, 225, 287, 301, 351, 352, 361, 362, 364, 365, 405, 406, 407, 422
Nature and Claims of Protection 358
Nature of Monopoly 222
Nature of Personal Distribution 293
Nature of Production 189
Nature of Wages 151
Need of organization 181
Net income 30, 42, 95, 96, 110, 345
Non-material wants 9
Normal price 27, 28
No unit of labor 164
N. P. Gilman 216

O

Objective income 30, 32, 95
Objective Physical Conditions 144
Obligations of railroad 391
Oil Trust 241
One-sided competition 24, 243
Open shop 183

INDEX 451

Organization and the Enterpriser's Function *195, 428*
Organization of workers *180*
Oriental competition *193*

P

Paper Money *315, 326, 327, 328, 329, 338, 340*
Par of exchange *316, 353, 354*
Pastoral stage *192*
Permanent possession *40, 91*
Persistence of competition *243*
Personal Distribution *263, 264, 293, 294, 305, 387*
Personal incomes *264, 347*
Philosophy of natural law *310*
Physical differences *131*
Physiocratic school *302*
Political and Economic Power of Railroad *391*
Political Economy *1, 2, 3, 4, 5, 22, 53, 82, 130, 148, 159, 209, 280, 300, 302, 303, 305, 310, 311, 401, 411, 412, 417, 422, 423, 436*
Political Money *326, 327, 328, 329, 340*
Political monopoly *224*
Political security *122, 146*
Population in Human Society *138*
Precious Metals as Money *314*
Present and future goods *104, 107, 108*
Present and future wants *161*
Price changes *321*
Primary money *320, 321*
Primitive society *267, 288*
Private income *30, 262, 346*
Private Property *122, 139, 162, 166, 225, 263, 265, 266, 267, 268, 269, 270, 271, 274, 275, 284, 343, 368, 388, 402, 432, 433, 437*
Privileges of Railroad *388*
Producers' Coöperation *217, 219, 220*
Production and the Combination of the Factors *189, 427*
Production vs. welfare *290*
Productive labor *32*
Productivity of labor *158, 159, 160*
Profit-sharing *215, 216, 217, 220, 429*
Profits of promoter *251*
Progress of social control *402*
Progress of the Masses *170*
Property and wealth *264, 265*
Property in land *122, 267, 274*
Property tax *346*
Protective Social and Labor Legislation *367, 439*
Protective Tariff *170, 273, 274, 356, 357, 358, 359, 360, 361, 362, 373, 391, 438*

Pseudo-profits *212*
Psychic cost *201, 289, 352*
Psychic Income *29, 30, 32, 33, 36, 80, 92, 93, 109, 131, 152, 165, 203, 247, 293, 294, 297, 374, 415*
Public charity *369*
Public control *393, 396*
Public Control of Industry *398*
Public debts *100, 334*
Public interests *268, 342, 388, 390, 398*
Public nature of railroad *388*
Public Ownership *274, 369, 374, 375, 376, 377, 378, 379, 380, 381, 395, 401, 439*
Public Policy as to Control of Industry *396, 441*
Public utilities *72, 379*
Public wants *183, 344*
Purposes of Taxation *303, 343, 344, 438*

Q

Quantity Theory of Money *318, 319*

R

Radical socialism *401, 402*
Railroad *27, 31, 62, 94, 111, 125, 163, 176, 193, 198, 202, 232, 233, 236, 255, 256, 268, 277, 280, 375, 383, 384, 385, 386, 387, 388, 389, 390, 391, 392, 393, 394, 396, 398, 400, 405, 414, 418, 420, 425, 440*
Rate of contract *103, 109, 111*
Rate of Interest *91, 92, 93, 97, 98, 99, 100, 103, 104, 107, 110, 111, 118, 123, 125, 161, 168, 211, 212, 257, 342, 346, 353, 370, 407, 420, 421, 422, 439*
Ratio of international demand *353*
R. C. Brooks *viii, 440*
Real and nominal wages *152*
Real wages *152, 156, 170, 177, 372*
Reciprocal demand *22, 364*
Relation of Labor to Value *158, 163, 426*
Remuneration *134, 216*
Rent and wages *130, 151, 162*
Rent-charges *43, 89, 90, 91, 92*
Renting Contract *40, 43, 44, 45, 50, 63, 83, 84, 87, 105, 151, 330, 416*
Rent of labor *151*
Rent of wealth *263*
Replenishing agents *114*
Resultant of many qualities *133*
Rewarding talent *277*
Risk-taking *246, 248*
Roundabout Process *422*
Russell Sage *276*

INDEX 453

S

Sale and purchase *89, 401*
Saturation point for coinage *323*
Scale of increasableness *117*
Scarcity of common materials *113*
Scarcity of human services *134*
Scarcity of labor *134*
Seigniorage *316, 323, 324, 325, 326*
Self-interest *8, 9, 24, 139, 142, 311, 340, 368, 372*
Serfdom *167, 169, 294, 311*
Series of goods *19, 29*
Services and wages *156*
Short-time loans *99, 102, 331*
Silver as money *77*
Single-tax *303*
Single-tax theory of value *303*
Slavery *4, 9, 12, 38, 129, 139, 147, 167, 169, 170, 196, 294, 309, 349, 399*
Smart *414, 415, 429*
S. N. Patten *433*
Social amelioration *369*
Social burden *240*
Social classes *140*
Social Conditions *132, 146, 172, 267, 275, 422, 424*
Social control *394, 402, 403*
Social effects *178, 272, 285, 311, 363*
Social income *30, 171, 240, 294, 441*
Social institutions *8, 122, 140, 159, 191, 263, 399, 409*
Social institutions and personal incomes *263*
Socialism *134, 275, 297, 303, 344, 374, 401, 434*
Socialistic theory of value *303*
Socialists *299, 303, 401, 402, 405*
Social Legislation *367, 370, 373, 399*
Social Limiting of Competition *312*
Social production *190, 305*
Social progress *178, 304, 399, 407*
Social prophecy *402, 404*
Social reform *302, 303, 402*
Social Sciences *2, 3*
Social service *251, 270, 271, 273, 274, 275, 276, 277, 278, 285, 429*
Social service of manual workers *277*
Sources of income *32, 40, 67, 251, 437*
Specialization *149, 193, 196, 230, 248, 249*
Speculating trustee *252*
Speculation in all business *249*
Stages of industry *43, 199*

Standard money *111, 315, 317, 325, 328, 335*
Standard of Deferred Payments *79, 105, 330, 331, 332, 333, 335, 436*
Standard of living *8, 141, 159*
State enterprise *375*
State ownership *274, 375, 393*
State socialism *401, 402, 403*
Storehouse of saving *79, 80, 83*
Strength of men and women *132*
Strikes *182, 184, 185, 216, 217*
Strike violence *184*
Subjective valuations *22, 26, 28*
Subsistence theory of wages *168*
Sugar trust *241*
Sumptuary laws *285*
Supply of gold *336, 436*
Supply of Labor *136, 138, 161, 423, 424, 425*
System of labor *376*

T

Talent and occupation *150*
Tariff for revenue *358*
Taxation *117, 122, 265, 269, 270, 281, 343, 344, 345, 346, 347, 348, 349, 389, 390, 391, 412, 437, 438*
Technical diminishing returns *51, 53*
Technical rank of goods *35*
Temperance legislation *369*
Temporary gratification *viii*
Temporary use *40, 45*
Tenement-house laws *368*
Territorial distribution *355*
Test of monopoly *226*
Theodore Roosevelt *397*
Theory of crises *258*
Theory of Foreign Exchanges *353*
Theory of Time-value *105, 108, 421*
Theory of Value *33, 263, 264, 300, 302, 303, 304, 317, 381, 414, 434*
Theory of wages *159, 166, 281, 304*
Time-discount *98, 103, 107, 111, 119, 302*
Time relations of goods to wants *35*
Time-value *74, 98, 104, 105, 106, 107, 108, 111, 112, 121, 160, 161, 162, 301, 302, 421*
Time-value and capital *263*
Tin-plate trust *242*
T. N. Carver *423*
Token coins *325*
Trade-unions *170, 180, 181, 182, 183, 185, 186, 187, 216, 240, 361, 427, 438*
Transportation as a Form of Production *382*

Trant *186*
Trustee *235, 251*
Two modes of approach *92*
Typical bank-notes *339, 340, 341, 342*
Typical gambling *246*

U

Unearned increments *72*
United States *69, 72, 82, 83, 143, 170, 174, 186, 216, 229, 230, 232, 233, 242, 255, 256, 257, 258, 274, 275, 295, 315, 316, 320, 327, 328, 333, 334, 338, 339, 341, 346, 357, 359, 360, 364, 365, 375, 386, 392, 406, 412, 422, 426, 430, 431, 440*
Unit of value *79, 87, 164*
Unproductive labor *32, 191, 423*
Unripe goods *15*
Use of authoritative distribution *299*
Use of Money *23, 30, 75, 77, 78, 79, 81, 82, 83, 84, 86, 255, 314, 315, 318, 320, 328, 330*
Usufruct *41, 42, 44, 55, 80, 83, 93, 162, 164, 263, 301*
Usury *85, 90, 100, 370*
Utilization *39, 48, 49, 51, 65, 117, 192*

V

Value Theories *302*
Volitional control *139, 140, 141, 142*

W

Wage contract *154, 164, 168*
Wages and efficiency *145*
Wages and profits *302*
Wages and rent *151, 152, 162*
Waste and Luxury *279, 433*
Waste in public outlay *281*
Waste of Wealth *279, 282*
Watch-factory *69*
Wealth and income *30, 83, 95, 287, 320*
Wealth and its Indirect Uses *35, 416*
Wealth and Welfare *10, 12, 13, 413*
Wealth concept *88*
Wealth of cities *90*
Wealth of Nations *310*
W. G. Sumner *411*
Widening markets *396*
Wieser *414, 415, 426, 429*
Worker in competition *168*
W. Z. Ripley *420*

Y

Years' purchase *90, 91, 92, 93*

www.ingramcontent.com/pod-product-compliance
Lightning Source LLC
Chambersburg PA
CBHW030242140725
29531CB00059B/1305